FuII MooN
o Sagashite

4

Story & Art by Arina Tanemura

Table of Contents

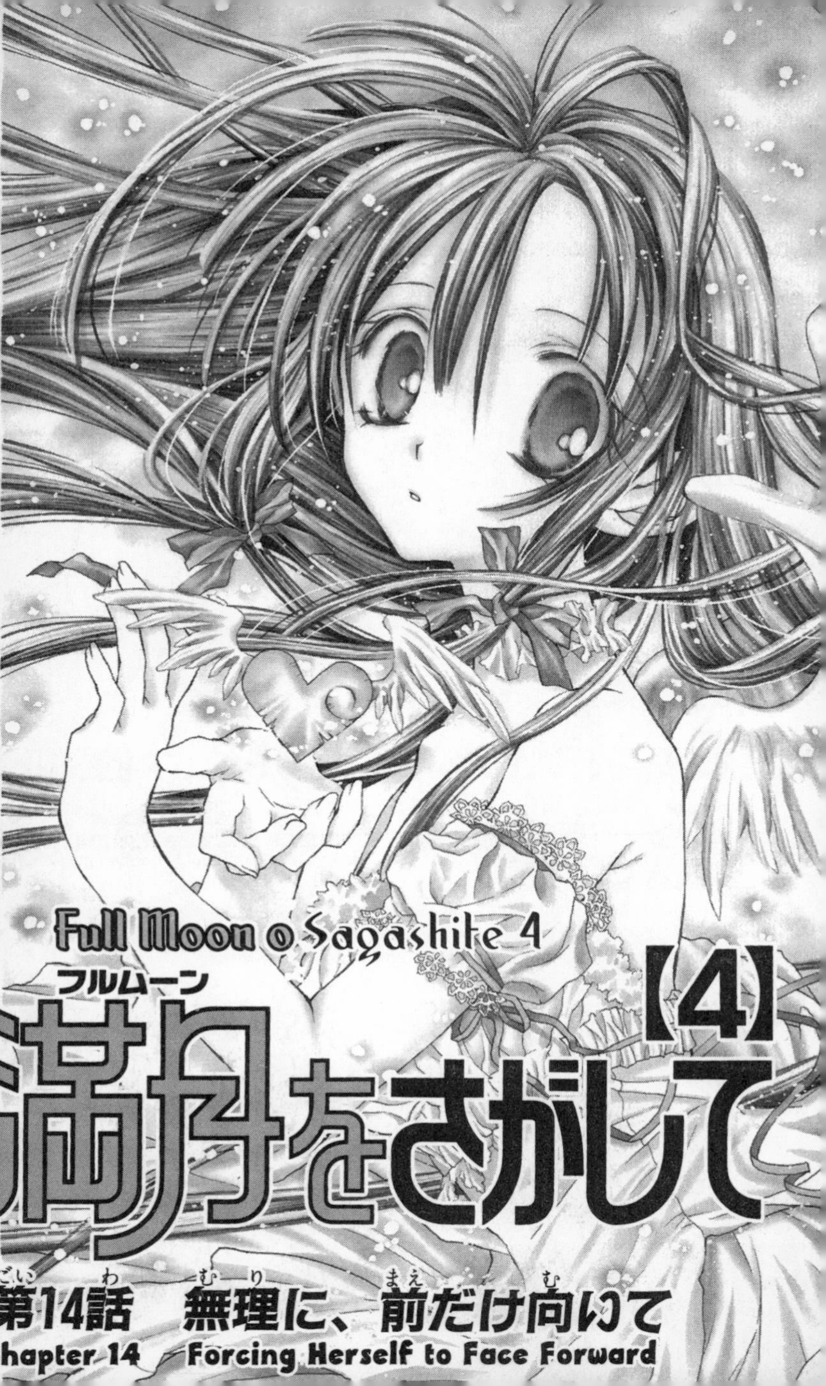
Full Moon o Sagashite 4
フルムーン
満月をさがして【4】
第14話　無理に、前だけ向いて
Chapter 14　Forcing Herself to Face Forward

CHARACTER INTRODUCTIONS

MEROKO
A Shinigami who turns into a rabbit. She likes her partner, Takuto.

TAKUTO
A Shinigami who turns into a cat.

EICHI
He's studying in the U.S. Mitsuki has loved him since she was little.

MITSUKI KOYAMA (AGE 12)
She has throat cancer, and can't talk or sing loud. She's not good at competing or quarreling.

MITSUKI KOYAMA (AGE 16)
Mitsuki's alter ego, who debuts as the singer "Fullmoon."

Full Moon o Sagashite

Mitsuki is 12. She loves Eichi, who's studying in the U.S., and she dreams of fulfilling her promise to him by becoming a singer. Mitsuki has a form of cancer in her throat called sarcoma, and Dr. Wakaoji has told her she has only one year to live. One day, a pair of Shinigami named Takuto and Meroko appears, and tries to stop Mitsuki from going to an audition. But, Takuto is moved by Mitsuki's ardent wish to become a singer, and helps her audition by transforming her into a healthy 16-year-old. Mitsuki is able to sing in her new body and wins the competition. She makes her musical debut as "Fullmoon." Mitsuki's singing career is going well, and Dr. Wakaoji appears as her new producer. Dr. Wakaoji used to be in a legendary band named "ROUTE..L" with Mitsuki's father. When Takuto sees Dr. Wakaoji, he remembers his past— he had the same throat illness as Mitsuki and eventually committed suicide. Takuto hasn't become a full Shinigami yet, so if he remembers his past, he will cease to exist. Mitsuki decides to give her soul to Takuto to free him from his past. But Takuto is beginning to love the pure Mitsuki, and decides to try to protect her instead of taking her life. He also starts to try to find Eichi to make her happy. The Shinigami find out that Eichi died in an airplane crash years ago, and that Mitsuki has known about it all along. But Mitsuki hasn't realized that the Shinigami know her secret...

STORY THUS FAR

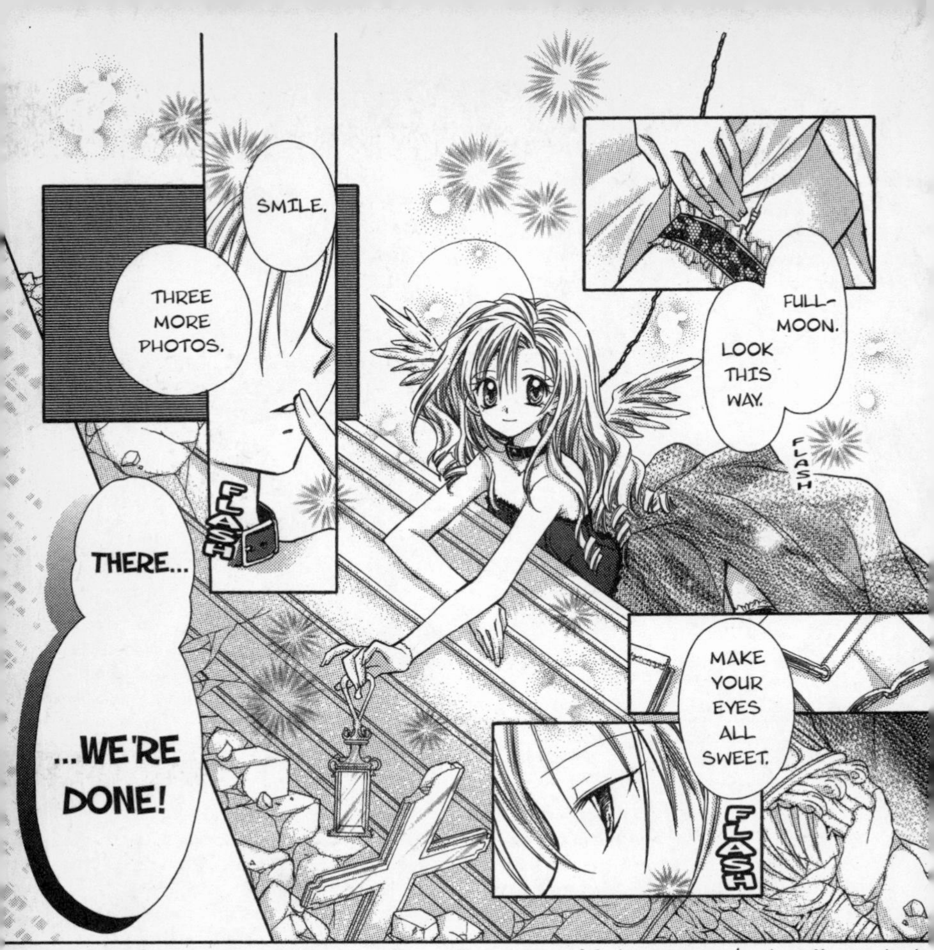
FULL-MOON. LOOK THIS WAY.
FLASH
MAKE YOUR EYES ALL SWEET.
FLASH
SMILE.
THREE MORE PHOTOS.
FLASH
THERE...
...WE'RE DONE!

Author's Comments About the Cover Illustrations: * Spoilers are contained in the stuff written here! (If you haven't read this chapter before, please read this section after reading it.)

Chapter 14: Forcing Herself to Face Forward

Cover Copy Where are her overflowing feelings going?

The cover illustration is Mitsuki-chan as an angel. It's difficult drawing her body. Sigh. The main character for my next series will be a senior high school girl with breasts and hips!! So do your best, me!

This chapter is the beginning of Mitsuki and the darkness in her heart. Oh dear.
In Yamanako-ko, where Fullmoon-chan went recording, there really is a record company studio (I wonder if people can stay there?), and I've always wanted to use it. (The outside and the inside of the buildings don't look the way I've drawn them.) I wonder if it's used only when recording albums? Hmmm...but Fullmoon-chan must have recorded songs other than her single... Nya!

Personally, I love Fullmoon-chan jumping around in the room! Ahaha, she's such a fool. And Wakaoji♥Oshige!! Oh, I love them.♥♥I want to draw this anxious couple!! Yes!!! Those two are good!! They make great material!!!

And look for Gut-chan being carried under Madoka-yan's arm. How lovely.♥

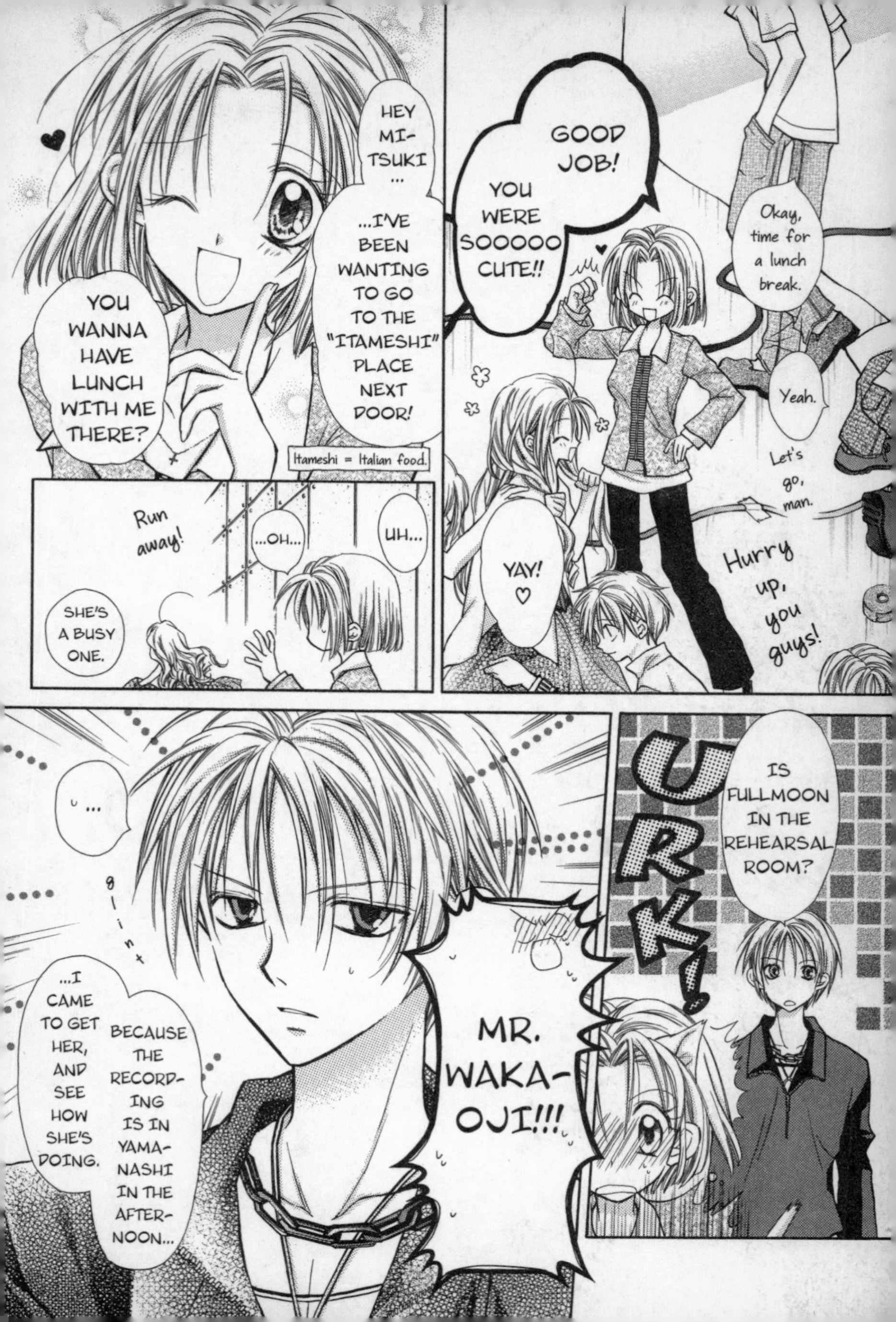
Okay, time for a lunch break.
Yeah.
Let's go, man.
GOOD JOB! YOU WERE SOOOOO CUTE!!
Hurry up, you guys!
YAY! ♡
HEY MI-TSUKI ...
...I'VE BEEN WANTING TO GO TO THE "ITAMESHI" PLACE NEXT DOOR!
YOU WANNA HAVE LUNCH WITH ME THERE?
Itameshi = Italian food.
UH...
...OH...
Run away!
SHE'S A BUSY ONE.
IS FULLMOON IN THE REHEARSAL ROOM?
URK!
MR. WAKA-OJI!!!
...
glint
BECAUSE THE RECORD-ING IS IN YAMA-NASHI IN THE AFTER-NOON...
...I CAME TO GET HER, AND SEE HOW SHE'S DOING.

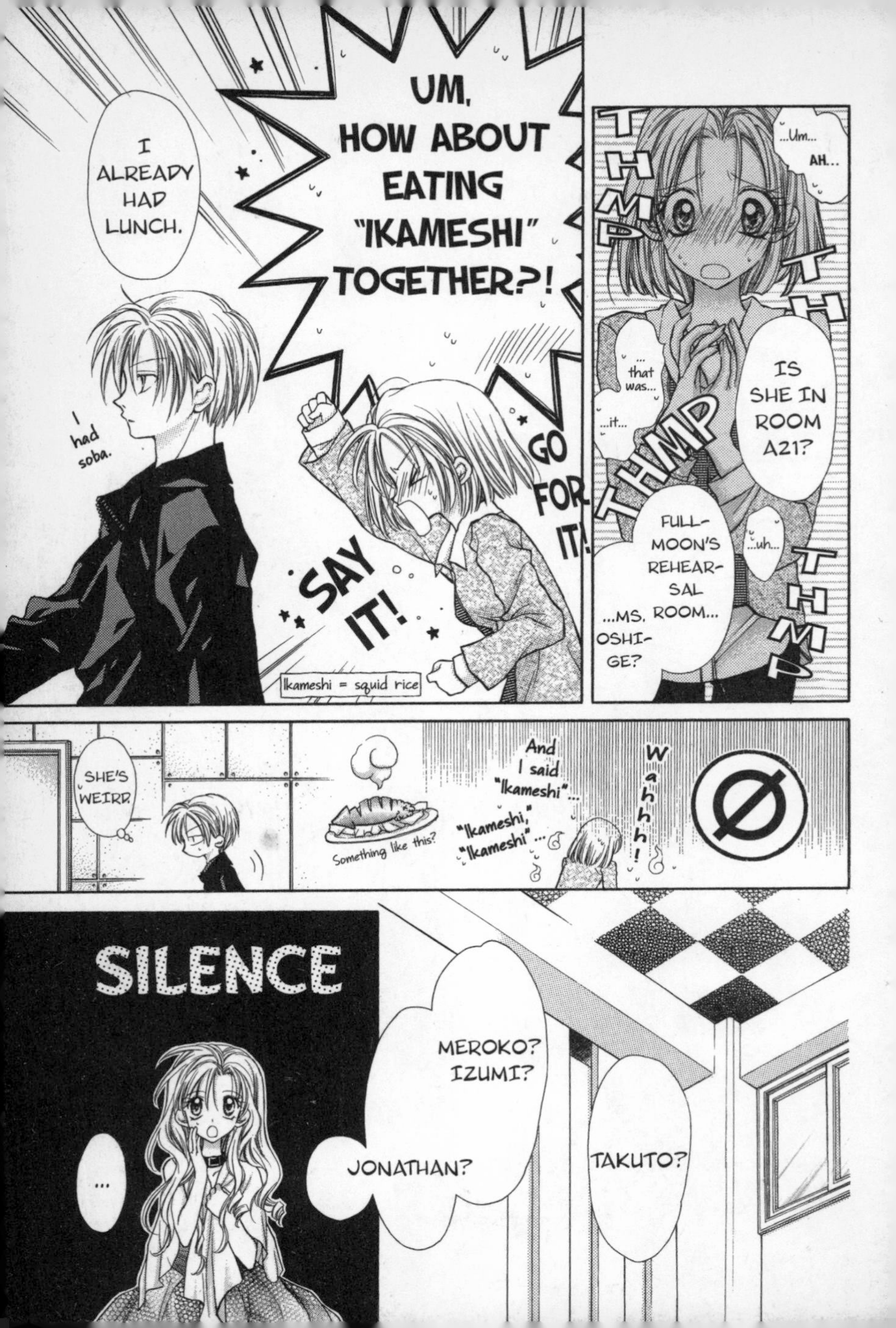
THMP THMP THMP THMP
...Um...
AH...
IS SHE IN ROOM A21?
...that was...
...it...
...uh...
FULL-MOON'S REHEARSAL ROOM... MS. OSHIGE?
UM, HOW ABOUT EATING "IKAMESHI" TOGETHER?!
GO FOR IT!
SAY IT!
I ALREADY HAD LUNCH.
I had soba.
Ikameshi = squid rice
Wahhh!
And I said "Ikameshi"...
"Ikameshi," "Ikameshi"...
Something like this?
SHE'S WEIRD.
TAKUTO?
MEROKO? IZUMI?
JONATHAN?
...
SILENCE

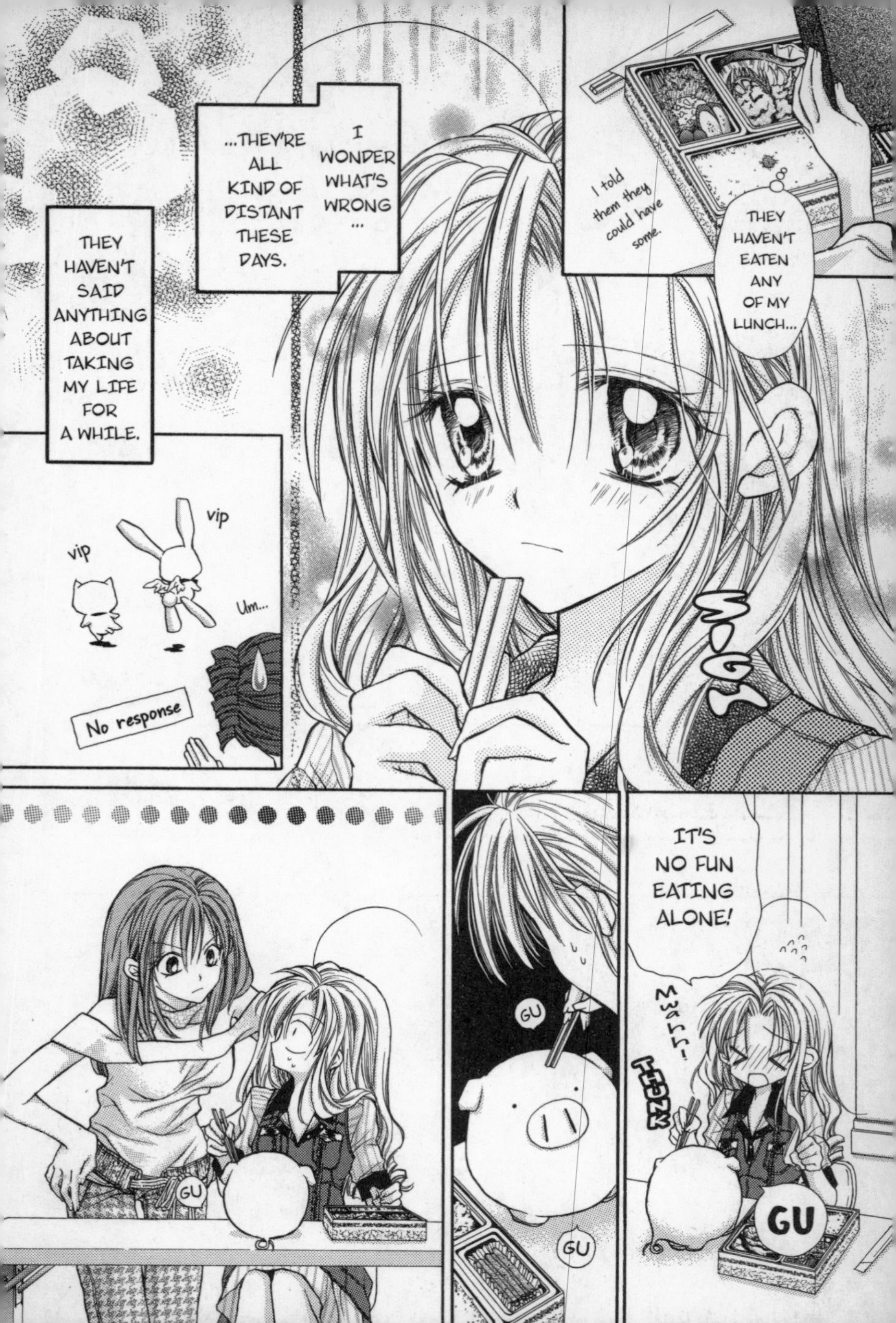
THEY HAVEN'T EATEN ANY OF MY LUNCH...
I told them they could have some.
I WONDER WHAT'S WRONG ...
...THEY'RE ALL KIND OF DISTANT THESE DAYS.
THEY HAVEN'T SAID ANYTHING ABOUT TAKING MY LIFE FOR A WHILE.
vip
vip
Um...
No response
IT'S NO FUN EATING ALONE!
Mwahh!
GU
GU
GU
GU

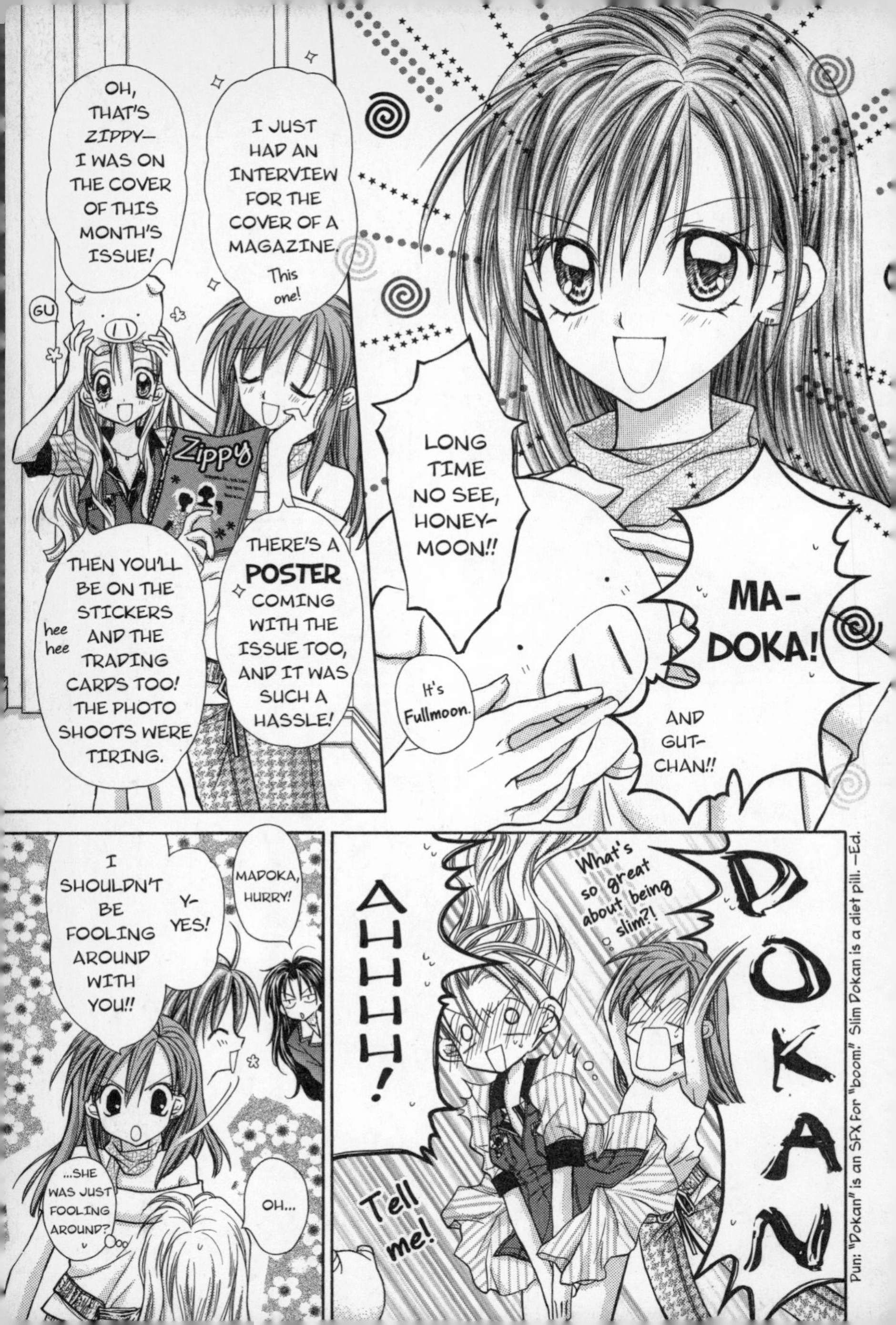
MA-DOKA!
AND GUT-CHAN!!
LONG TIME NO SEE, HONEYMOON!!
It's Fullmoon.
I JUST HAD AN INTERVIEW FOR THE COVER OF A MAGAZINE.
This one!
OH, THAT'S ZIPPY— I WAS ON THE COVER OF THIS MONTH'S ISSUE!
GU
Zippy
THERE'S A POSTER COMING WITH THE ISSUE TOO, AND IT WAS SUCH A HASSLE!
THEN YOU'LL BE ON THE STICKERS AND THE TRADING CARDS TOO! THE PHOTO SHOOTS WERE TIRING.
hee hee
DOKAN
What's so great about being slim?!
AHHHH!
Tell me!
MADOKA, HURRY!
Y-YES!
I SHOULDN'T BE FOOLING AROUND WITH YOU!!
OH...
...SHE WAS JUST FOOLING AROUND?

Pun: "Dokan" is an SFX for "boom." Slim Dokan is a diet pill. —Ed.

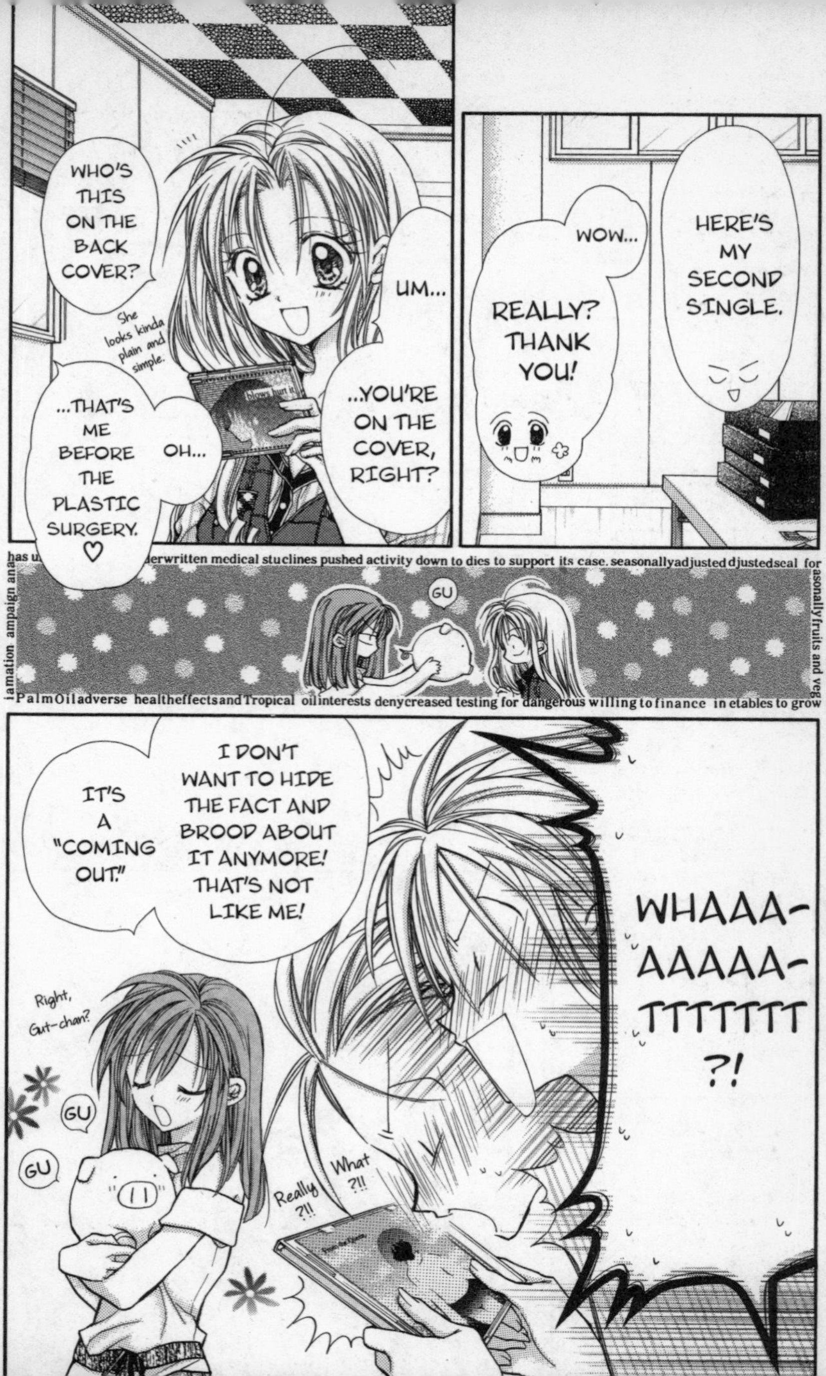
HERE'S MY SECOND SINGLE.
WOW... REALLY? THANK YOU!
UM...
...YOU'RE ON THE COVER, RIGHT?
WHO'S THIS ON THE BACK COVER?
She looks kinda plain and simple.
OH...
...THAT'S ME BEFORE THE PLASTIC SURGERY. ♡
has u... derwritten medical stuclines pushed activity down to dies to support its case. seasonallyadjusted djustedseal for
asonally fruits and veg
iamation ampaign ana
GU
PalmOiladverse healtheffectsandTropical oilinterests denycreased testing for dangerous willing to finance in etables to grow
WHAAA-AAAAA-TTTTTTT?!
I DON'T WANT TO HIDE THE FACT AND BROOD ABOUT IT ANYMORE! THAT'S NOT LIKE ME!
IT'S A "COMING OUT."
Right, Gut-chan?
GU
GU
What?!!
Really?!!

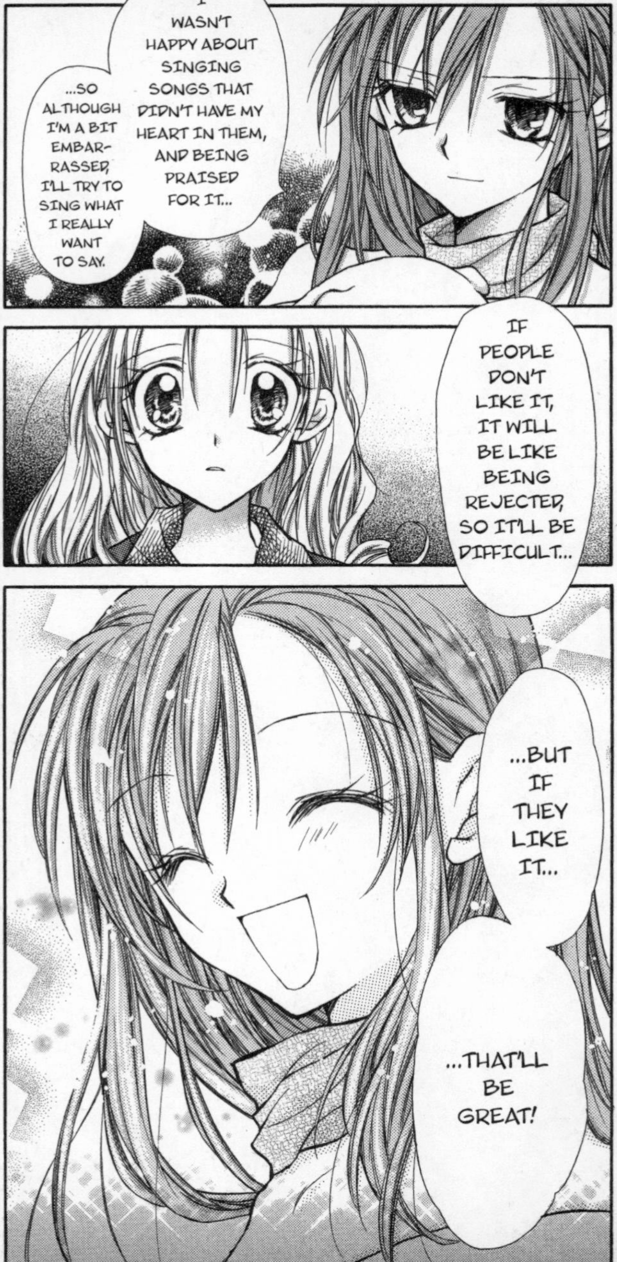
I WASN'T HAPPY ABOUT SINGING SONGS THAT DIDN'T HAVE MY HEART IN THEM, AND BEING PRAISED FOR IT...
...SO ALTHOUGH I'M A BIT EMBARRASSED, I'LL TRY TO SING WHAT I REALLY WANT TO SAY.
IF PEOPLE DON'T LIKE IT, IT WILL BE LIKE BEING REJECTED, SO IT'LL BE DIFFICULT...
...BUT IF THEY LIKE IT...
...THAT'LL BE GREAT!

Arina Tanemura's

Penchi de Shakin

Episode 56 ☆

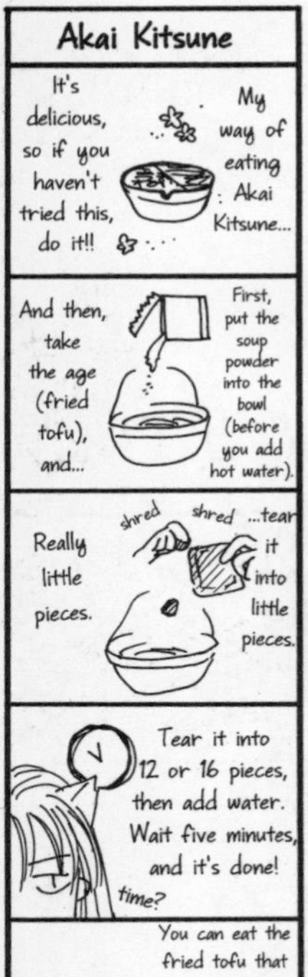
Akai Kitsune
My way of eating Akai Kitsune...
It's delicious, so if you haven't tried this, do it!!
First, put the soup powder into the bowl (before you add hot water).
And then, take the age (fried tofu), and...
shred shred ...tear it into little pieces.
Really little pieces.
Tear it into 12 or 16 pieces, then add water. Wait five minutes, and it's done!
time?
You can eat the fried tofu that absorbed the soup, and it's delicious. (If you bite on the big fried tofu, it's hot and you get burned.)
Definitely, try it out.
Ummm good!!

I love Akai Kitsune. ˅
(I ate it today, too.)

By the way, there are episodes of "Penshaki" drawn for the *Ribon* website. If you don't own a computer, please wait awhile. I'll include them in the manga.

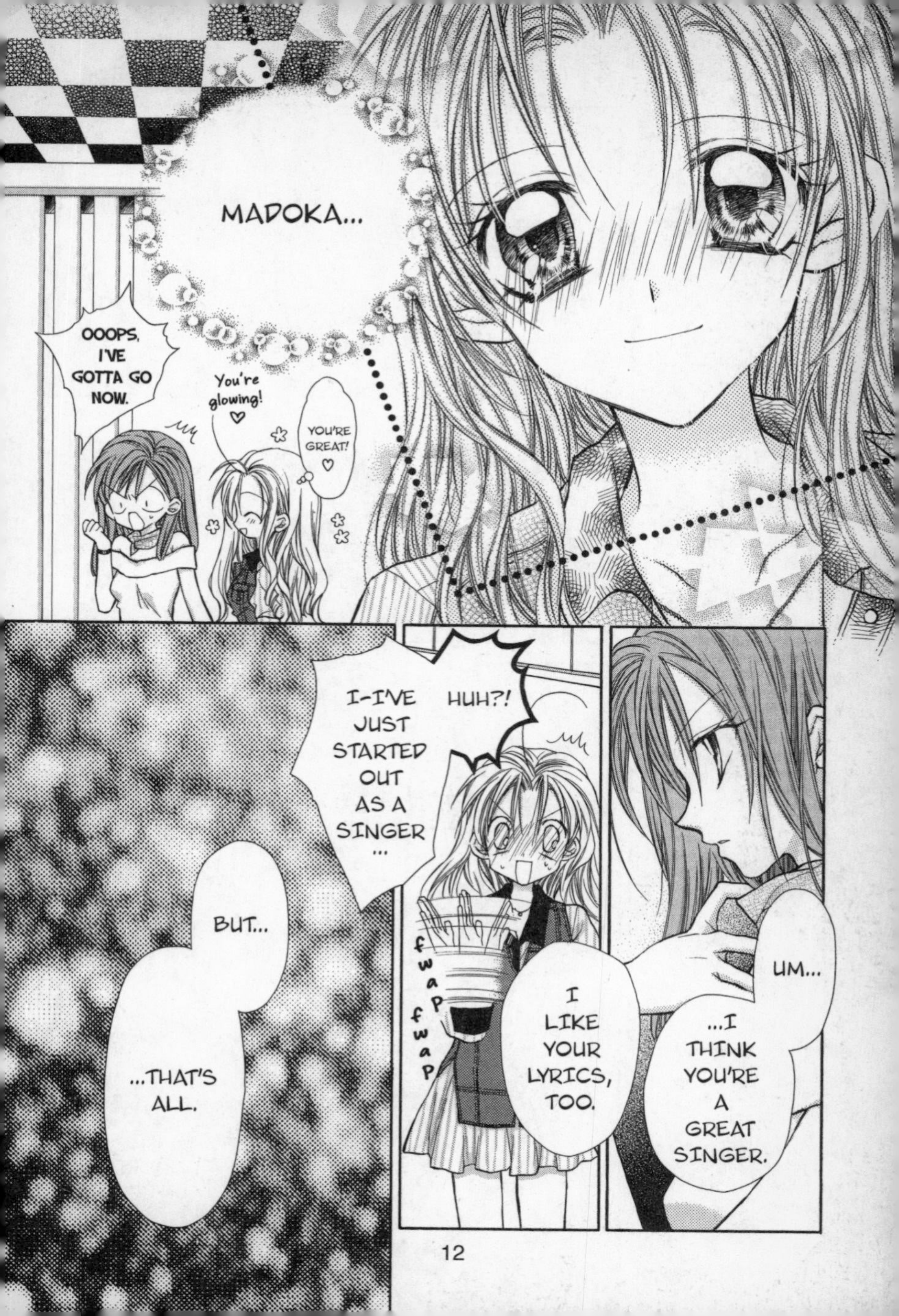

MADOKA...
You're glowing!
YOU'RE GREAT!
OOOPS, I'VE GOTTA GO NOW.
UM...
...I THINK YOU'RE A GREAT SINGER.
I LIKE YOUR LYRICS, TOO.
HUH?!
I-I'VE JUST STARTED OUT AS A SINGER...
fwap fwap
BUT...
...THAT'S ALL.

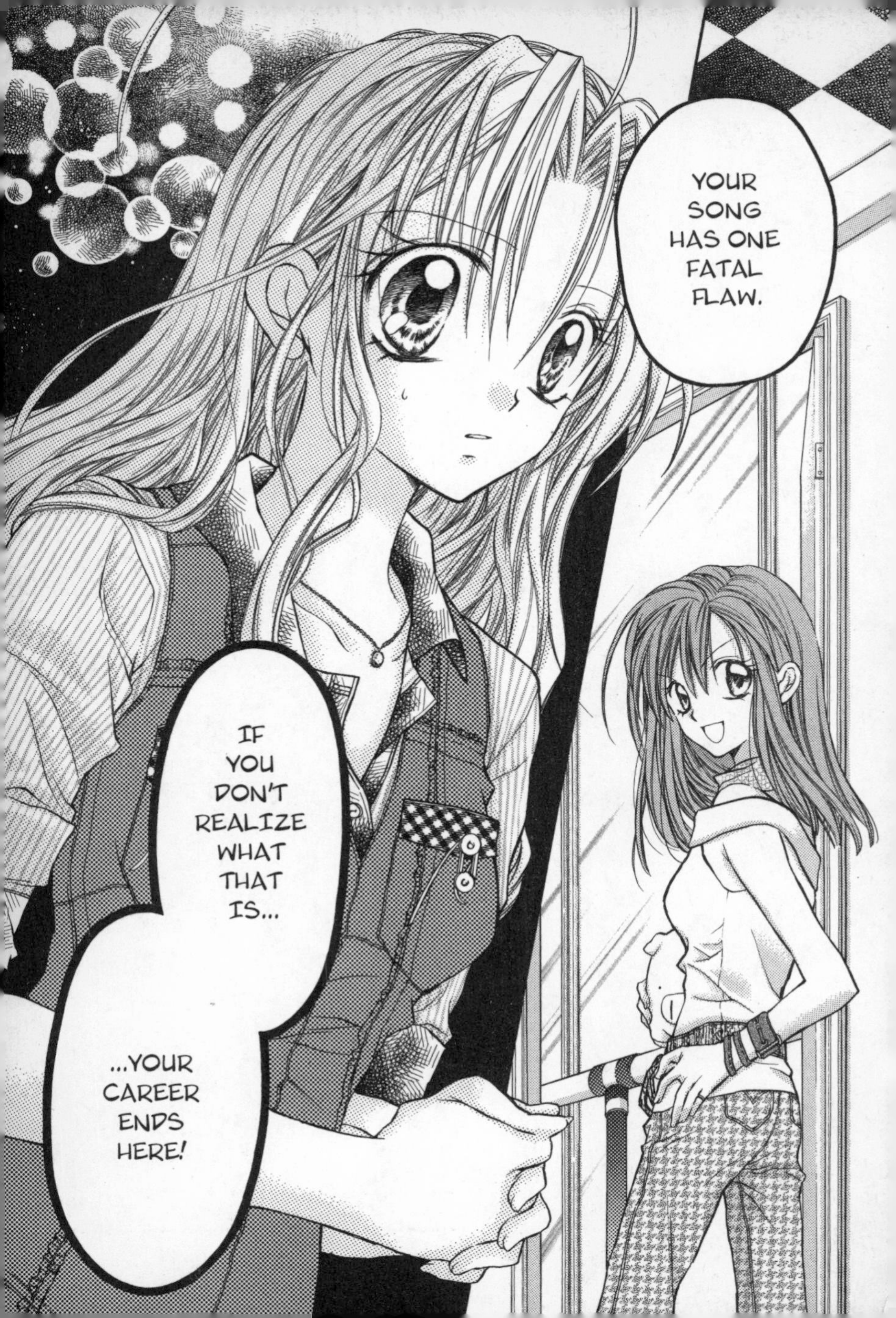
YOUR SONG HAS ONE FATAL FLAW.
IF YOU DON'T REALIZE WHAT THAT IS...
...YOUR CAREER ENDS HERE!

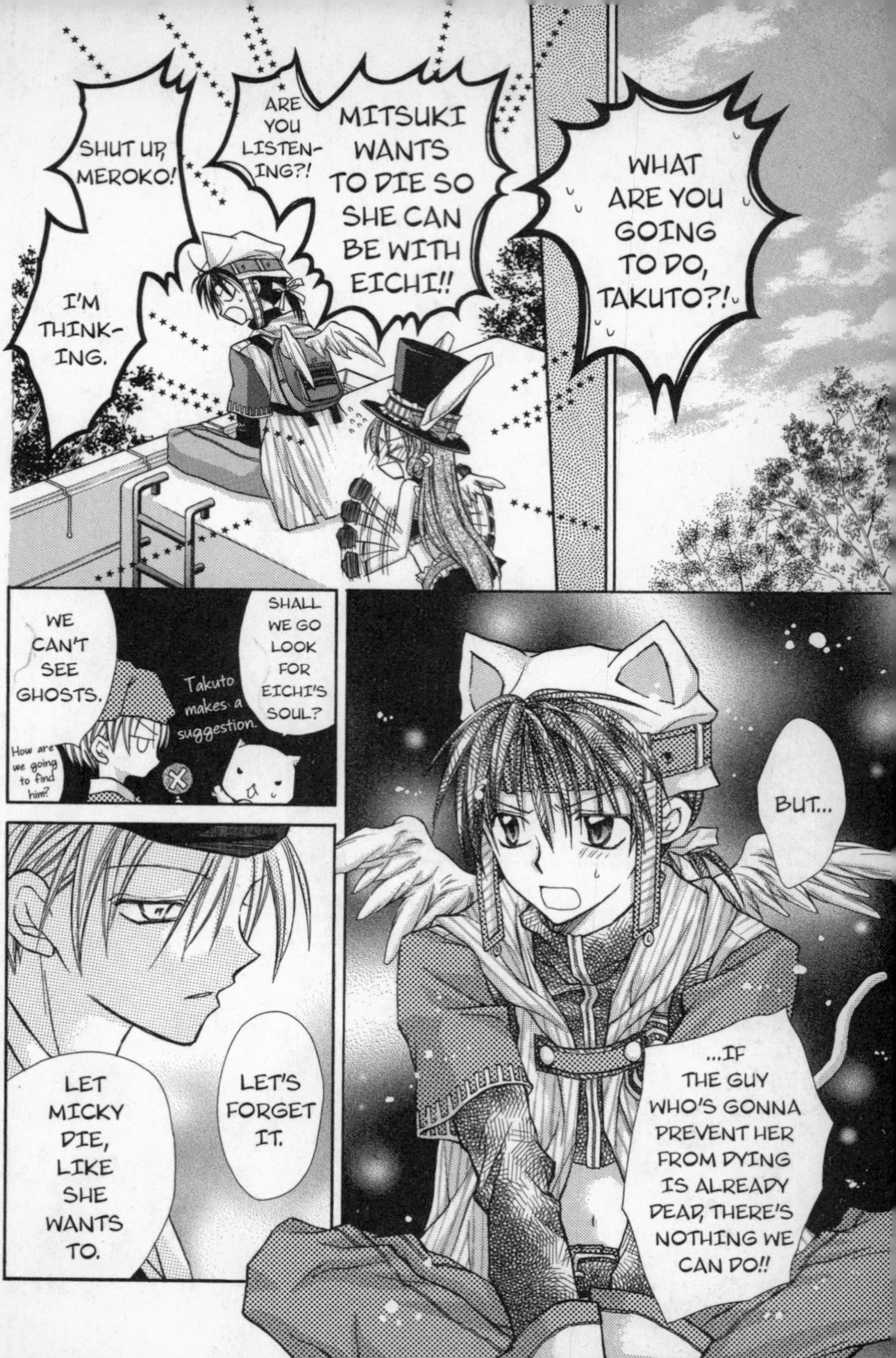
WHAT ARE YOU GOING TO DO, TAKUTO?!
MITSUKI WANTS TO DIE SO SHE CAN BE WITH EICHI!!
ARE YOU LISTENING?!
SHUT UP, MEROKO!
I'M THINKING.
BUT...
...IF THE GUY WHO'S GONNA PREVENT HER FROM DYING IS ALREADY DEAD, THERE'S NOTHING WE CAN DO!!
SHALL WE GO LOOK FOR EICHI'S SOUL?
Takuto makes a suggestion.
WE CAN'T SEE GHOSTS.
How are we going to find him?
LET'S FORGET IT.
LET MICKY DIE, LIKE SHE WANTS TO.

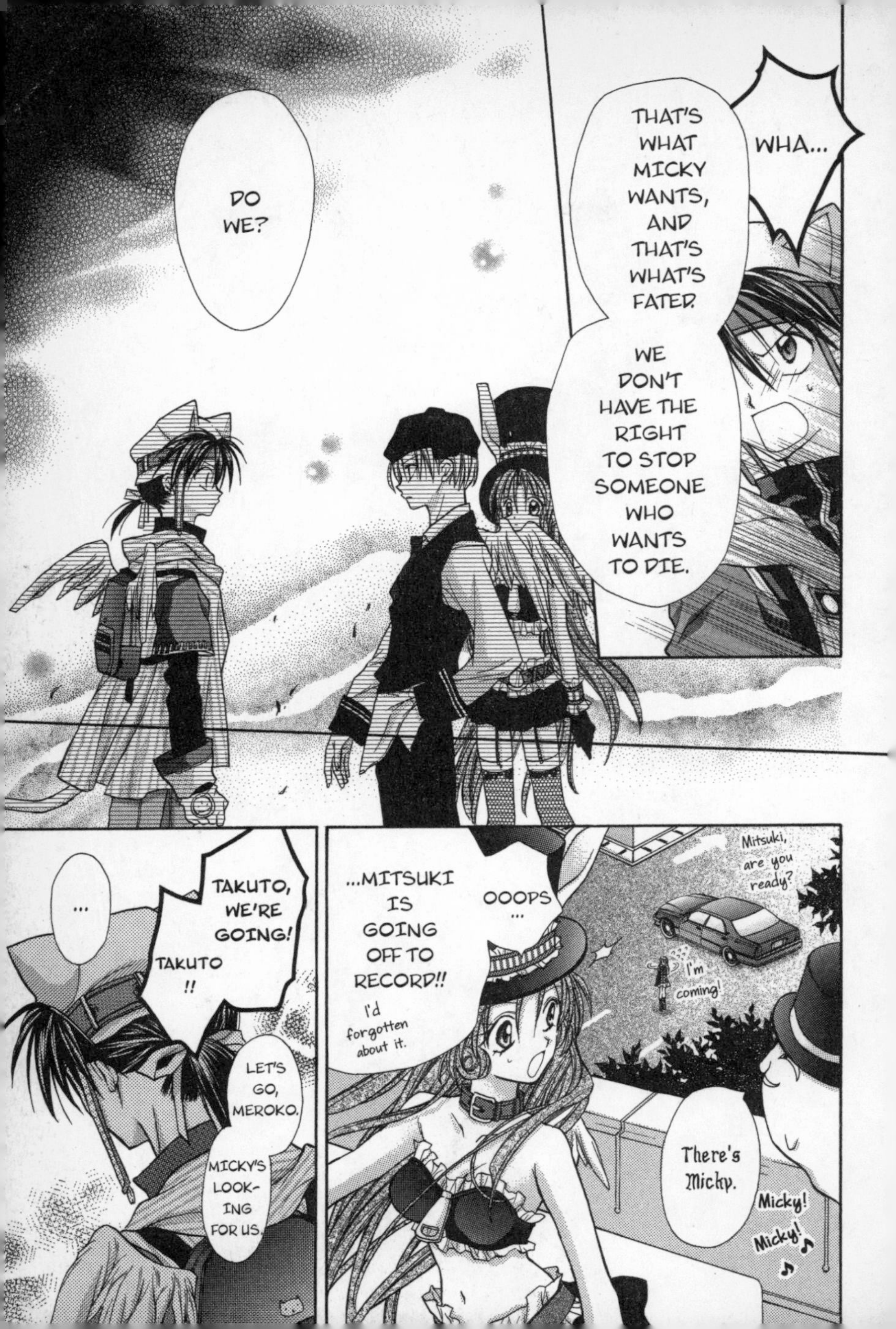
WHA...
THAT'S WHAT MICKY WANTS, AND THAT'S WHAT'S FATED.
WE DON'T HAVE THE RIGHT TO STOP SOMEONE WHO WANTS TO DIE.
DO WE?
Mitsuki, are you ready?
OOOPS...
...MITSUKI IS GOING OFF TO RECORD!!
I'd forgotten about it.
I'm coming!
There's Micky.
Micky! Micky!
TAKUTO, WE'RE GOING!
TAKUTO !!
...
LET'S GO, MEROKO.
MICKY'S LOOK-ING FOR US.

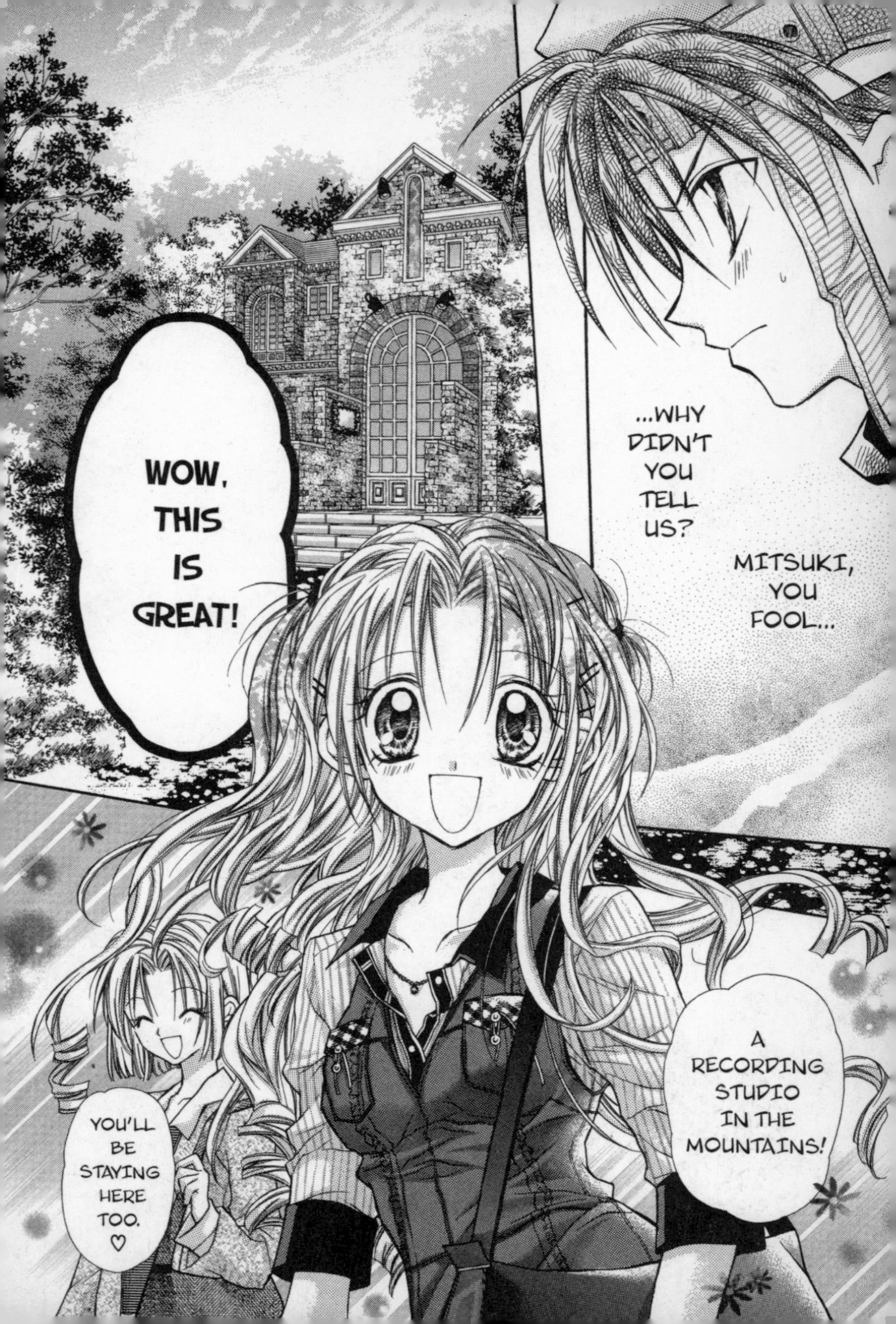
...WHY DIDN'T YOU TELL US?
MITSUKI, YOU FOOL...
WOW, THIS IS GREAT!
A RECORDING STUDIO IN THE MOUNTAINS!
YOU'LL BE STAYING HERE TOO. ♡

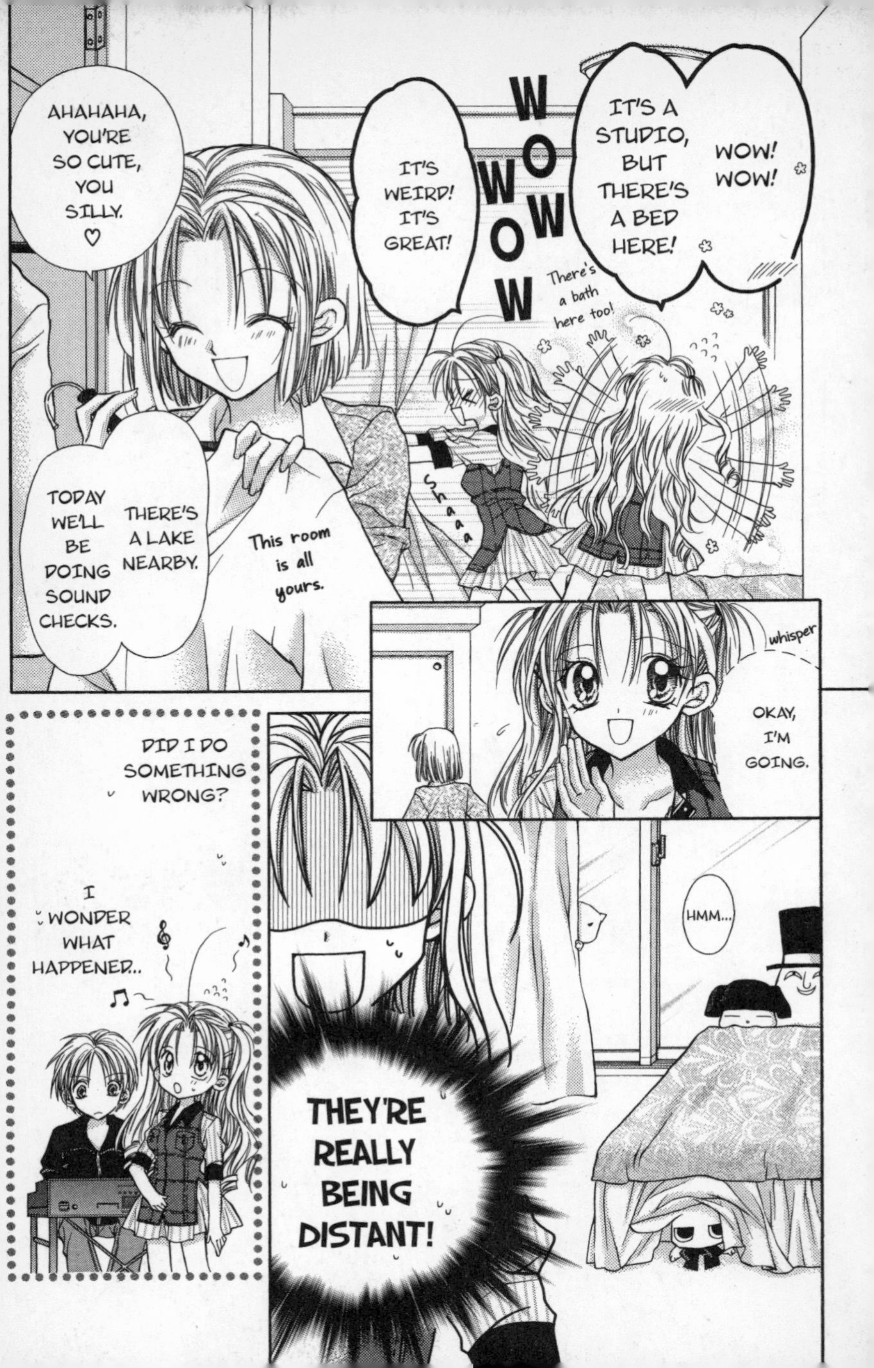
IT'S A STUDIO, BUT THERE'S A BED HERE!
WOW! WOW!
WOWOWOWOW
IT'S WEIRD! IT'S GREAT!
There's a bath here too!
Shaaa
AHAHAHA, YOU'RE SO CUTE, YOU SILLY. ♡
THERE'S A LAKE NEARBY.
TODAY WE'LL BE DOING SOUND CHECKS.
This room is all yours.
whisper
OKAY, I'M GOING.
HMM...
THEY'RE REALLY BEING DISTANT!
DID I DO SOMETHING WRONG?
I WONDER WHAT HAPPENED...

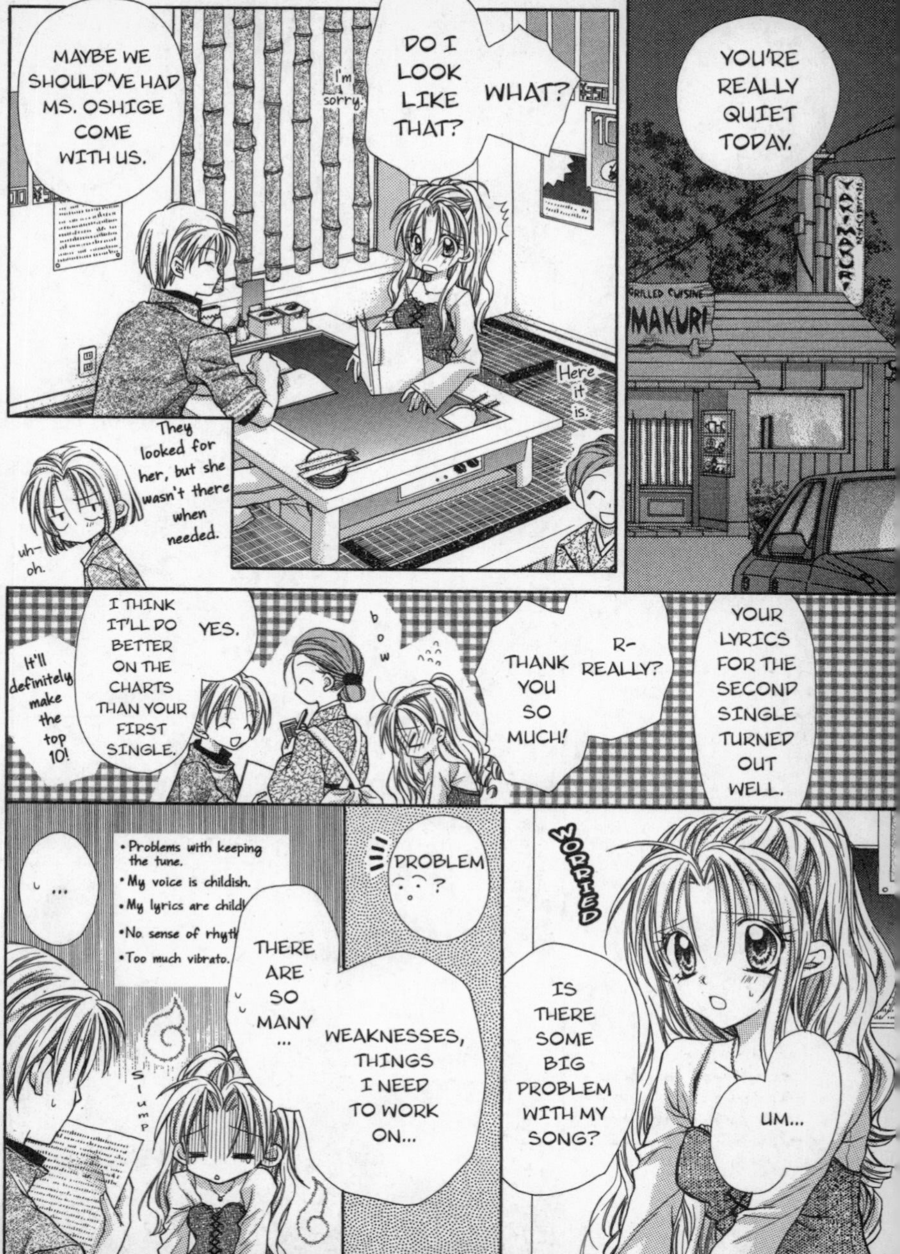
YOU'RE REALLY QUIET TODAY.
GRILLED CUISINE
WHAT?
DO I LOOK LIKE THAT?
I'm sorry.
MAYBE WE SHOULD'VE HAD MS. OSHIGE COME WITH US.
Here it is.
They looked for her, but she wasn't there when needed.
uh-oh.
YOUR LYRICS FOR THE SECOND SINGLE TURNED OUT WELL.
R-REALLY?
THANK YOU SO MUCH!
bow
YES.
I THINK IT'LL DO BETTER ON THE CHARTS THAN YOUR FIRST SINGLE.
It'll definitely make the top 10!
WORRIED
UM...
IS THERE SOME BIG PROBLEM WITH MY SONG?
PROBLEM?
THERE ARE SO MANY...
WEAKNESSES, THINGS I NEED TO WORK ON...
slump
...
• Problems with keeping the tune.
• My voice is childish.
• Too much vibrato.

Hellooooo.

Hey, it's A-chan.

I'm a bit tired today, and I'm not as lively as usual, but let's go!!

In an email from the Ribon Web site, I was asked, "Is it true that you've been sick since you were a child?" That's not true. It's just a rumor. What I say is the only truth. Please believe me.

I'm getting old, so...I don't recover from fatigue very fast. But I love my work!! So I will take care of my body, build up my physical strength, and do my best!!
Yes!

Doing your best is good!! It's cool!

Nowadays, I like See-Saw and "Akatsuki no Kuruma." I love them.

I like doing my color illustrations while playing DVDs of "Hamtaro," "Gundam SEED," and "Tanoshii Moomin Ikka."
Yay.

Ari-ham.

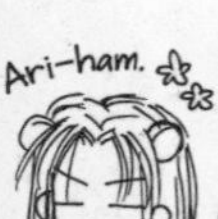

←Aaa!

Ham-chans. LOVE
Lacus and Yzak and Kira and Athrun and Dearka
Miriallia, Cagalli and Flay LOVE
Little My and Snufkin LOVE

Some of the sidebars are intentionally left blank because this volume has lots of serious stories. But I've drawn extra stuff for the end, so please forgive me.

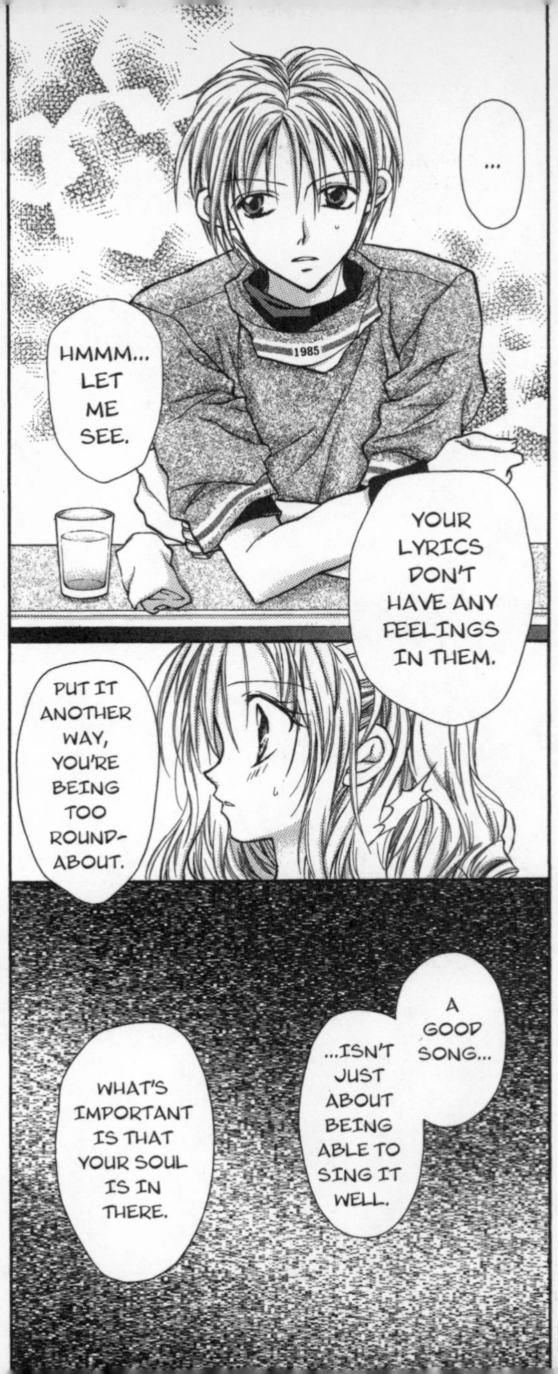
...
HMMM... LET ME SEE.
YOUR LYRICS DON'T HAVE ANY FEELINGS IN THEM.
PUT IT ANOTHER WAY, YOU'RE BEING TOO ROUND-ABOUT.
A GOOD SONG...
...ISN'T JUST ABOUT BEING ABLE TO SING IT WELL.
WHAT'S IMPORTANT IS THAT YOUR SOUL IS IN THERE.

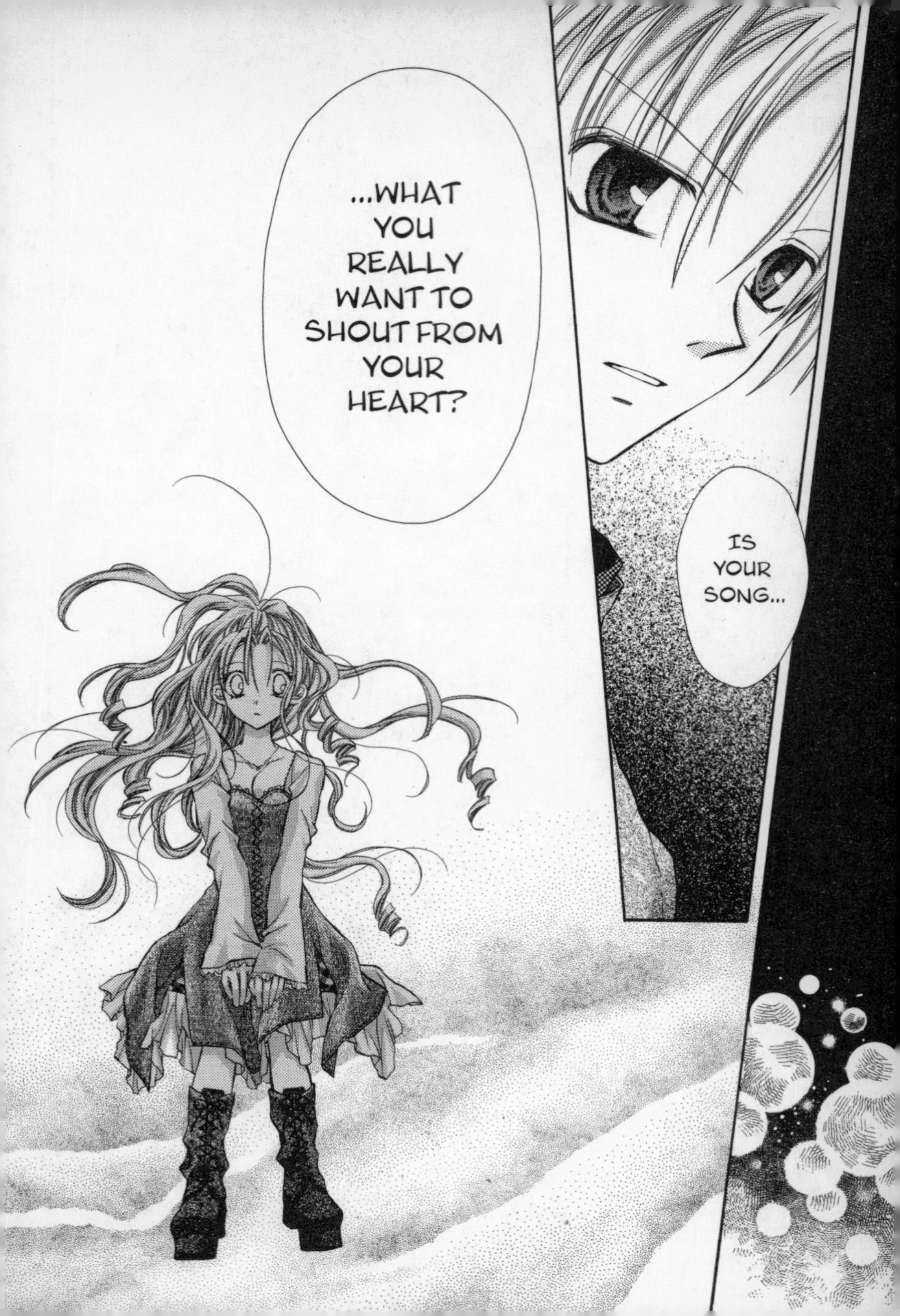
IS YOUR SONG...
...WHAT YOU REALLY WANT TO SHOUT FROM YOUR HEART?

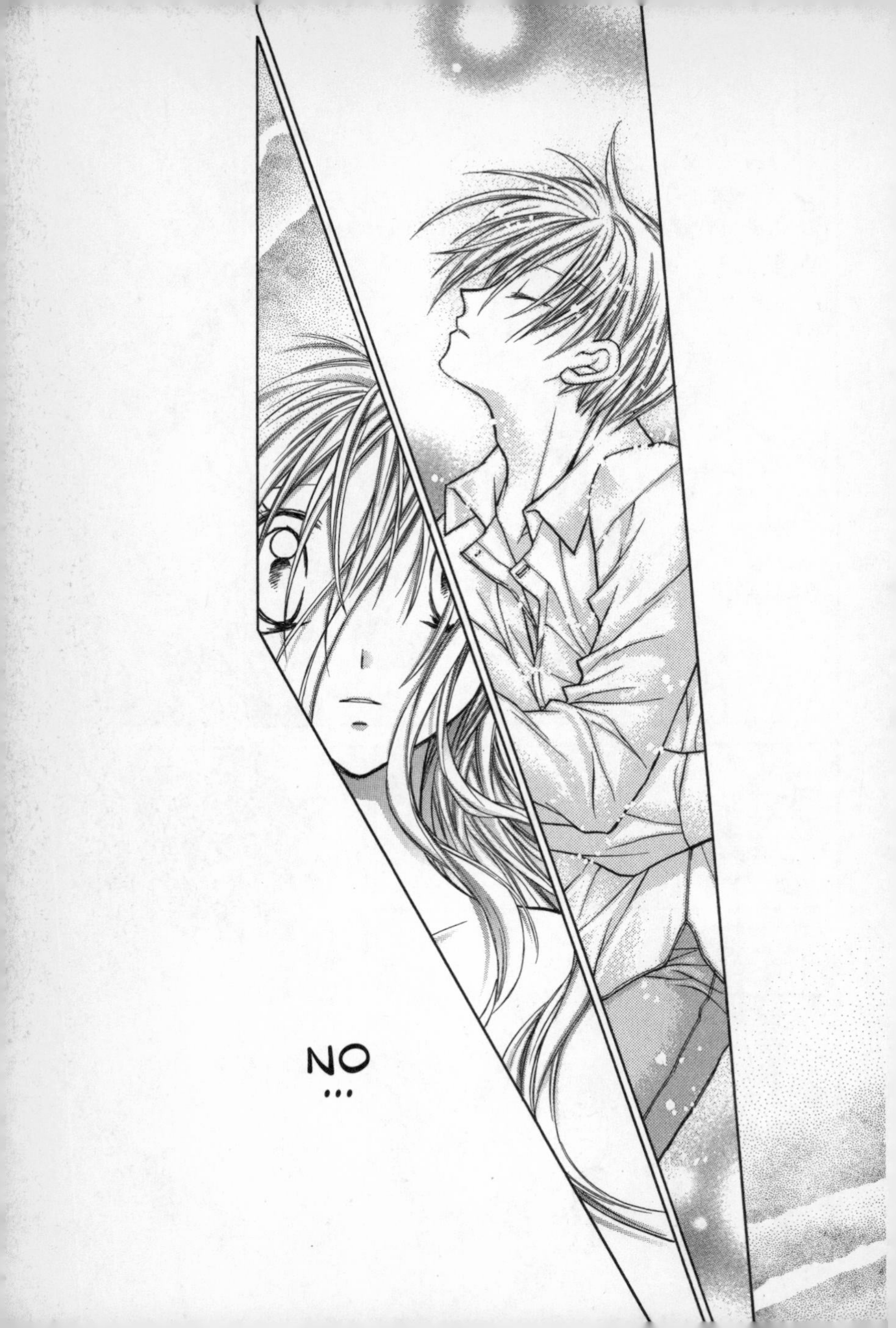
NO
...

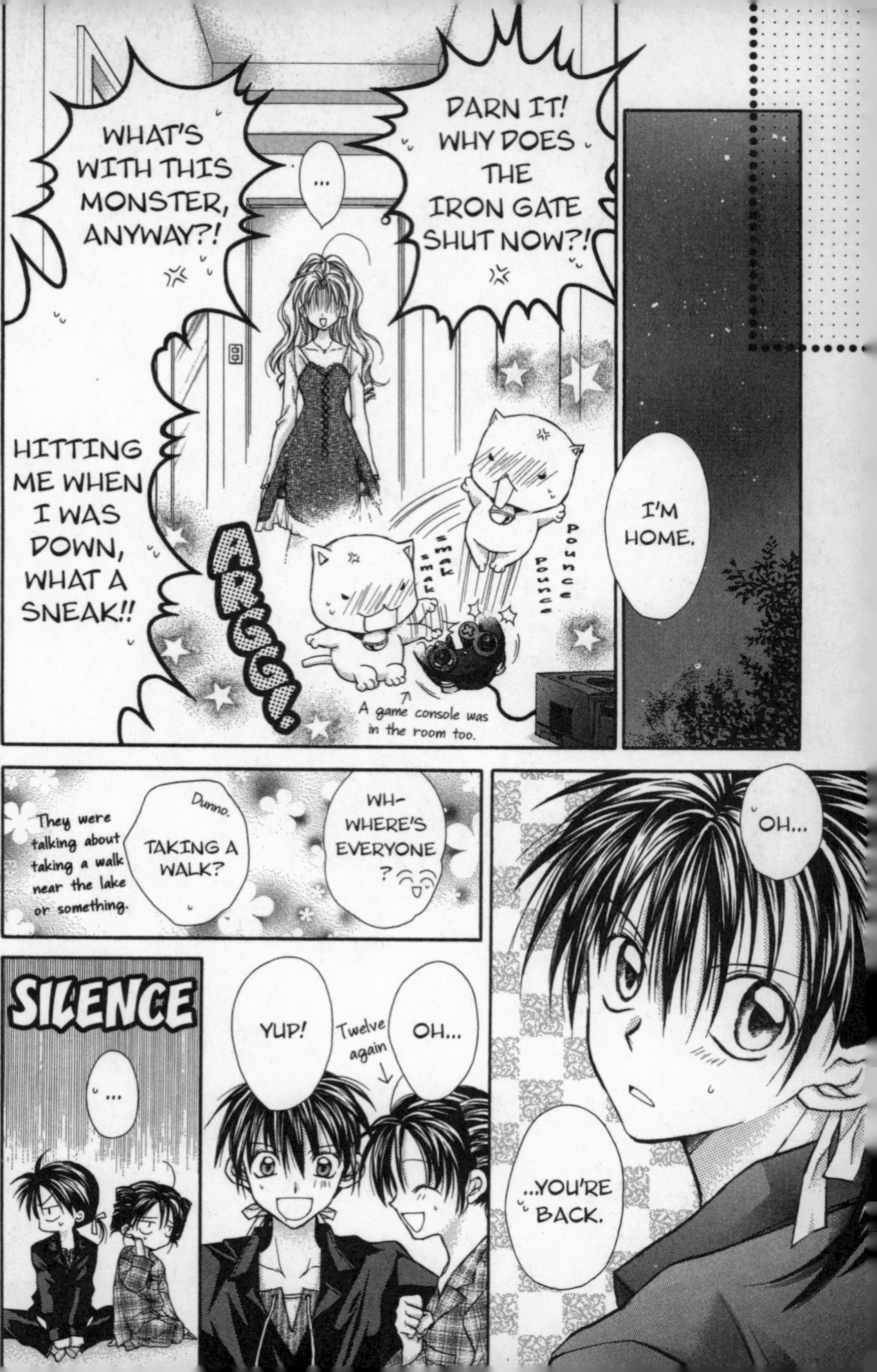
I'M HOME.
DARN IT! WHY DOES THE IRON GATE SHUT NOW?!
...
WHAT'S WITH THIS MONSTER, ANYWAY?!
pounce pounce
smak smak
HITTING ME WHEN I WAS DOWN, WHAT A SNEAK!!
ARGG!
A game console was in the room too.
OH...
...YOU'RE BACK.
WH-WHERE'S EVERYONE?
TAKING A WALK?
Dunno.
They were talking about taking a walk near the lake or something.
OH...
Twelve again
YUP!
SILENCE
...

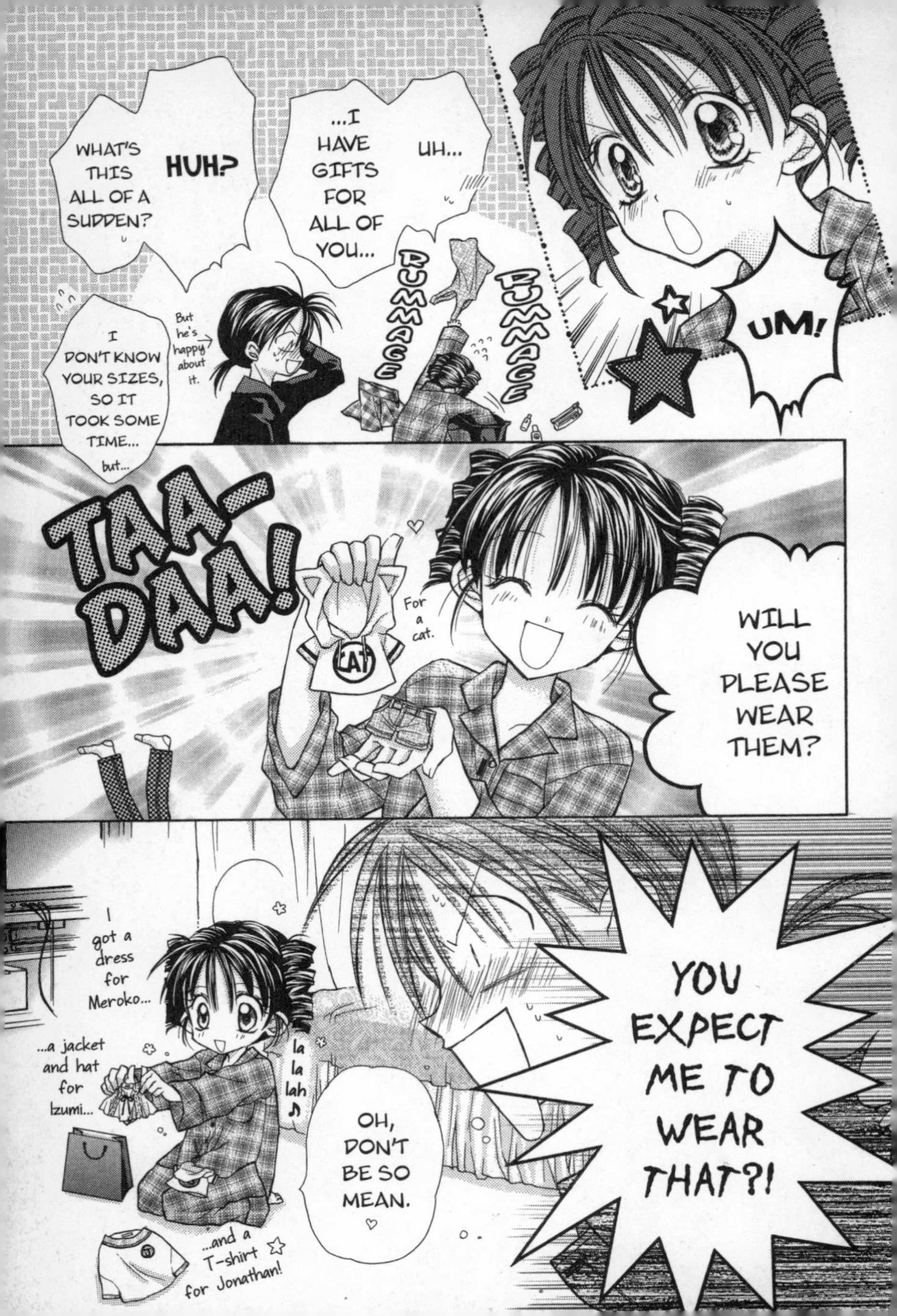
UM!
UH...
...I HAVE GIFTS FOR ALL OF YOU...
HUH?
WHAT'S THIS ALL OF A SUDDEN?
RUMMAGE
RUMMAGE
But he's happy about it.
I DON'T KNOW YOUR SIZES, SO IT TOOK SOME TIME... but...
WILL YOU PLEASE WEAR THEM?
For a cat.
CAT
TAA-DAA!
YOU EXPECT ME TO WEAR THAT?!
OH, DON'T BE SO MEAN.
la la lah ♪
I got a dress for Meroko...
...a jacket and hat for Izumi...
...and a T-shirt for Jonathan!

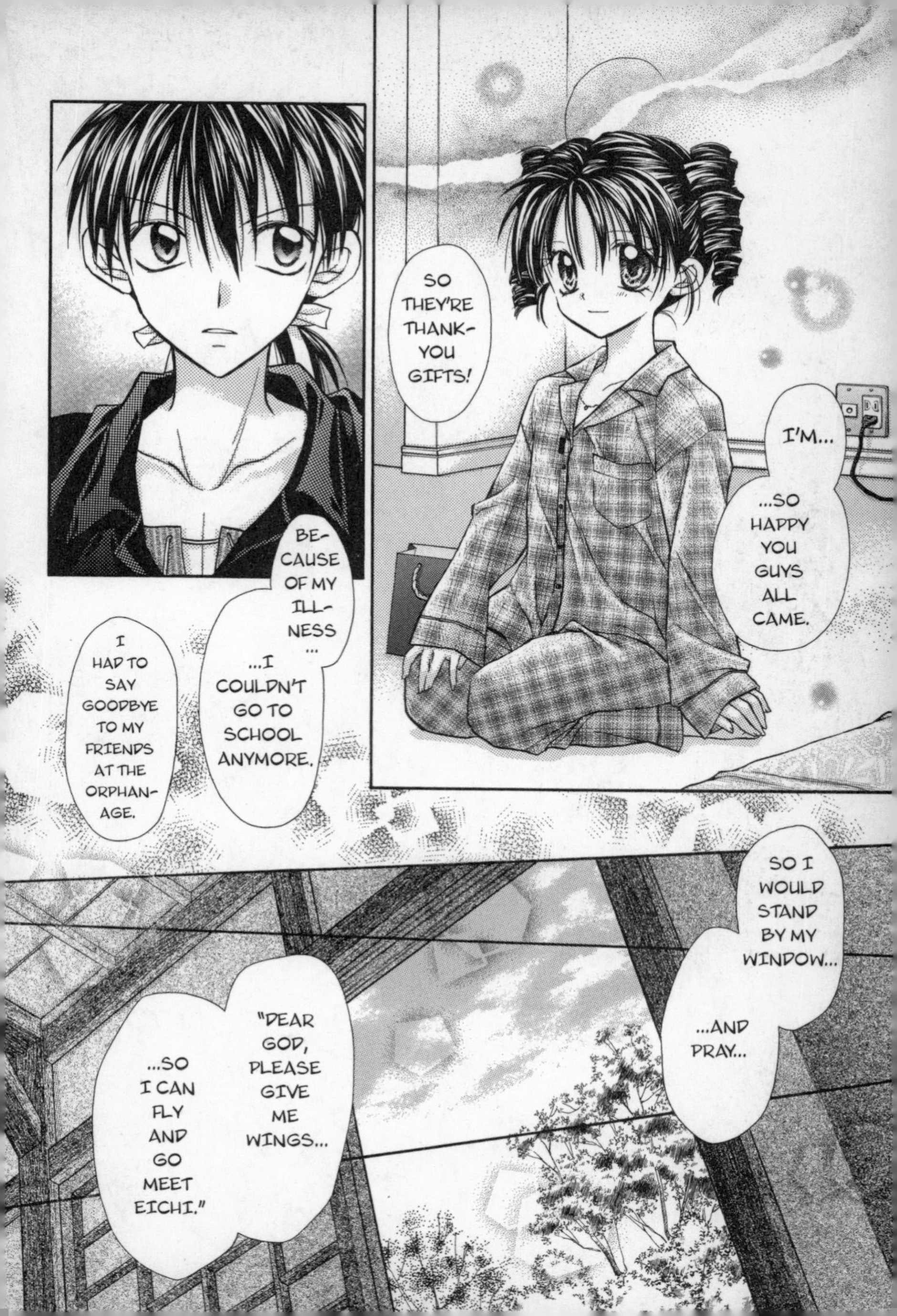
SO THEY'RE THANK-YOU GIFTS!
I'M...
...SO HAPPY YOU GUYS ALL CAME.
BECAUSE OF MY ILLNESS...
...I COULDN'T GO TO SCHOOL ANYMORE.
I HAD TO SAY GOODBYE TO MY FRIENDS AT THE ORPHANAGE.
SO I WOULD STAND BY MY WINDOW...
...AND PRAY...
"DEAR GOD, PLEASE GIVE ME WINGS...
...SO I CAN FLY AND GO MEET EICHI."

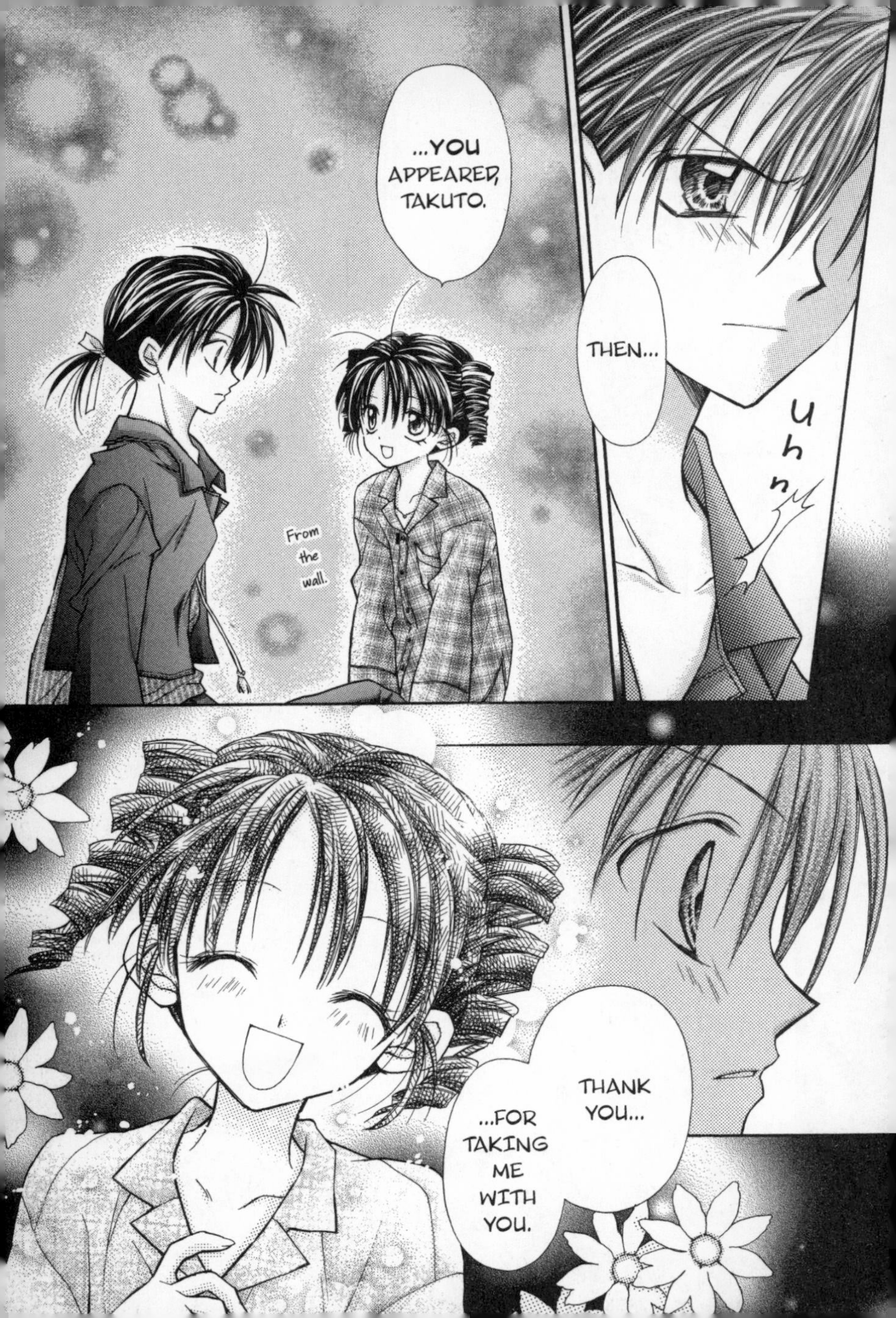
THEN...
Uhn
...YOU APPEARED, TAKUTO.
From the wall.
THANK YOU...
...FOR TAKING ME WITH YOU.

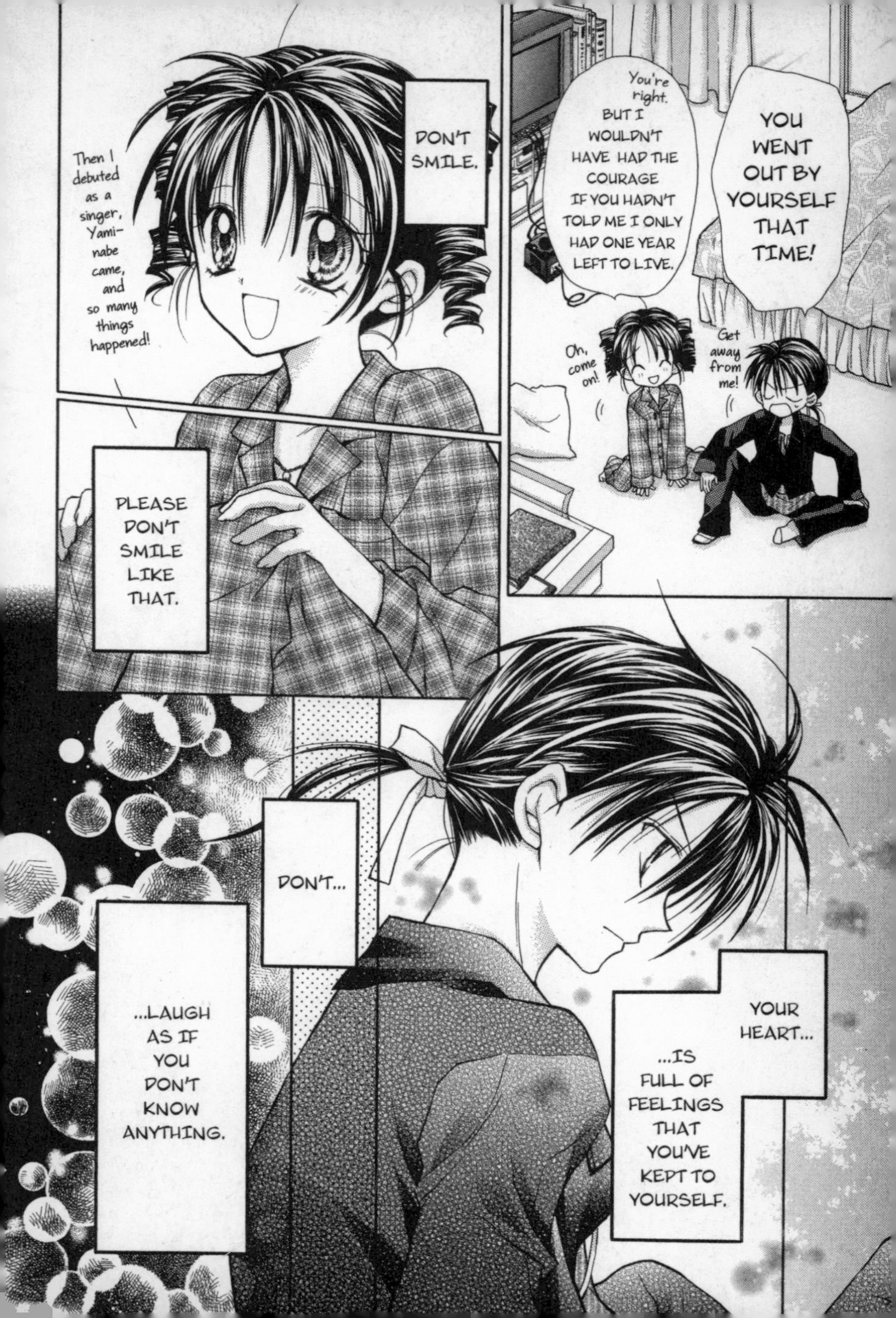
YOU WENT OUT BY YOURSELF THAT TIME!
You're right. BUT I WOULDN'T HAVE HAD THE COURAGE IF YOU HADN'T TOLD ME I ONLY HAD ONE YEAR LEFT TO LIVE.
Get away from me!
Oh, come on!
DON'T SMILE.
Then I debuted as a singer, Yami-nabe came, and so many things happened!
PLEASE DON'T SMILE LIKE THAT.
YOUR HEART...
...IS FULL OF FEELINGS THAT YOU'VE KEPT TO YOURSELF.
DON'T...
...LAUGH AS IF YOU DON'T KNOW ANYTHING.

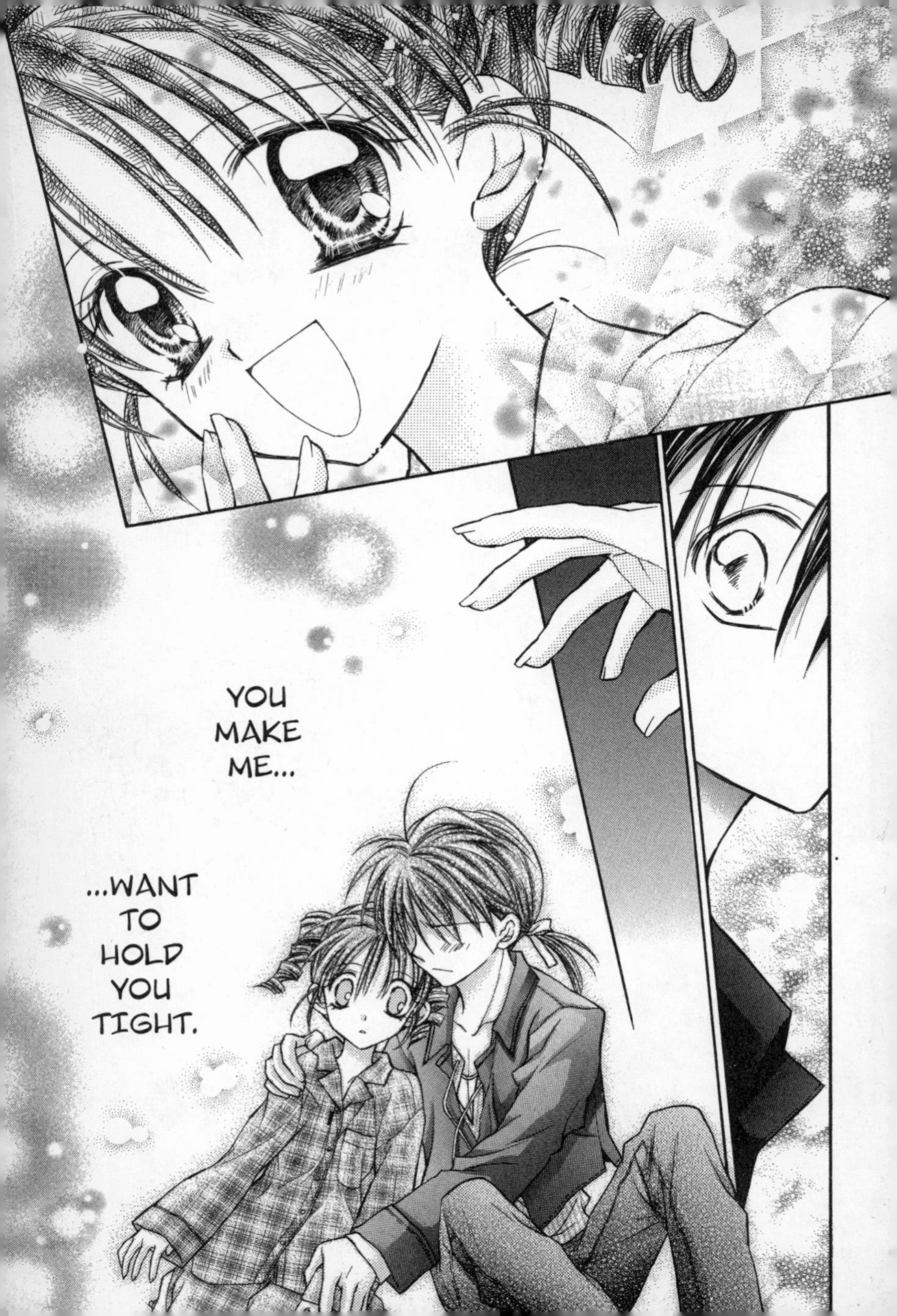
YOU MAKE ME...
...WANT TO HOLD YOU TIGHT.

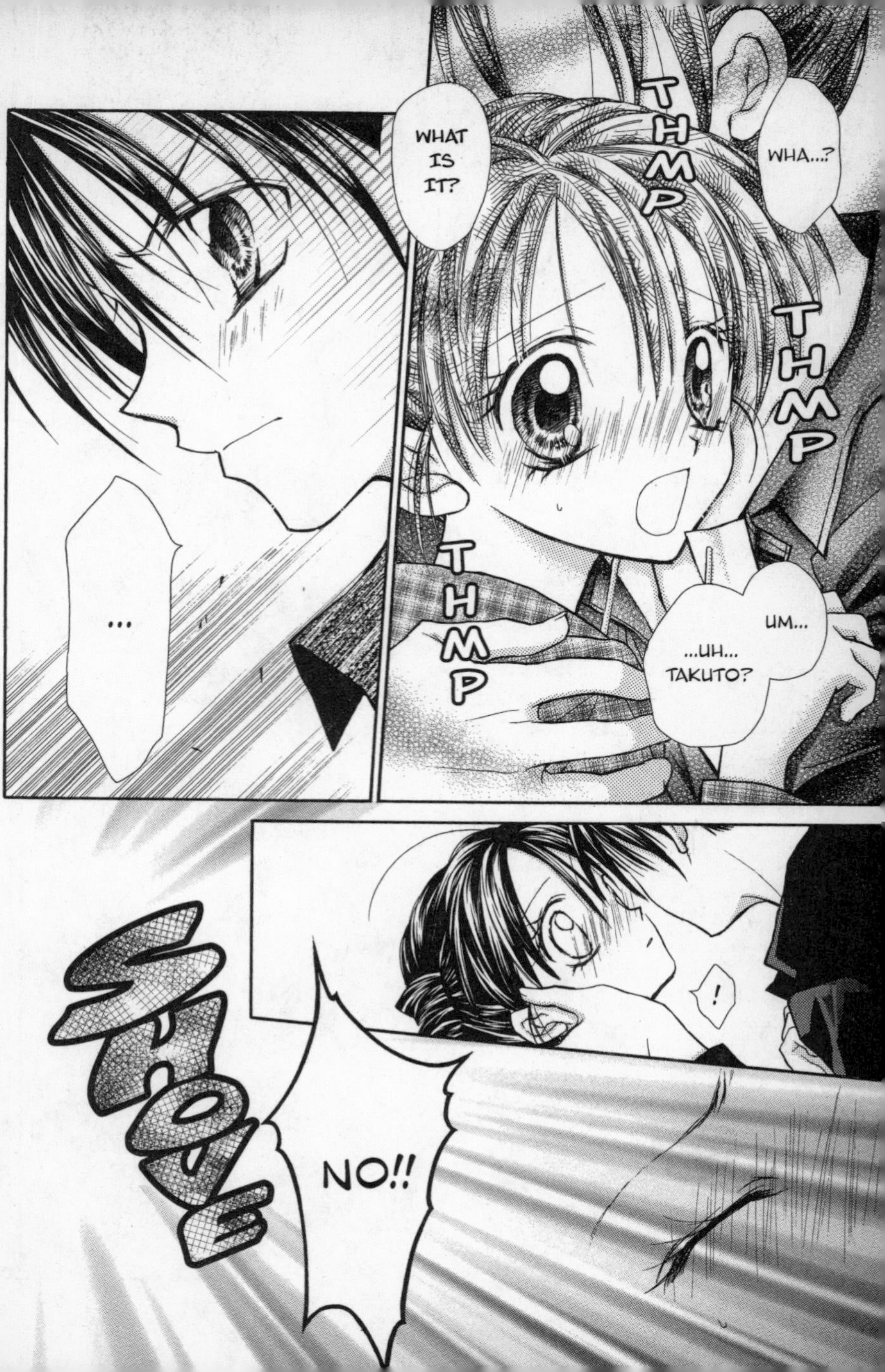
WHA...?
THMP
WHAT IS IT?
THMP
UM... ...UH... TAKUTO?
THMP
...
!
NO!!
SHOVE

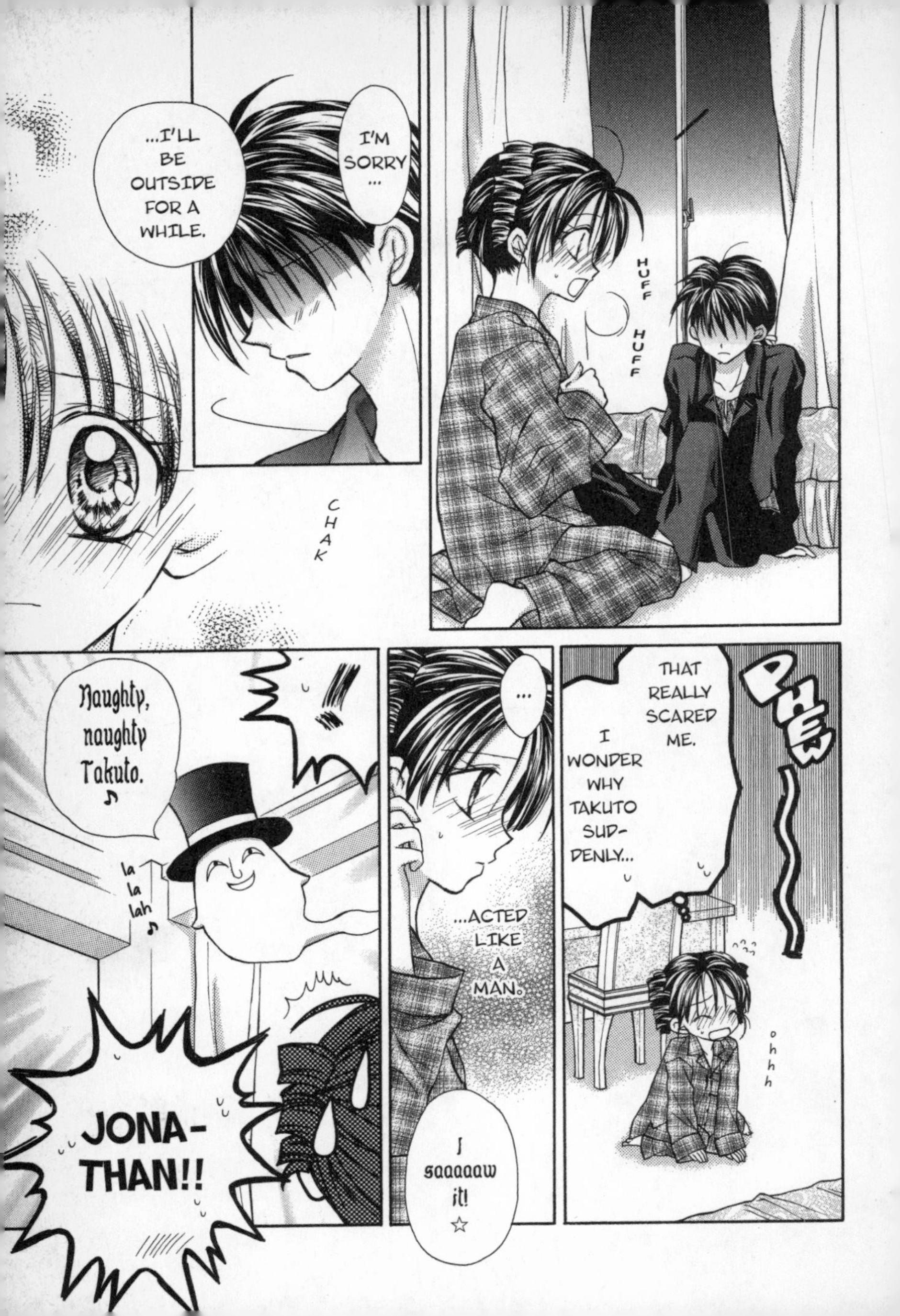
HUFF HUFF
I'M SORRY ...
...I'LL BE OUTSIDE FOR A WHILE.
CHAK
PHEW
THAT REALLY SCARED ME.
I WONDER WHY TAKUTO SUD-DENLY...
ohhh
...
...ACTED LIKE A MAN.
I saaaaaw it! ☆
!
Naughty, naughty Takuto. ♪
la la lah ♪
JONA-THAN!!

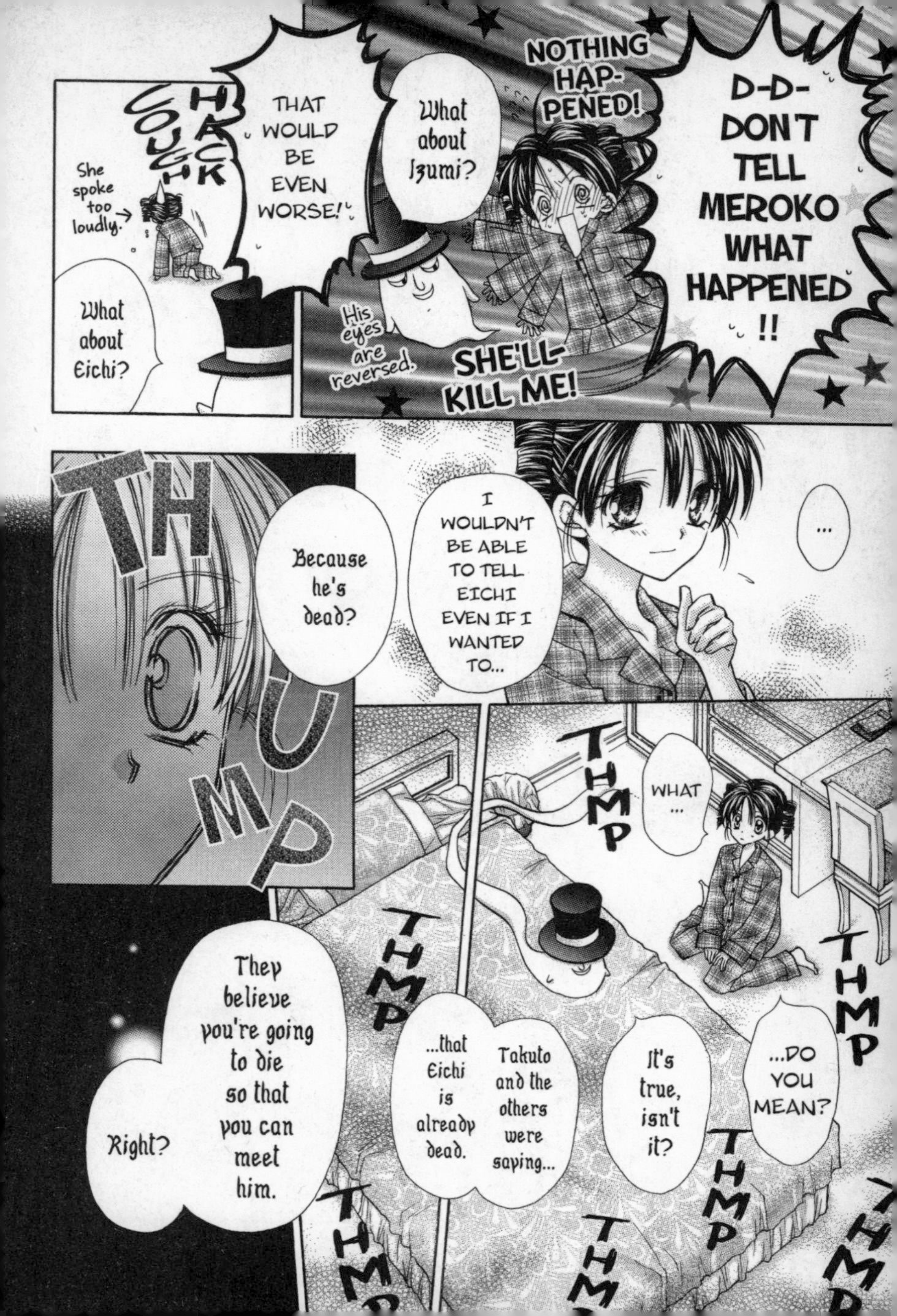
D-D-DON'T TELL MEROKO WHAT HAPPENED!!
NOTHING HAPPENED!
What about Izumi?
SHE'LL-KILL ME!
His eyes are reversed.
THAT WOULD BE EVEN WORSE!
HACK
COUGH
She spoke too loudly.
What about Eichi?
...
I WOULDN'T BE ABLE TO TELL EICHI EVEN IF I WANTED TO...
Because he's dead?
THUMP
THMP
WHAT ...
THMP
...DO YOU MEAN?
It's true, isn't it?
Takuto and the others were saying...
...that Eichi is already dead.
THMP
They believe you're going to die so that you can meet him.
Right?
THMP
THMP
THMP
THMP

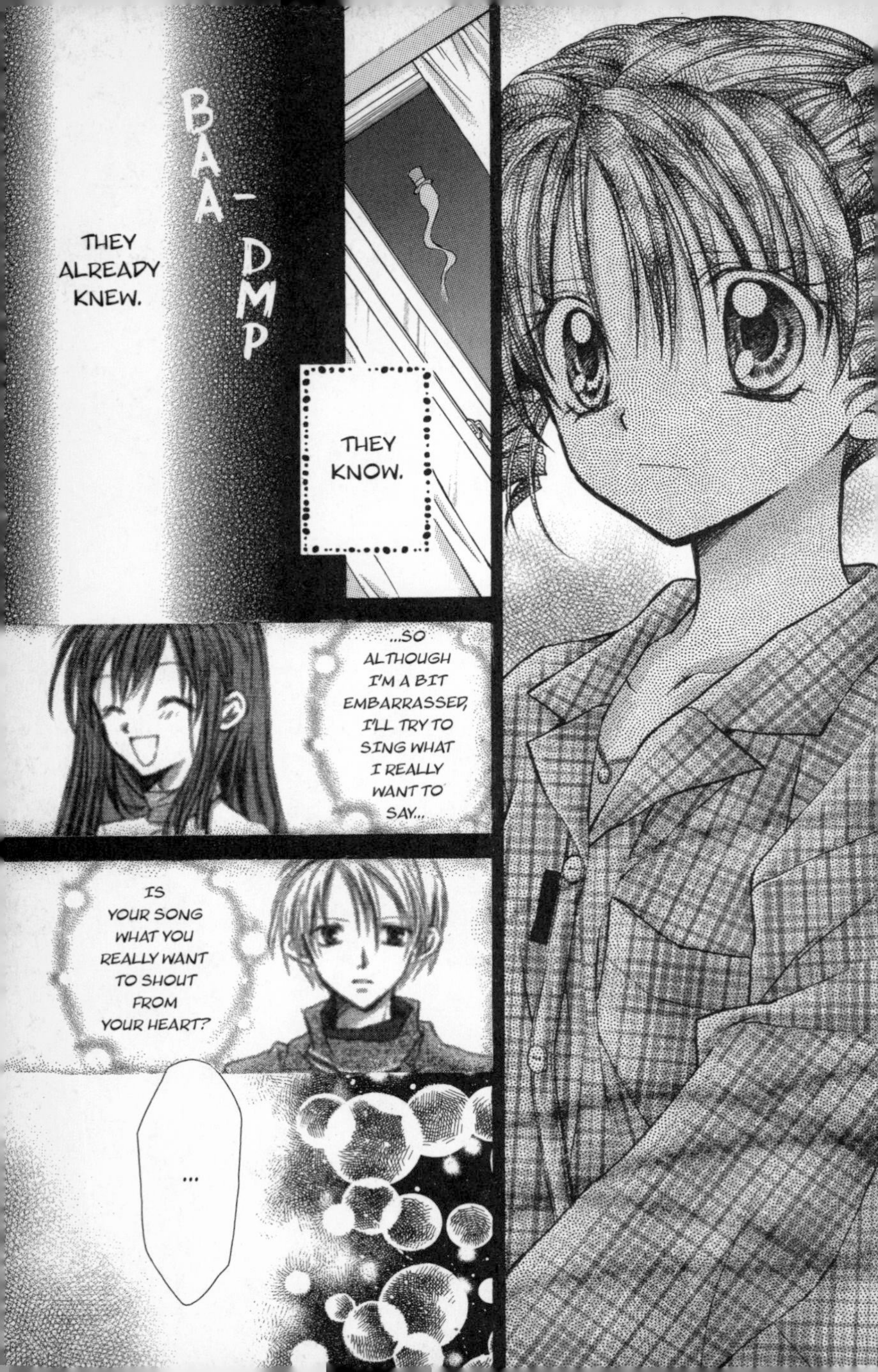
THEY KNOW.
BAA-DMP
THEY ALREADY KNEW.
...SO ALTHOUGH I'M A BIT EMBARRASSED, I'LL TRY TO SING WHAT I REALLY WANT TO SAY...
IS YOUR SONG WHAT YOU REALLY WANT TO SHOUT FROM YOUR HEART?
...

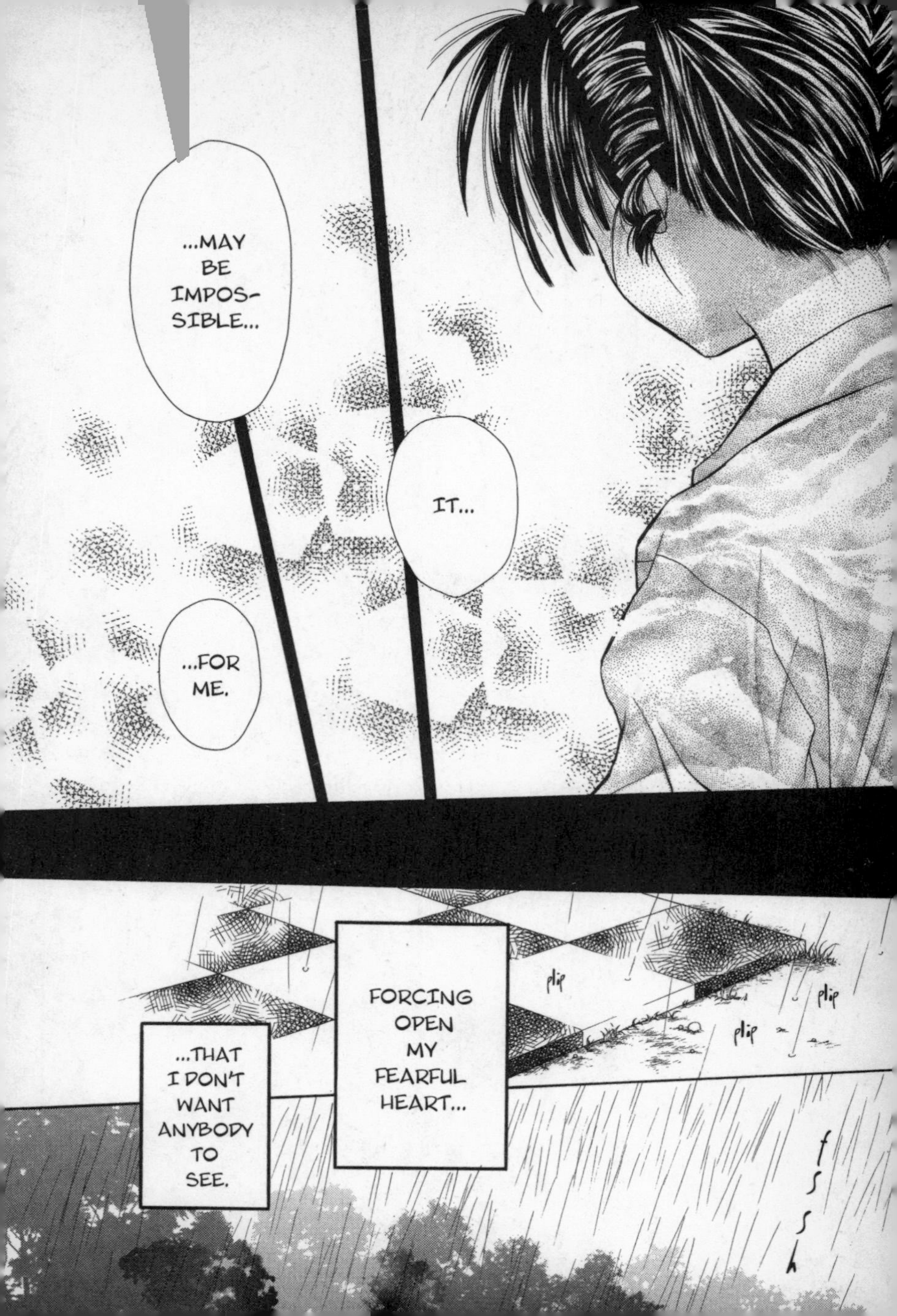
IT...
...MAY BE IMPOSSIBLE...
...FOR ME.
plip
plip
plip
FORCING OPEN MY FEARFUL HEART...
...THAT I DON'T WANT ANYBODY TO SEE.
fssh

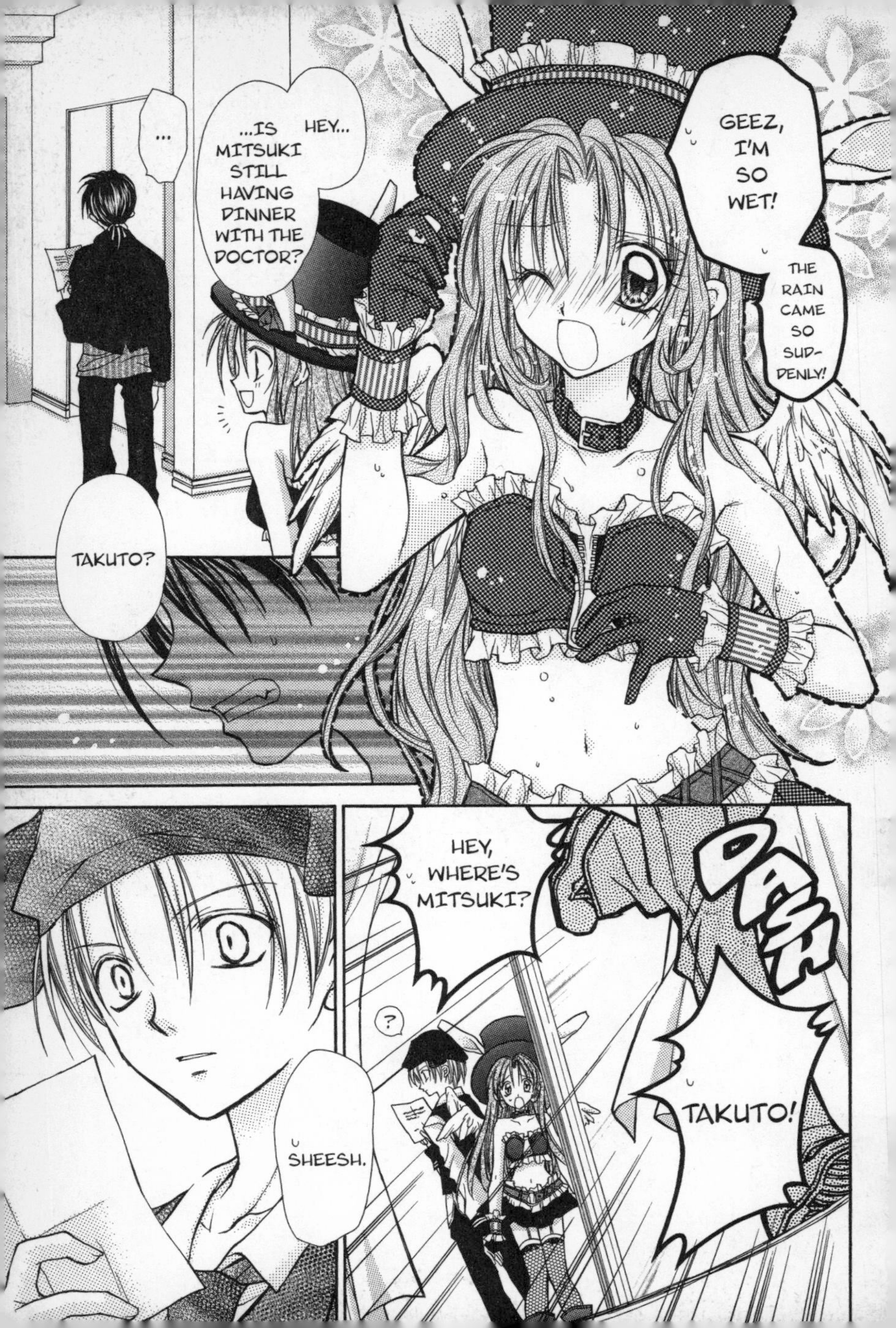
GEEZ, I'M SO WET!
THE RAIN CAME SO SUD-DENLY!
HEY...
...IS MITSUKI STILL HAVING DINNER WITH THE DOCTOR?
...
TAKUTO?
HEY, WHERE'S MITSUKI?
DASH
?
TAKUTO!
SHEESH.

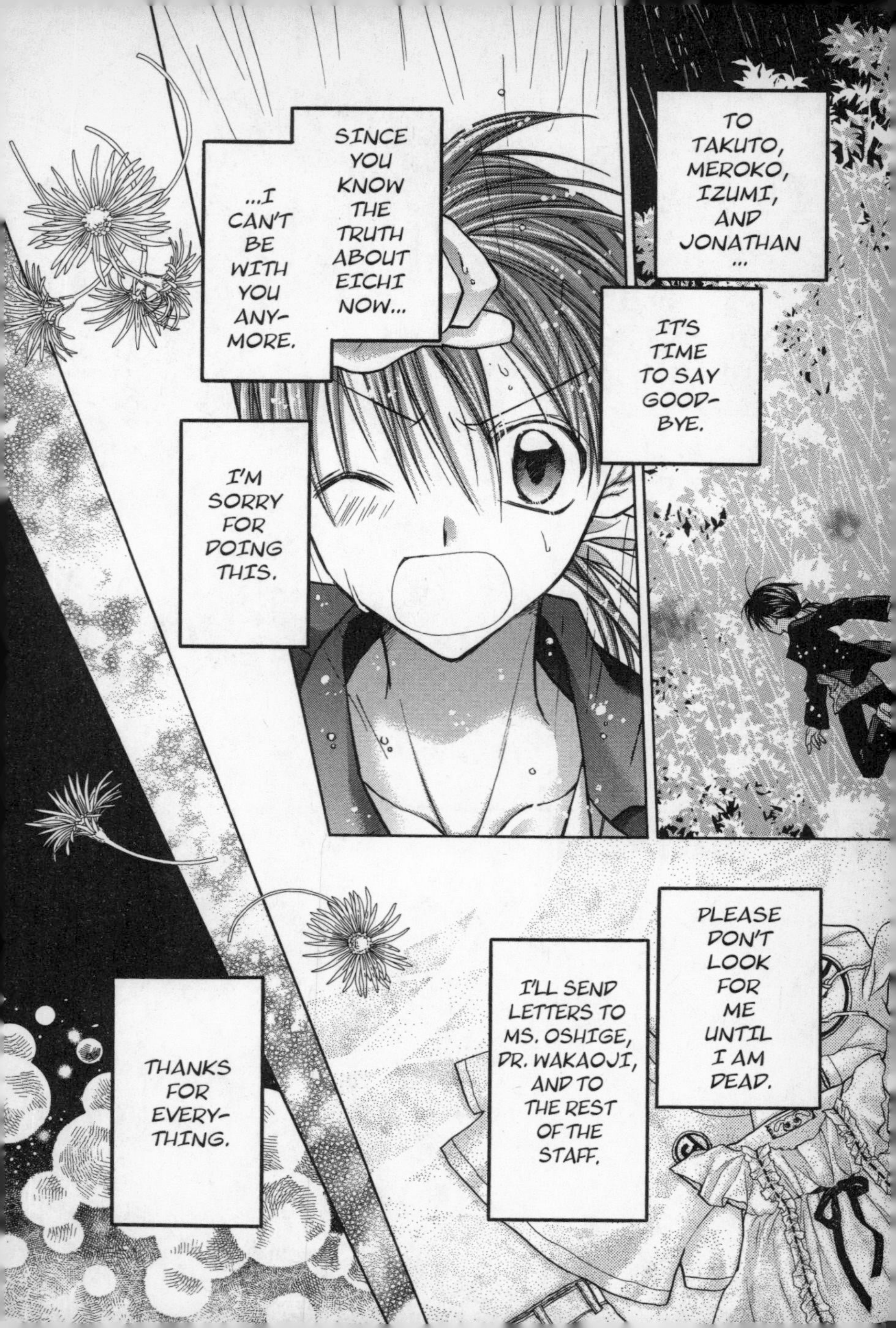
TO TAKUTO, MEROKO, IZUMI, AND JONATHAN ...
IT'S TIME TO SAY GOOD-BYE.
SINCE YOU KNOW THE TRUTH ABOUT EICHI NOW...
...I CAN'T BE WITH YOU ANY-MORE.
I'M SORRY FOR DOING THIS.
PLEASE DON'T LOOK FOR ME UNTIL I AM DEAD.
I'LL SEND LETTERS TO MS. OSHIGE, DR. WAKAOJI, AND TO THE REST OF THE STAFF.
THANKS FOR EVERY-THING.

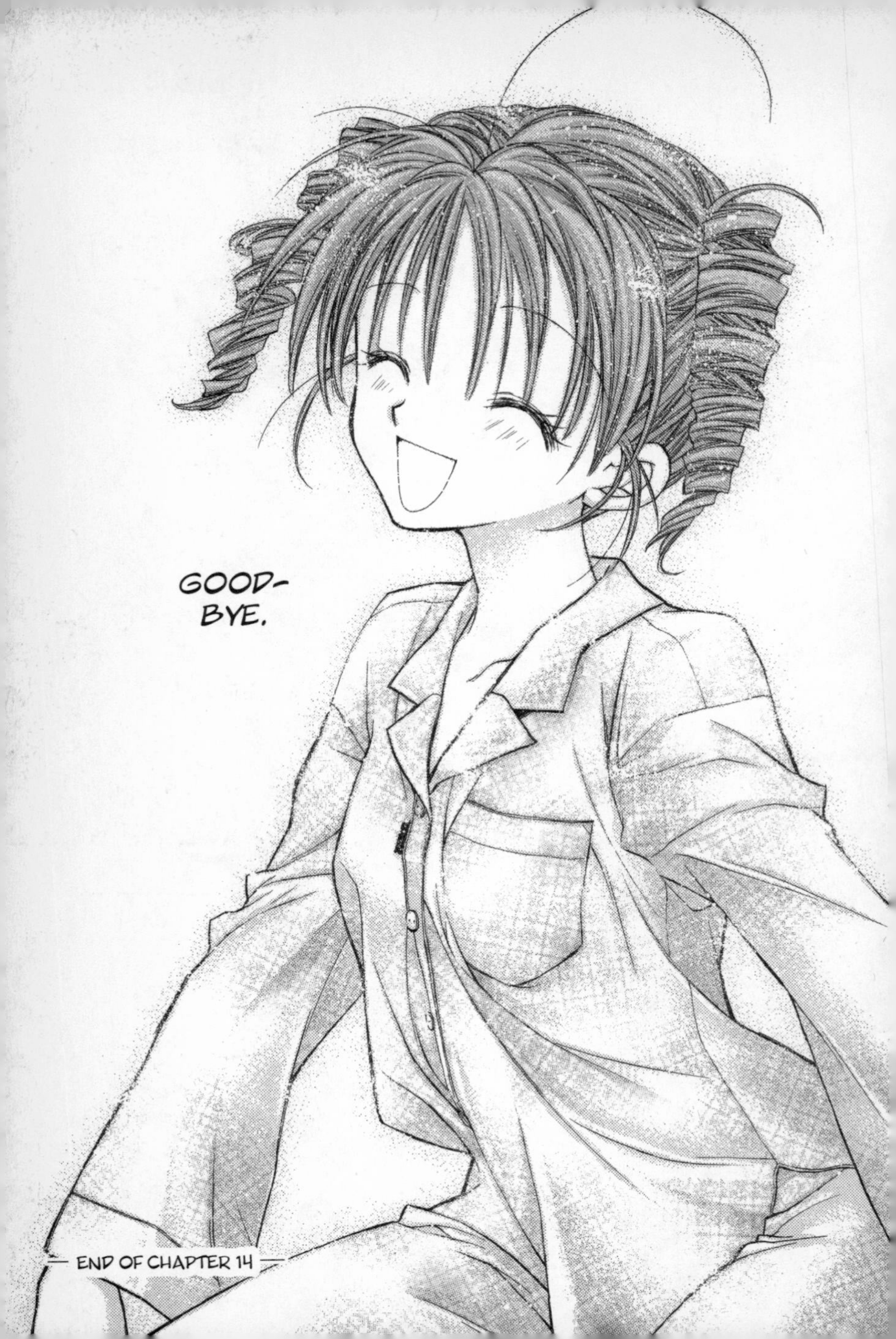
GOOD-BYE.
END OF CHAPTER 14

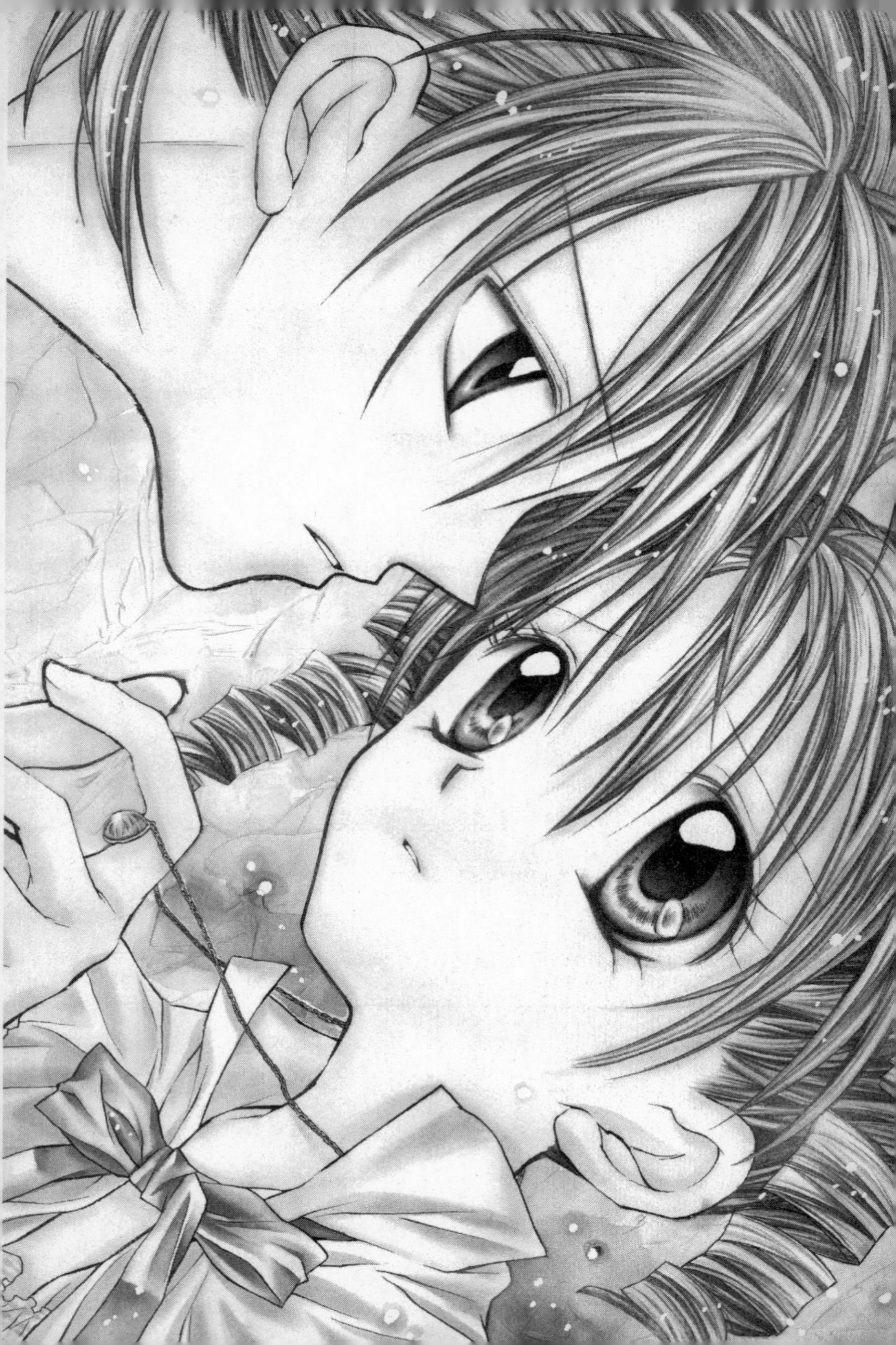

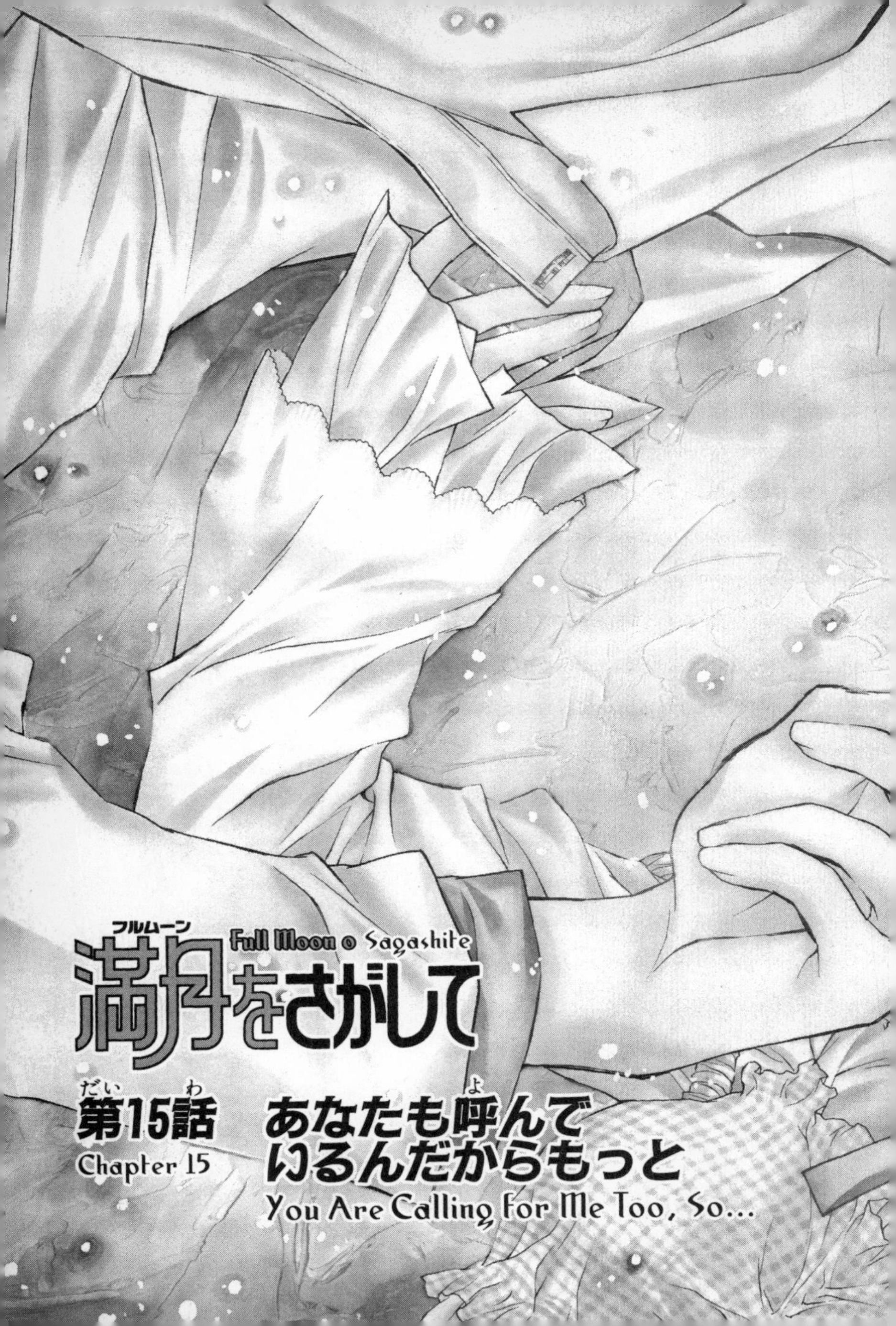

満月をさがして
Full Moon o Sagashite
第15話
Chapter 15
あなたも呼んでいるんだからもっと
You Are Calling For Me Too, So...

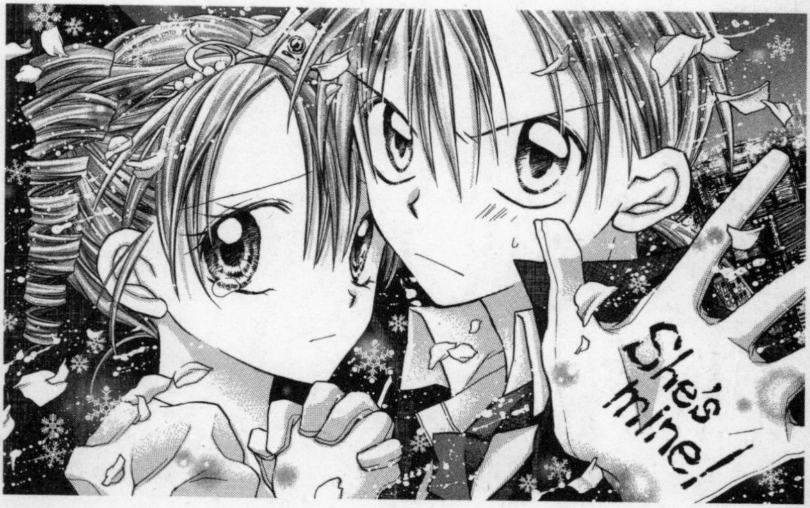
She's mine!

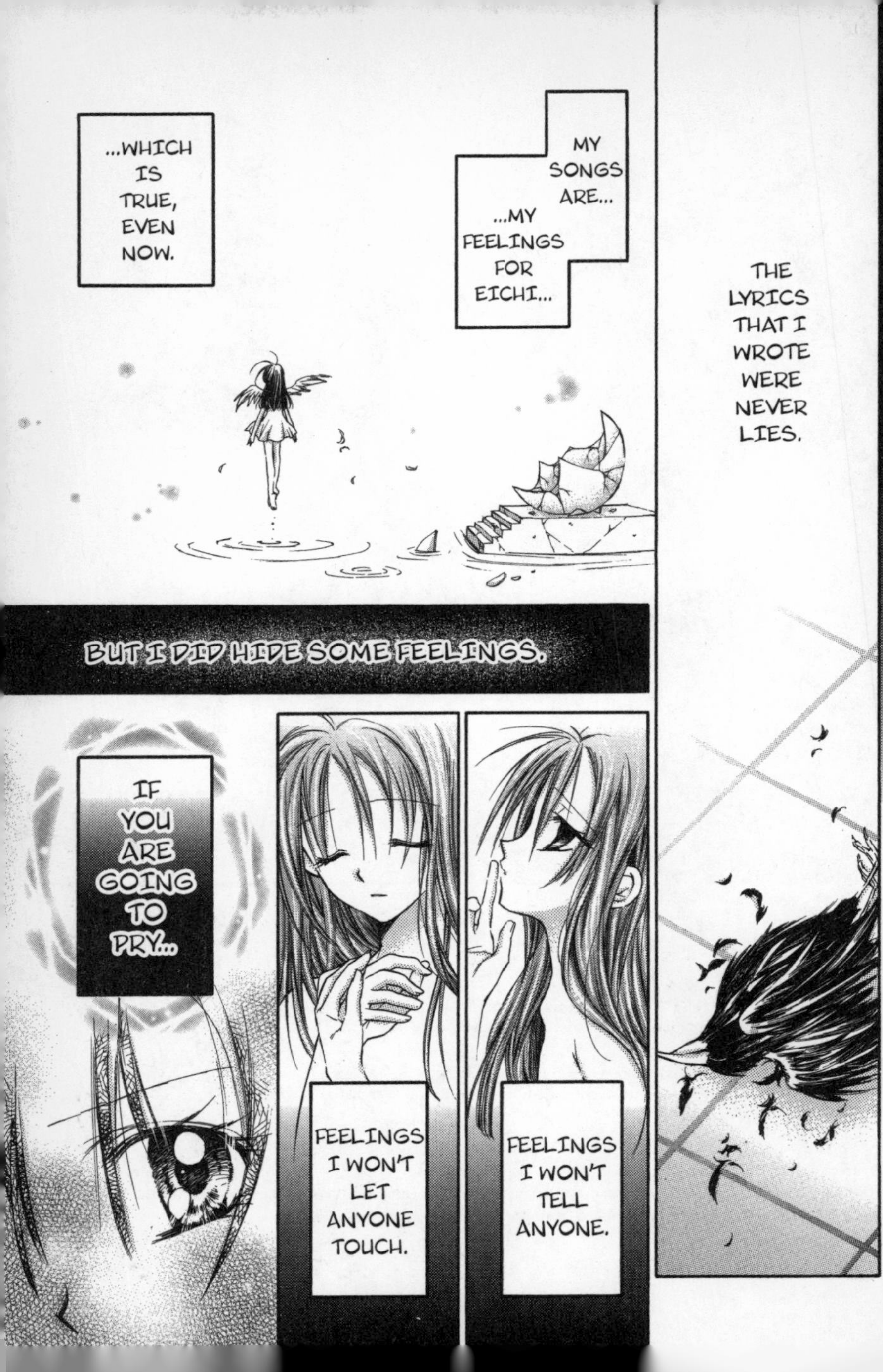
THE LYRICS THAT I WROTE WERE NEVER LIES.
MY SONGS ARE...
...MY FEELINGS FOR EICHI...
...WHICH IS TRUE, EVEN NOW.
BUT I DID HIDE SOME FEELINGS.
FEELINGS I WON'T TELL ANYONE.
FEELINGS I WON'T LET ANYONE TOUCH.
IF YOU ARE GOING TO PRY...

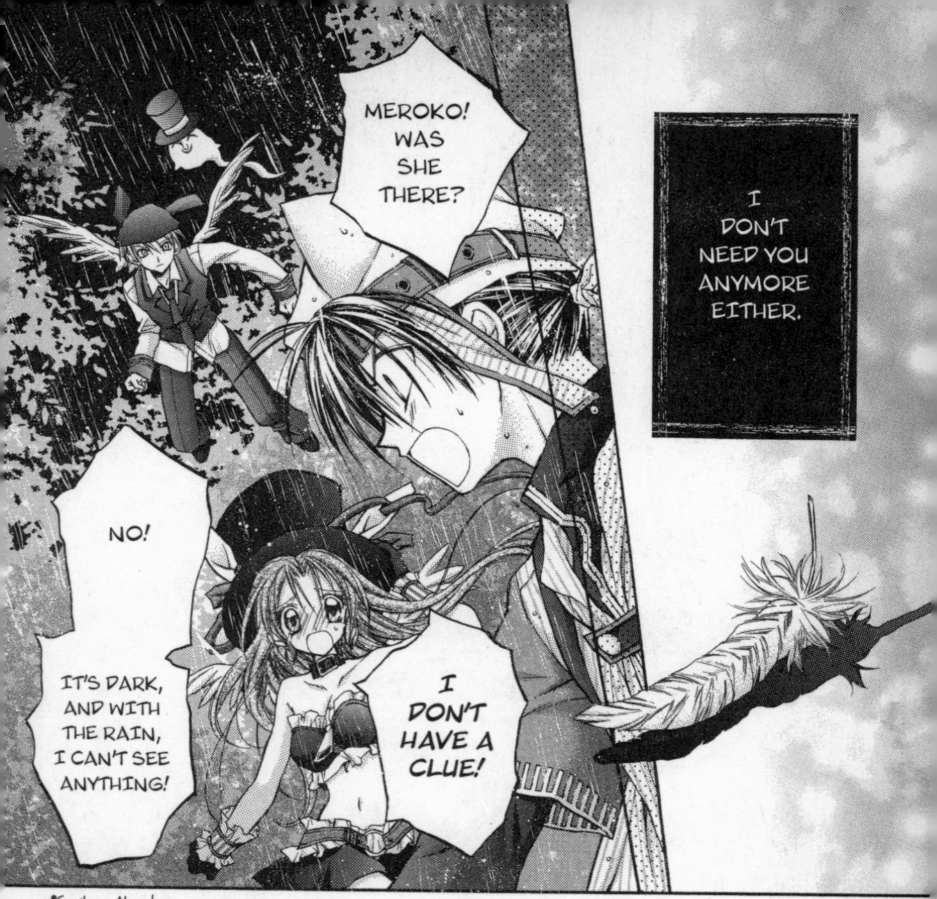
I DON'T NEED YOU ANYMORE EITHER.
MEROKO! WAS SHE THERE?
I DON'T HAVE A CLUE!
NO!
IT'S DARK, AND WITH THE RAIN, I CAN'T SEE ANYTHING!

*Spoilers Ahead.

Chapter 15 You are Calling for Me, Too, So...

Cover Copy

Their feelings come and go.

A lot of people said this illustration is too sexy, but Takuto is not lying on top of Mitsuki. Um...it's more like they're floating? There was really no time, and I have bitter memories of drawing this under pressure. Takuto pulling the pendant that Eichi gave Mitsuki...nooooo! (That's why Eichi-fans hate you, Takuto.) ☺

About this chapter! Before the tankobons come out, I sometimes apply extra screentones, but I'd completely forgotten about "that scene" with Takuto and Izumi, and I was really surprised when I turned the page.

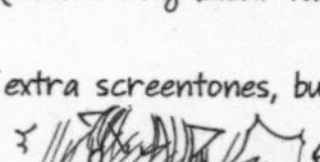
Ahhh!
← She forgets easily.

When I was drawing that scene...I was right in the middle of my period (I'm sorry), and I was feeling irritated, and because Tak-kun started saying stupid things...I got mad (I was sympathizing with Izumi-kun), so I did a little mischief. Sorry, Tak-kun. Mee-chan is "old," so she was feeling something like "these guys..."

It's heartwarming to see the four looking for Mitsuki.

From this chapter, I suddenly started to love Izumi.♡ He's good.

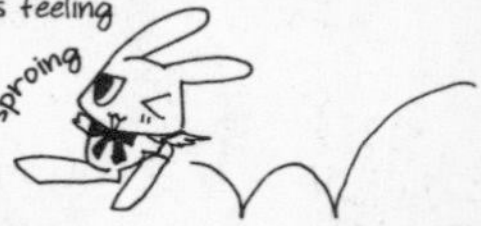
sproing

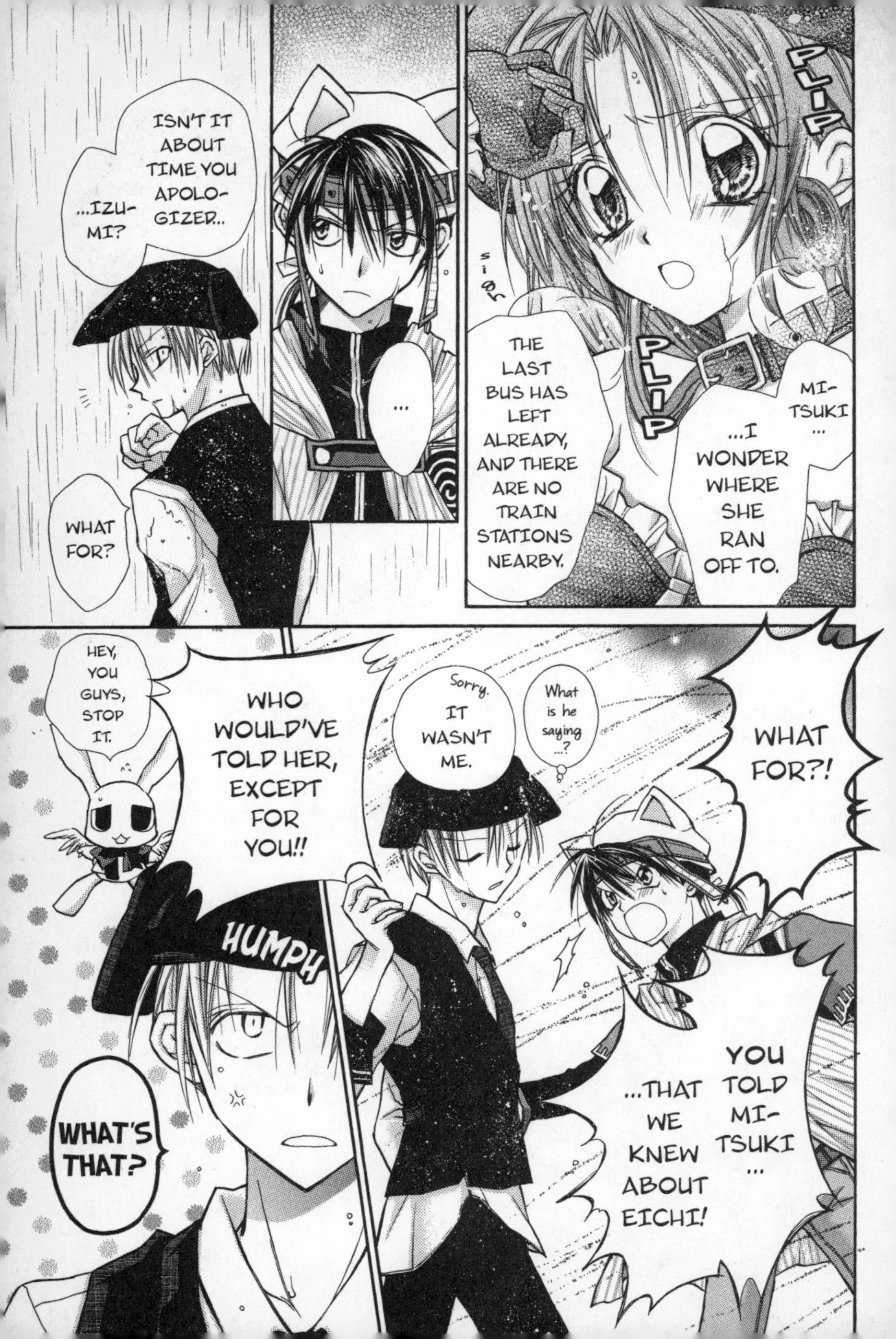
PLIP
MI-TSUKI...
...I WONDER WHERE SHE RAN OFF TO.
PLIP
THE LAST BUS HAS LEFT ALREADY, AND THERE ARE NO TRAIN STATIONS NEARBY.
sigh
...
...IZU-MI?
ISN'T IT ABOUT TIME YOU APOLO-GIZED...
WHAT FOR?
WHAT FOR?!
YOU TOLD MI-TSUKI...
...THAT WE KNEW ABOUT EICHI!
What is he saying...?
Sorry.
IT WASN'T ME.
WHO WOULD'VE TOLD HER, EXCEPT FOR YOU!!
HEY, YOU GUYS, STOP IT.
HUMPH
WHAT'S THAT?

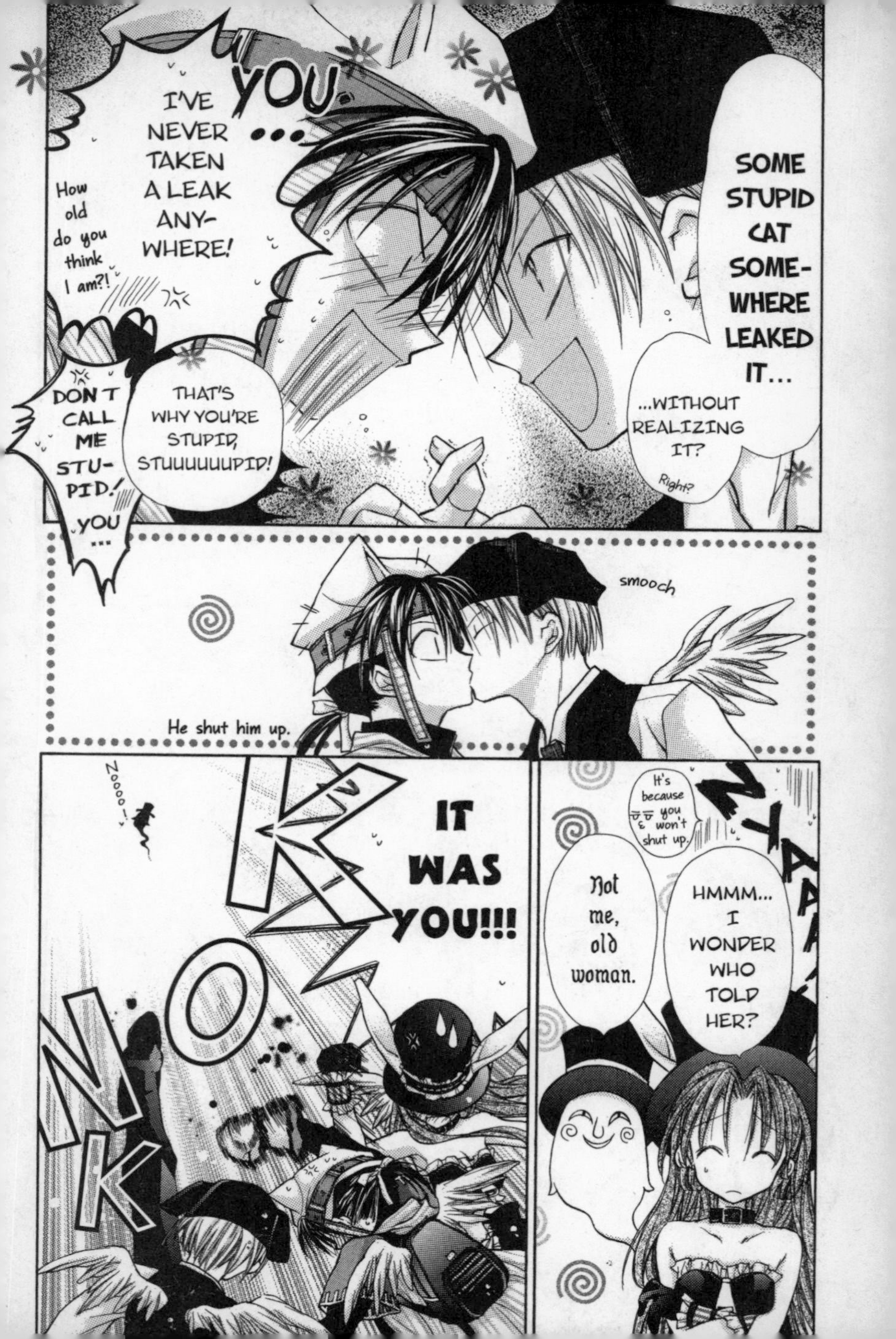
SOME STUPID CAT SOMEWHERE LEAKED IT...
...WITHOUT REALIZING IT?
Right?
YOU...
I'VE NEVER TAKEN A LEAK ANYWHERE!
How old do you think I am?!
THAT'S WHY YOU'RE STUPID, STUUUUUUPID!
DON'T CALL ME STUPID! YOU...
smooch
He shut him up.
NYAA
It's because you won't shut up.
HMMM... I WONDER WHO TOLD HER?
Not me, old woman.
IT WAS YOU!!!
KNOCK
Noooo!

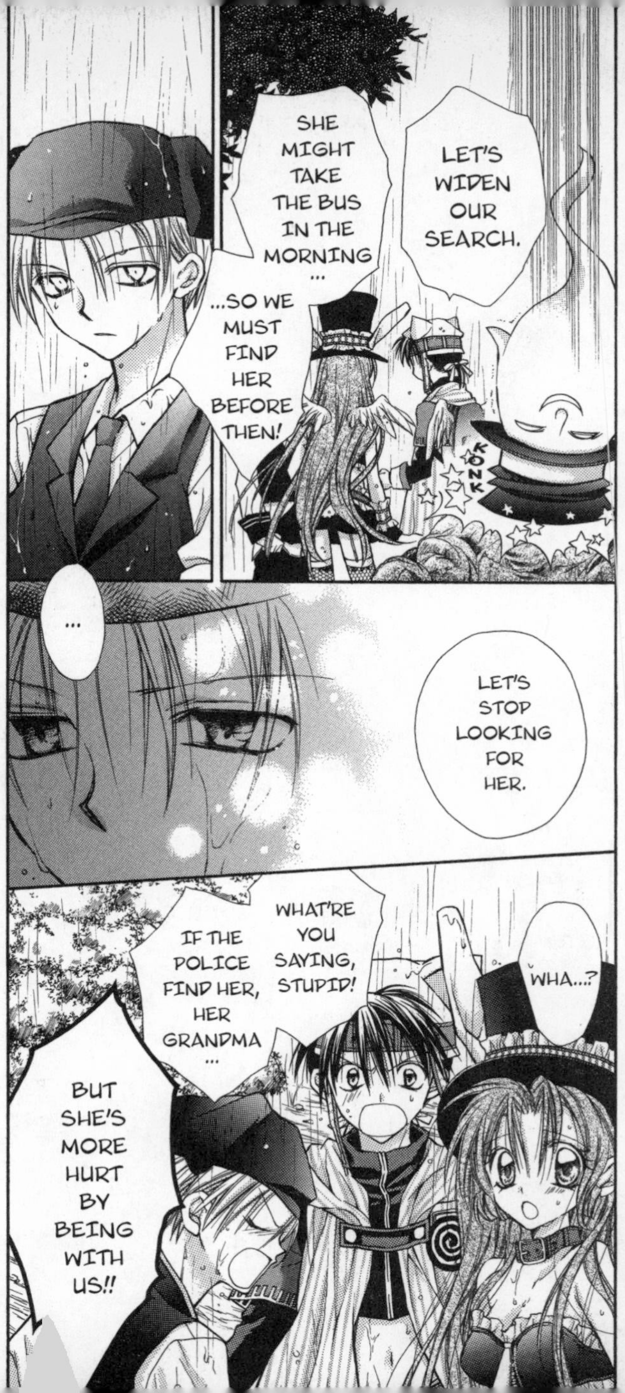
LET'S WIDEN OUR SEARCH.
SHE MIGHT TAKE THE BUS IN THE MORNING ...
...SO WE MUST FIND HER BEFORE THEN!
KONK
...
LET'S STOP LOOKING FOR HER.
WHA...?
WHAT'RE YOU SAYING, STUPID!
IF THE POLICE FIND HER, HER GRANDMA ...
BUT SHE'S MORE HURT BY BEING WITH US!!

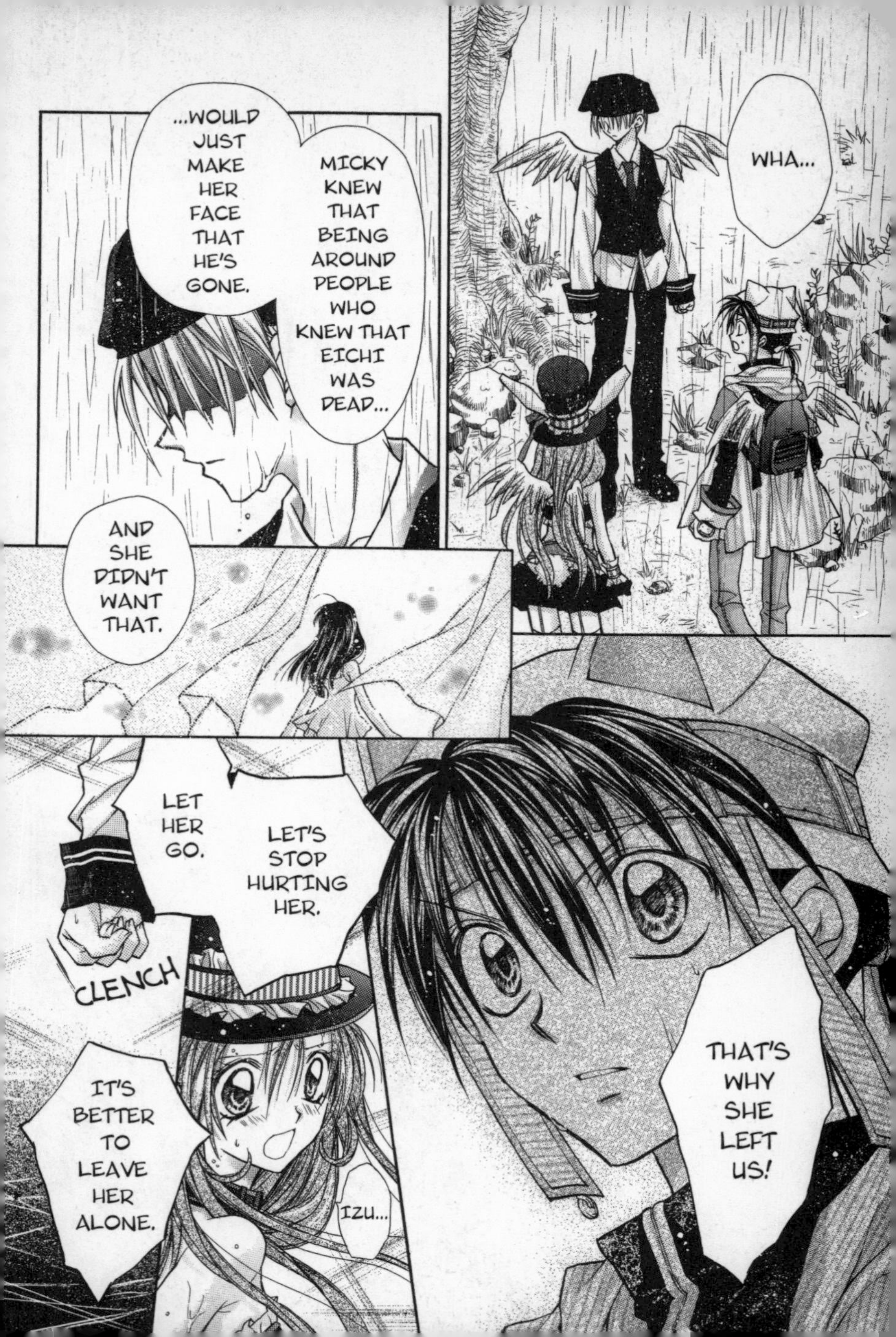
WHA...
MICKY KNEW THAT BEING AROUND PEOPLE WHO KNEW THAT EICHI WAS DEAD...
...WOULD JUST MAKE HER FACE THAT HE'S GONE.
AND SHE DIDN'T WANT THAT.
THAT'S WHY SHE LEFT US!
LET'S STOP HURTING HER.
LET HER GO.
CLENCH
IZU...
IT'S BETTER TO LEAVE HER ALONE.

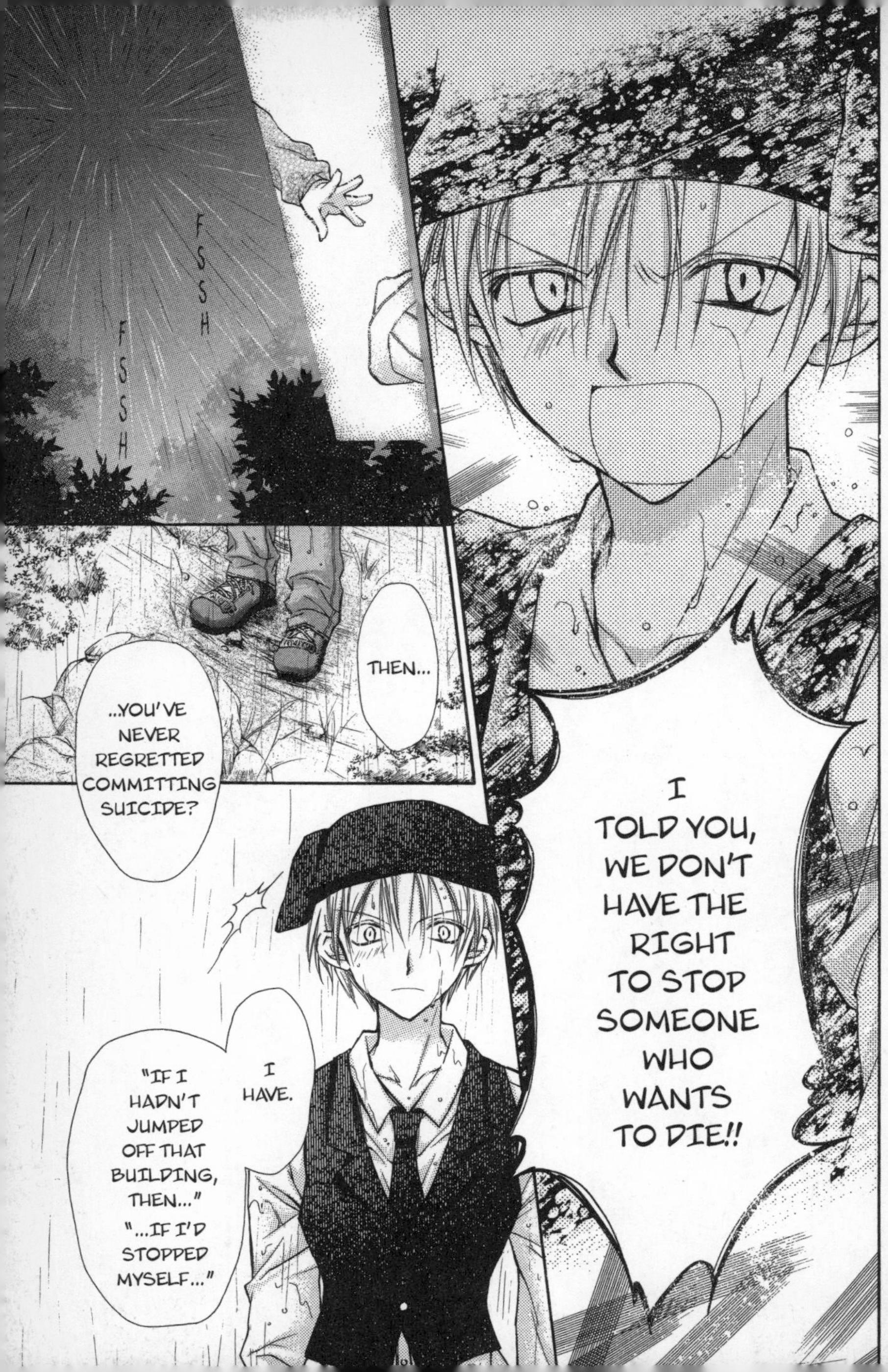
I TOLD YOU, WE DON'T HAVE THE RIGHT TO STOP SOMEONE WHO WANTS TO DIE!!
FSSH
FSSH
THEN...
...YOU'VE NEVER REGRETTED COMMITTING SUICIDE?
I HAVE.
"IF I HADN'T JUMPED OFF THAT BUILDING, THEN..."
"...IF I'D STOPPED MYSELF..."

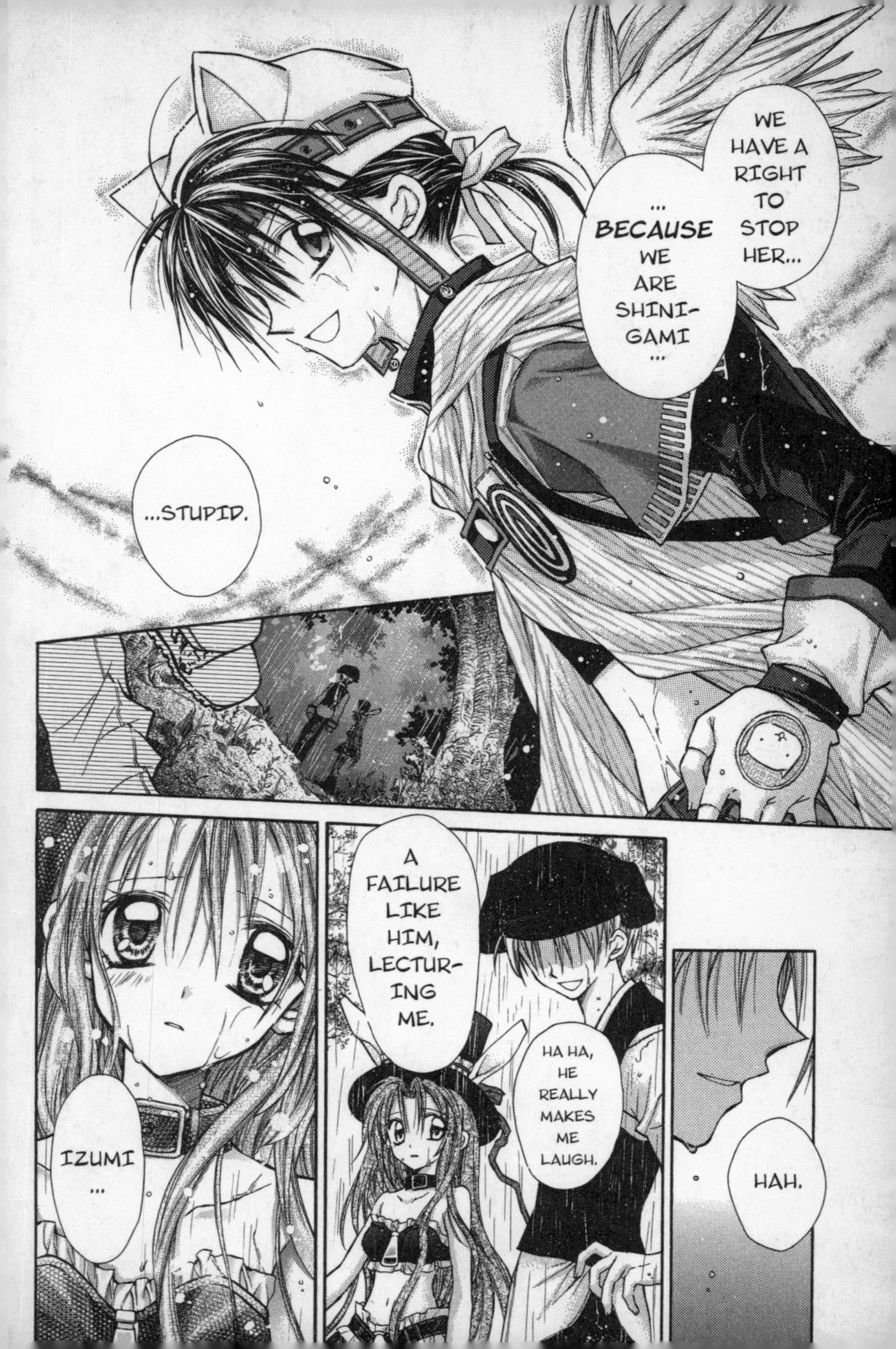
WE HAVE A RIGHT TO STOP HER...
...BECAUSE WE ARE SHINI-GAMI...
...STUPID.
HAH.
A FAILURE LIKE HIM, LECTUR-ING ME.
HA HA, HE REALLY MAKES ME LAUGH.
IZUMI...

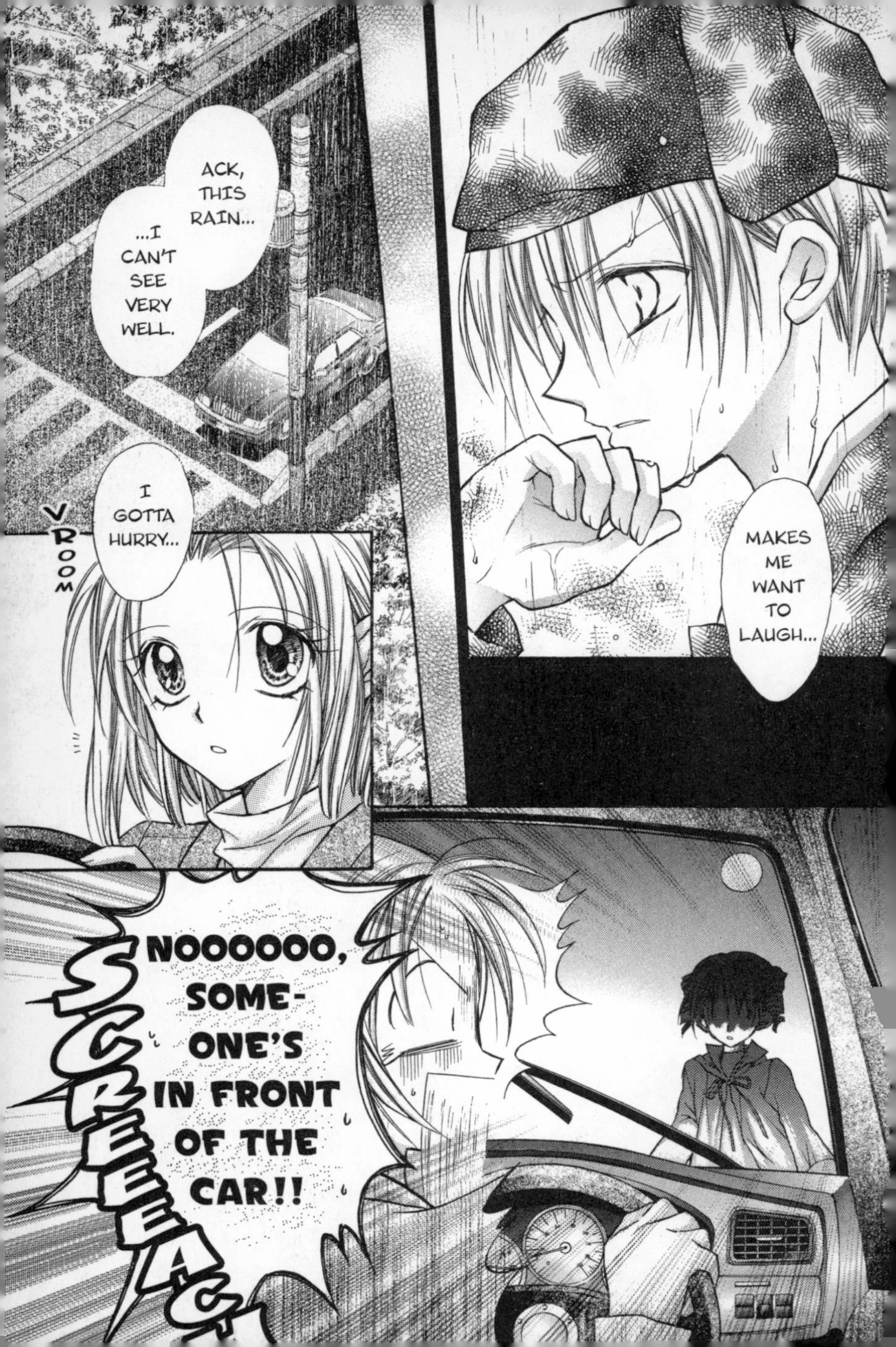

MAKES ME WANT TO LAUGH...
ACK, THIS RAIN...
...I CAN'T SEE VERY WELL.
VROOM
I GOTTA HURRY...
SCREEEAC
NOOOOOO, SOME-ONE'S IN FRONT OF THE CAR!!

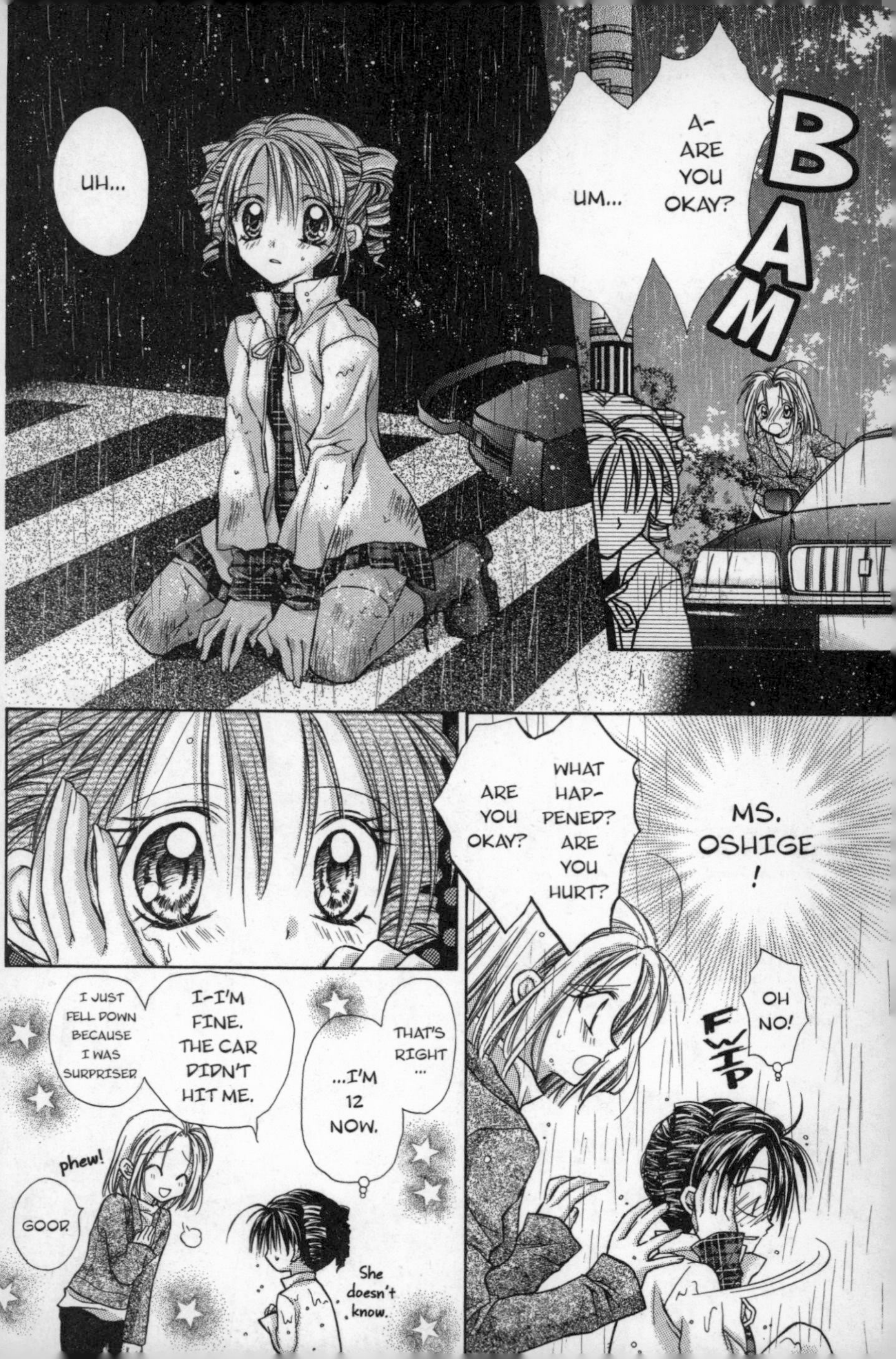
BAM
A- ARE YOU OKAY?
UM...
UH...
MS. OSHIGE!
WHAT HAPPENED? ARE YOU HURT?
ARE YOU OKAY?
OH NO!
FWIP
THAT'S RIGHT ...
...I'M 12 NOW.
I-I'M FINE. THE CAR DIDN'T HIT ME.
I JUST FELL DOWN BECAUSE I WAS SURPRISED.
phew!
GOOD.
She doesn't know.

"Full Moon" Information

There are several things to mention here.

These items are no longer available ⊗—Ed.

The first thing.

Starting July 3rd, various "Full Moon o Sagashite" goods are on sale at the Ito Yokado and Esupa stores (not all locations will be carrying the goods, though.)

The prices may be subject to change.

- Coffee mug — 800 yen
- Transparent tote bag — 980 yen
- Paper fan — 400 yen
- Mini-size towel — 400 yen (2 types)
- Vinyl pouch — 600 yen
- Face towel — 700 yen
- Postcards — 400 yen
  (3 cards in one set, 2 sets available)
- Denim bag (price to be determined)
- Wallet — 720 yen
- Folding umbrella — 1,980 yen

Arinacchi's recommendations are the paper fan, postcards, and the denim bag. The denim bag is really cute.
Please take a look at them.

The second thing.

There will be a 2003 calendar coming out!! Please reserve it if you want to spend next year with Mitsuki (the deadline for reserving the calendar is end of September, and the calendar will be on sale in November).

You also can reserve it on the Internet, at
→ http://www.s-book.com/.

If you don't have Internet access, please reserve a copy at your neighborhood bookstore. The cover is a new illustration (Mitsuki + 3 Shinigami), and I chose which illustrations to use in the calendar.

The third thing.
The September issue of *Ribon* will come with a CD-ROM.
I don't know how this happened, but ////
there is a typing game using my voice, and you can make your own letter sets by combining illustrations included in the CD-ROM.

Please buy *Ribon*!

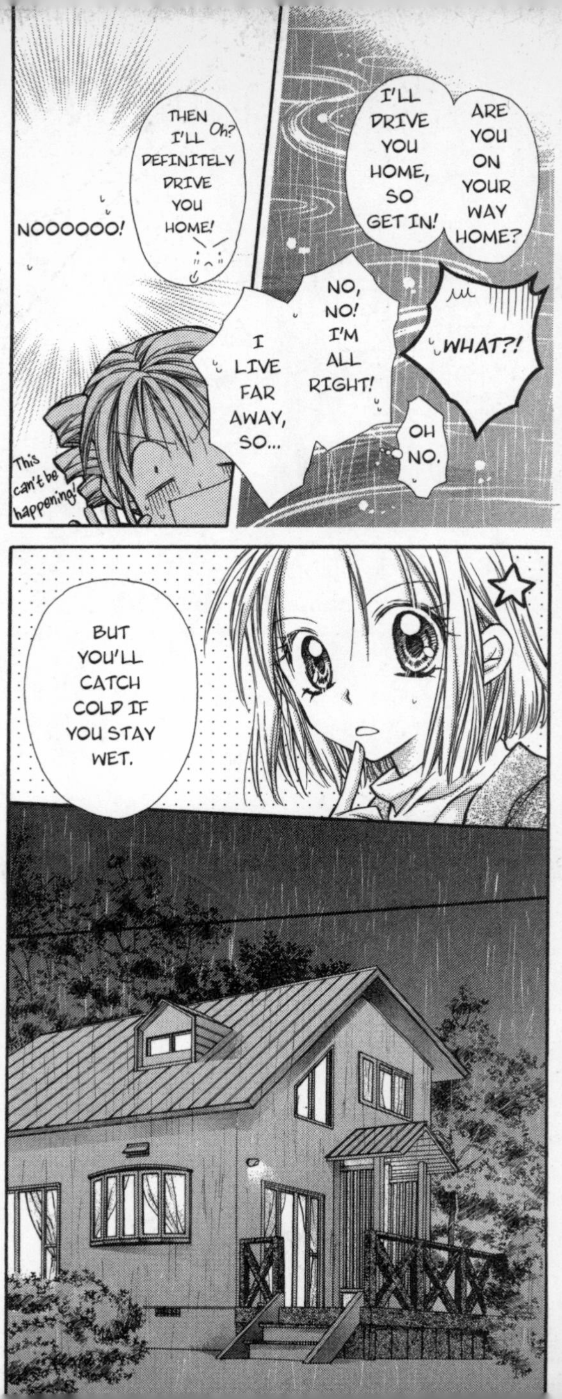
ARE YOU ON YOUR WAY HOME?
I'LL DRIVE YOU HOME, SO GET IN!
WHAT?!
NO, NO! I'M ALL RIGHT!
I LIVE FAR AWAY, SO...
OH NO.
Oh?
THEN I'LL DEFINITELY DRIVE YOU HOME!
NOOOOOO!
This can't be happening!
BUT YOU'LL CATCH COLD IF YOU STAY WET.

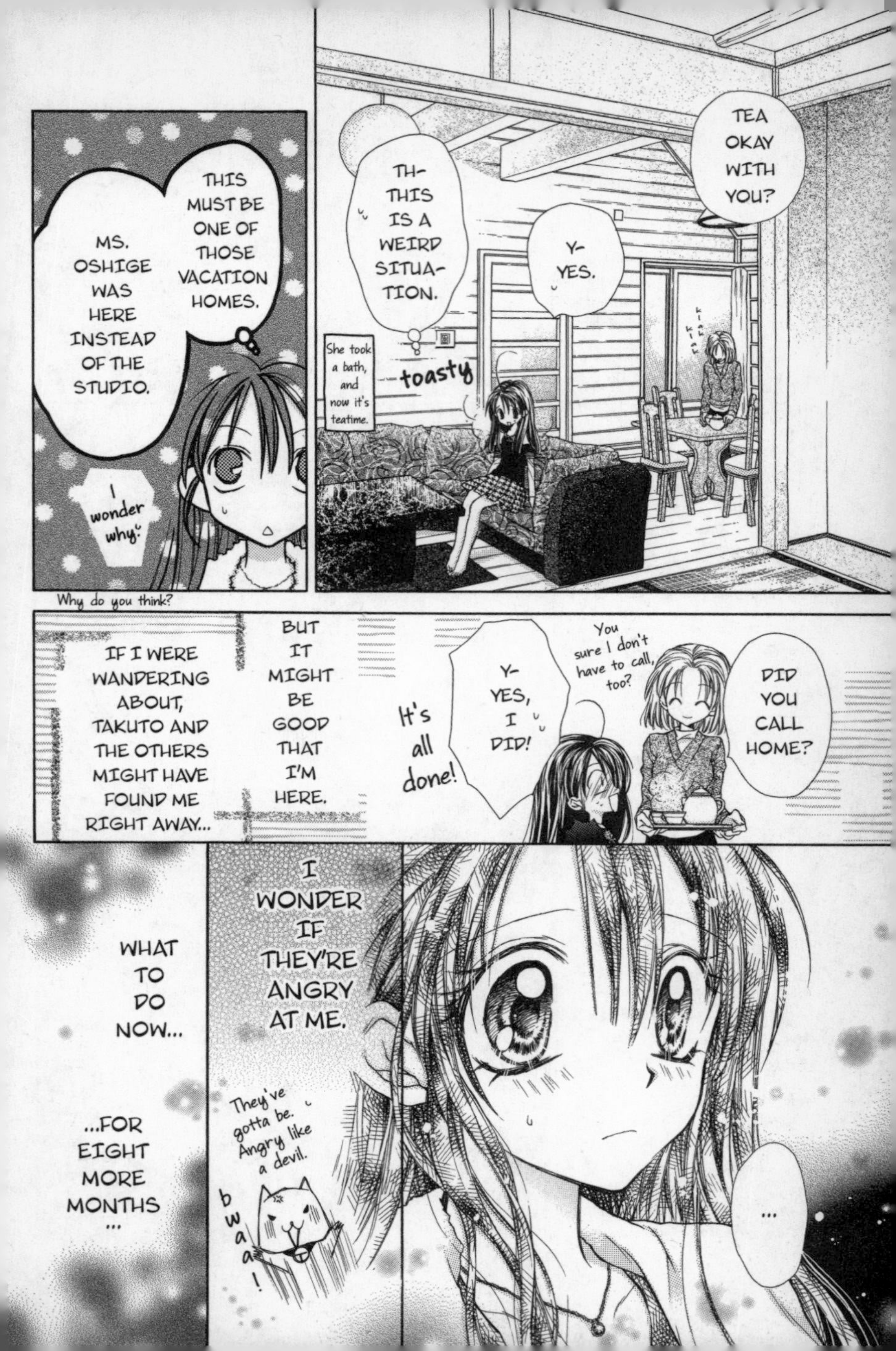
TEA OKAY WITH YOU?
Y-YES.
TH-THIS IS A WEIRD SITUATION.
She took a bath, and now it's teatime.
toasty
klak klak
THIS MUST BE ONE OF THOSE VACATION HOMES.
MS. OSHIGE WAS HERE INSTEAD OF THE STUDIO.
I wonder why.
Why do you think?
DID YOU CALL HOME?
You sure I don't have to call, too?
Y-YES, I DID!
It's all done!
BUT IT MIGHT BE GOOD THAT I'M HERE.
IF I WERE WANDERING ABOUT, TAKUTO AND THE OTHERS MIGHT HAVE FOUND ME RIGHT AWAY...
...
I WONDER IF THEY'RE ANGRY AT ME.
They've gotta be. Angry like a devil.
bwaa!
WHAT TO DO NOW...
...FOR EIGHT MORE MONTHS...

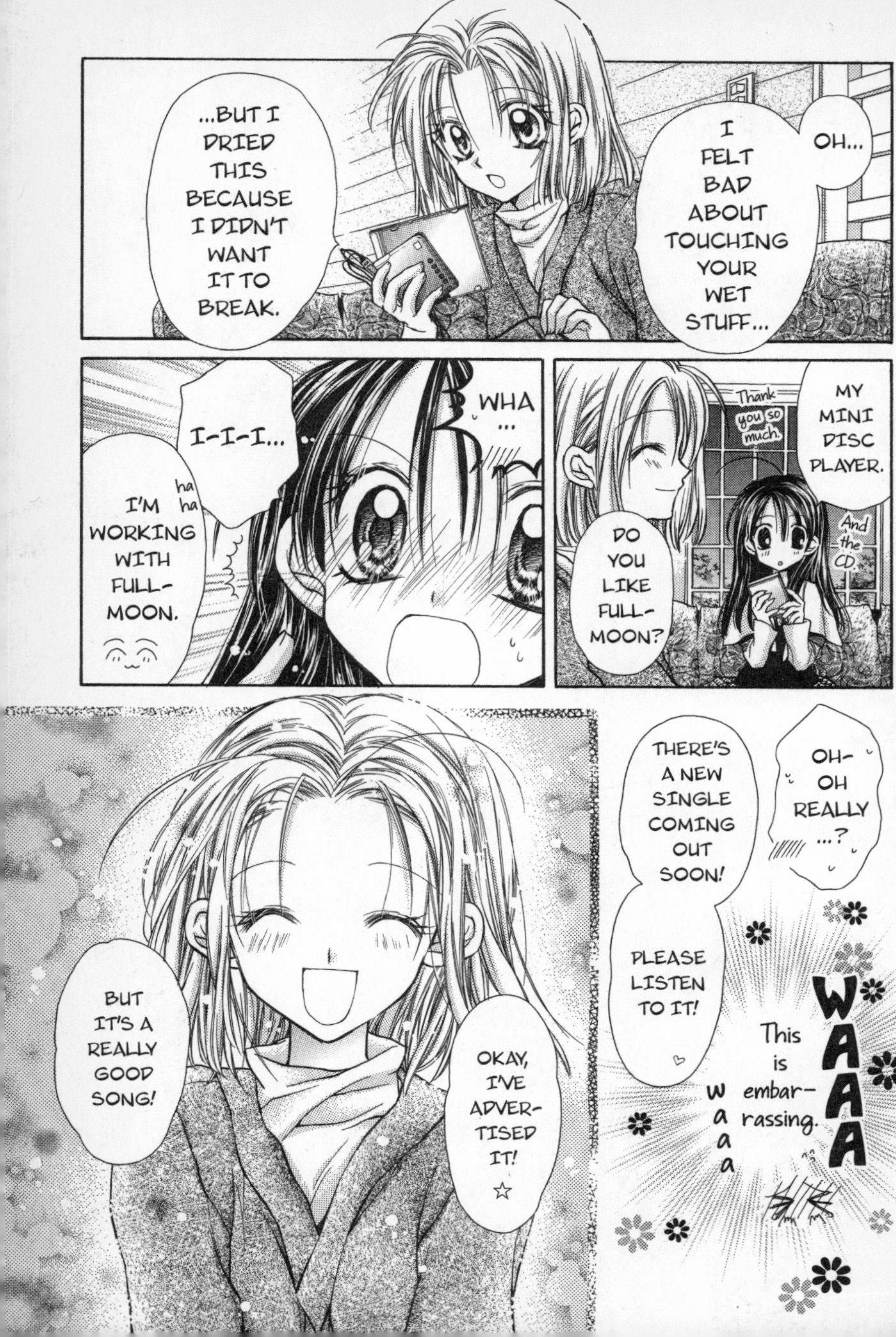
OH...
I FELT BAD ABOUT TOUCHING YOUR WET STUFF...
...BUT I DRIED THIS BECAUSE I DIDN'T WANT IT TO BREAK.
MY MINI DISC PLAYER.
Thank you so much.
And the CD.
DO YOU LIKE FULL-MOON?
WHA ...
I-I-I...
ha ha
I'M WORKING WITH FULL-MOON.
OH-OH REALLY ...?
THERE'S A NEW SINGLE COMING OUT SOON!
PLEASE LISTEN TO IT!
WAAA
This is embarrassing.
waaa
OKAY, I'VE ADVERTISED IT! ☆
BUT IT'S A REALLY GOOD SONG!

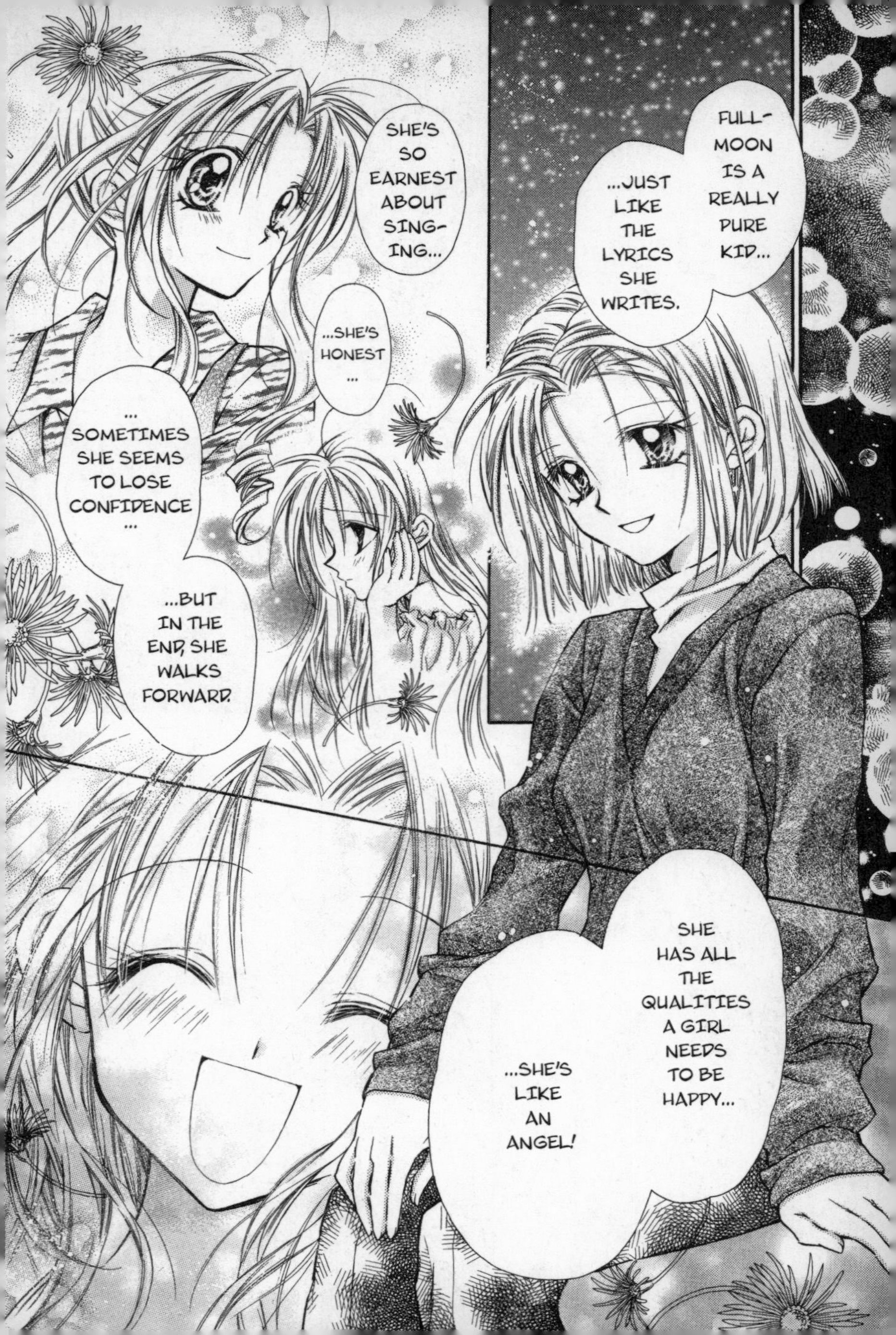
FULL-MOON IS A REALLY PURE KID...
...JUST LIKE THE LYRICS SHE WRITES.
SHE'S SO EARNEST ABOUT SINGING...
...SHE'S HONEST...
...SOMETIMES SHE SEEMS TO LOSE CONFIDENCE...
...BUT IN THE END, SHE WALKS FORWARD.
SHE HAS ALL THE QUALITIES A GIRL NEEDS TO BE HAPPY...
...SHE'S LIKE AN ANGEL!

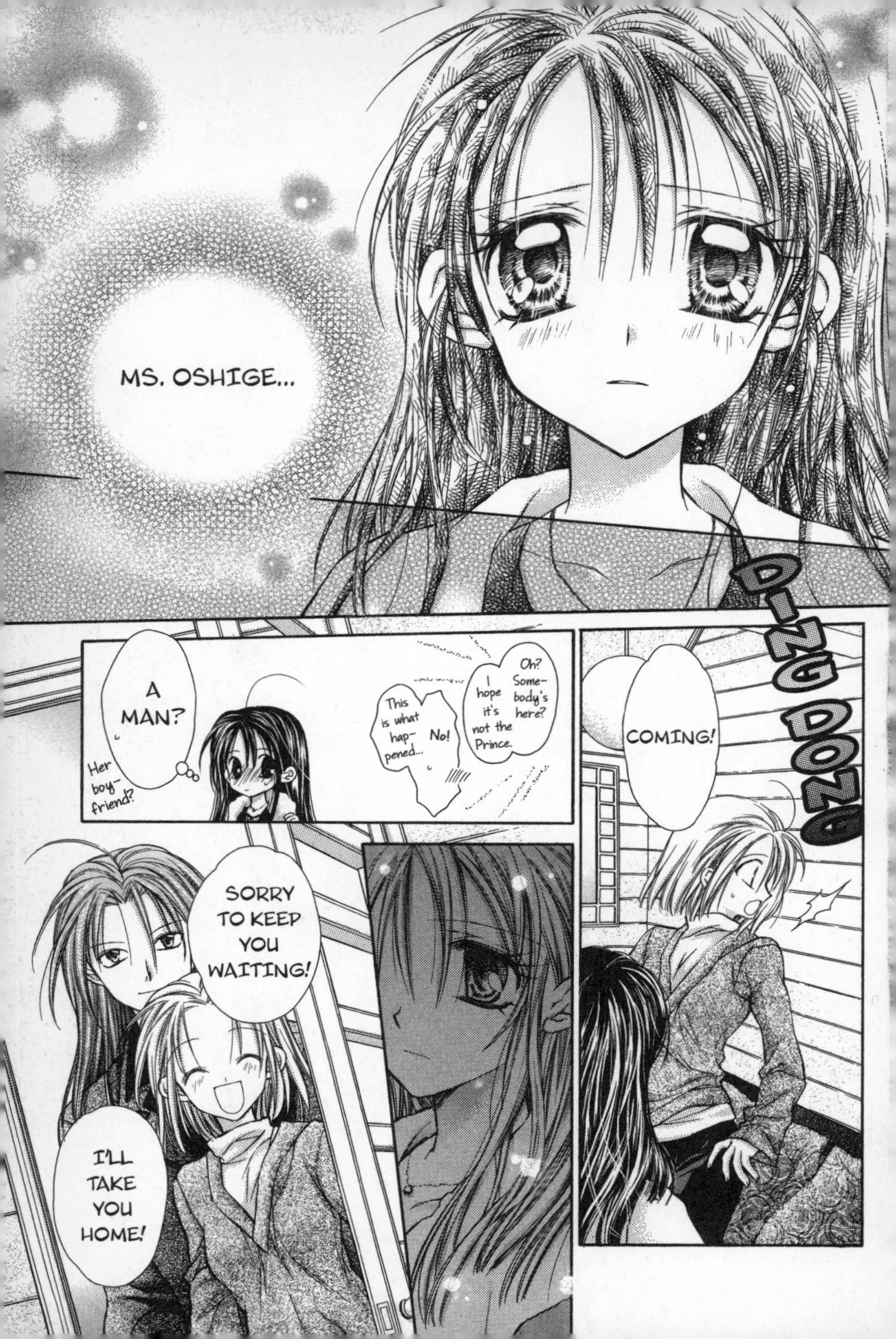
MS. OSHIGE...
DING DONG
COMING!
Oh? Somebody's here?
I hope it's not the Prince.
No!
This is what happened...
A MAN?
Her boyfriend?
SORRY TO KEEP YOU WAITING!
I'LL TAKE YOU HOME!

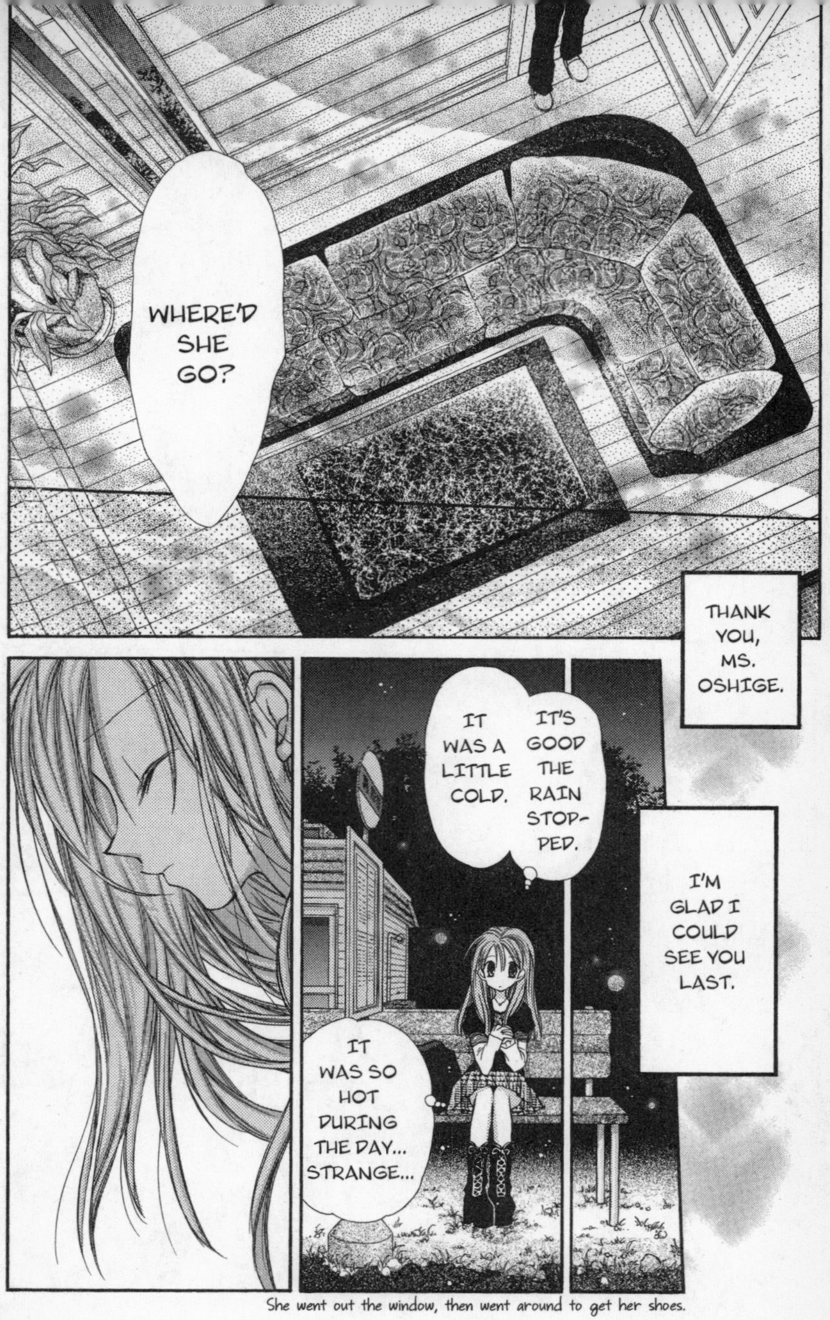
WHERE'D SHE GO?
THANK YOU, MS. OSHIGE.
I'M GLAD I COULD SEE YOU LAST.
IT'S GOOD THE RAIN STOP-PED.
IT WAS A LITTLE COLD.
IT WAS SO HOT DURING THE DAY... STRANGE...

She went out the window, then went around to get her shoes.

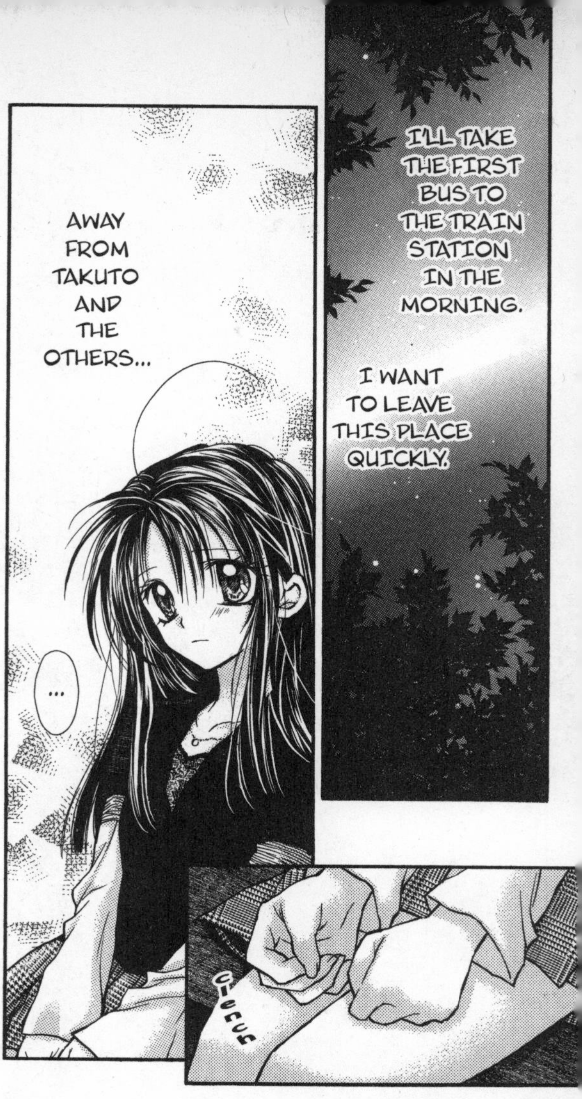
I'LL TAKE THE FIRST BUS TO THE TRAIN STATION IN THE MORNING.
I WANT TO LEAVE THIS PLACE QUICKLY.
AWAY FROM TAKUTO AND THE OTHERS...
...
CLENCH
NO, MITSUKI.
DON'T SAY "I'M LONELY."

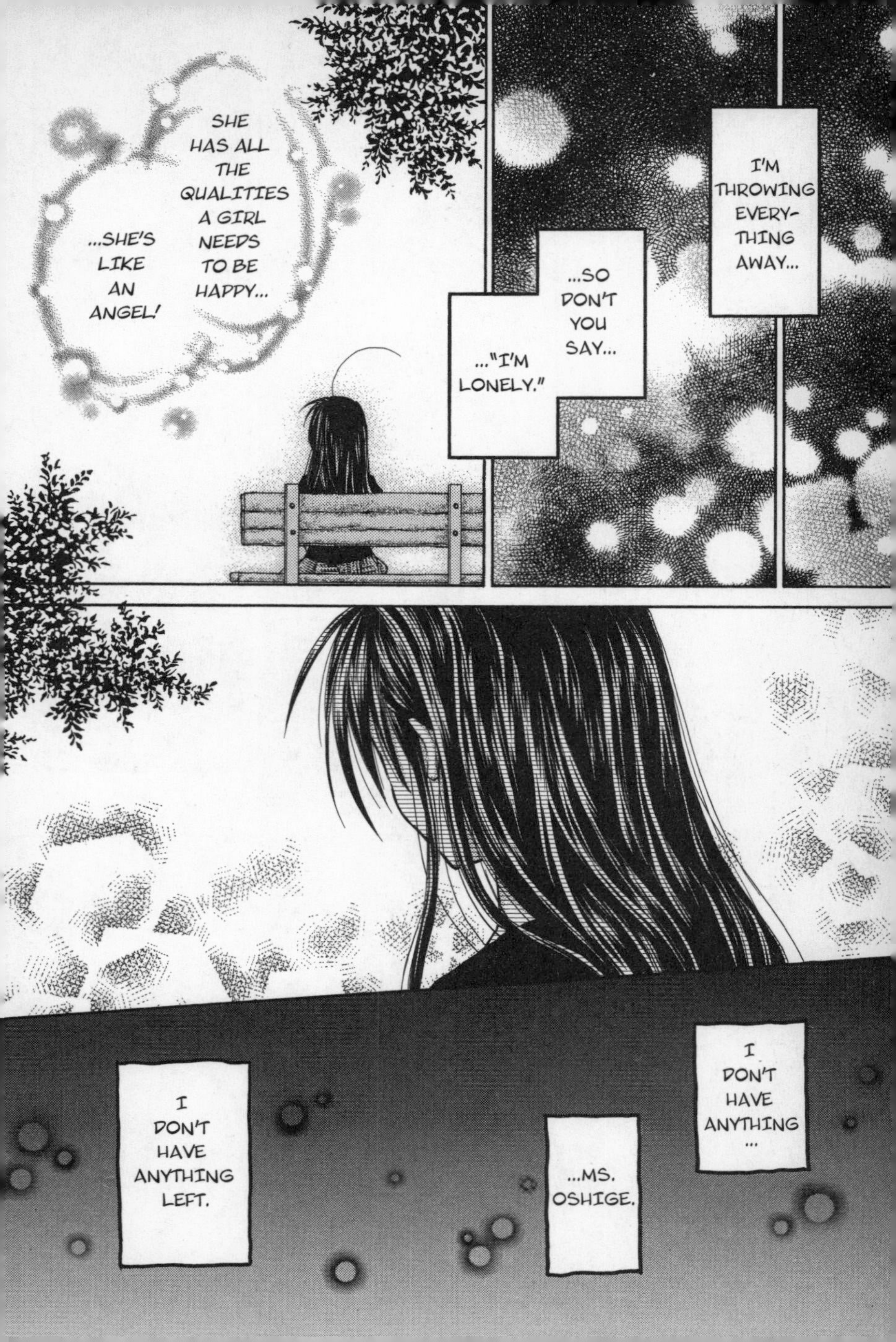
I'M THROWING EVERY-THING AWAY...
...SO DON'T YOU SAY...
..."I'M LONELY."
SHE HAS ALL THE QUALITIES A GIRL NEEDS TO BE HAPPY...
...SHE'S LIKE AN ANGEL!
I DON'T HAVE ANYTHING ...
...MS. OSHIGE.
I DON'T HAVE ANYTHING LEFT.

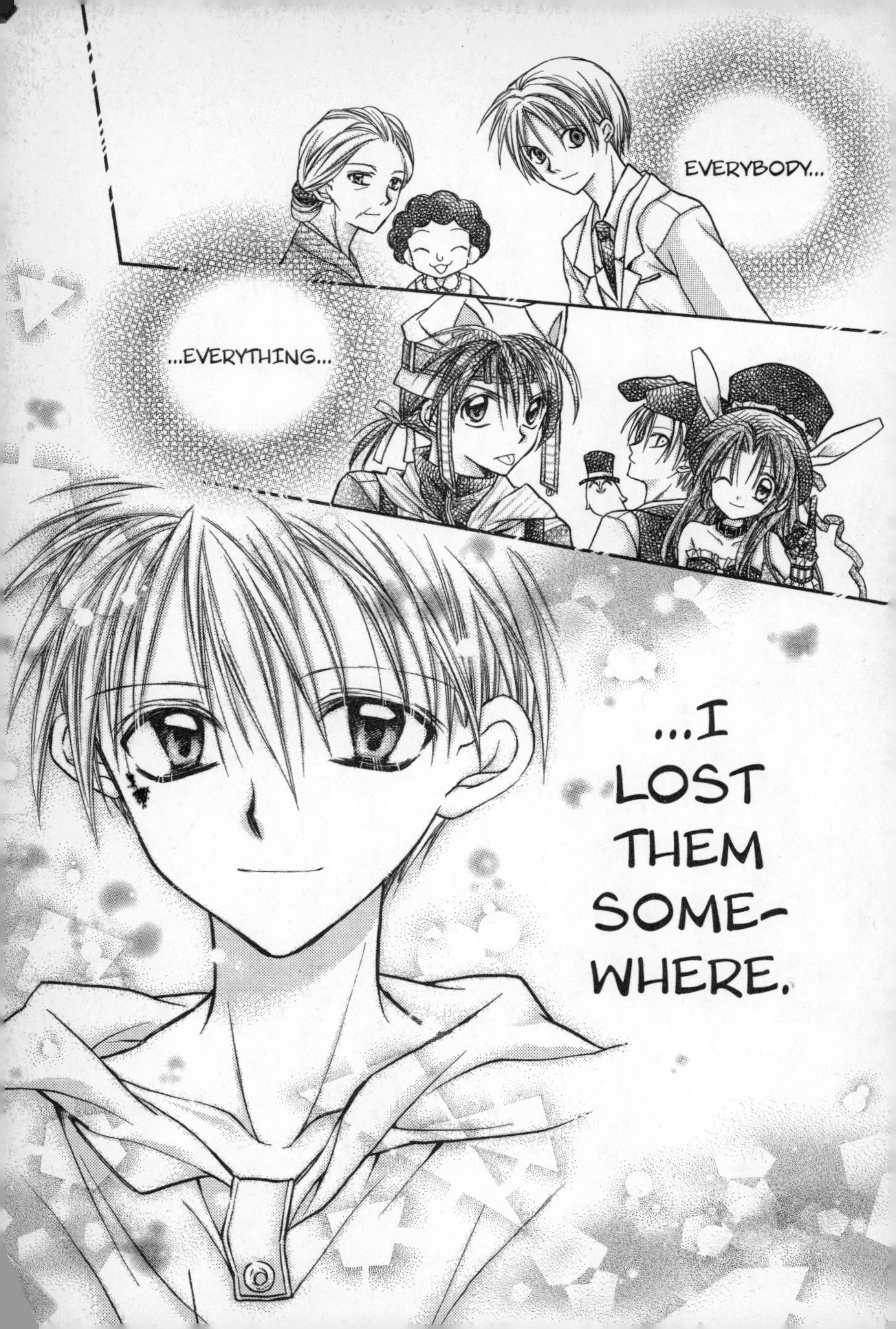
EVERYBODY...
...EVERYTHING...
...I LOST THEM SOME-WHERE.

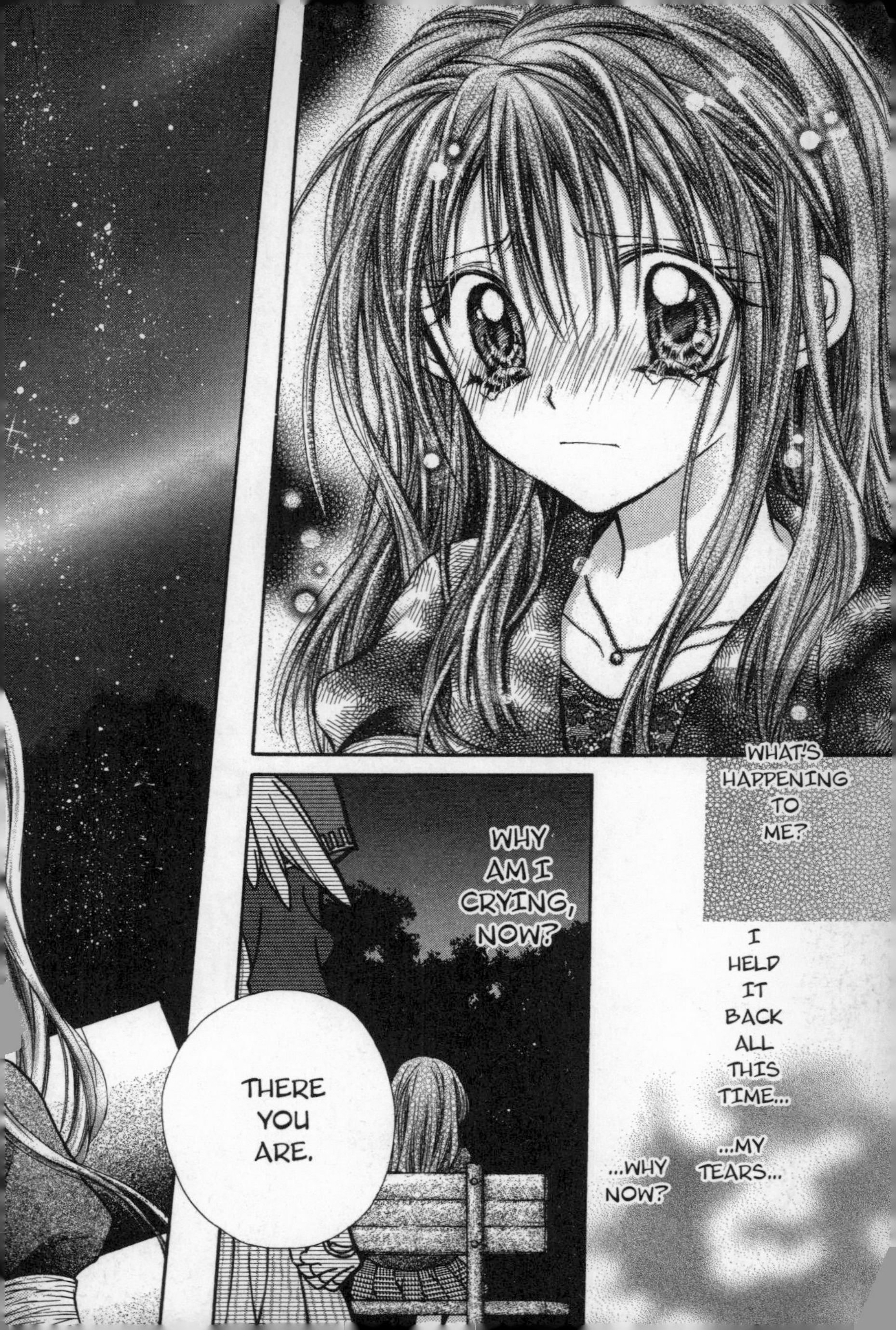
WHAT'S HAPPENING TO ME?
I HELD IT BACK ALL THIS TIME...
...MY TEARS...
...WHY NOW?
WHY AM I CRYING, NOW?
THERE YOU ARE.

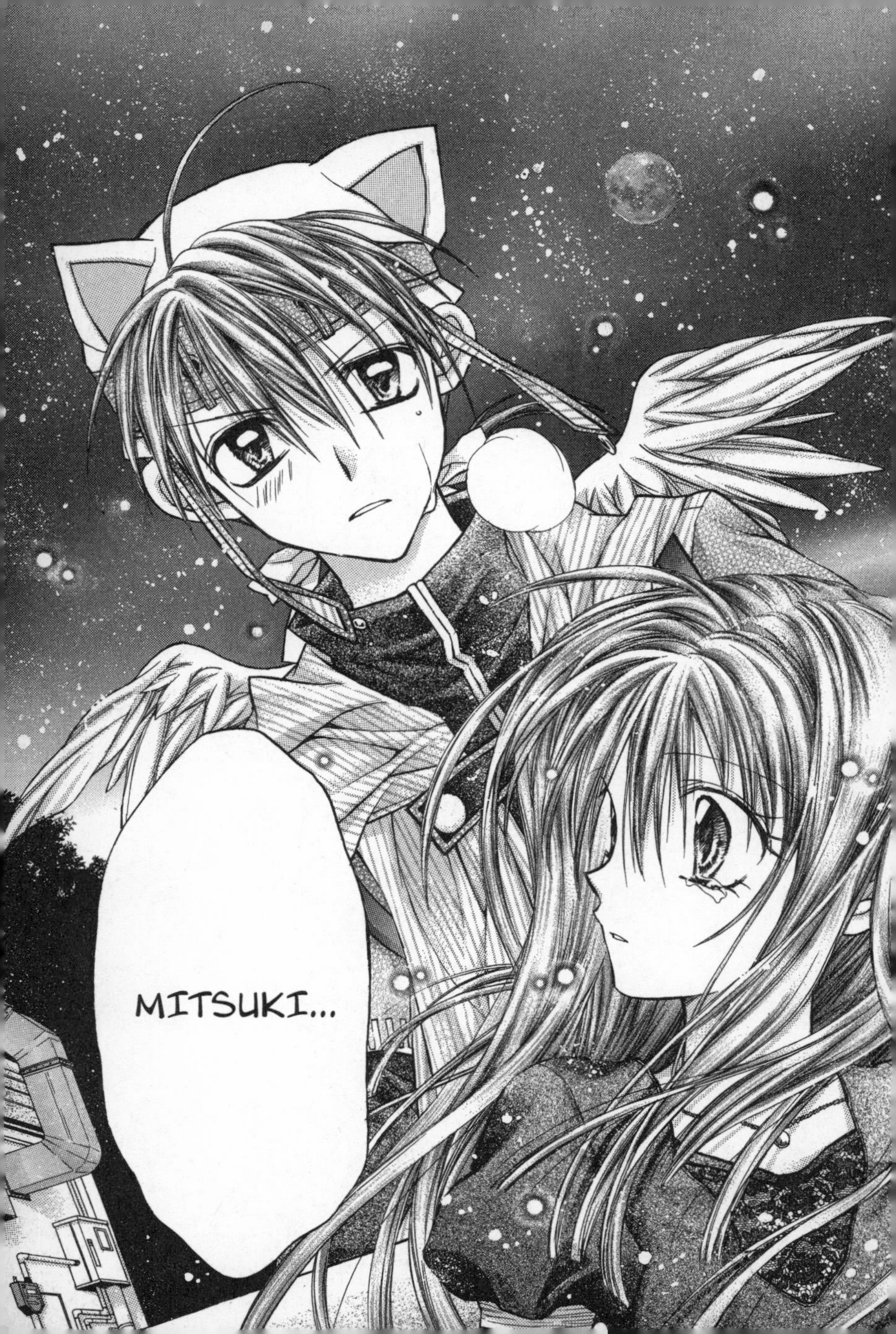
MITSUKI...

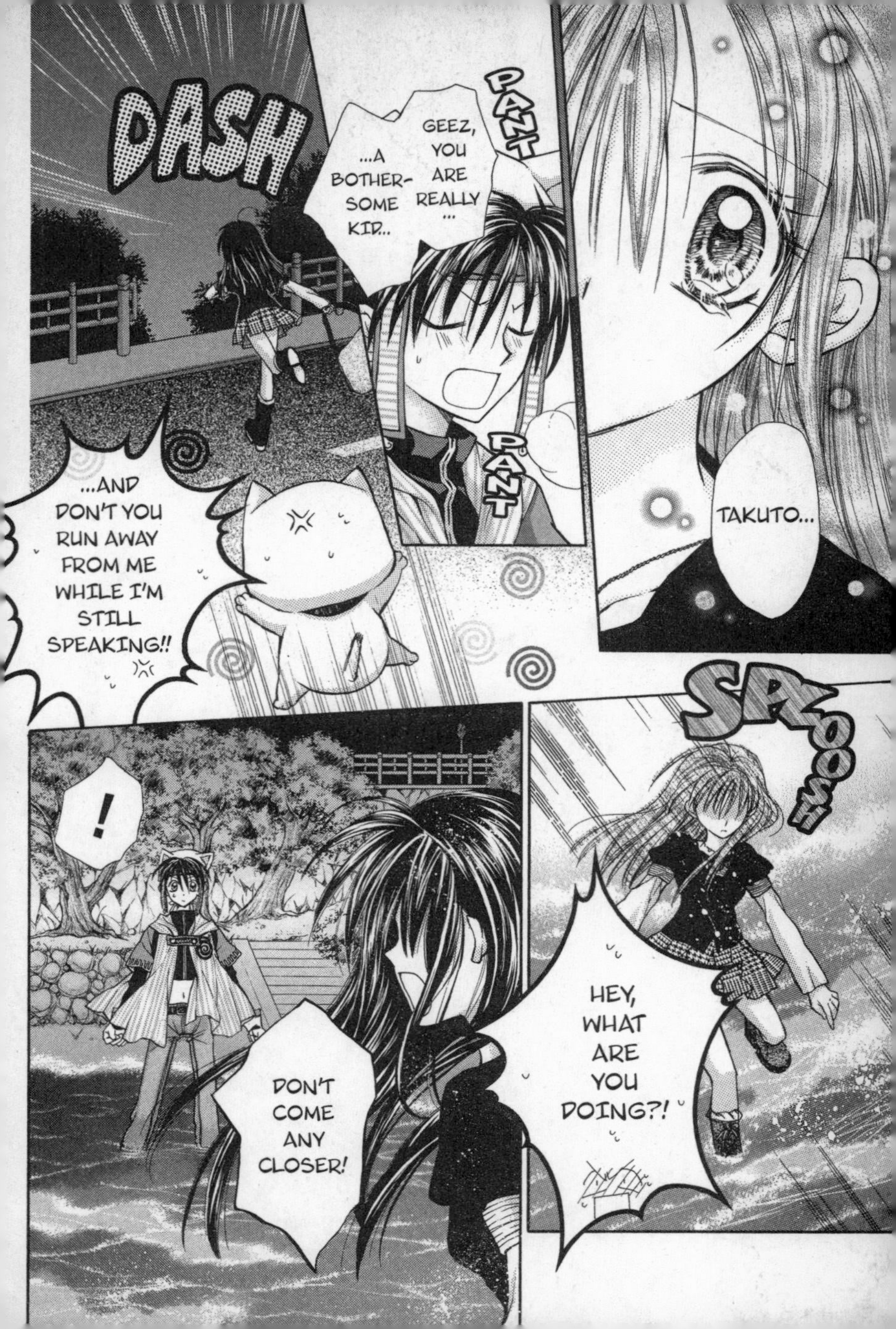
TAKUTO...
PANT
GEEZ, YOU ARE REALLY...
...A BOTHER-SOME KID...
PANT
DASH
...AND DON'T YOU RUN AWAY FROM ME WHILE I'M STILL SPEAKING!!
SPROOSH!!
HEY, WHAT ARE YOU DOING?!
!
DON'T COME ANY CLOSER!

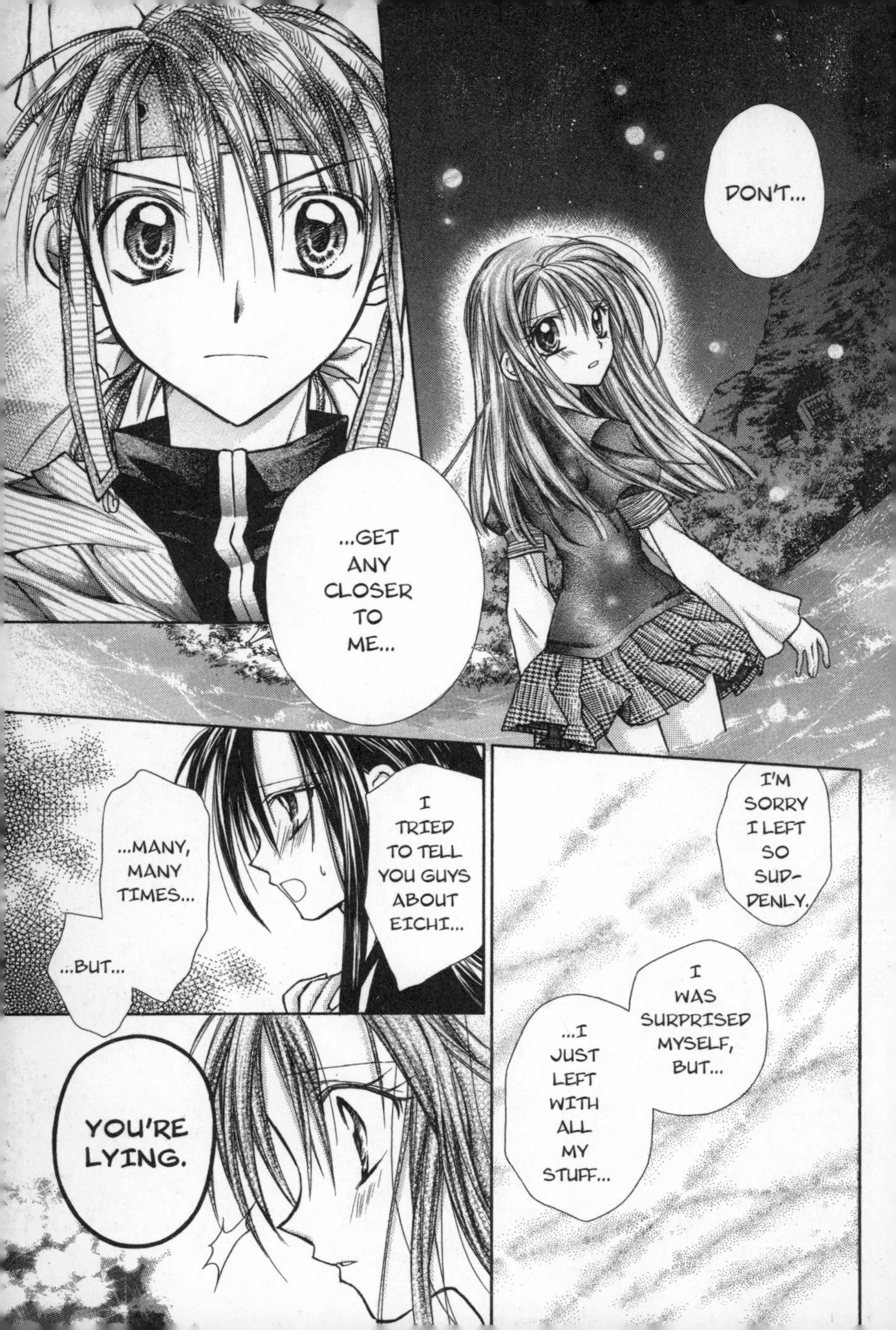
DON'T...
...GET ANY CLOSER TO ME...
I'M SORRY I LEFT SO SUD-DENLY.
I WAS SURPRISED MYSELF, BUT...
...I JUST LEFT WITH ALL MY STUFF...
I TRIED TO TELL YOU GUYS ABOUT EICHI...
...MANY, MANY TIMES...
...BUT...
YOU'RE LYING.

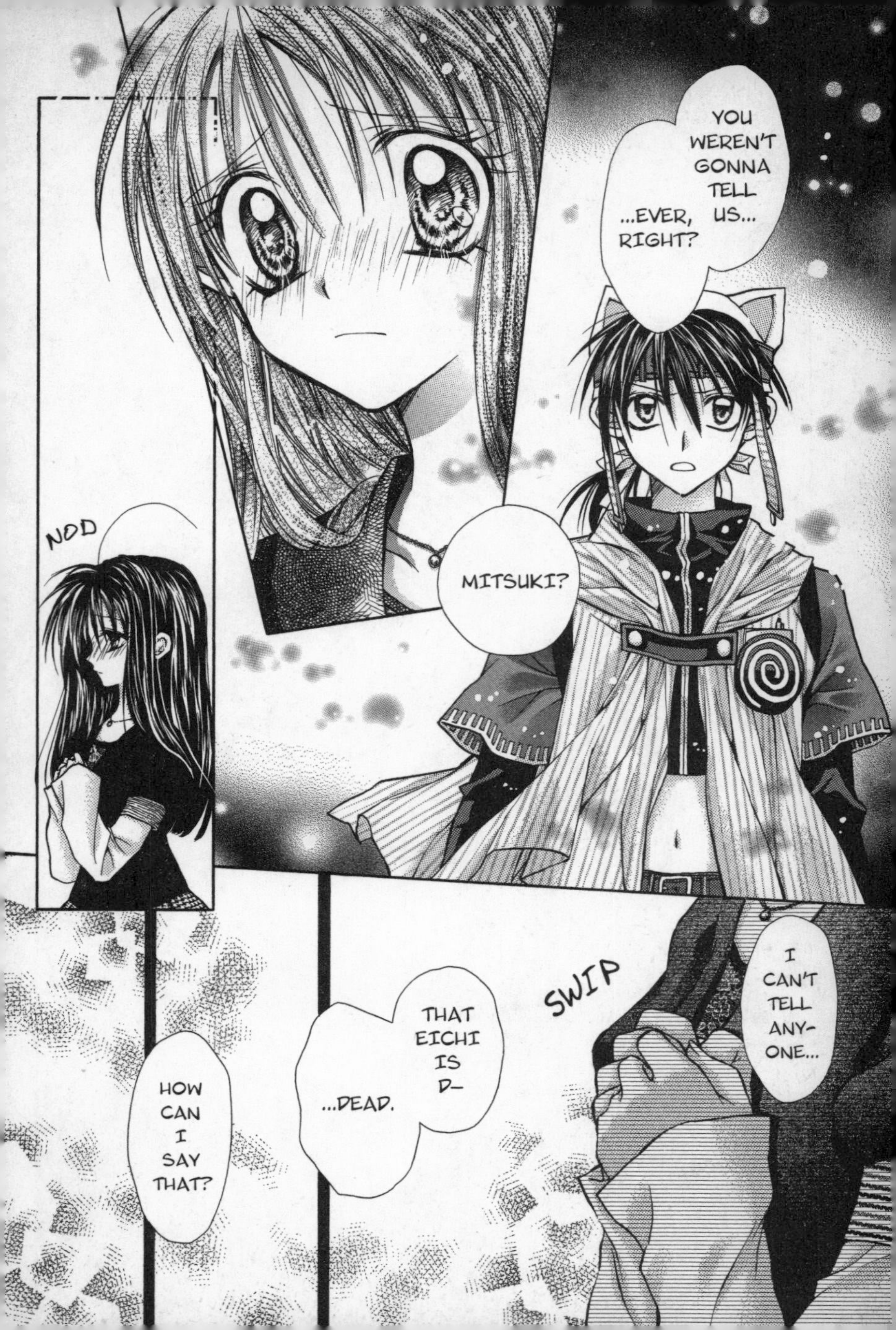
YOU WEREN'T GONNA TELL US... ...EVER, RIGHT?
MITSUKI?
NOD
SWIP
I CAN'T TELL ANY-ONE...
THAT EICHI IS D—
...DEAD.
HOW CAN I SAY THAT?

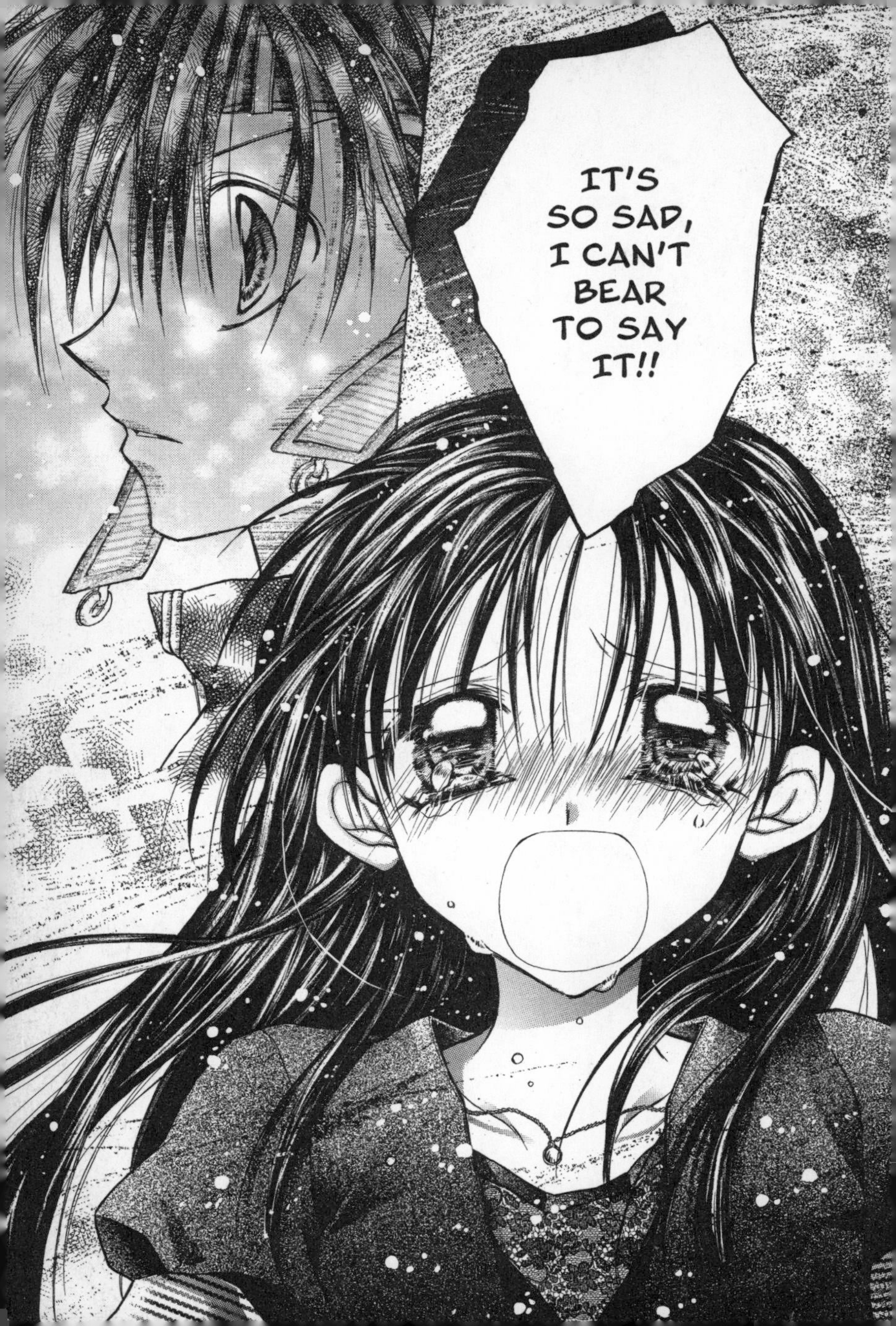
IT'S SO SAD, I CAN'T BEAR TO SAY IT!!

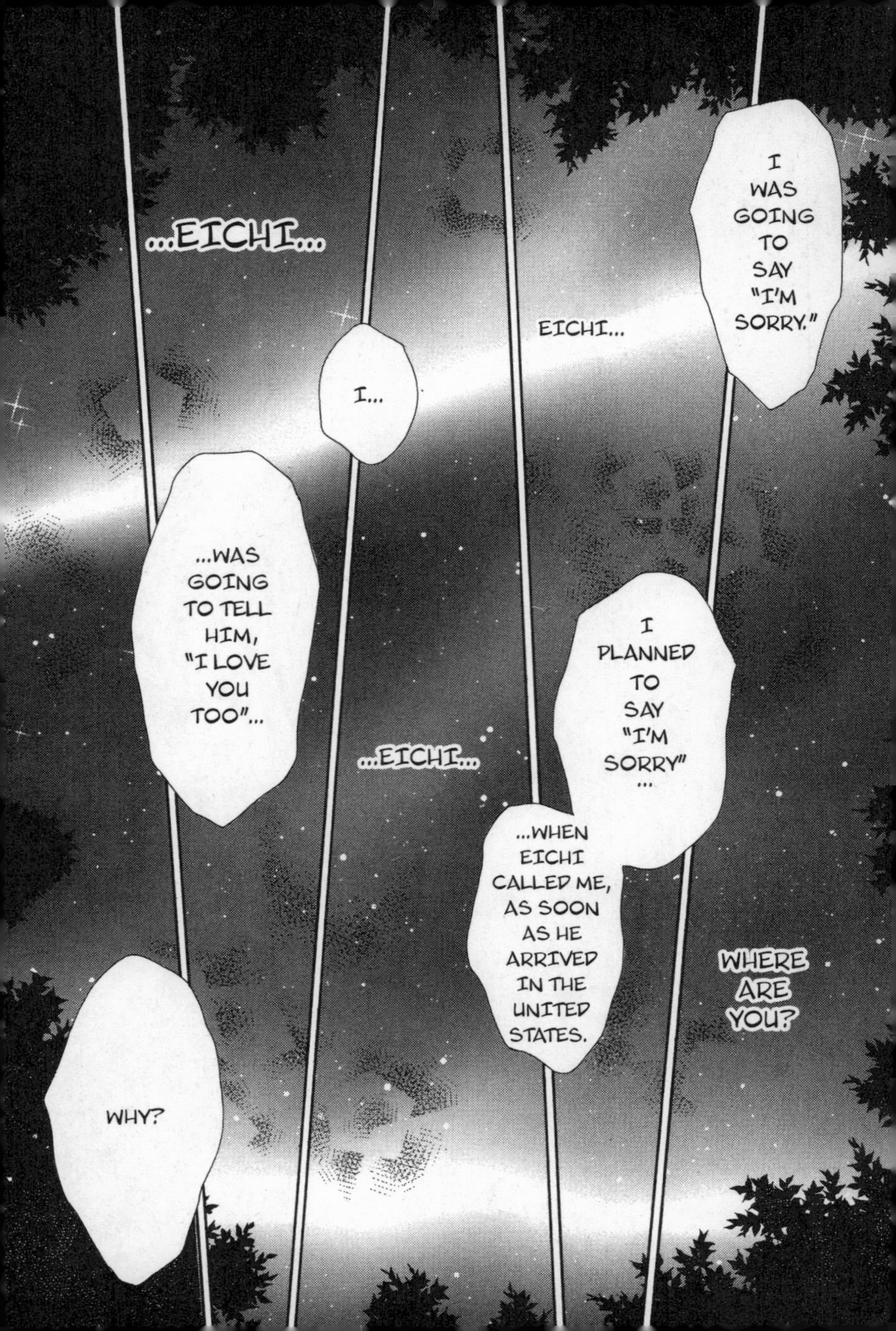

I WAS GOING TO SAY "I'M SORRY."
WHERE ARE YOU?
EICHI...
I PLANNED TO SAY "I'M SORRY"...
...WHEN EICHI CALLED ME, AS SOON AS HE ARRIVED IN THE UNITED STATES.
I...
...EICHI...
...EICHI...
...WAS GOING TO TELL HIM, "I LOVE YOU TOO"...
WHY?

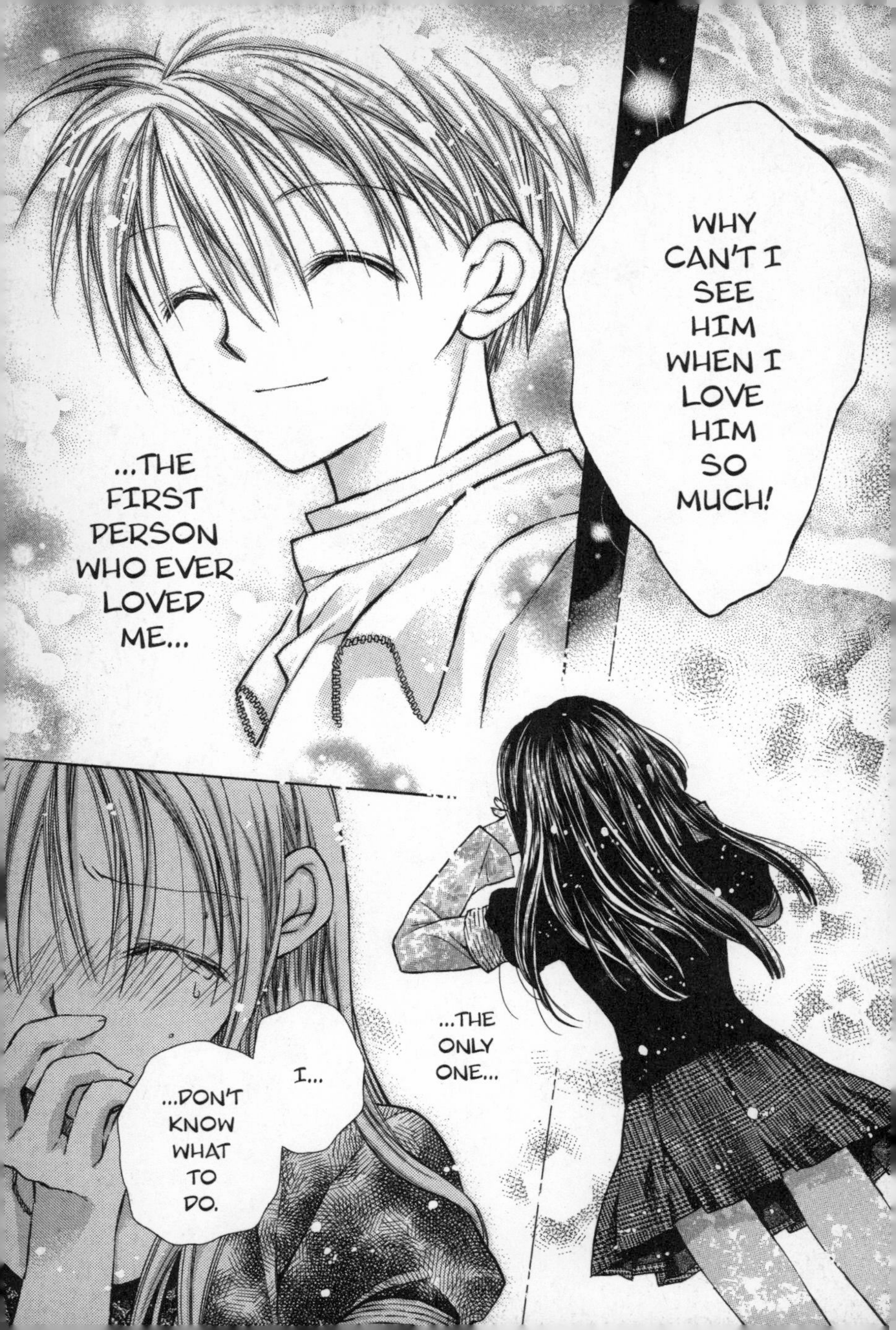
WHY CAN'T I SEE HIM WHEN I LOVE HIM SO MUCH!
...THE FIRST PERSON WHO EVER LOVED ME...
...THE ONLY ONE...
I...
...DON'T KNOW WHAT TO DO.

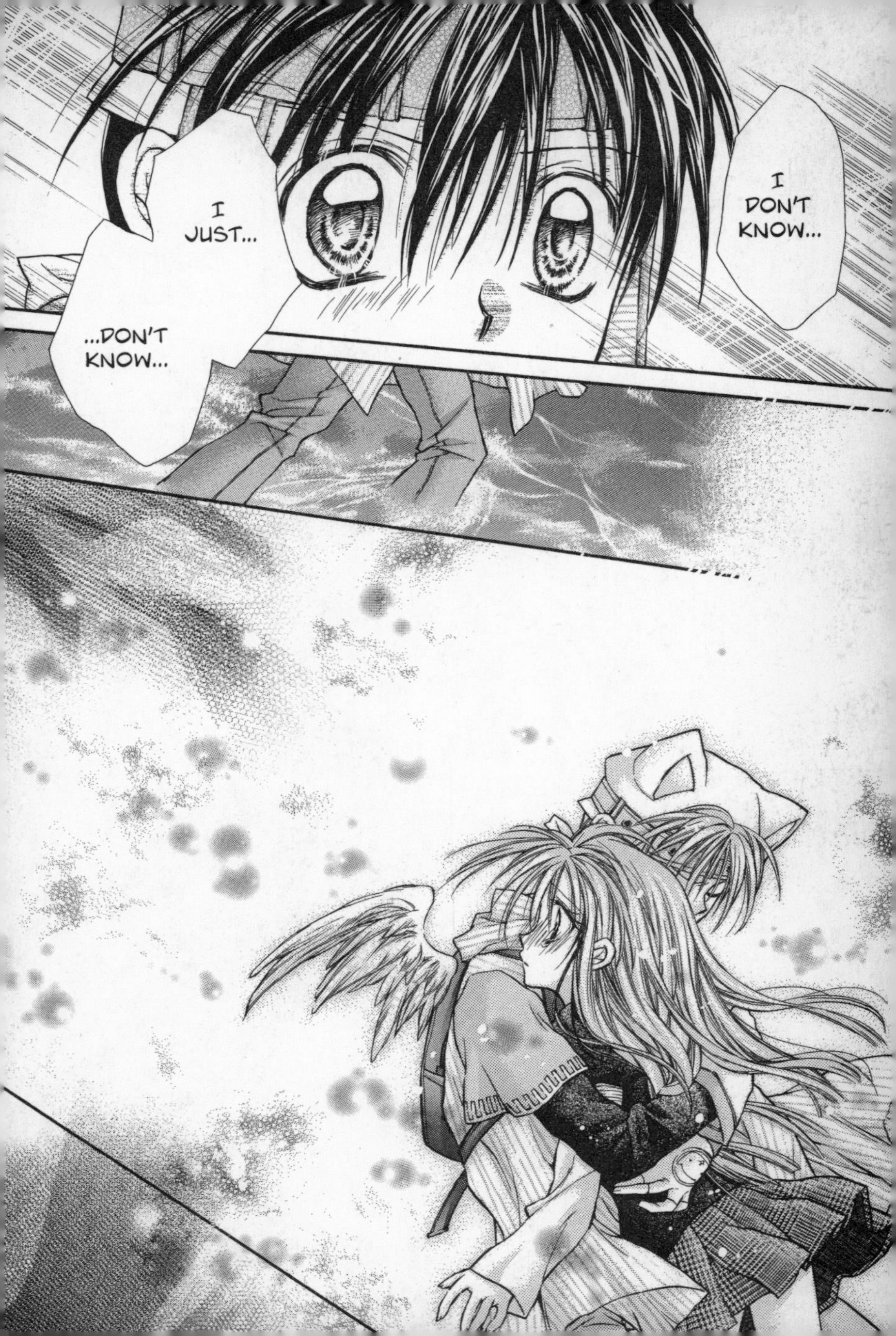
I DON'T KNOW...
I JUST...
...DON'T KNOW...

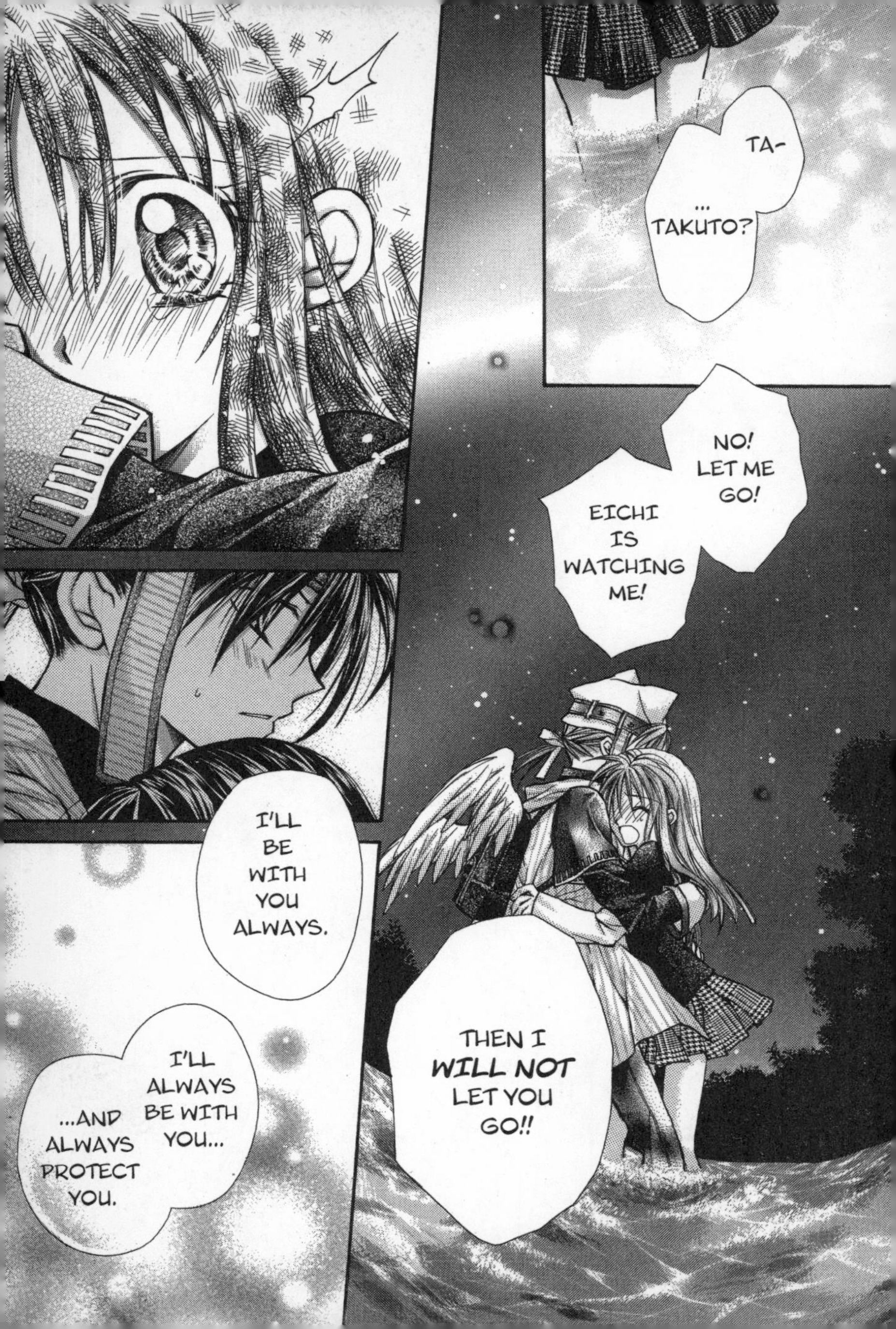
TA-
...TAKUTO?
NO! LET ME GO!
EICHI IS WATCHING ME!
THEN I **WILL NOT** LET YOU GO!!
I'LL BE WITH YOU ALWAYS.
I'LL ALWAYS BE WITH YOU...
...AND ALWAYS PROTECT YOU.

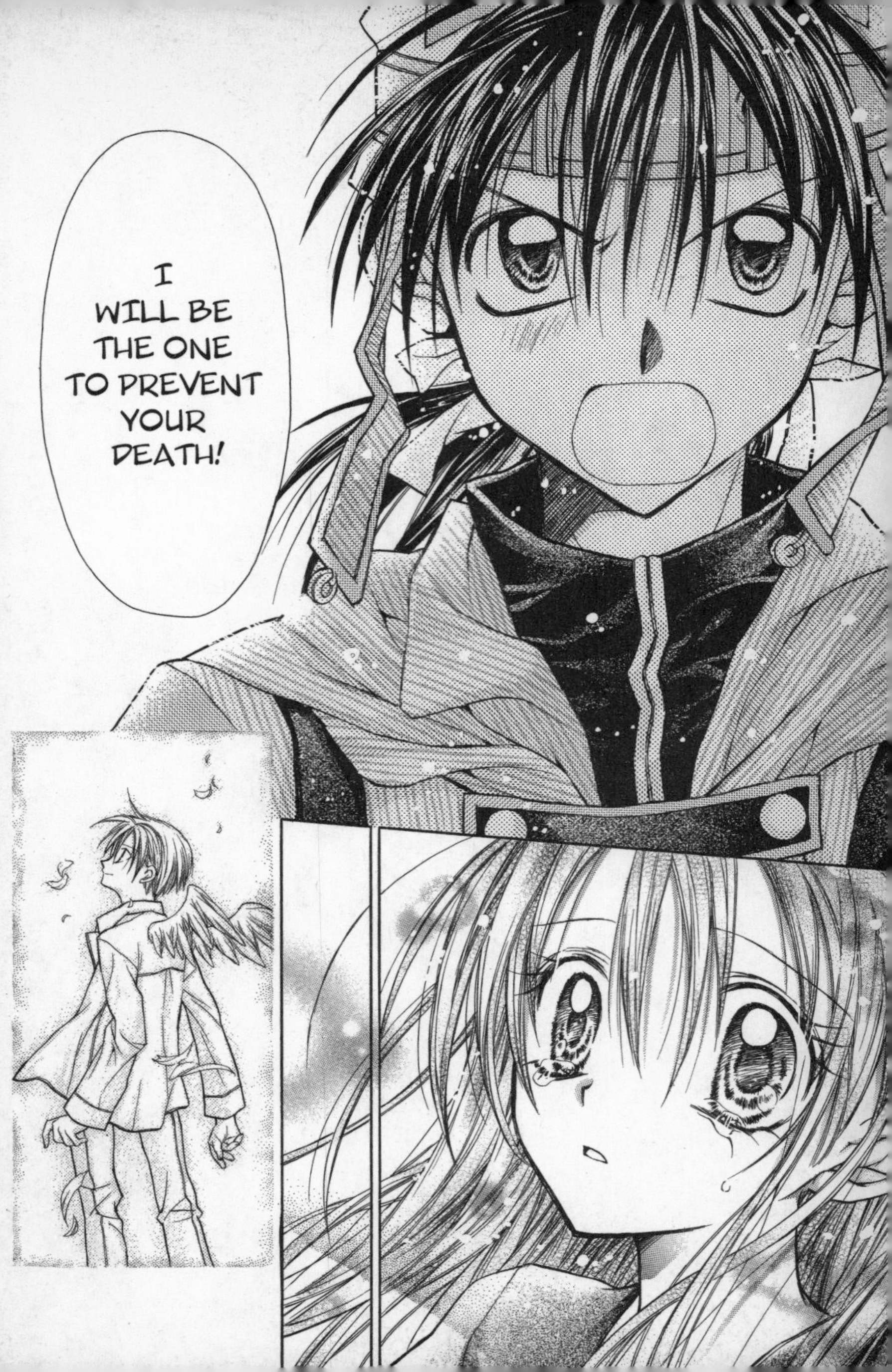
I WILL BE THE ONE TO PREVENT YOUR DEATH!

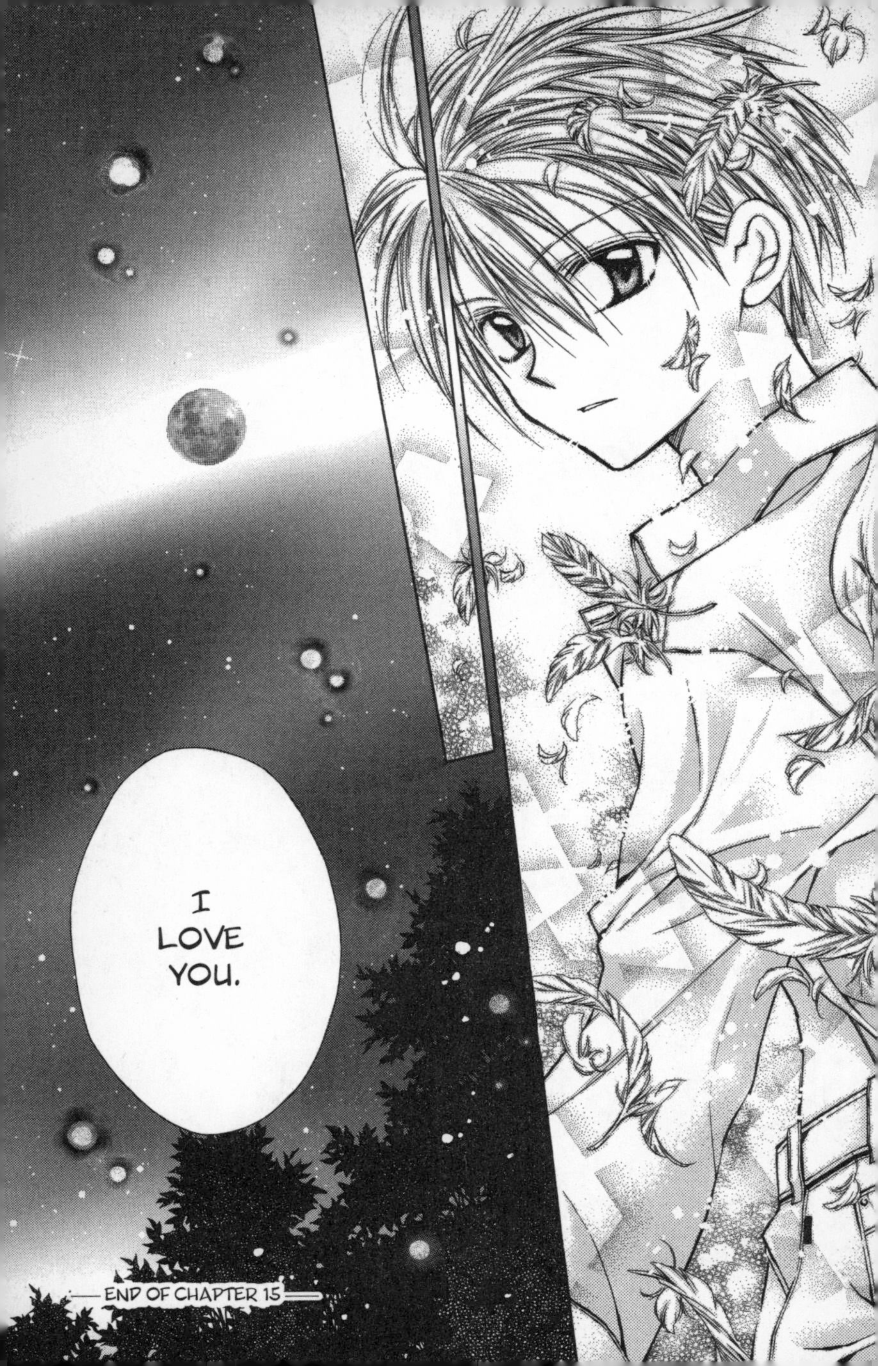
I LOVE YOU.
END OF CHAPTER 15

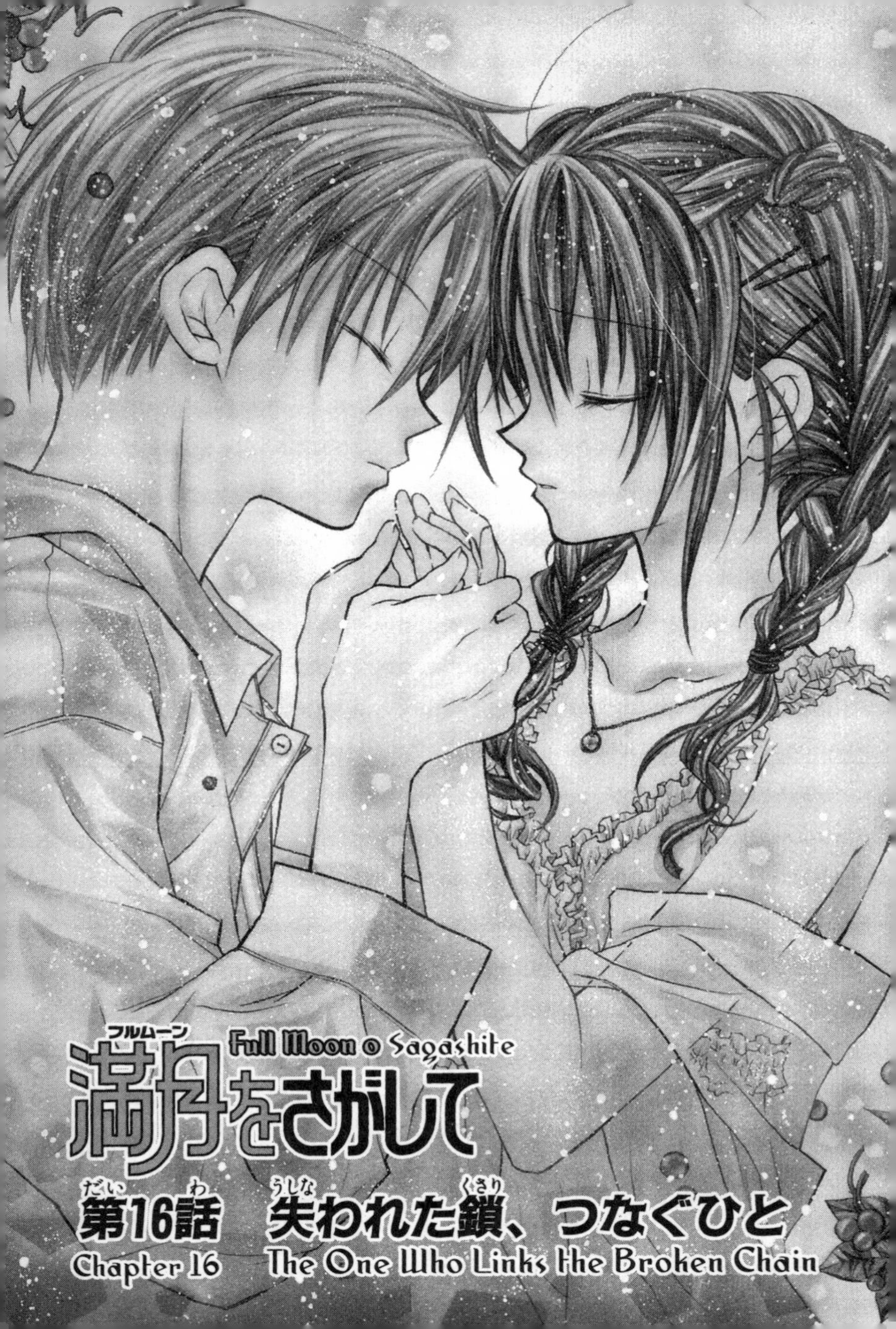

満月をさがして
Full Moon o Sagashite

第16話 失われた鎖、つなぐひと
Chapter 16 The One Who Links the Broken Chain

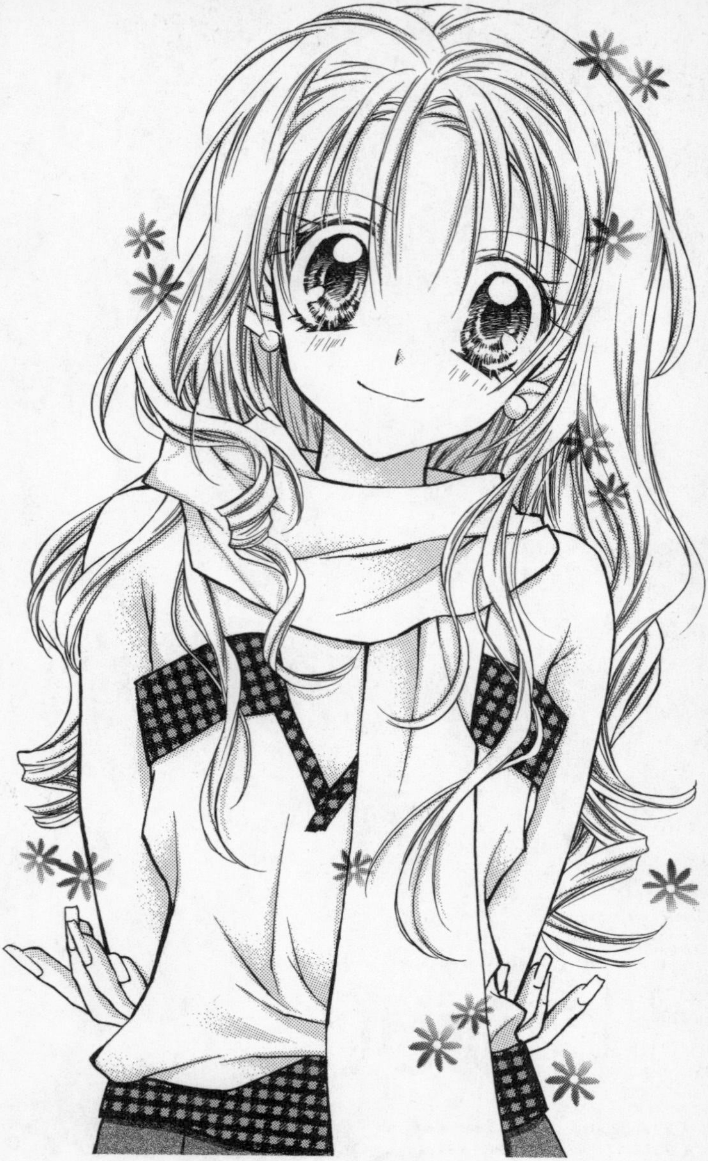

I...

...LOVE YOU!

*Spoilers ahead

Cover Copy · I can still feel your warmth in my hands.

Chapter 16 The One Who Links the Broken Chain

I like this illustration. Somehow Eichi ♥ Mitsuki is easy to do in color. I really put my feelings in them.

In this chapter, there's a scene where Eichi-kun and Mitsuki-yan are holding each other, and their hairstyle and clothes are the ones on the cover.

I really enjoyed this chapter. ♪ Drawing it, ♥ I feel like I've matured as a mangaka.

There, I'm praising myself! ♪ It's really true that when a quiet person explodes, she really explodes! Yes, yes.

Um, the song Mitsuki-chan talks about is "Metropolitan Museum," a classic on NHK's "Minna no Uta (Songs for Everybody)," that show with animated songs. ♥

The book's title is "From the Mixed-Up Files of Mrs. Basil E. Frankweiler." It's a good book. Please read it if you're curious.

Eichi-kun probably had a great influence on Mitsuki-chan, so there's no way she can be cheerful again right away...you might have to be patient, but let's see what happens to her. Together with the Shinigami...

I feel relieved when I see Mitsuki not being cheerful. It's so much better than watching her pretending to be cheerful.

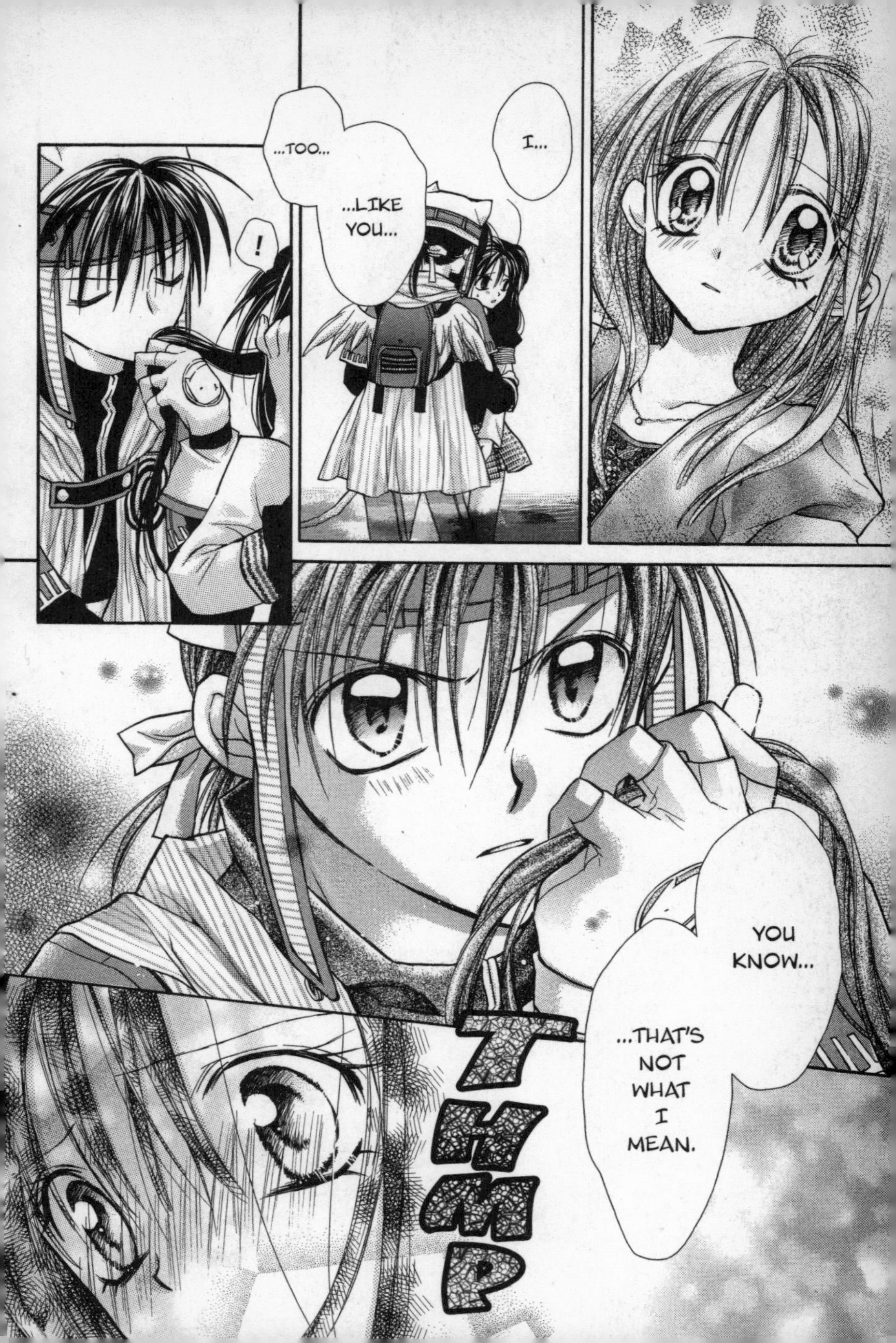
I...
...LIKE YOU...
...TOO...
!
YOU KNOW...
...THAT'S NOT WHAT I MEAN.
THMP

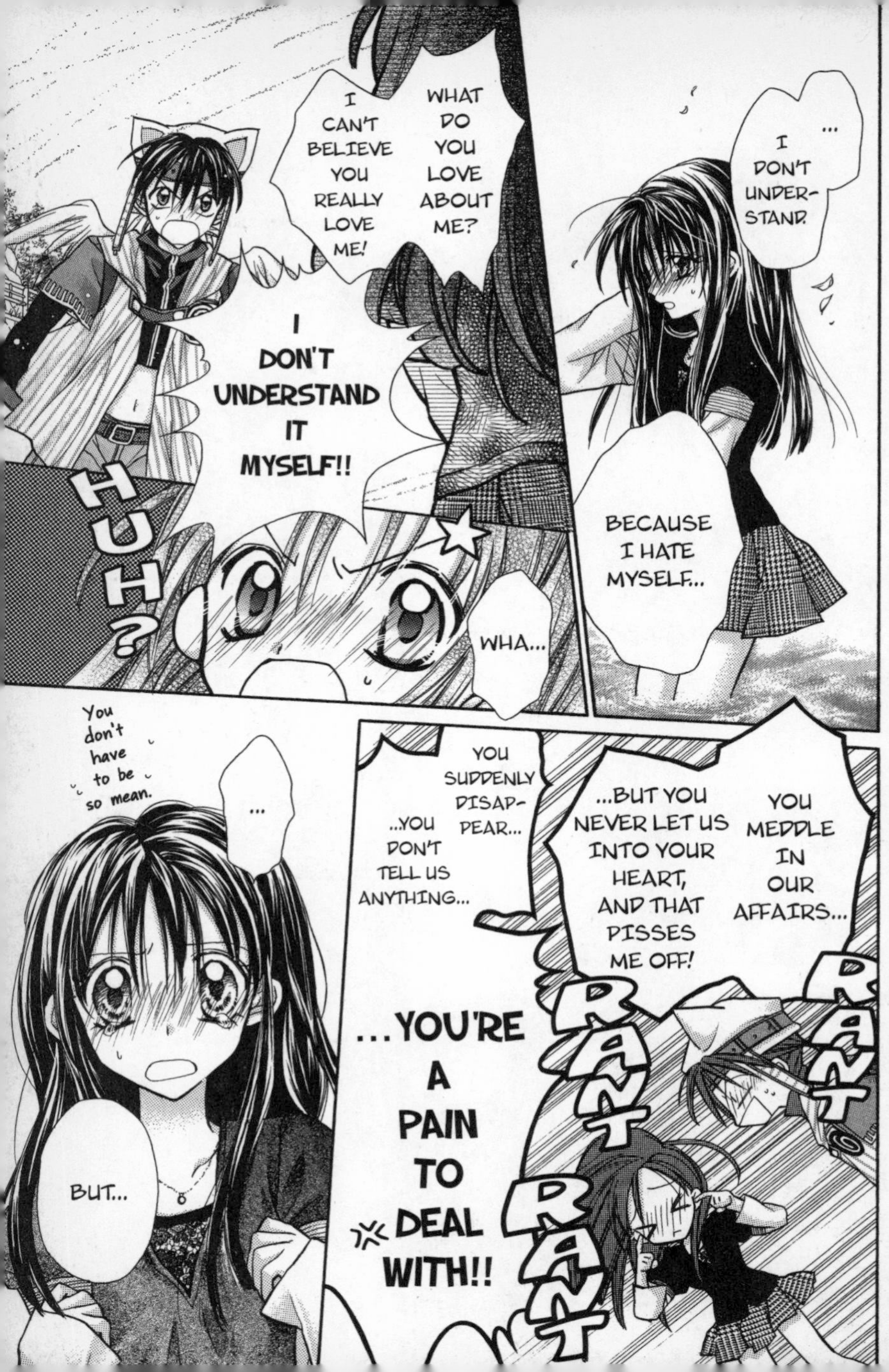
...
I DON'T UNDERSTAND.
BECAUSE I HATE MYSELF...
WHAT DO YOU LOVE ABOUT ME?
I CAN'T BELIEVE YOU REALLY LOVE ME!
I DON'T UNDERSTAND IT MYSELF!!
HUH?
WHA...
YOU MEDDLE IN OUR AFFAIRS...
...BUT YOU NEVER LET US INTO YOUR HEART, AND THAT PISSES ME OFF!
YOU SUDDENLY DISAPPEAR...
...YOU DON'T TELL US ANYTHING...
RANT RANT
RANT RANT
...YOU'RE A PAIN TO DEAL WITH!!
...
BUT...
You don't have to be so mean.

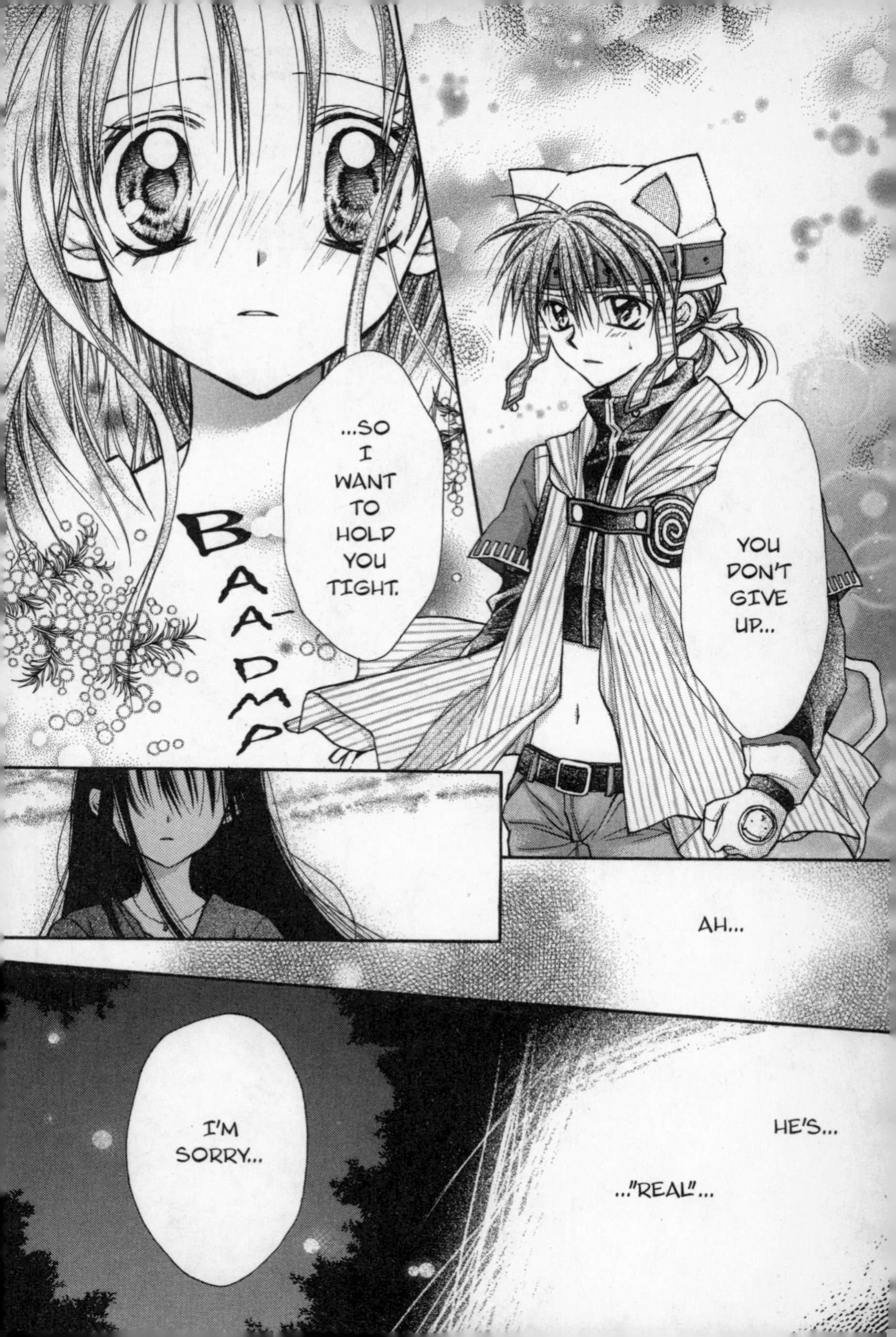
YOU DON'T GIVE UP...
...SO I WANT TO HOLD YOU TIGHT.
BAADMP
AH...
HE'S...
..."REAL"...
I'M SORRY...

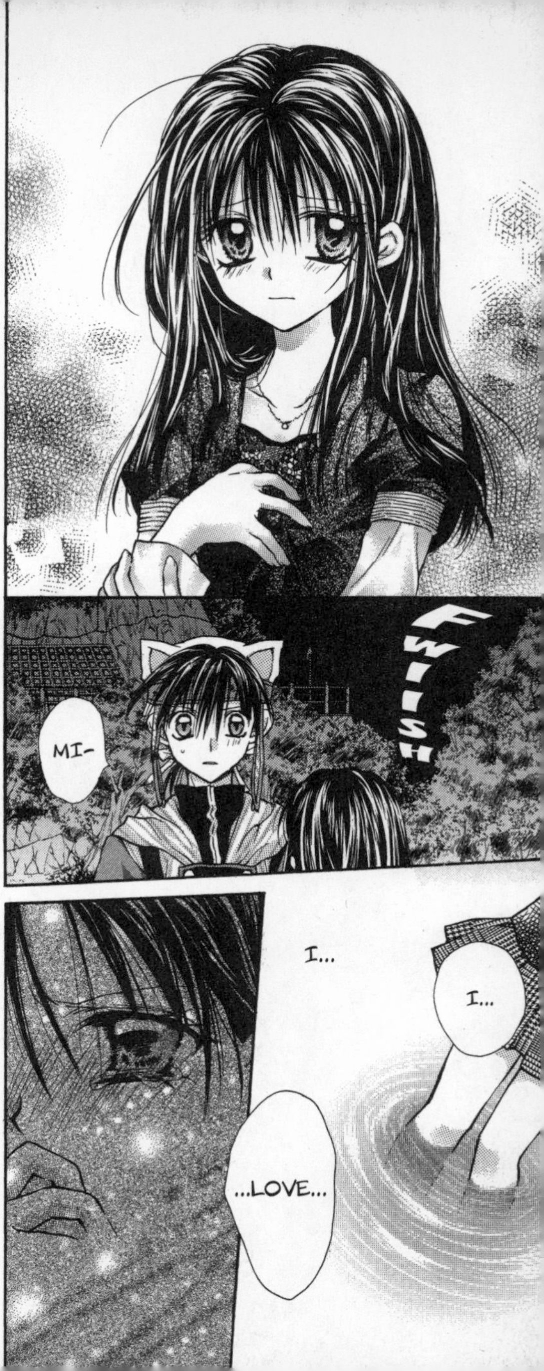
FWISH
MI-
I...
I...
...LOVE...

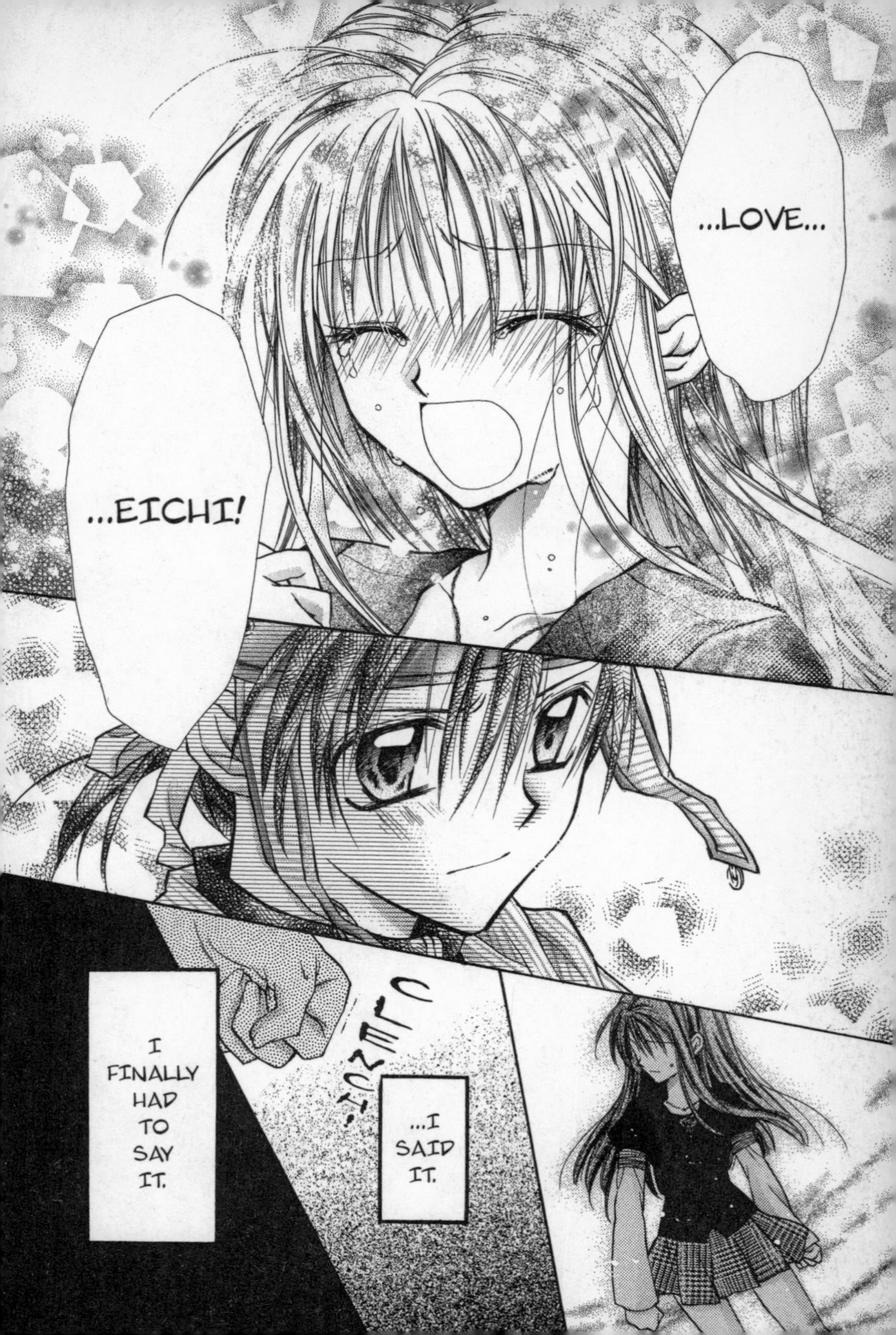
...LOVE...
...EICHI!
CLENCH!
...I SAID IT.
I FINALLY HAD TO SAY IT.

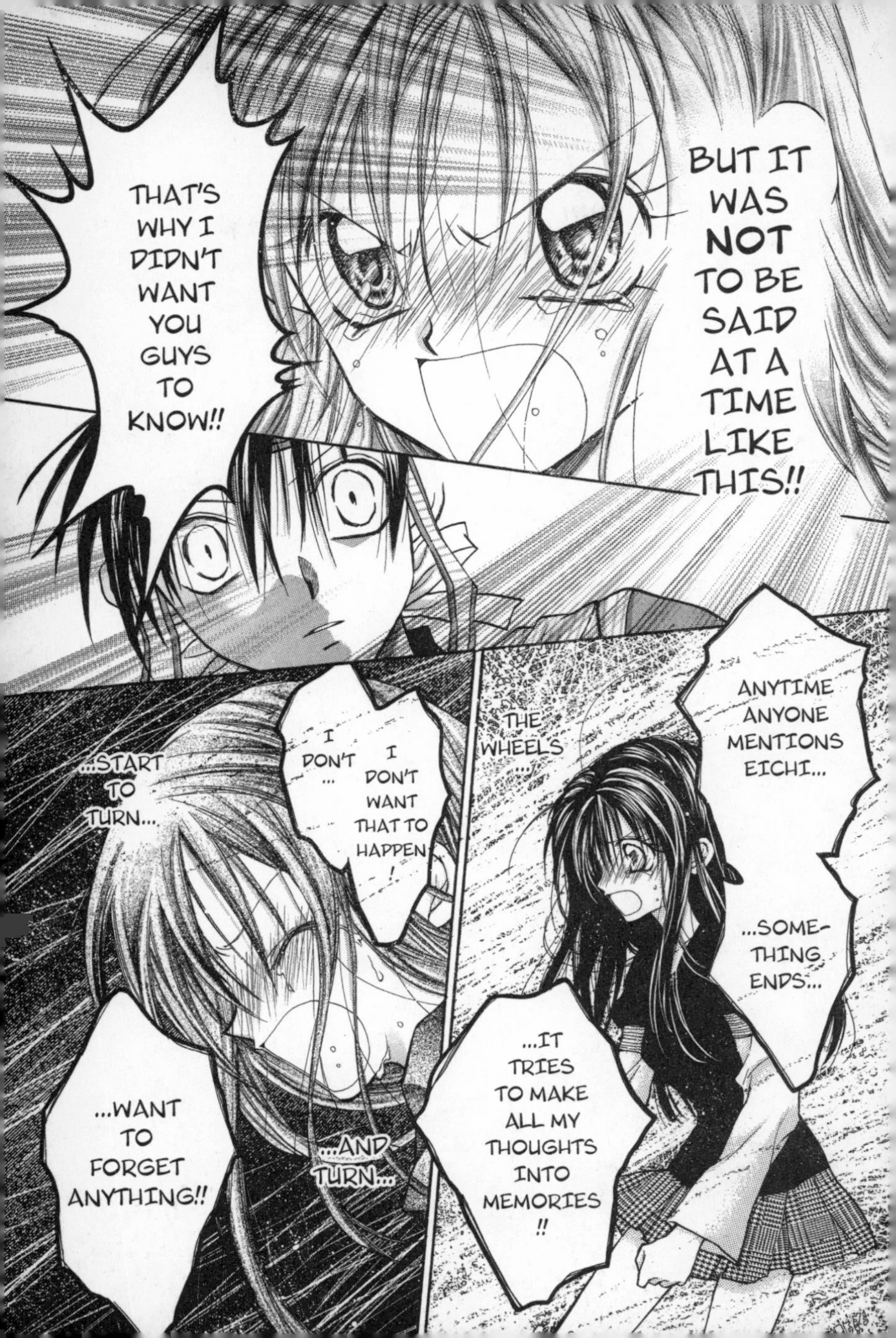
BUT IT WAS NOT TO BE SAID AT A TIME LIKE THIS!!
THAT'S WHY I DIDN'T WANT YOU GUYS TO KNOW!!
ANYTIME ANYONE MENTIONS EICHI...
THE WHEELS...
...SOME-THING ENDS...
...IT TRIES TO MAKE ALL MY THOUGHTS INTO MEMORIES!!
I DON'T ... I DON'T WANT THAT TO HAPPEN!
...START TO TURN...
...AND TURN...
...WANT TO FORGET ANYTHING!!

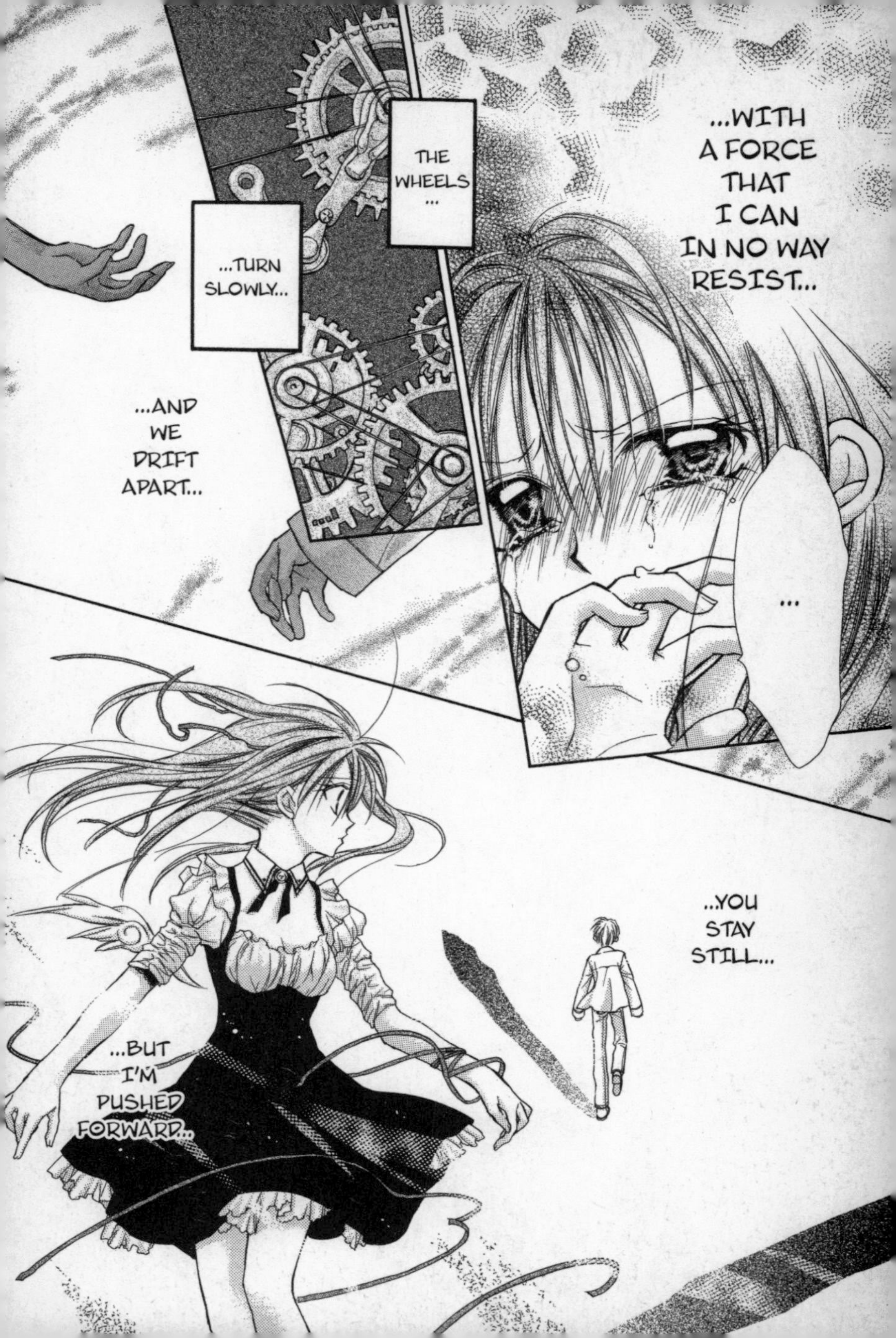
...WITH A FORCE THAT I CAN IN NO WAY RESIST...
...
THE WHEELS...
...TURN SLOWLY...
...AND WE DRIFT APART...
...YOU STAY STILL...
...BUT I'M PUSHED FORWARD...

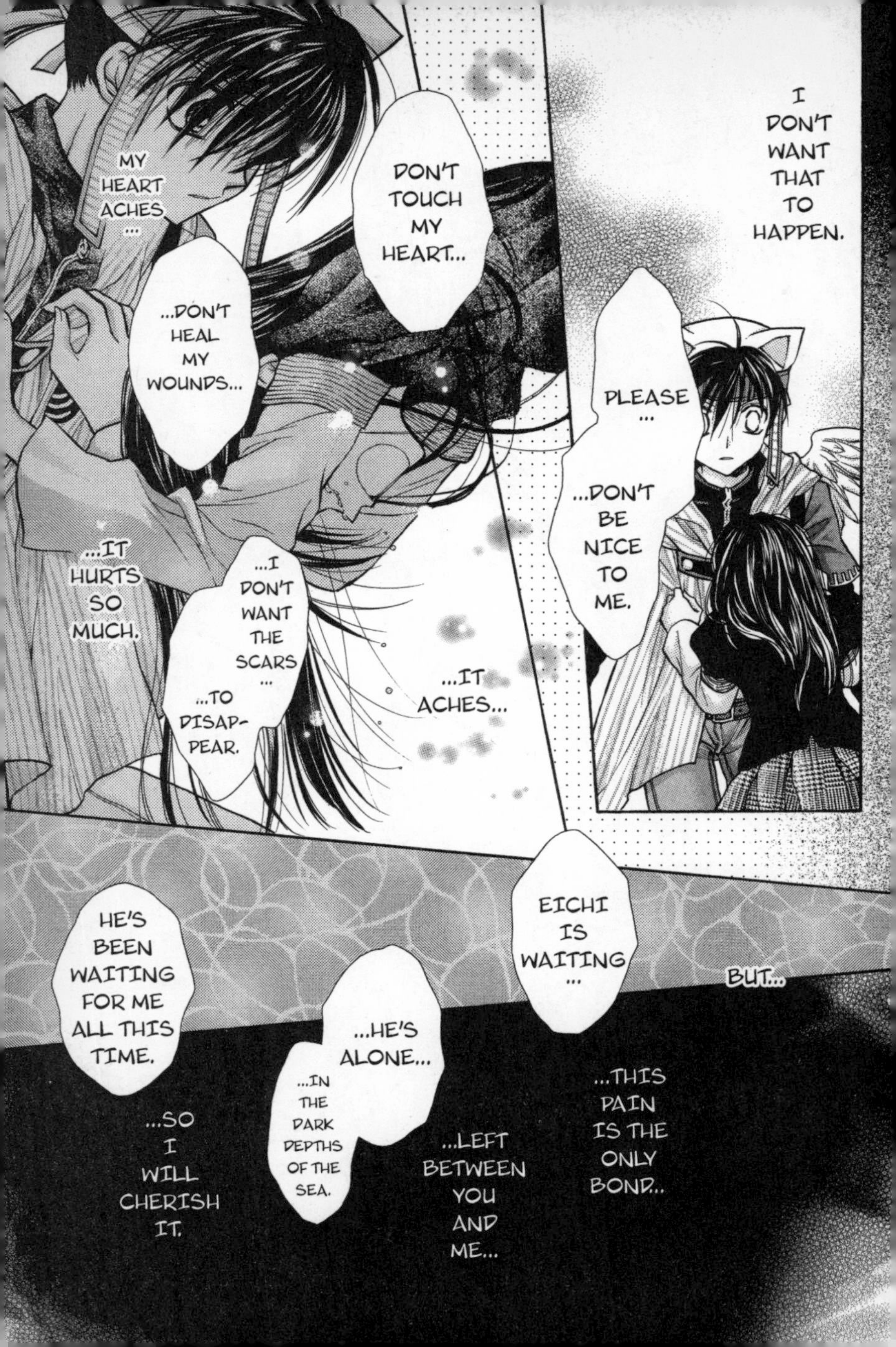
I DON'T WANT THAT TO HAPPEN.
PLEASE...
...DON'T BE NICE TO ME.
DON'T TOUCH MY HEART...
MY HEART ACHES...
...DON'T HEAL MY WOUNDS...
...IT ACHES...
...I DON'T WANT THE SCARS...
...TO DISAPPEAR.
...IT HURTS SO MUCH.
BUT...
EICHI IS WAITING...
...HE'S ALONE...
...IN THE DARK DEPTHS OF THE SEA.
HE'S BEEN WAITING FOR ME ALL THIS TIME.
...THIS PAIN IS THE ONLY BOND..
...LEFT BETWEEN YOU AND ME...
...SO I WILL CHERISH IT.

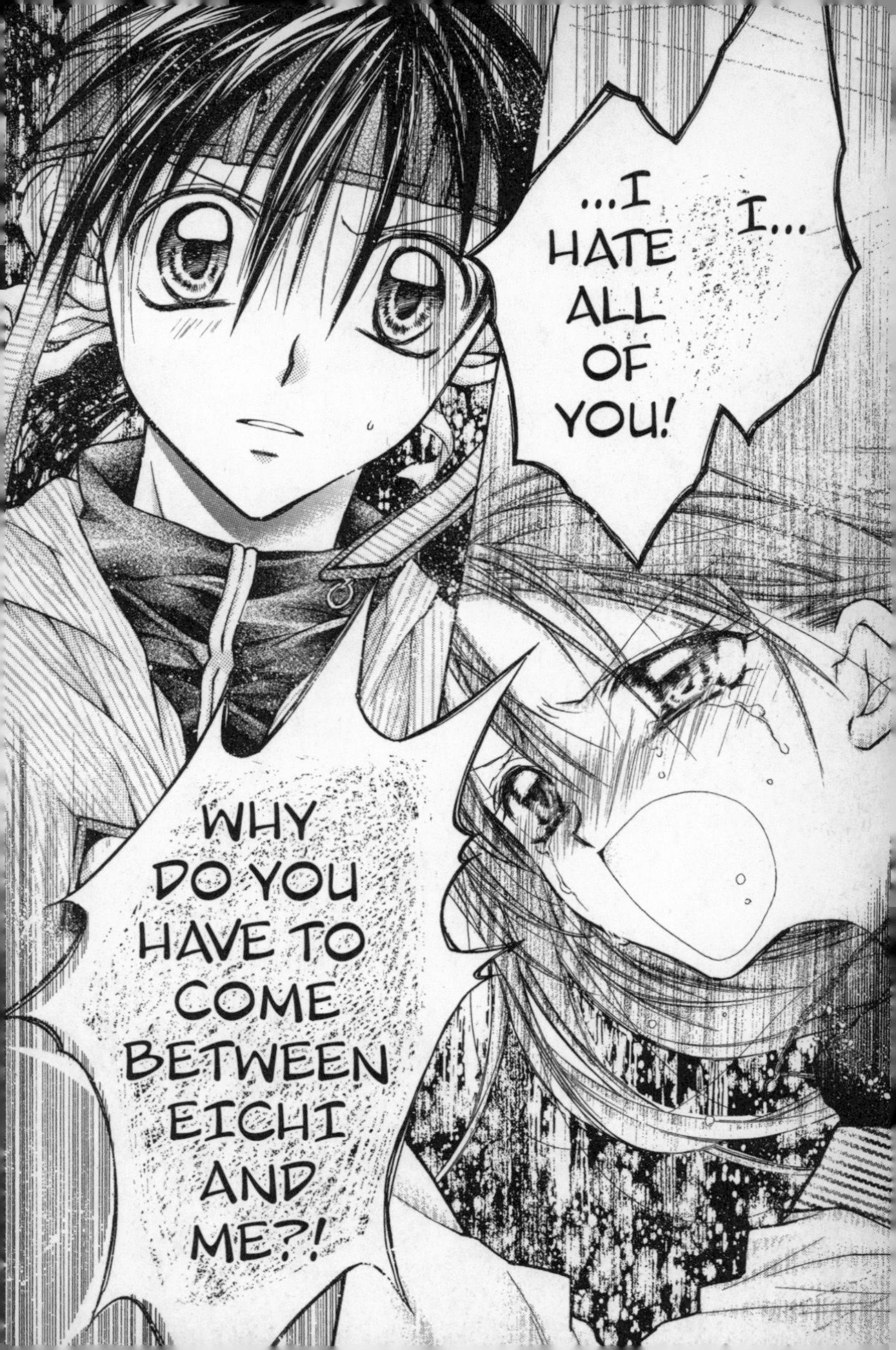
I...
...I HATE ALL OF YOU!
WHY DO YOU HAVE TO COME BETWEEN EICHI AND ME?!

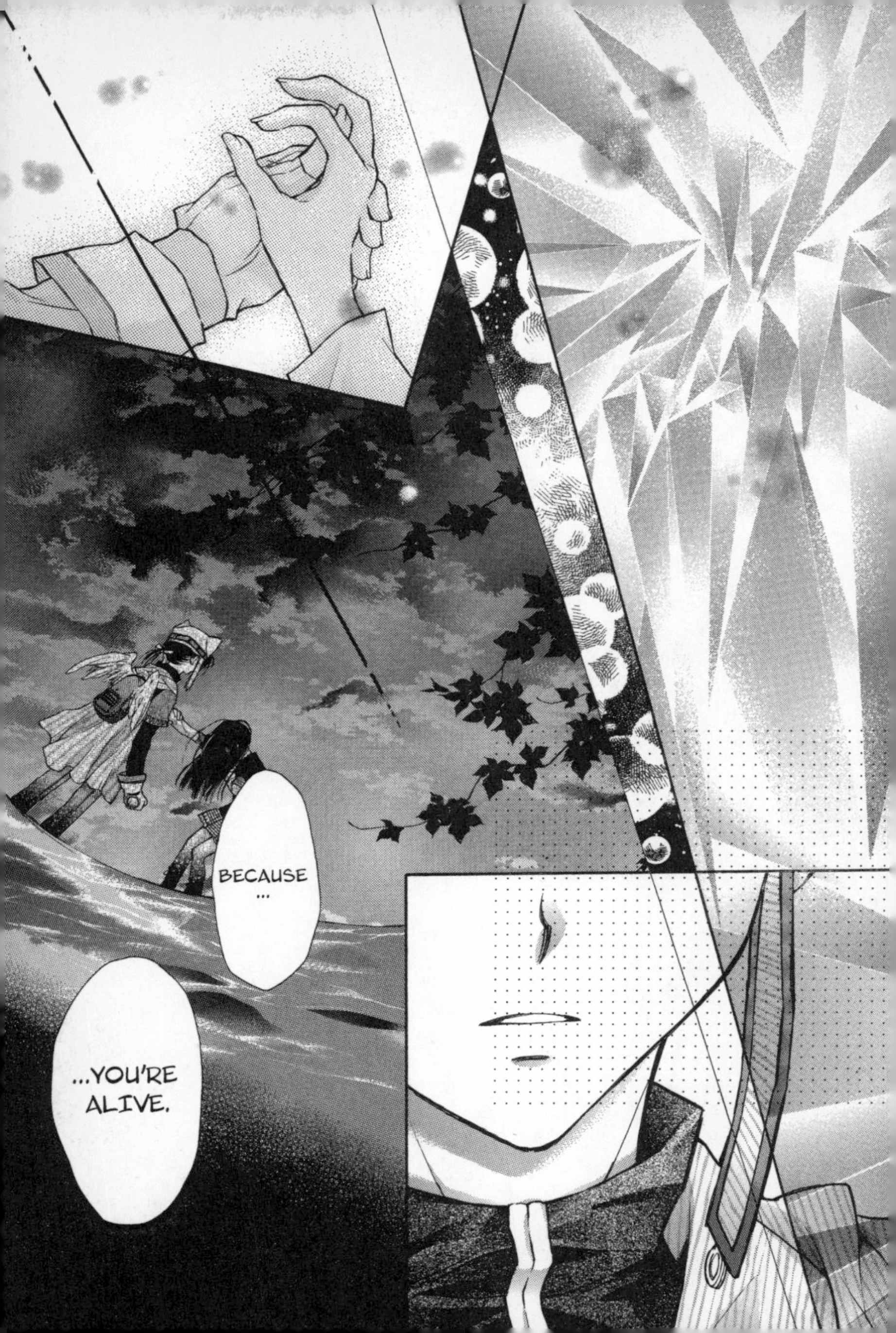
BECAUSE ...
...YOU'RE ALIVE.

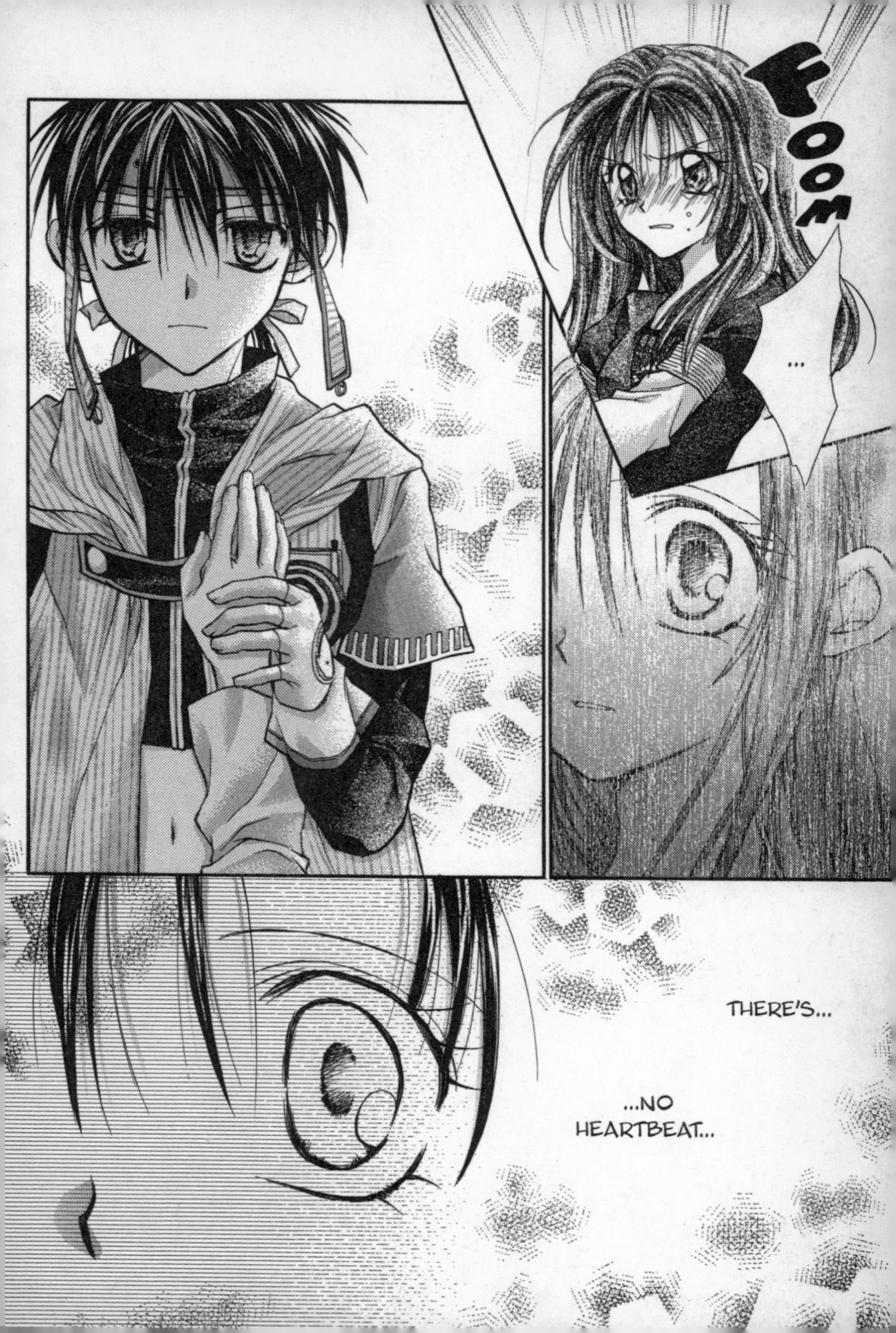
FOOM
...
THERE'S...
...NO
HEARTBEAT...

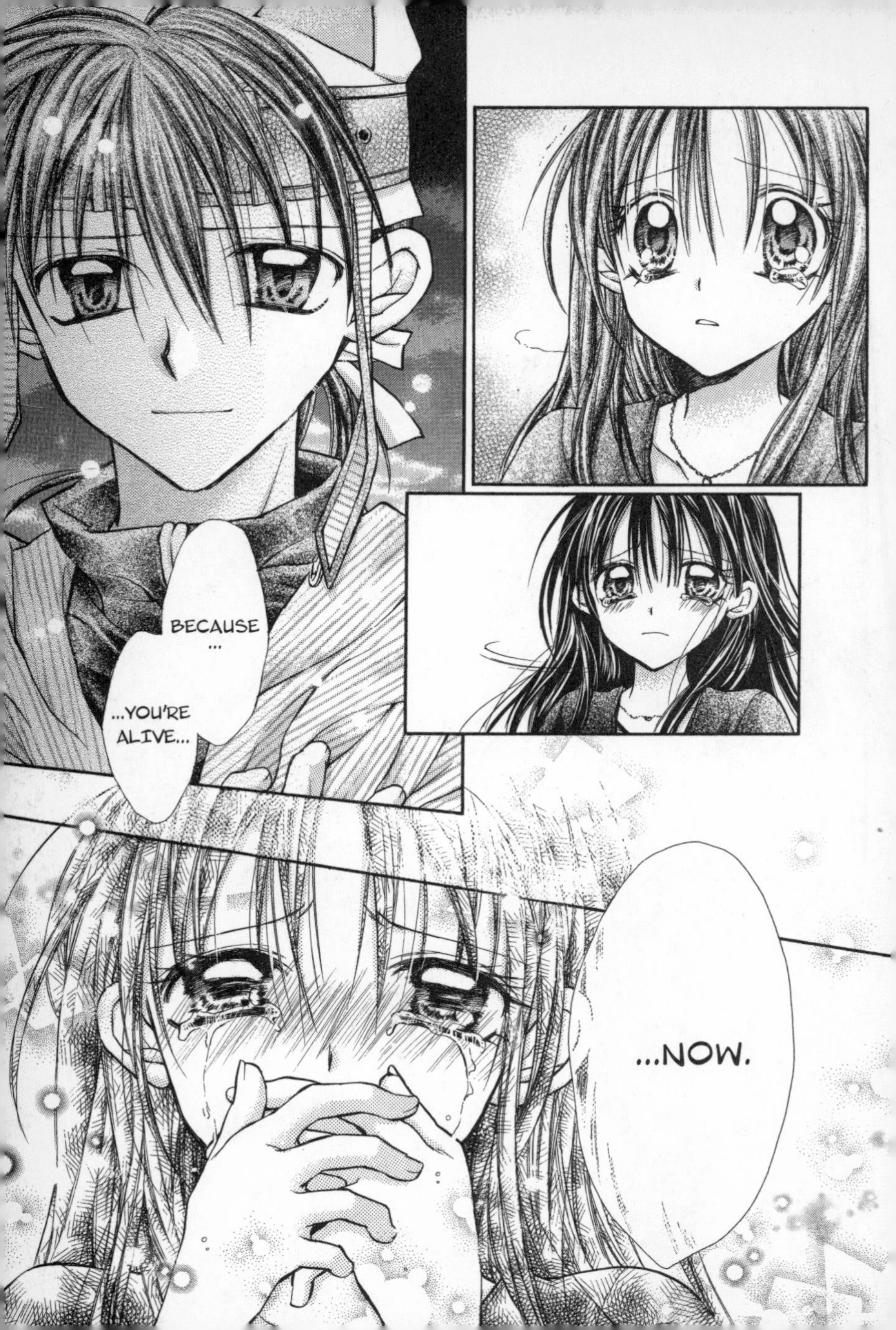
BECAUSE ...
...YOU'RE ALIVE...
...NOW.

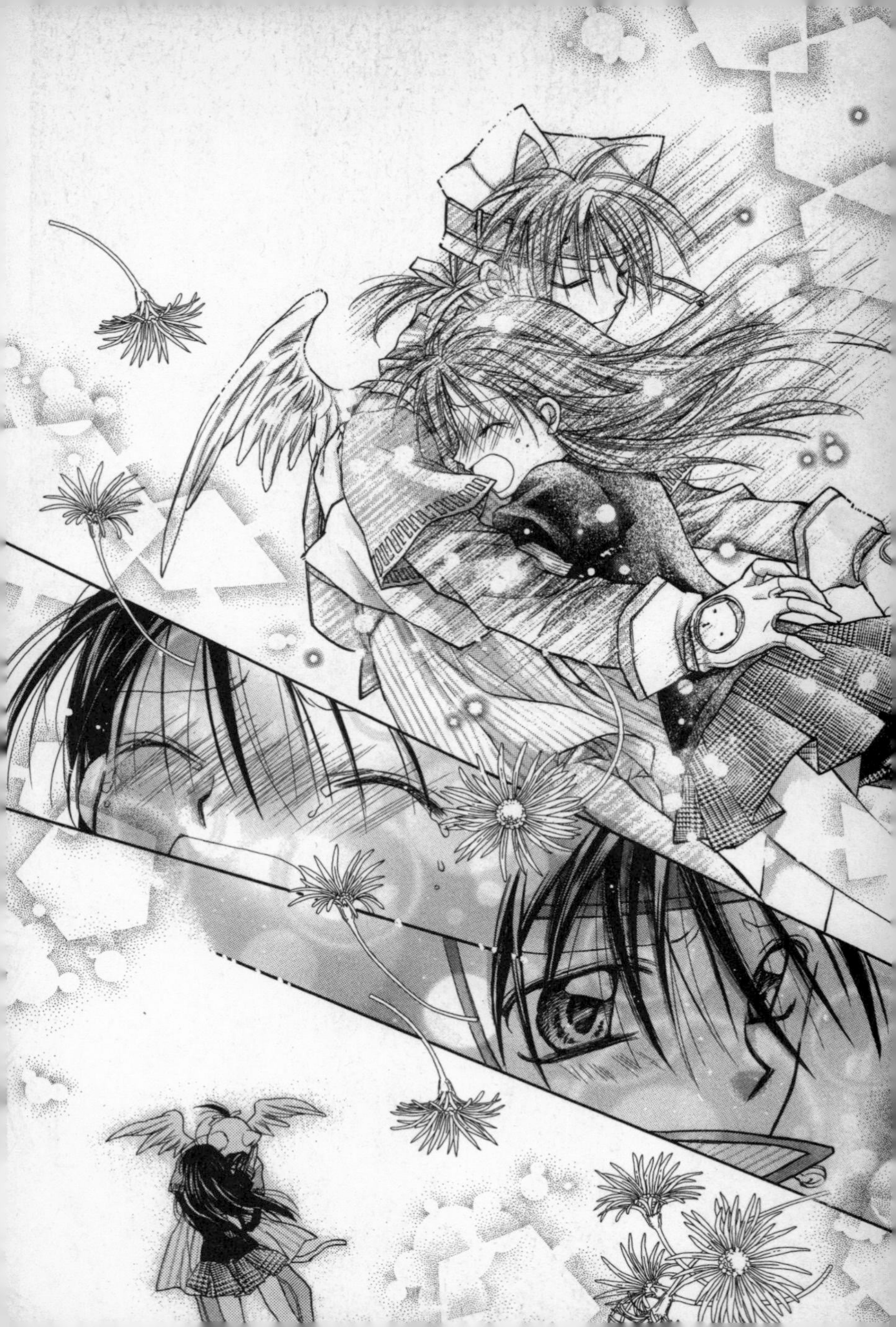

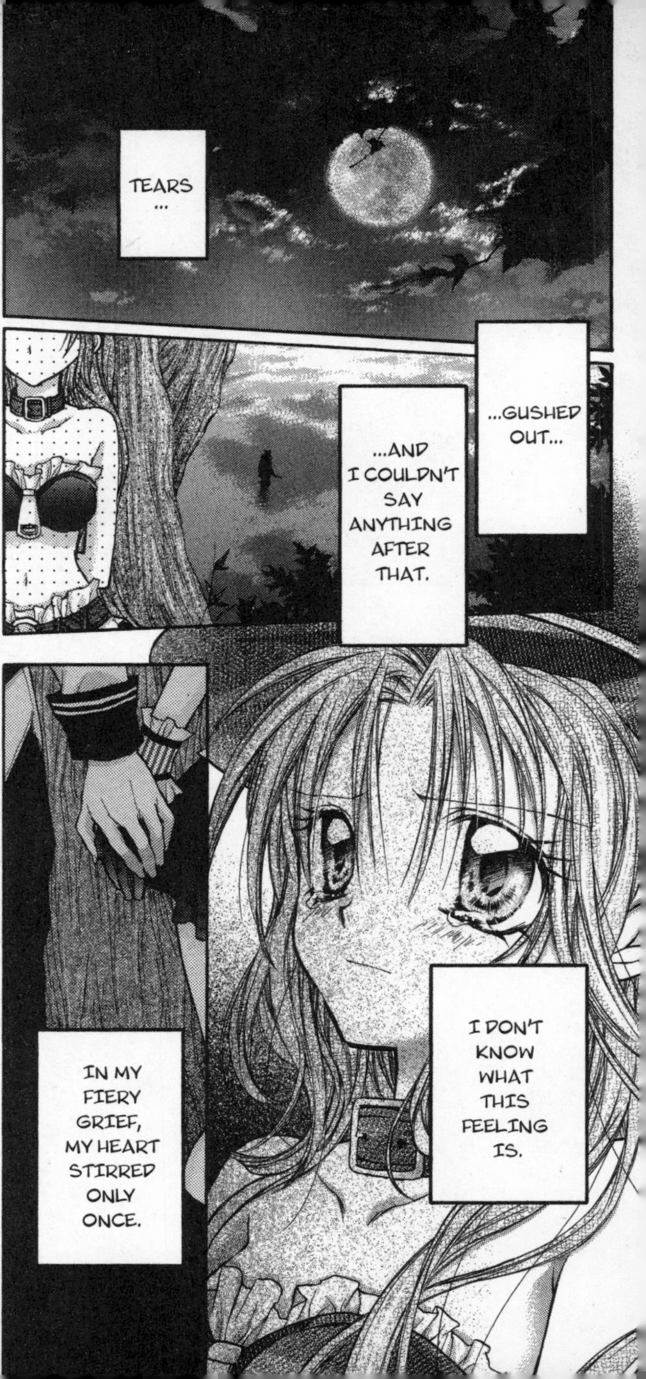
TEARS ...
...GUSHED OUT...
...AND I COULDN'T SAY ANYTHING AFTER THAT.
I DON'T KNOW WHAT THIS FEELING IS.
IN MY FIERY GRIEF, MY HEART STIRRED ONLY ONCE.

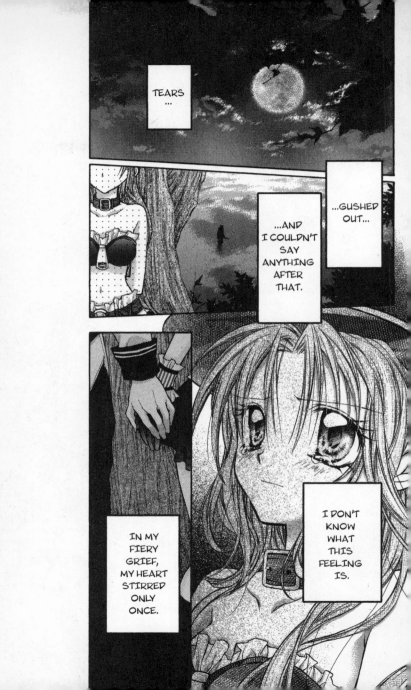

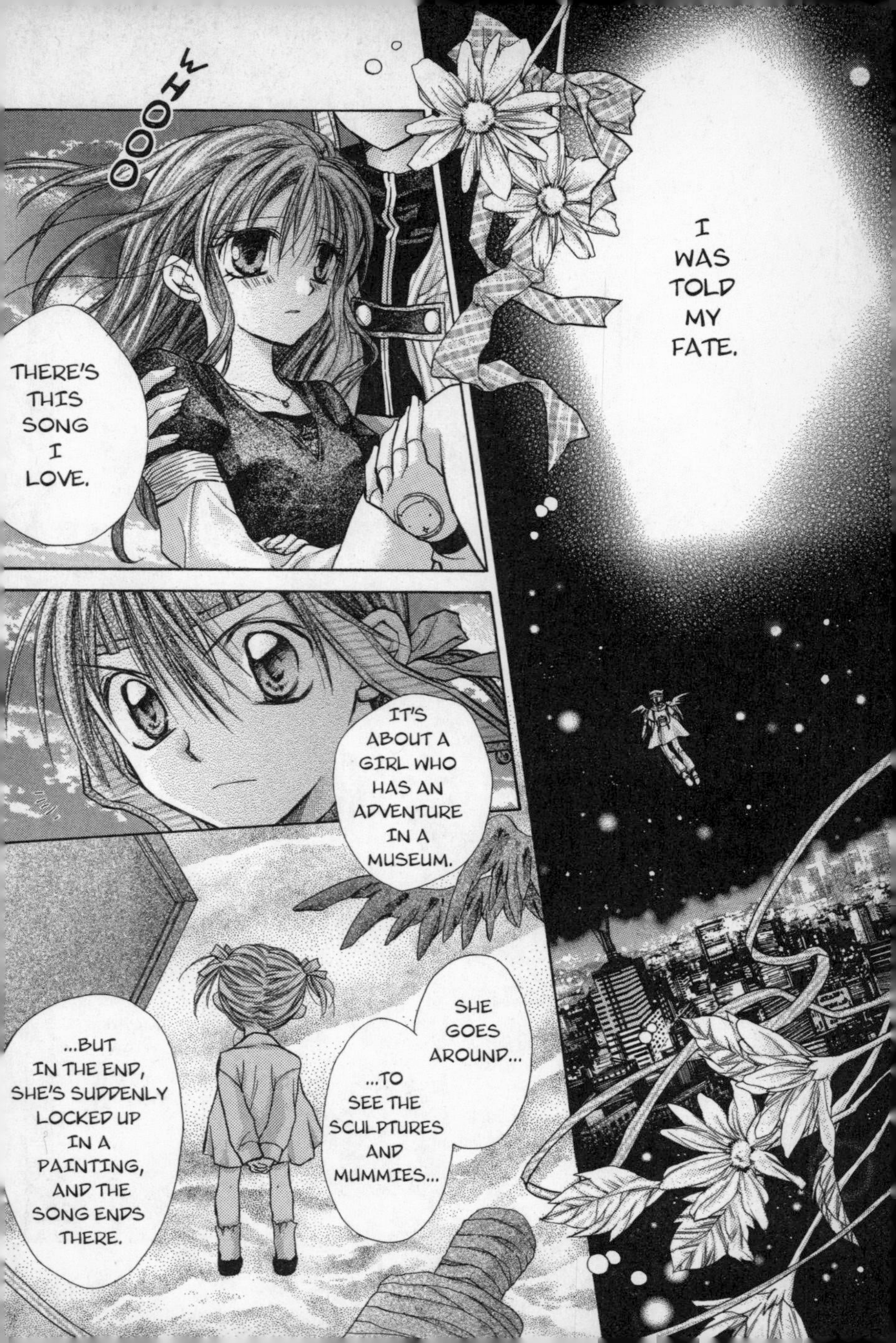
I WAS TOLD MY FATE.
THERE'S THIS SONG I LOVE.
IT'S ABOUT A GIRL WHO HAS AN ADVENTURE IN A MUSEUM.
SHE GOES AROUND...
...TO SEE THE SCULPTURES AND MUMMIES...
...BUT IN THE END, SHE'S SUDDENLY LOCKED UP IN A PAINTING, AND THE SONG ENDS THERE.

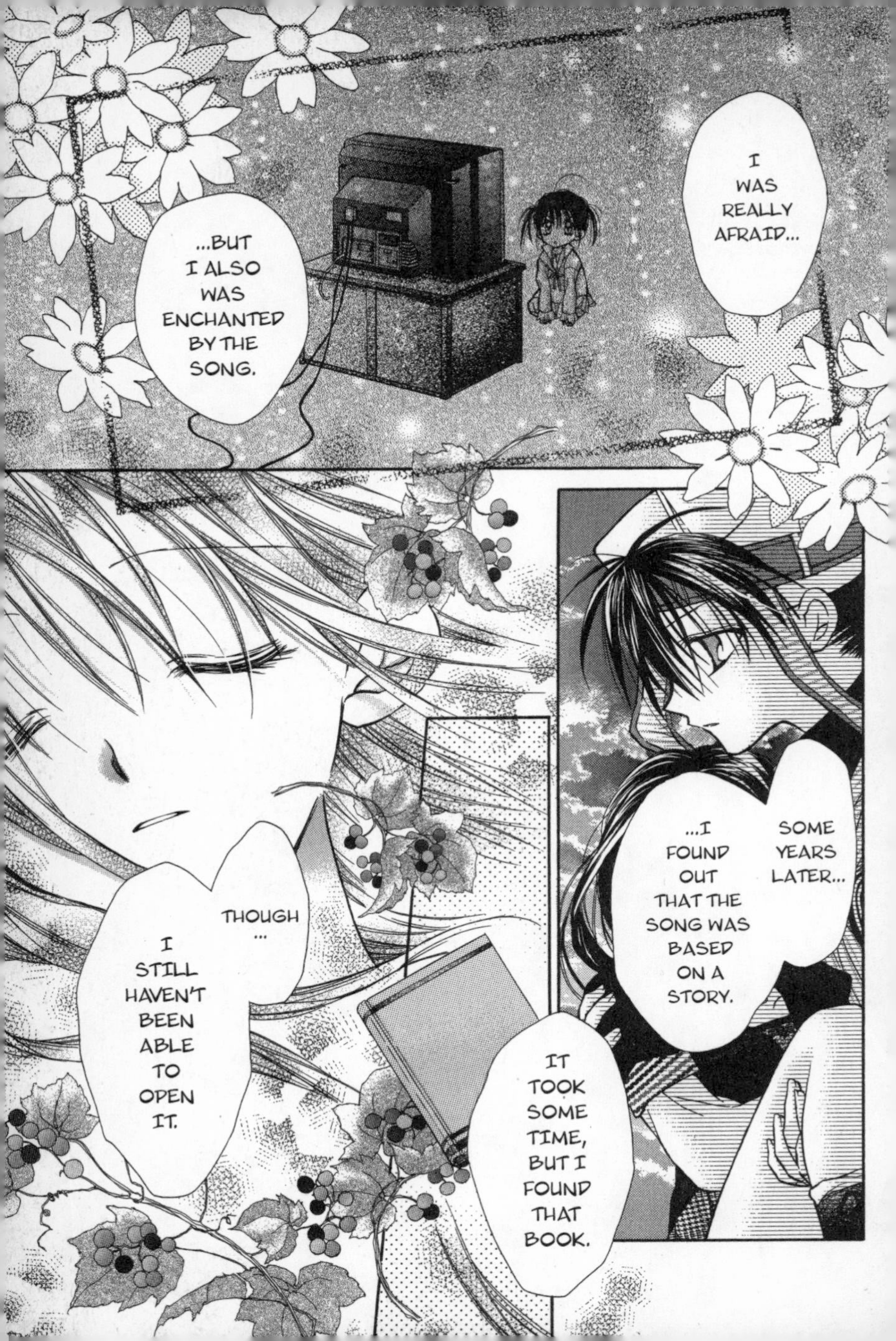
I WAS REALLY AFRAID...
...BUT I ALSO WAS ENCHANTED BY THE SONG.
SOME YEARS LATER...
...I FOUND OUT THAT THE SONG WAS BASED ON A STORY.
IT TOOK SOME TIME, BUT I FOUND THAT BOOK.
THOUGH...
I STILL HAVEN'T BEEN ABLE TO OPEN IT.

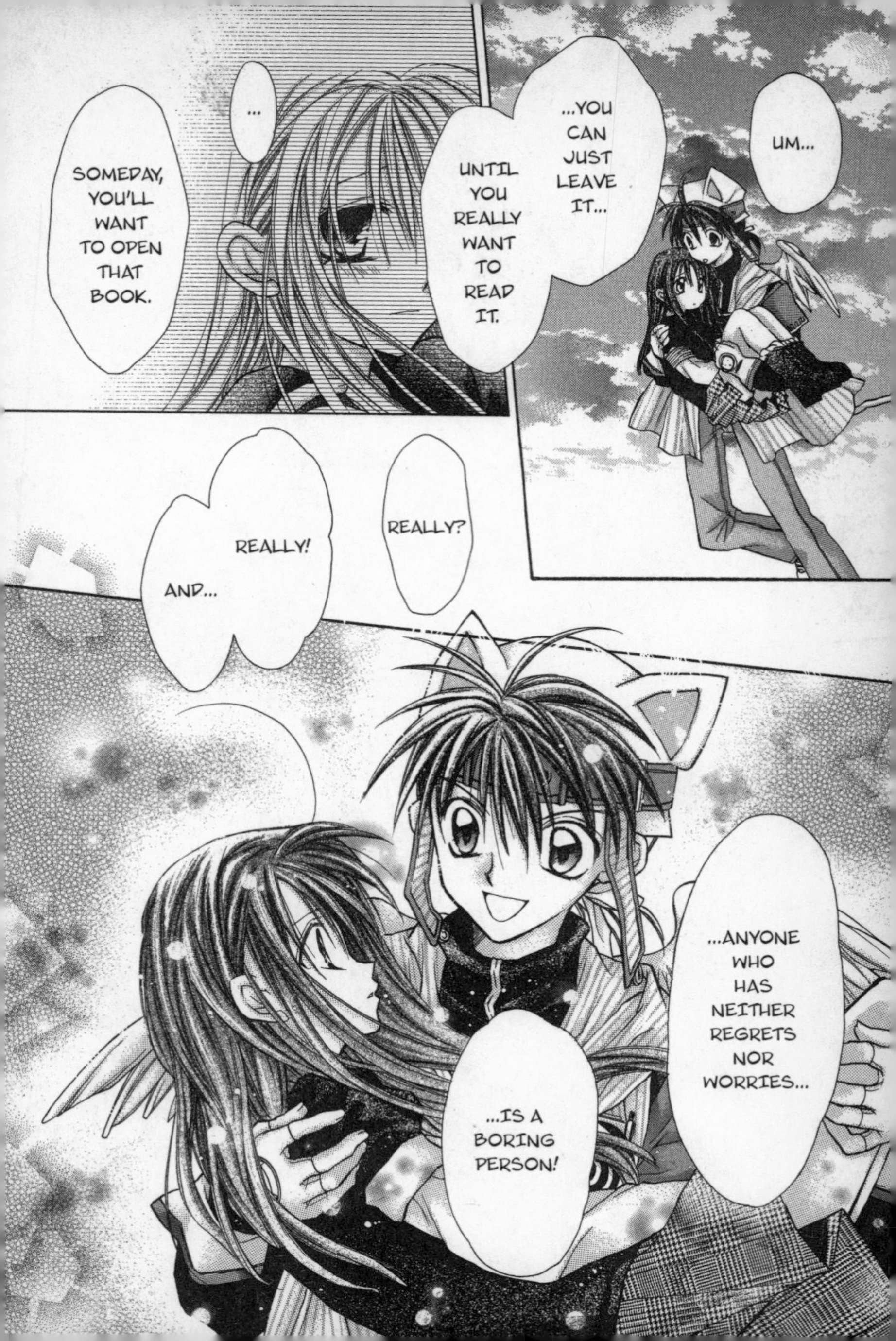
UM...
...YOU CAN JUST LEAVE IT...
UNTIL YOU REALLY WANT TO READ IT.
...
SOMEDAY, YOU'LL WANT TO OPEN THAT BOOK.
REALLY?
REALLY!
AND...
...ANYONE WHO HAS NEITHER REGRETS NOR WORRIES...
...IS A BORING PERSON!

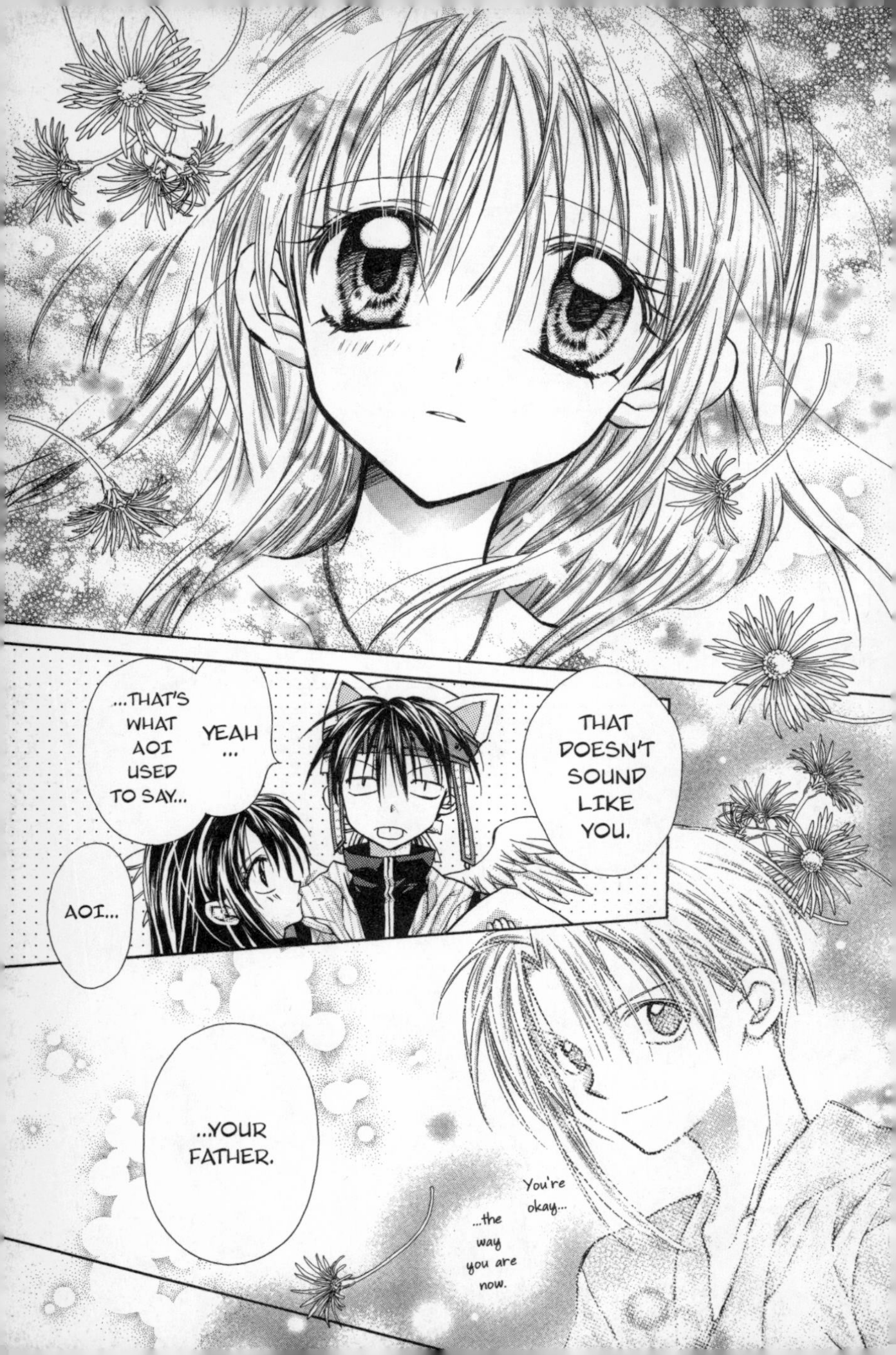
THAT DOESN'T SOUND LIKE YOU.
YEAH ...
...THAT'S WHAT AOI USED TO SAY...
AOI...
...YOUR FATHER.
You're okay...
...the way you are now.

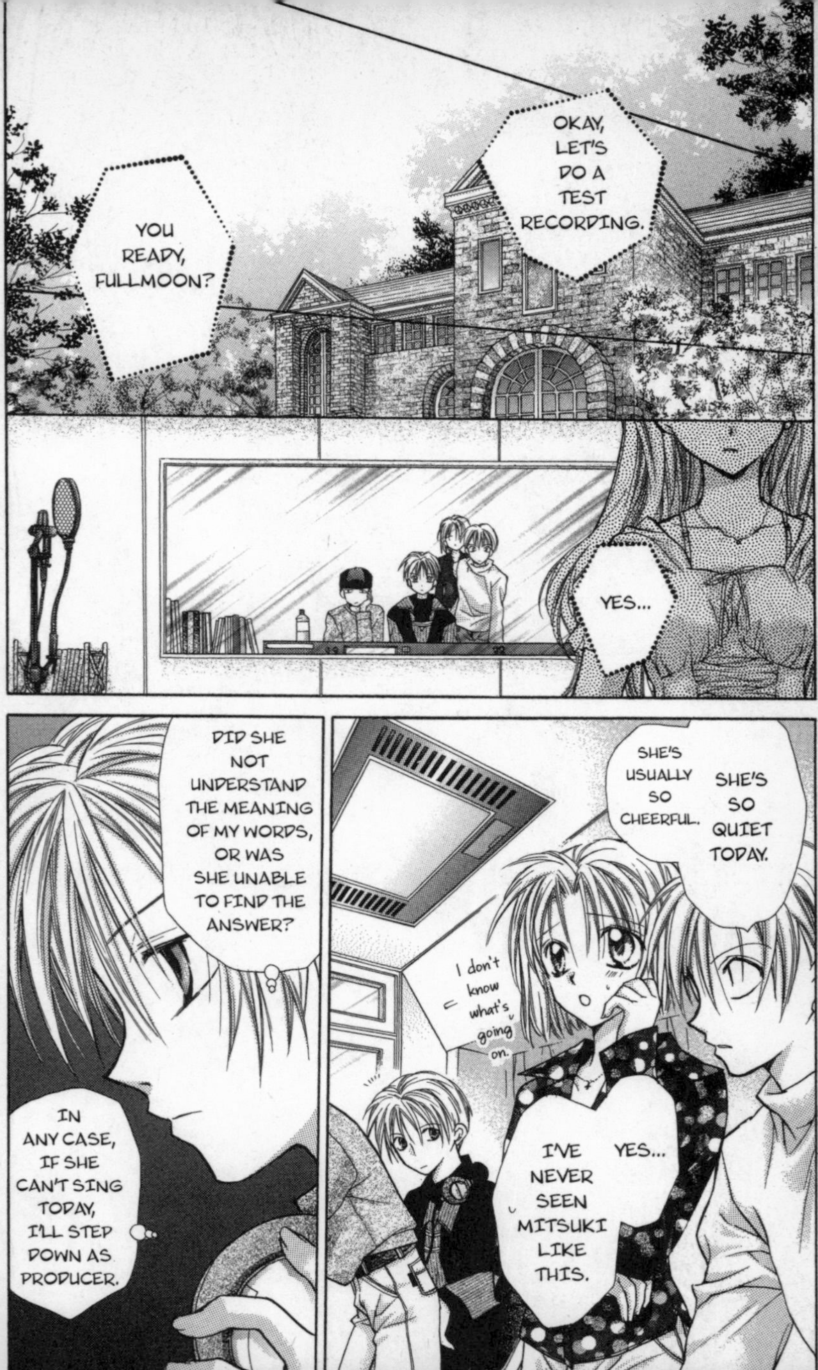

OKAY, LET'S DO A TEST RECORDING.
YOU READY, FULLMOON?
YES...
SHE'S SO QUIET TODAY.
SHE'S USUALLY SO CHEERFUL.
I don't know what's going on.
YES...
I'VE NEVER SEEN MITSUKI LIKE THIS.
DID SHE NOT UNDERSTAND THE MEANING OF MY WORDS, OR WAS SHE UNABLE TO FIND THE ANSWER?
IN ANY CASE, IF SHE CAN'T SING TODAY, I'LL STEP DOWN AS PRODUCER.

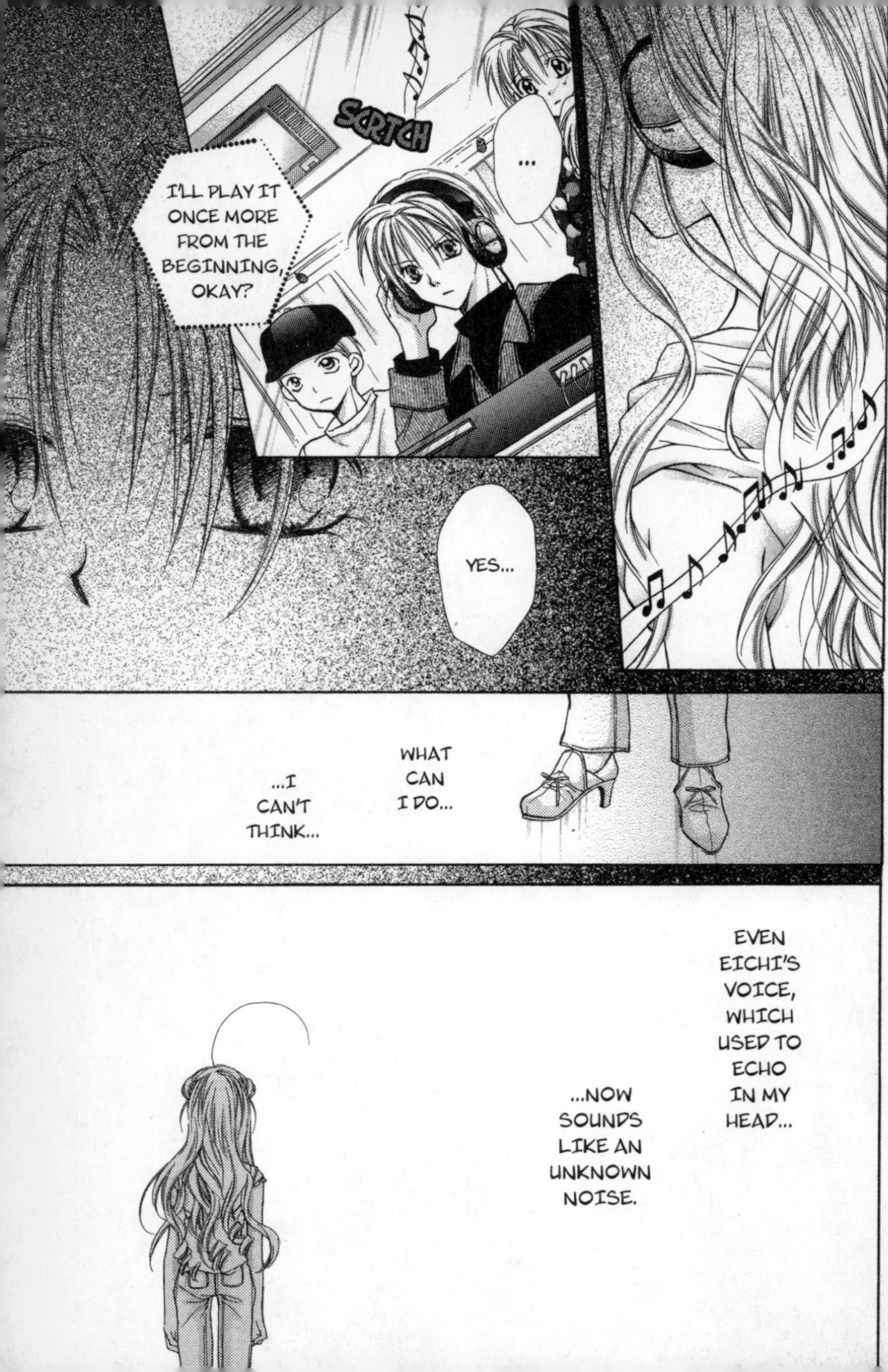
...
SCRTCH
I'LL PLAY IT ONCE MORE FROM THE BEGINNING, OKAY?
YES...
WHAT CAN I DO...
...I CAN'T THINK...
EVEN EICHI'S VOICE, WHICH USED TO ECHO IN MY HEAD...
...NOW SOUNDS LIKE AN UNKNOWN NOISE.

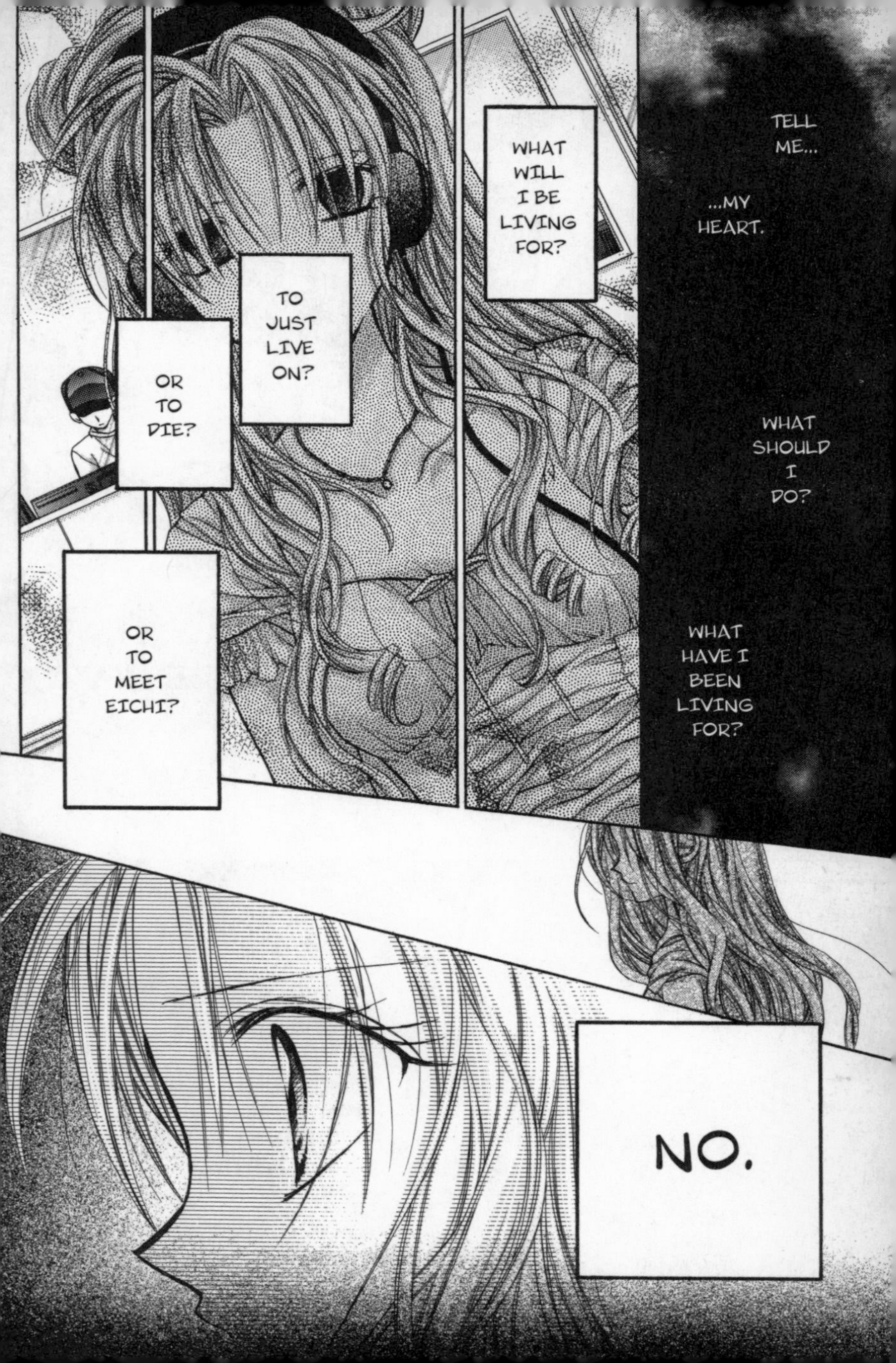
TELL ME...
...MY HEART.
WHAT SHOULD I DO?
WHAT HAVE I BEEN LIVING FOR?
WHAT WILL I BE LIVING FOR?
TO JUST LIVE ON?
OR TO DIE?
OR TO MEET EICHI?
NO.

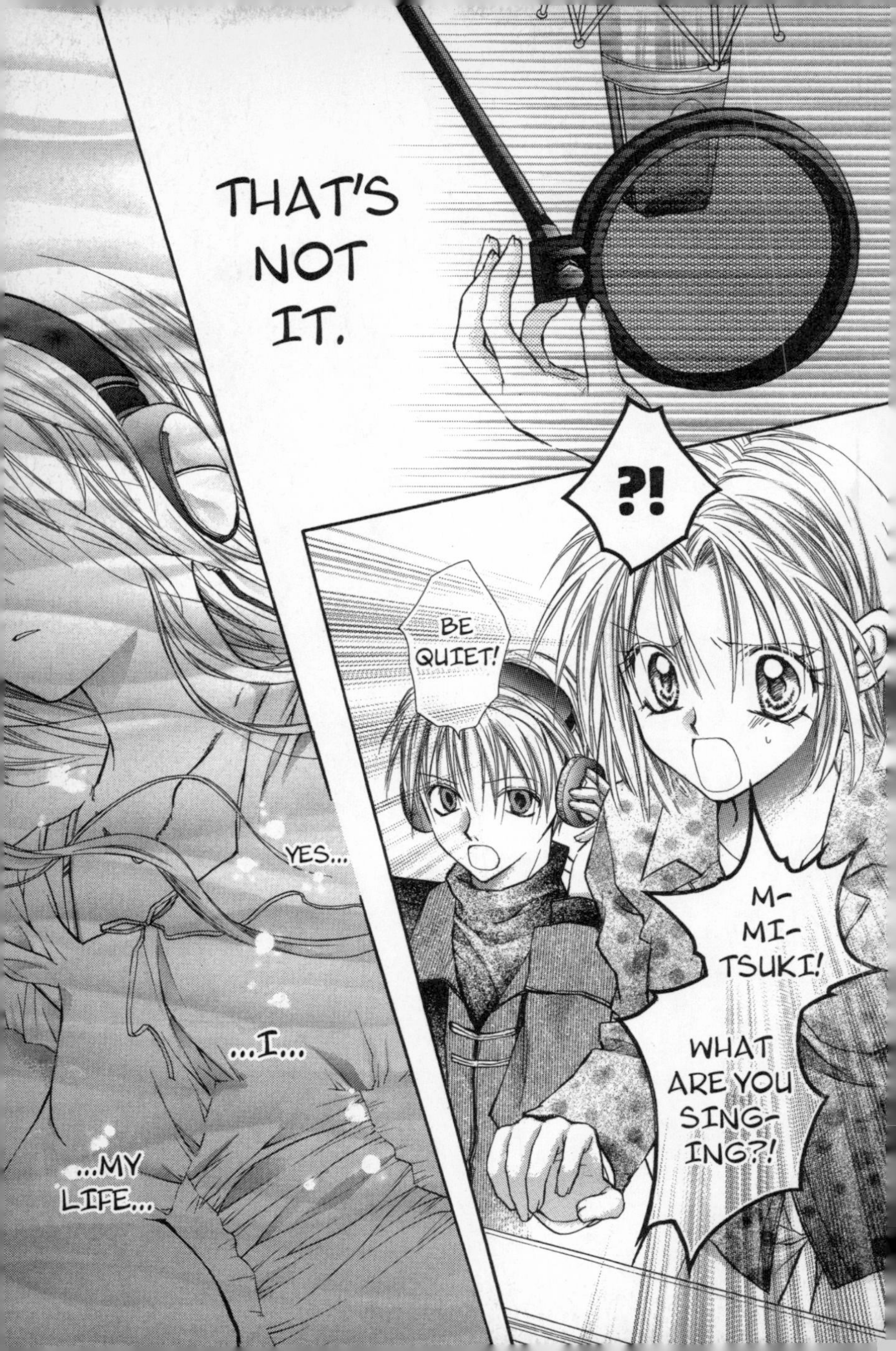
THAT'S NOT IT.
?!
M-MI-TSUKI!
WHAT ARE YOU SING-ING?!
BE QUIET!
YES...
...I...
...MY LIFE...

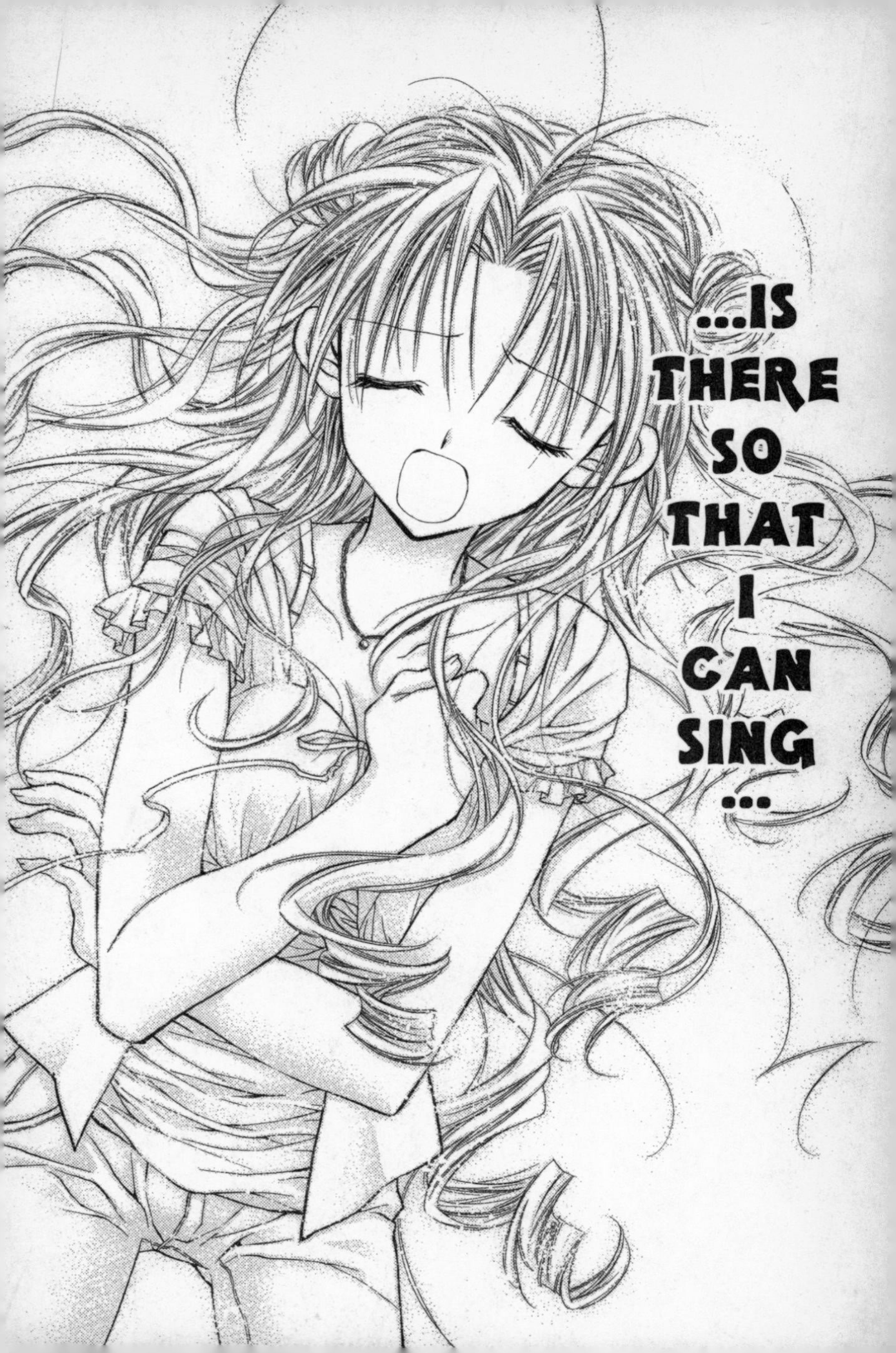
...IS THERE SO THAT I CAN SING...

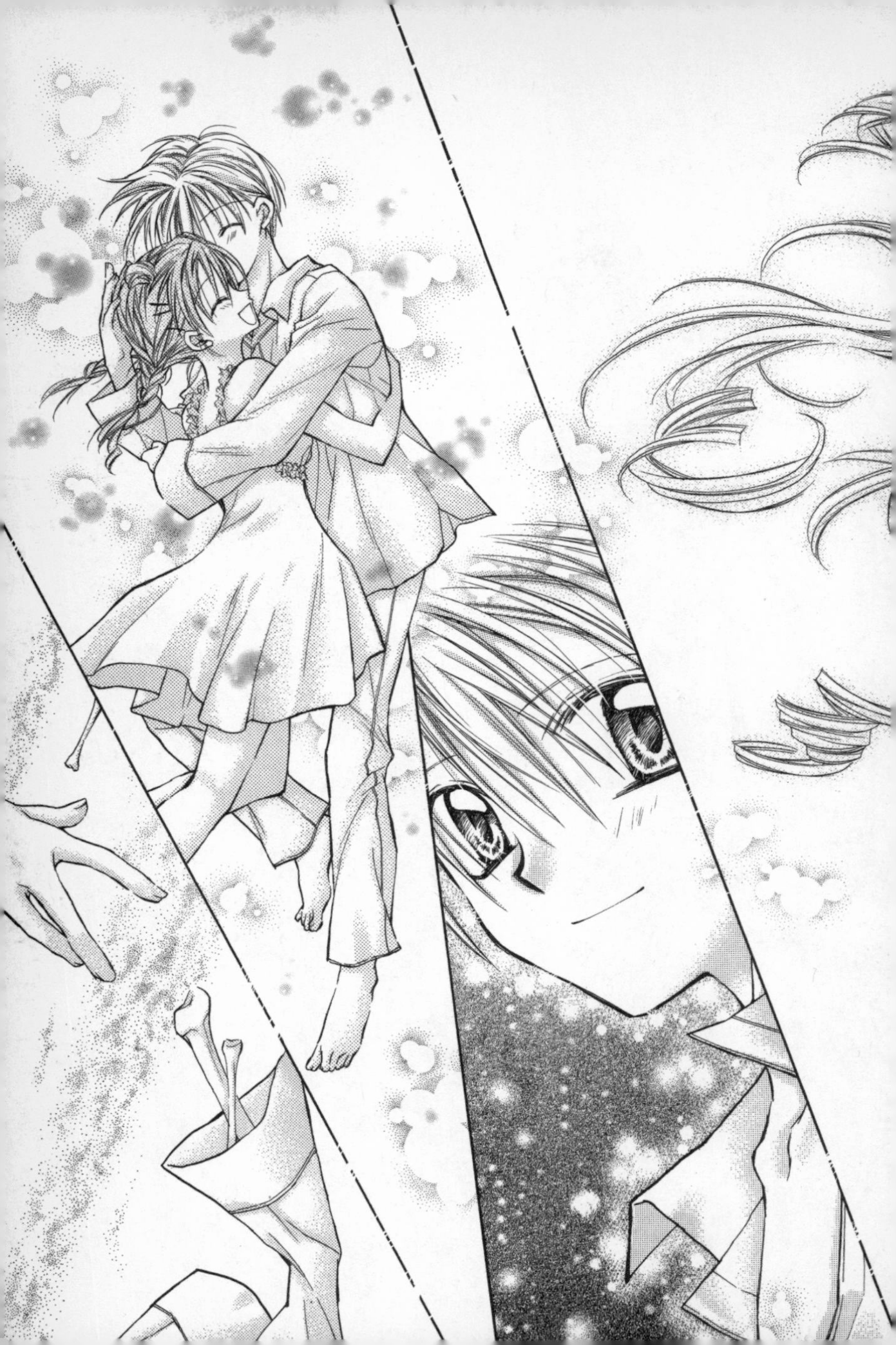

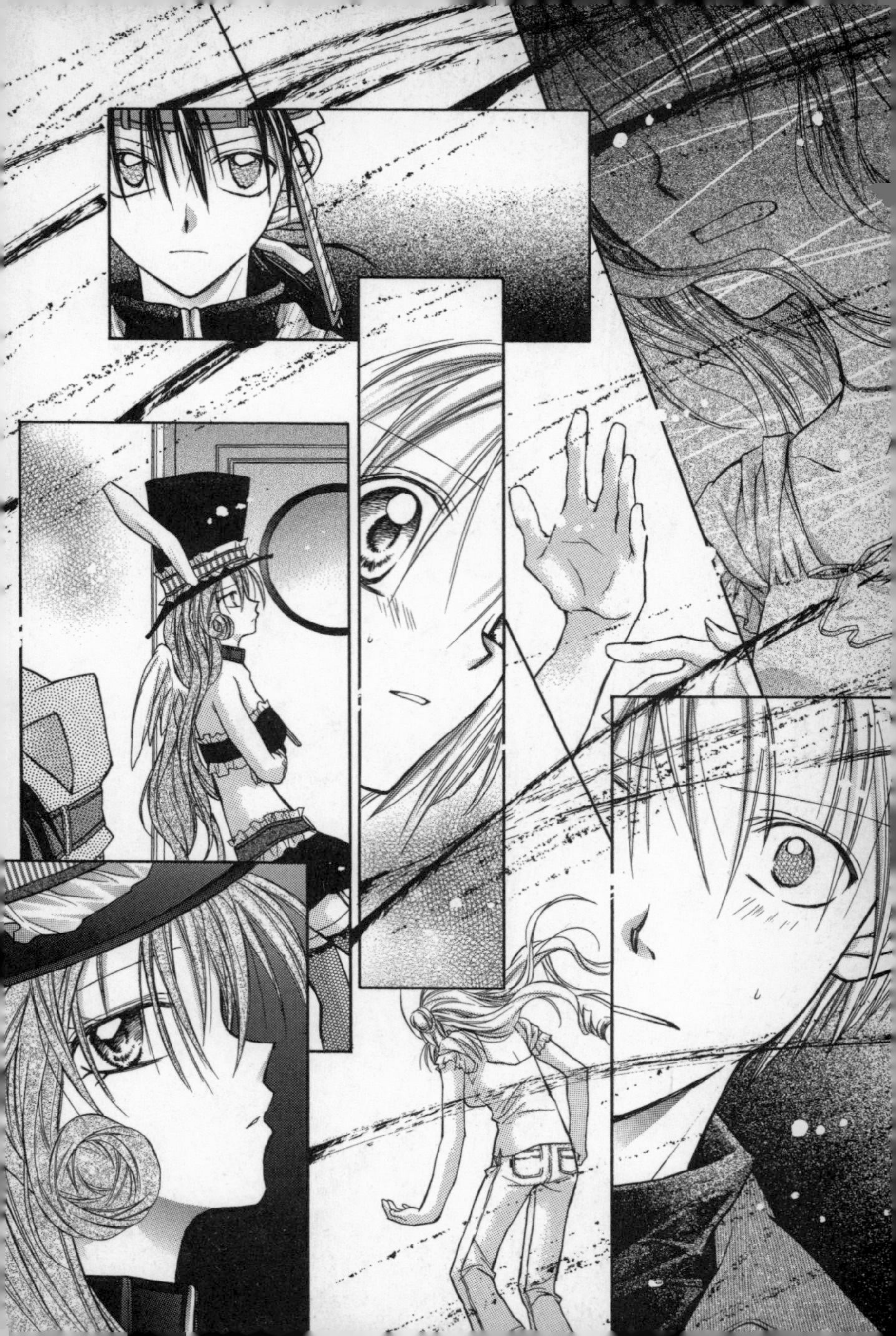

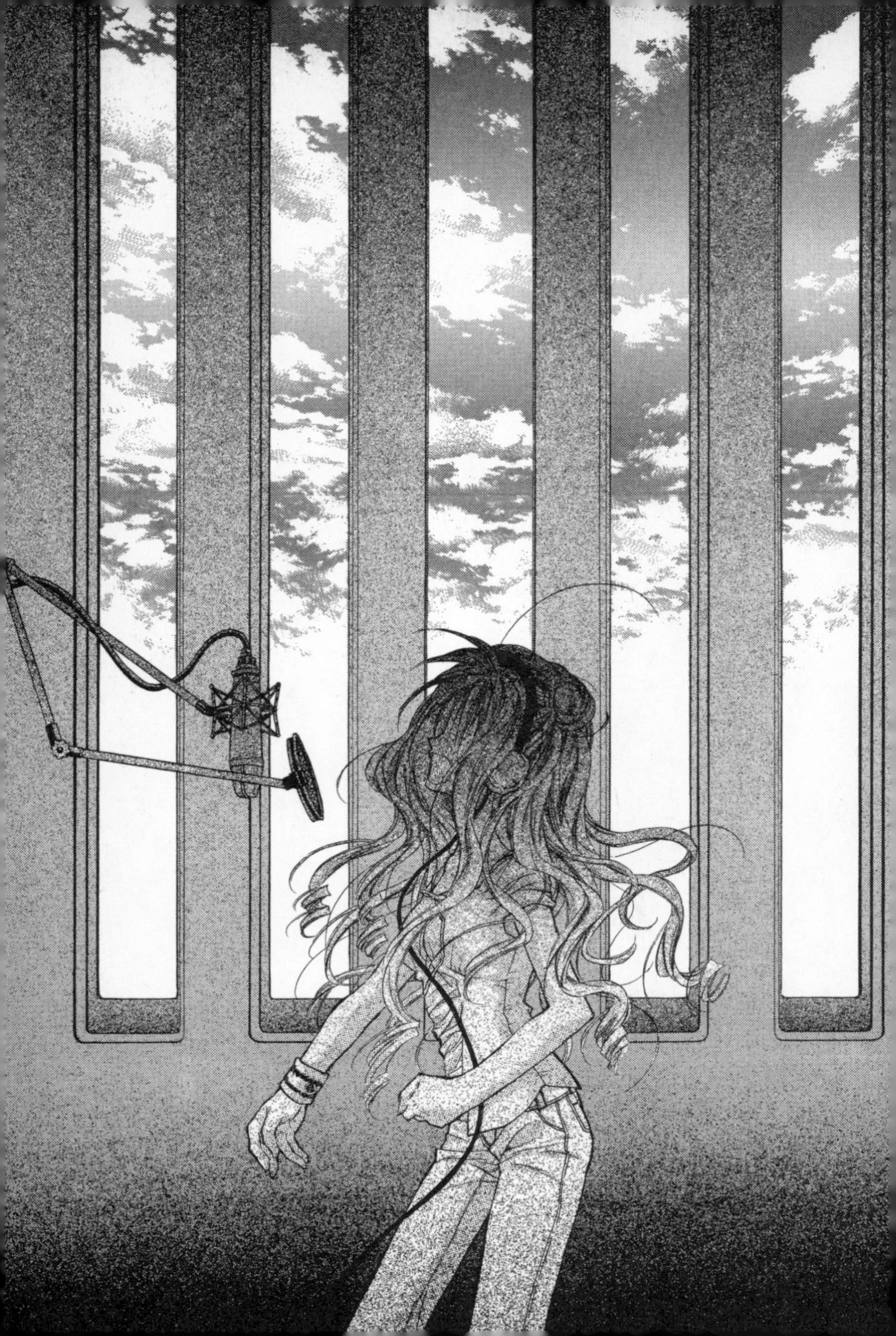

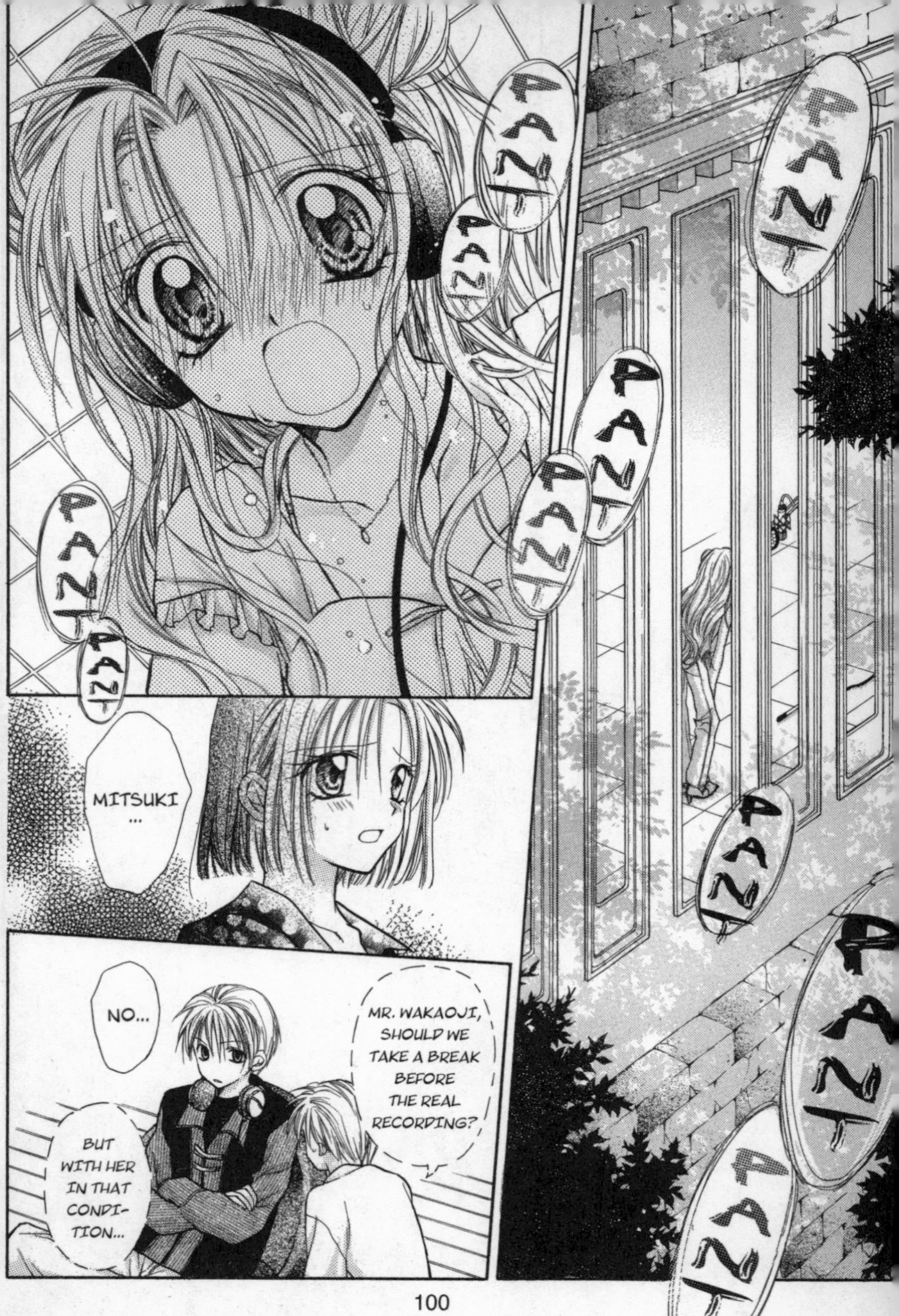
PANT
PANT
PANT
PANT
PANT
PANT
PANT
PANT
PANT
PANT
PANT
MITSUKI ...
MR. WAKAOJI, SHOULD WE TAKE A BREAK BEFORE THE REAL RECORDING?
NO...
BUT WITH HER IN THAT CONDI- TION...

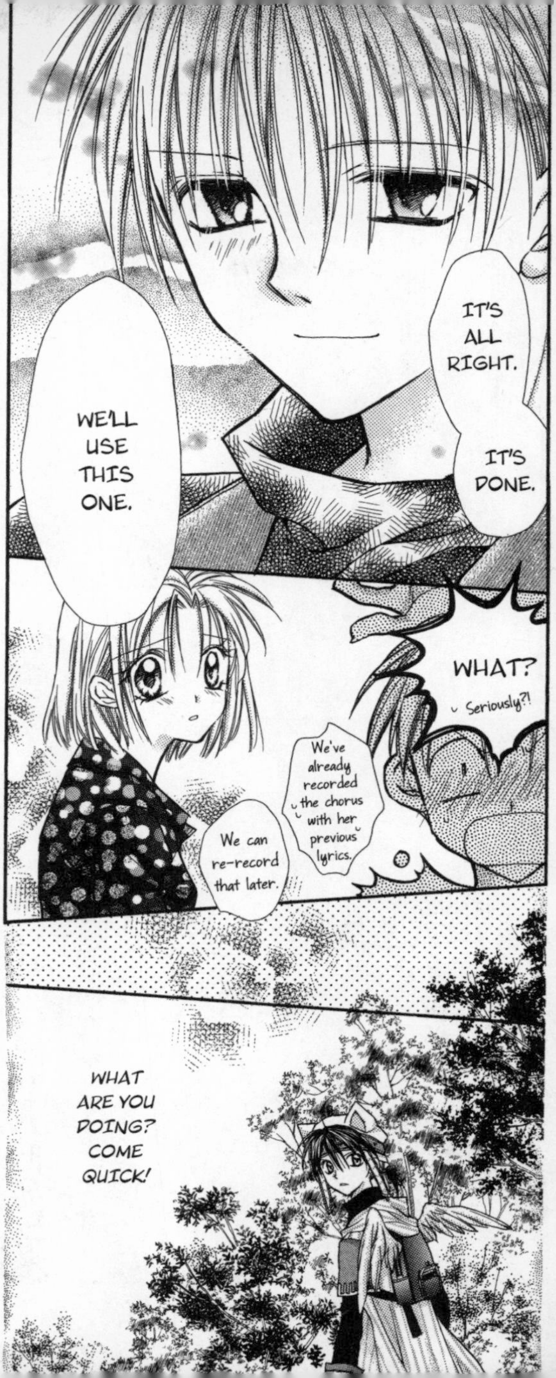
IT'S ALL RIGHT.
IT'S DONE.
WE'LL USE THIS ONE.
WHAT?
Seriously?!
We've already recorded the chorus with her previous lyrics.
We can re-record that later.
WHAT ARE YOU DOING? COME QUICK!

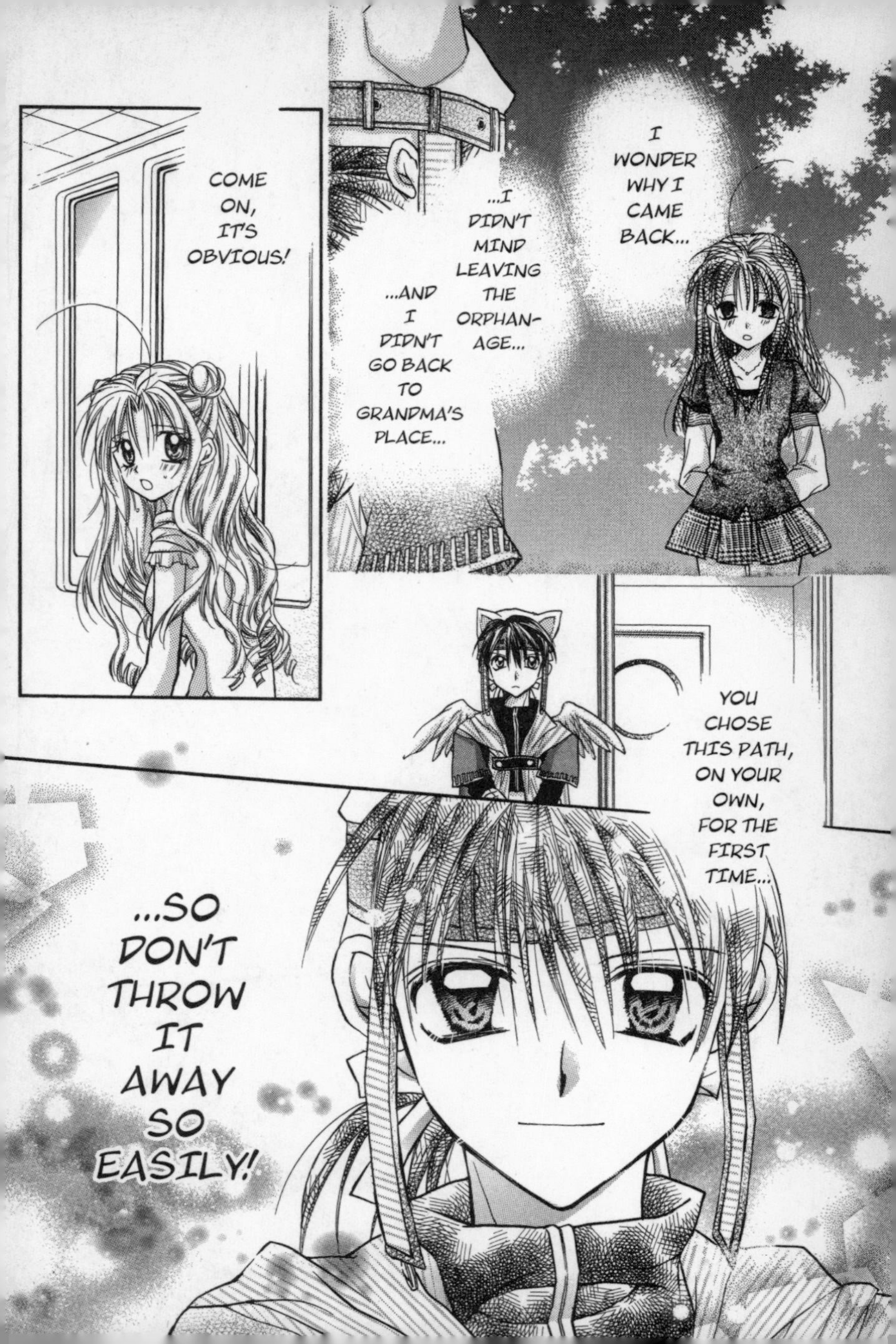
I WONDER WHY I CAME BACK...
...I DIDN'T MIND LEAVING THE ORPHANAGE...
...AND I DIDN'T GO BACK TO GRANDMA'S PLACE...
COME ON, IT'S OBVIOUS!
YOU CHOSE THIS PATH, ON YOUR OWN, FOR THE FIRST TIME...
...SO DON'T THROW IT AWAY SO EASILY!

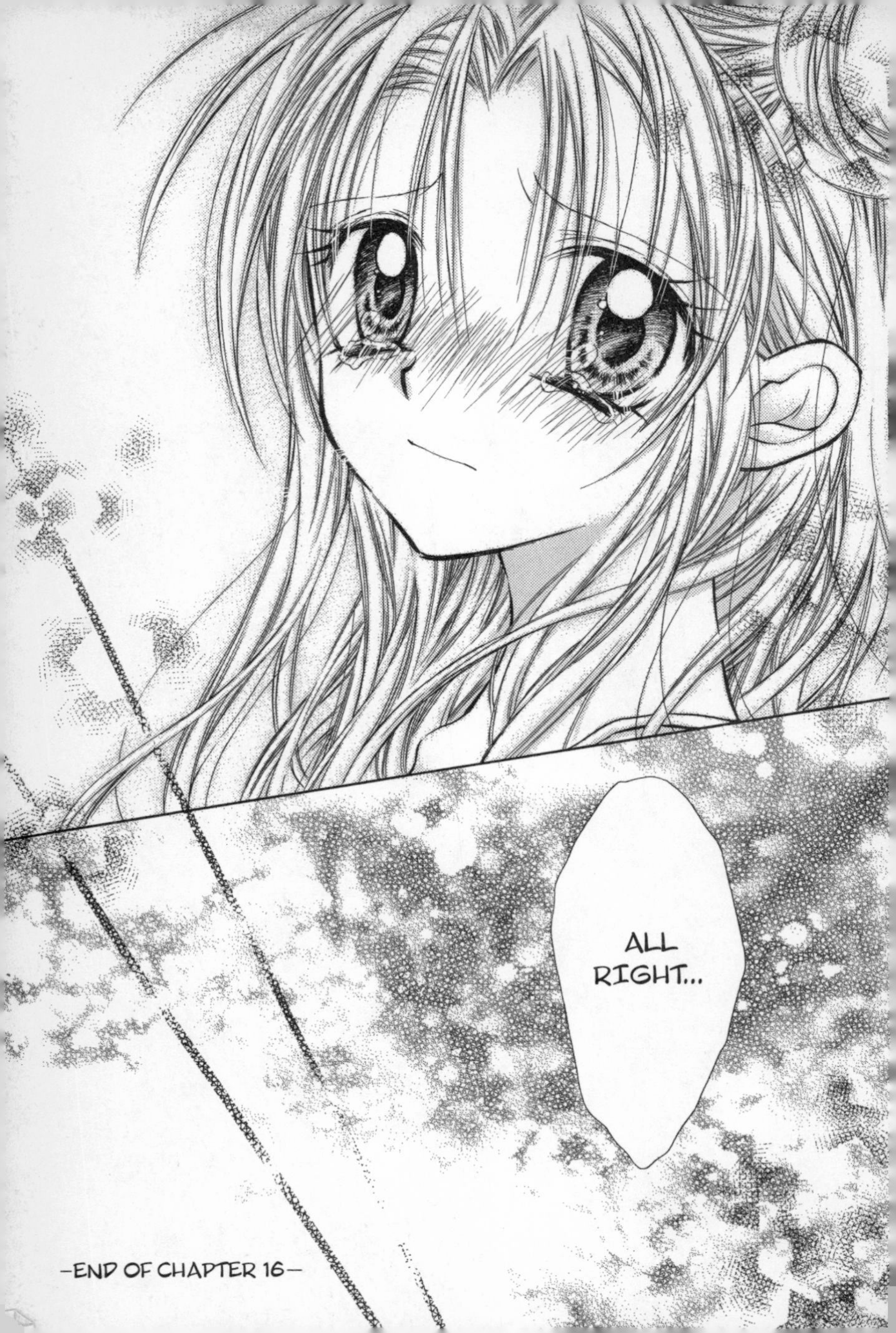
ALL RIGHT...
-END OF CHAPTER 16-

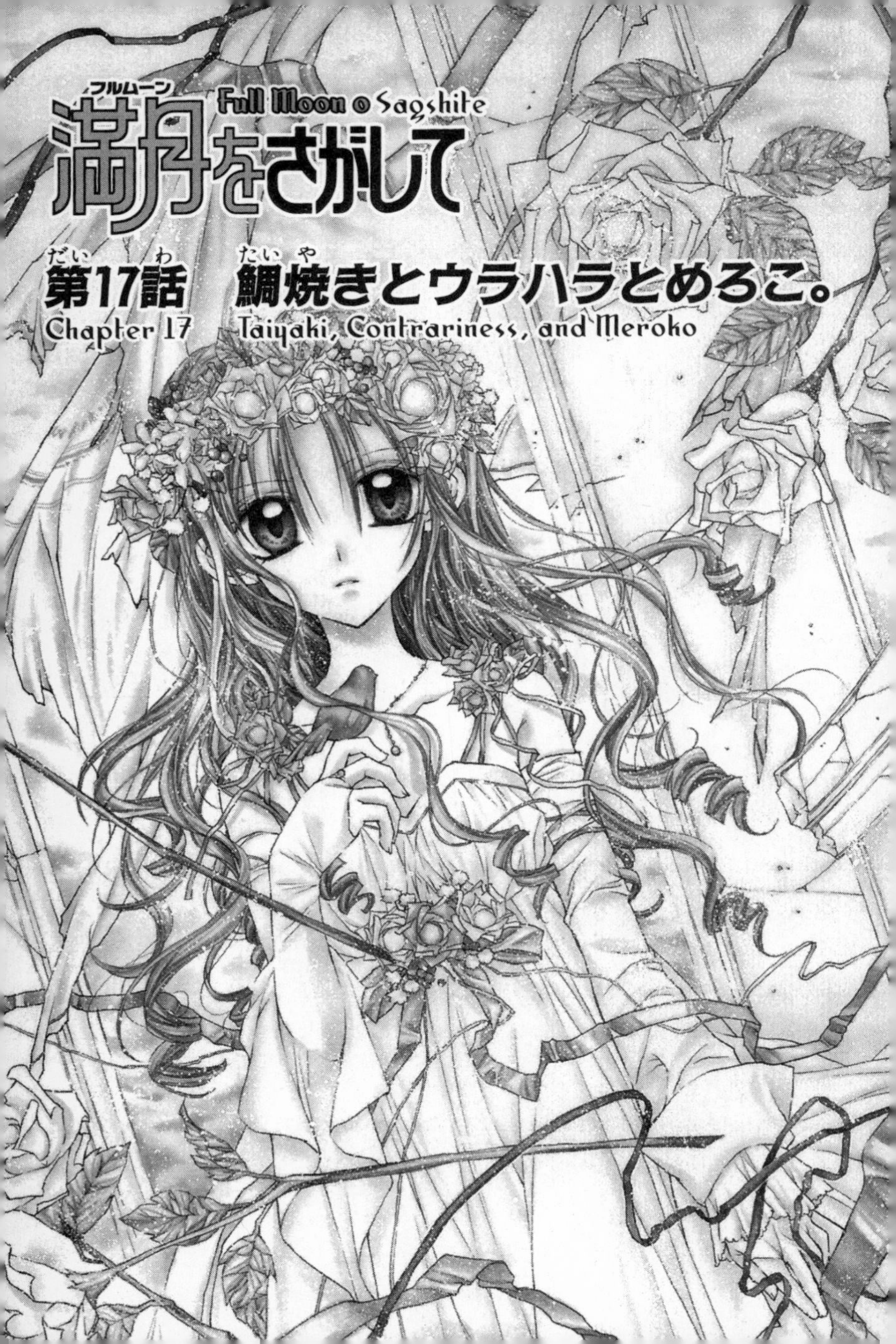
フルムーン
満月をさがして
Full Moon o Sagashite
第17話　鯛焼きとウラハラとめろこ。
Chapter 17　Taiyaki, Contrariness, and Meroko

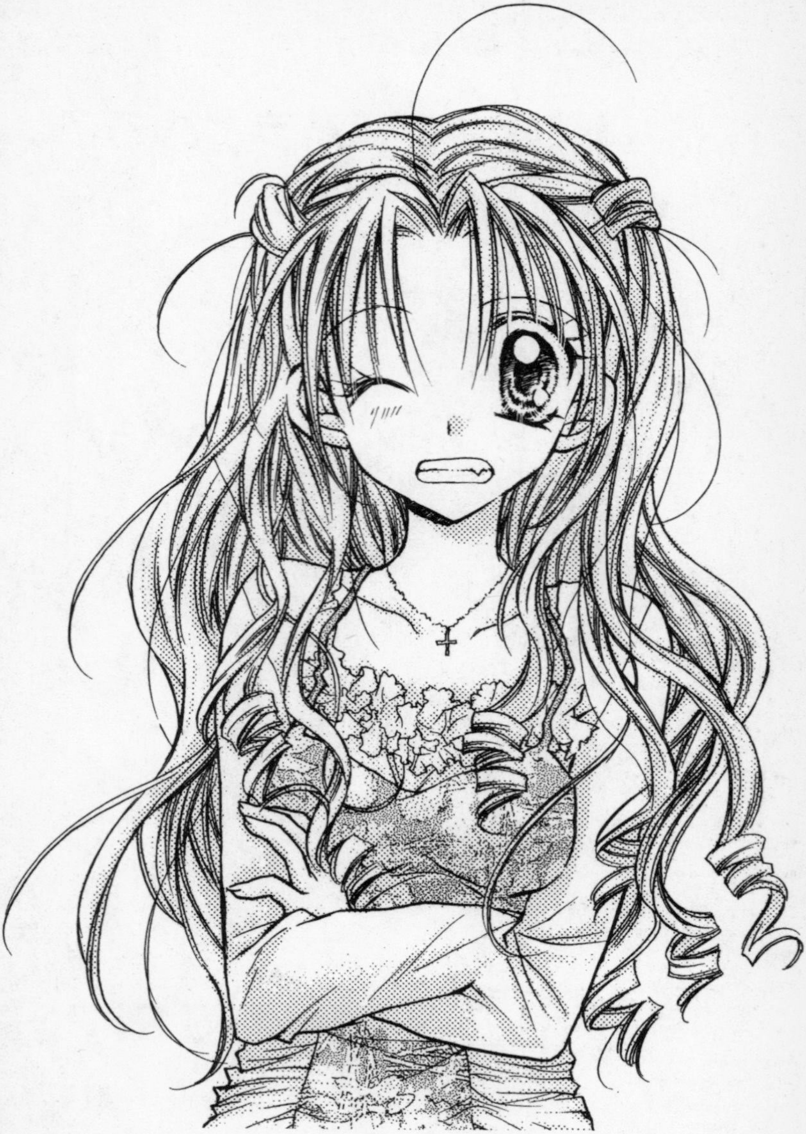

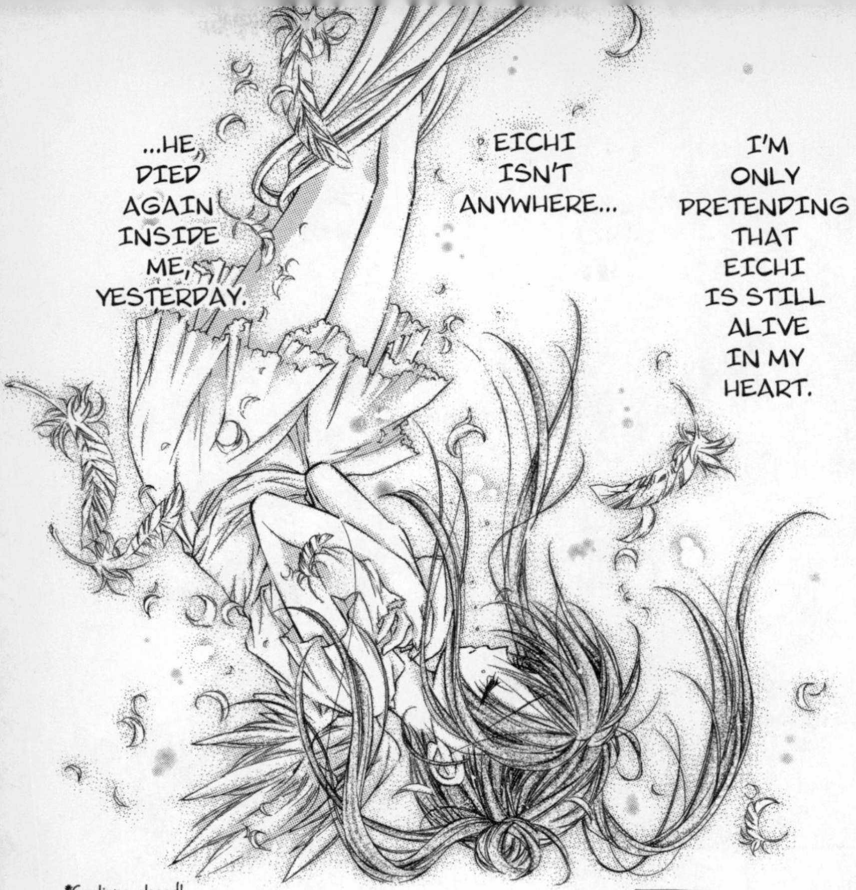
I'M ONLY PRETENDING THAT EICHI IS STILL ALIVE IN MY HEART.
EICHI ISN'T ANYWHERE...
...HE, DIED AGAIN INSIDE ME, YESTERDAY.

*Spoliers ahead!

Chapter 17: Taiyaki, Contrariness, and Meroko

Cover Copy

Mitsuki's love is stronger and sadder than anybody's...

This illustration...I don't like it too much. I think I watched Lord of the Rings 2, and Eowyn was really cute, and I wanted to draw a dress like hers, and I drew this, and it was a failure. ← Illustrations I draw like this are usually not good.

And I started drawing roses again (I'd forbidden myself to draw them, because I draw them often.)

The story is the beginning of the Meroko segment. (There were opinions that the title doesn't match the story...but it does exactly.) Usa-Mero's expressions are always kinda subtle. I like the face when she says "Why?" Meroko, you look weird. You're cute, yes!

I'd been thinking a lot about Grandma and Meroko's story, so I'm glad I could draw it. You might think "Mitsuki doesn't appear much in it," but the story is structured so that if you're reading the tankobon, it makes sense. after all. (For those who read this in Ribon, please bear with me. I've decided to draw in this manner.)

You might have realized already, but the cover of the tankobon has "Mitsuki and XXX (character name)" as the concept. I've put the character linked to the contents on the cover. Vol. 5 will have Zumi-yan (Izumi).

I haven't decided who'll be on the cover of Vol. 6 yet. The character cards, as long as they're continued, will have pairs or couples.

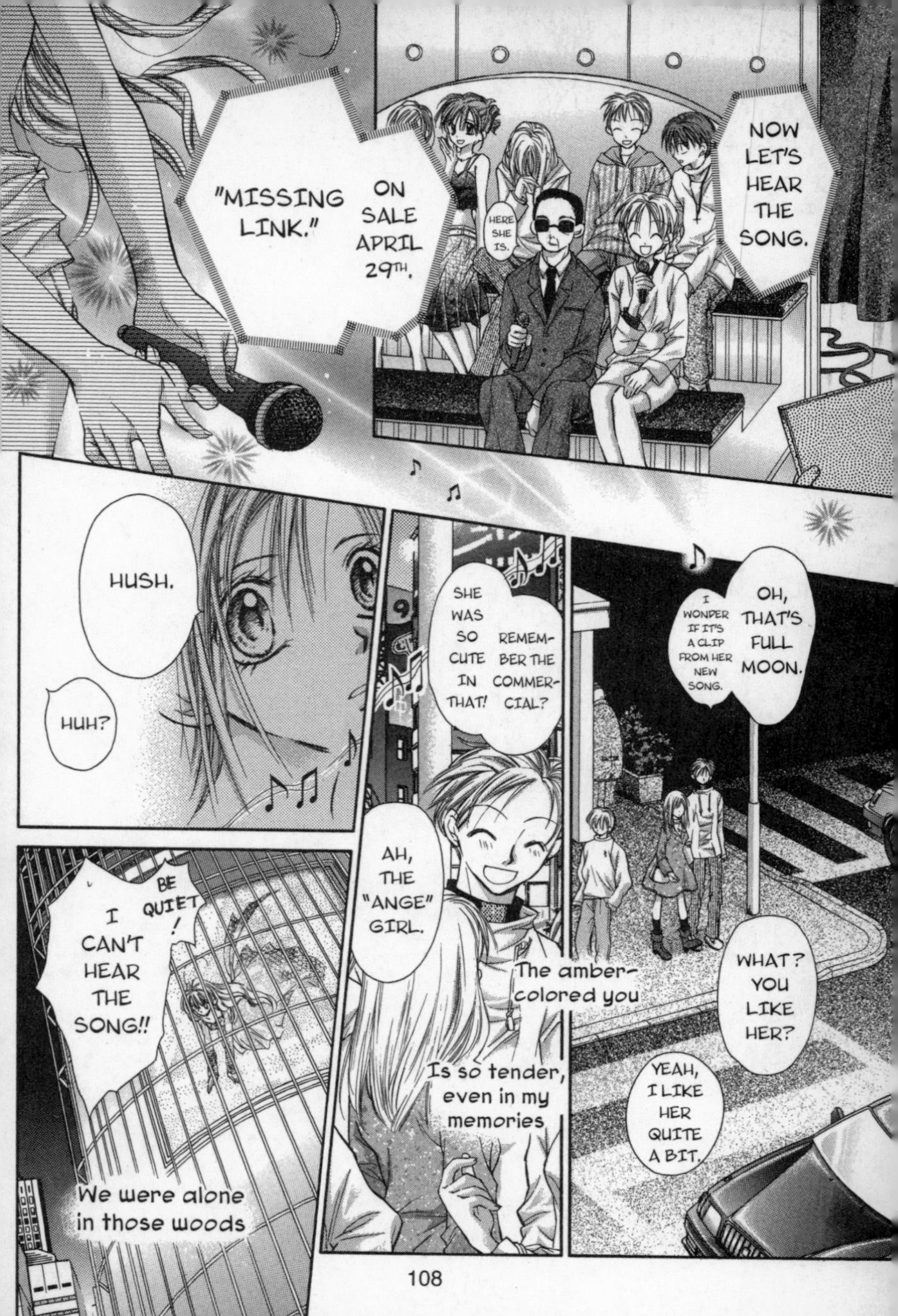
NOW LET'S HEAR THE SONG.
HERE SHE IS.
ON SALE APRIL 29TH.
"MISSING LINK."
OH, THAT'S FULL MOON.
I WONDER IF IT'S A CLIP FROM HER NEW SONG.
WHAT? YOU LIKE HER?
YEAH, I LIKE HER QUITE A BIT.
REMEMBER THE COMMERCIAL?
SHE WAS SO CUTE IN THAT!
AH, THE "ANGE" GIRL.
The amber-colored you
Is so tender, even in my memories
HUSH.
HUH?
BE QUIET!
I CAN'T HEAR THE SONG!!
We were alone in those woods

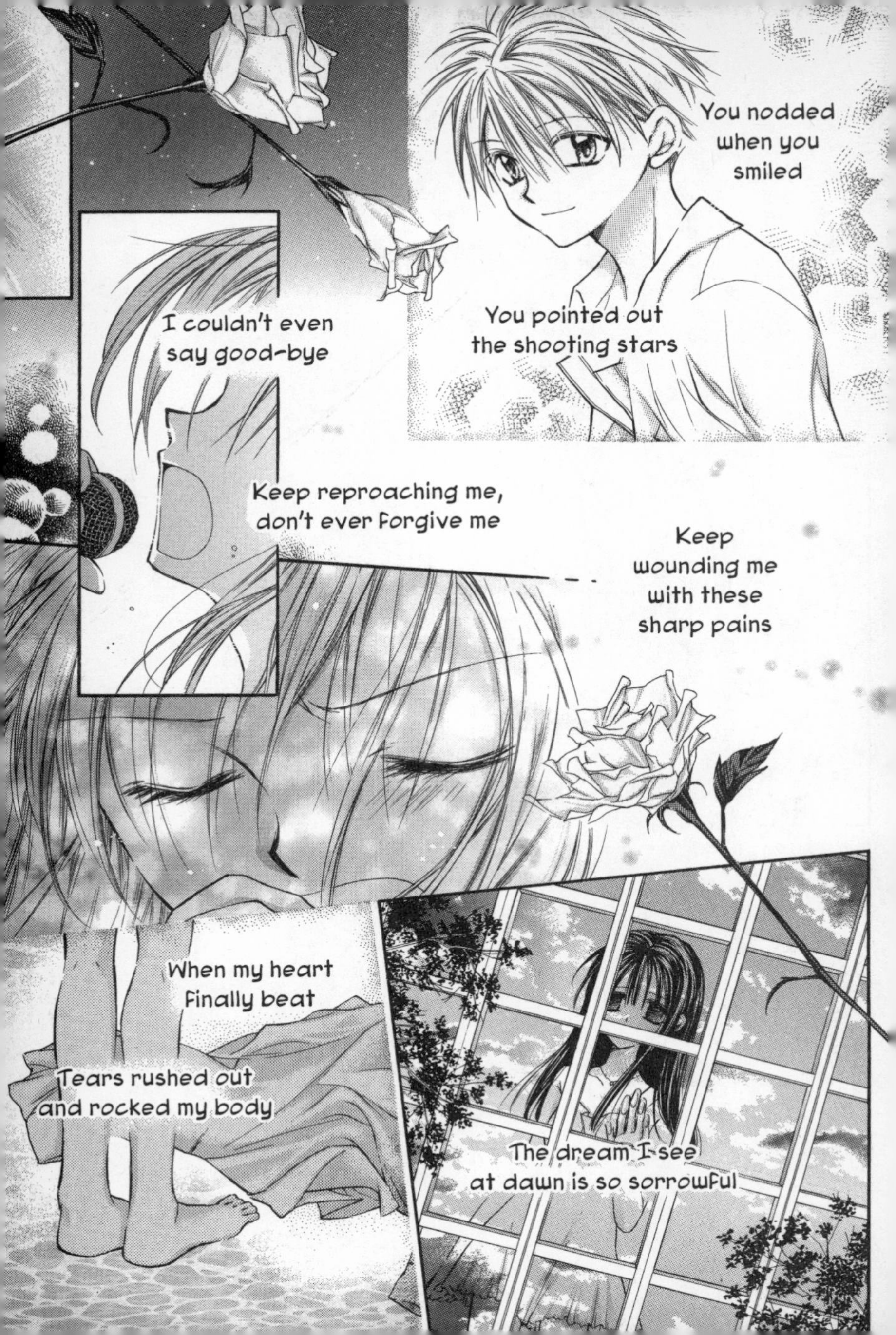
You nodded when you smiled
You pointed out the shooting stars
I couldn't even say good-bye
Keep reproaching me, don't ever forgive me
Keep wounding me with these sharp pains
The dream I see at dawn is so sorrowful
When my heart finally beat
Tears rushed out and rocked my body

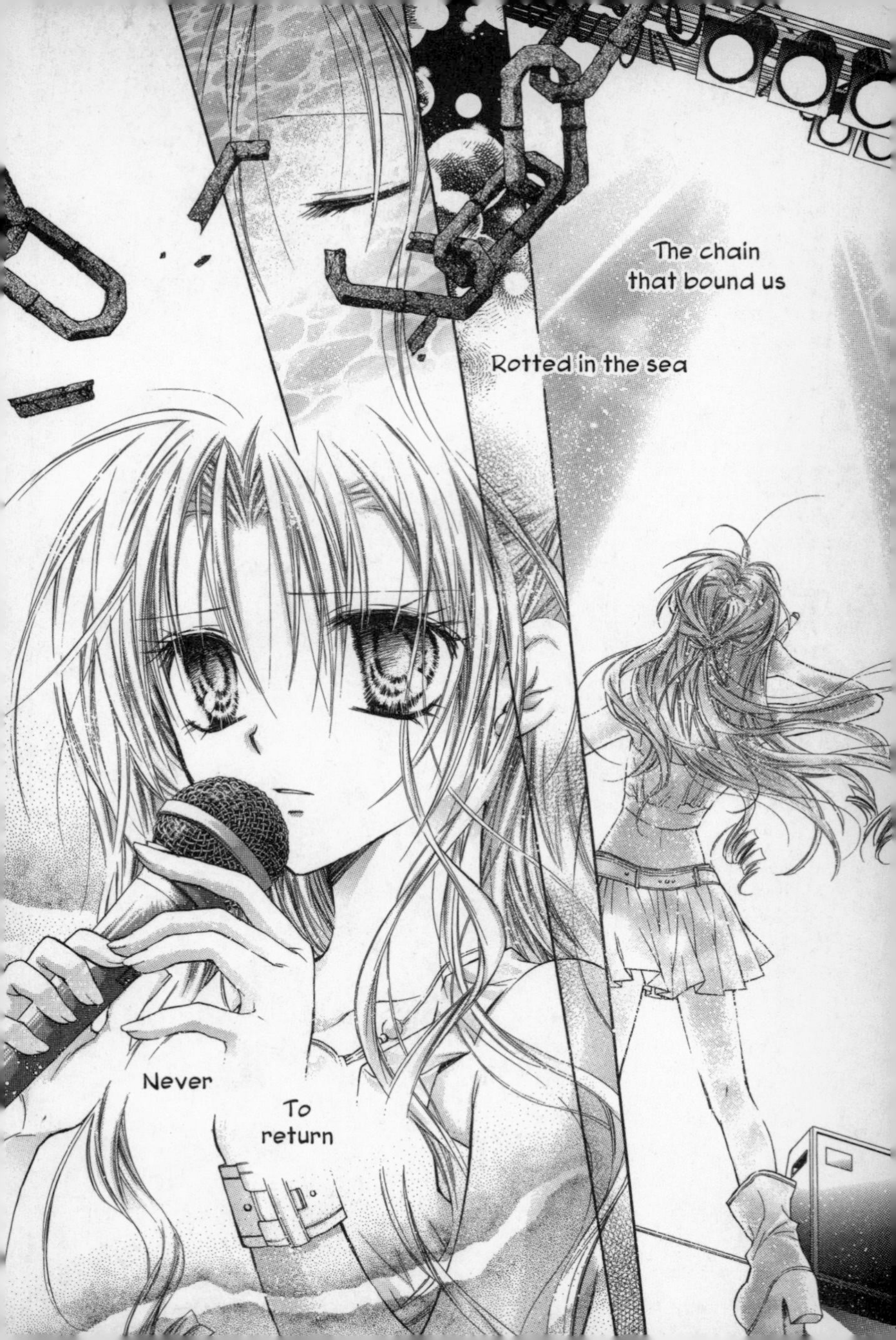
The chain that bound us
Rotted in the sea
Never
To return

Mansion

I had to decide between buying a house and a condo, but I bought a condo. It's goodbye to Meguro. The reason is, I'm getting married... that's a lie. (I'm sorry! I'm really sorry!! But I couldn't help it!!!)

The reason is that I want to keep a cat!! I want to smile with it, be surprised by its vomit, find its litter box smelly. I want to oversee the life of a cat from beginning to end.

Another reason is that my current place is small (since I have a lot of assistants). The new place is great!! It has three rooms, with a combined living/dining room and kitchen, and I can see the sea! A real high♢rise tower.

My work room is 8 tatami mats, my private room is 8 tatami mats, the bedroom for my assistants is 6.5 tatami mats, 2 walk-in closets are 1.5 tatami mats each, and there's a 1.7 tatami mat shoes-in-closet!! The living/dining room is 18 tatami mats.

It's huge ~ Boast boast

But as a result I have a loan for the first time in my life. A 10-year loan. Oh no!

I've still yet to get the cat, but I'm looking forward to it so much that I see it in my dreams.

Room sizes in Japan are measured in "tatami mats," i.e., how many tatami mats it would take to fill the room. -Ed.

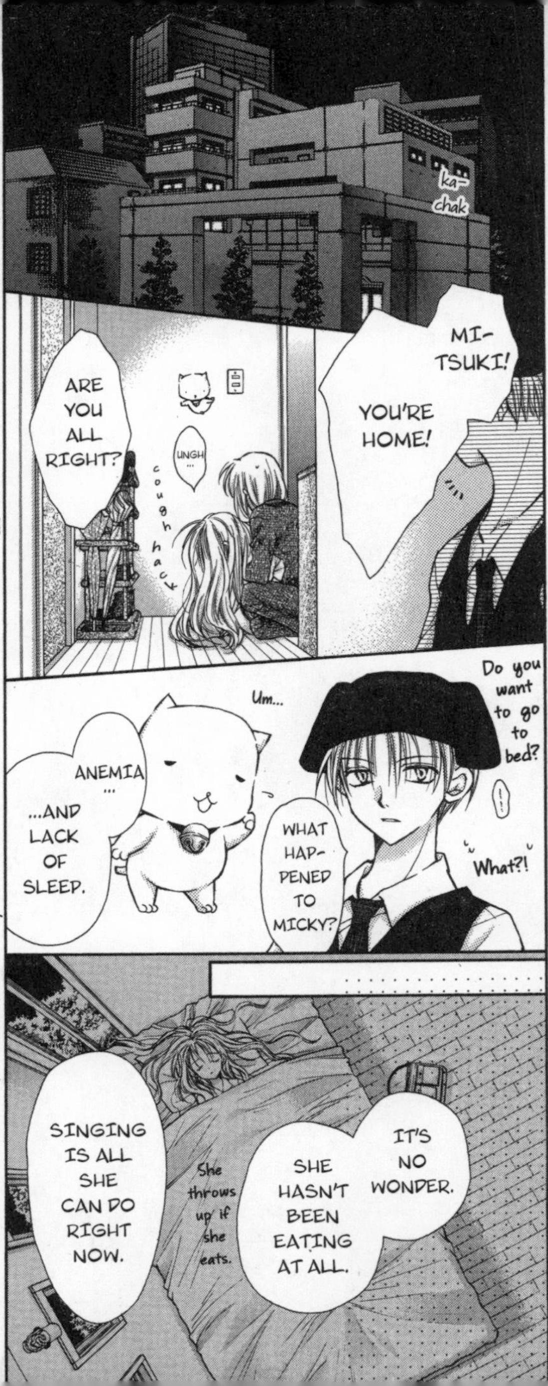

ka-chak
MI-TSUKI!
YOU'RE HOME!
ARE YOU ALL RIGHT?
UNGH...
cough hack
Do you want to go to bed?
!!
What?!
WHAT HAPPENED TO MICKY?
Um...
ANEMIA...
...AND LACK OF SLEEP.
IT'S NO WONDER.
SHE HASN'T BEEN EATING AT ALL.
She throws up if she eats.
SINGING IS ALL SHE CAN DO RIGHT NOW.

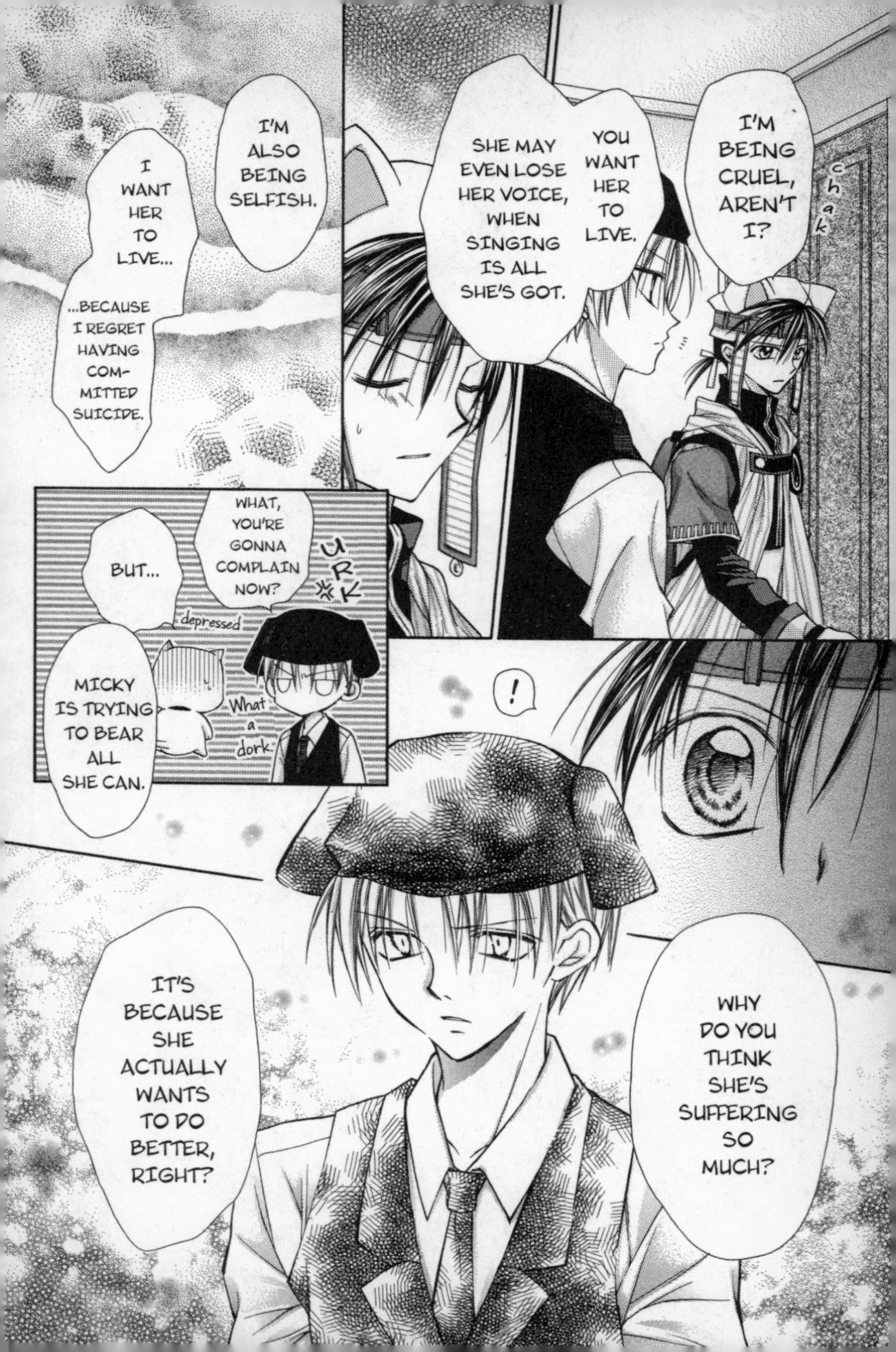
I'M BEING CRUEL, AREN'T I?
chak
YOU WANT HER TO LIVE.
SHE MAY EVEN LOSE HER VOICE, WHEN SINGING IS ALL SHE'S GOT.
I'M ALSO BEING SELFISH.
I WANT HER TO LIVE...
...BECAUSE I REGRET HAVING COM-MITTED SUICIDE.
!
WHAT, YOU'RE GONNA COMPLAIN NOW?
URK
BUT...
depressed
What a dork.
MICKY IS TRYING TO BEAR ALL SHE CAN.
WHY DO YOU THINK SHE'S SUFFERING SO MUCH?
IT'S BECAUSE SHE ACTUALLY WANTS TO DO BETTER, RIGHT?

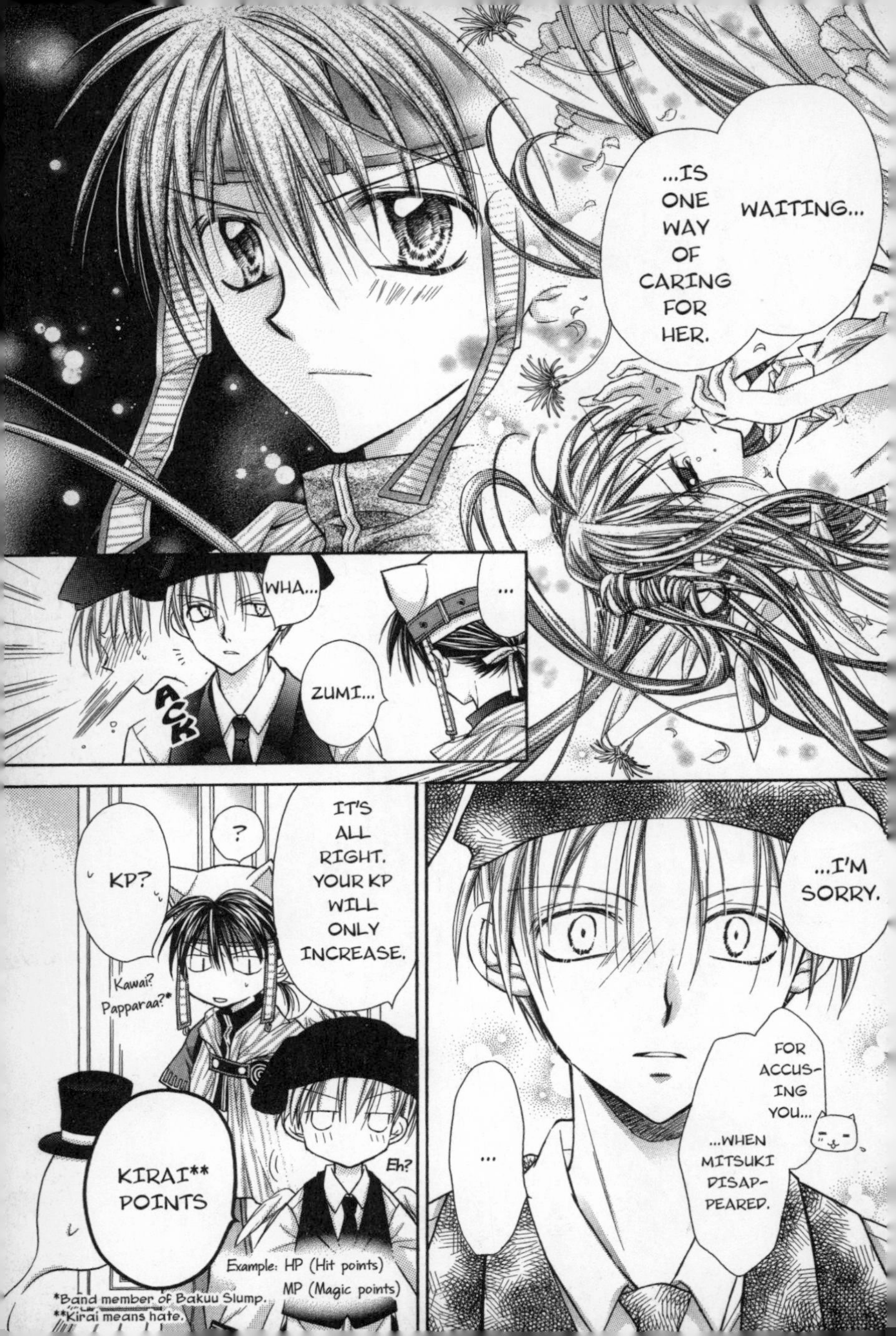
WAITING...
...IS ONE WAY OF CARING FOR HER.
...
WHA...
ZUMI...
ACK
...I'M SORRY.
FOR ACCUS-ING YOU...
...WHEN MITSUKI DISAP-PEARED.
...
IT'S ALL RIGHT. YOUR KP WILL ONLY INCREASE.
?
KP?
Kawai? Papparaa?*
Eh?
KIRAI** POINTS
Example: HP (Hit points)
MP (Magic points)

*Band member of Bakuu Slump.
**Kirai means hate.

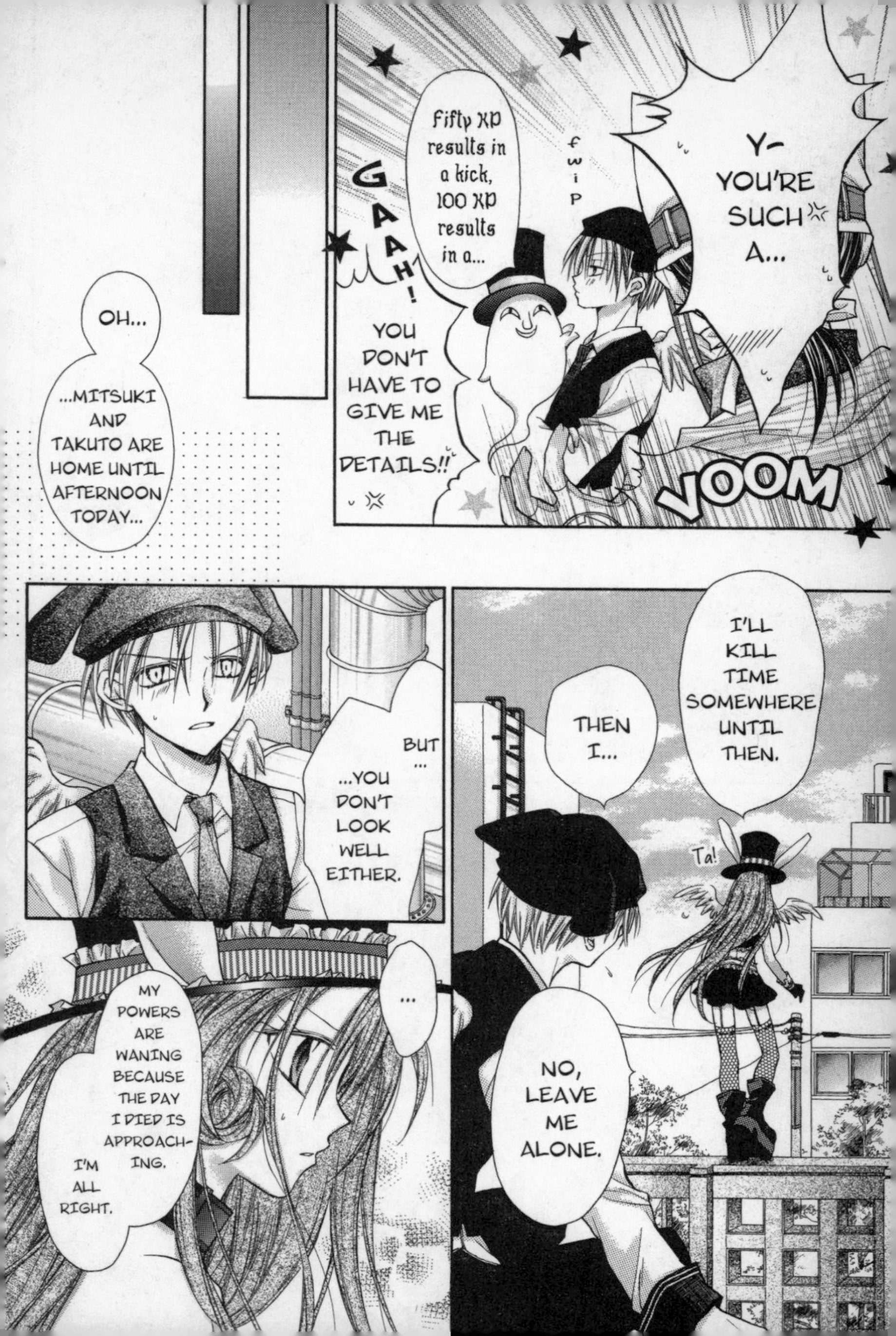
Y-YOU'RE SUCH A...
VOOM
fwip
Fifty xp results in a kick, 100 xp results in a...
GAAH!
YOU DON'T HAVE TO GIVE ME THE DETAILS!!
OH...
...MITSUKI AND TAKUTO ARE HOME UNTIL AFTERNOON TODAY...
I'LL KILL TIME SOMEWHERE UNTIL THEN.
Ta!
THEN I...
NO, LEAVE ME ALONE.
BUT ...
...YOU DON'T LOOK WELL EITHER.
...
MY POWERS ARE WANING BECAUSE THE DAY I DIED IS APPROACHING.
I'M ALL RIGHT.

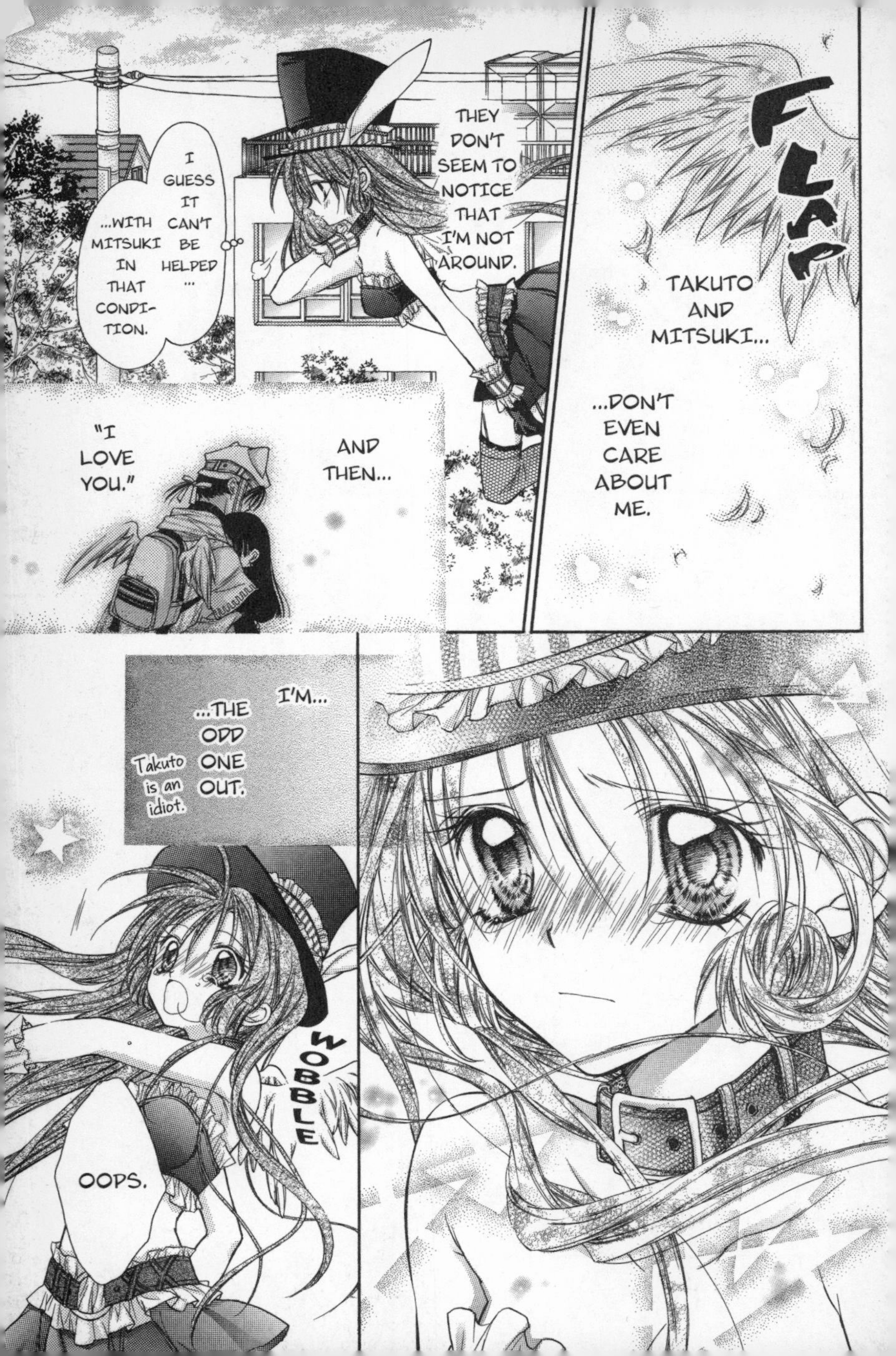
FLAP
TAKUTO AND MITSUKI...
...DON'T EVEN CARE ABOUT ME.
THEY DON'T SEEM TO NOTICE THAT I'M NOT AROUND.
I GUESS IT CAN'T BE HELPED...
...WITH MITSUKI IN THAT CONDITION.
AND THEN...
"I LOVE YOU."
I'M...
...THE ODD ONE OUT.
Takuto is an idiot.
WOBBLE
OOPS.

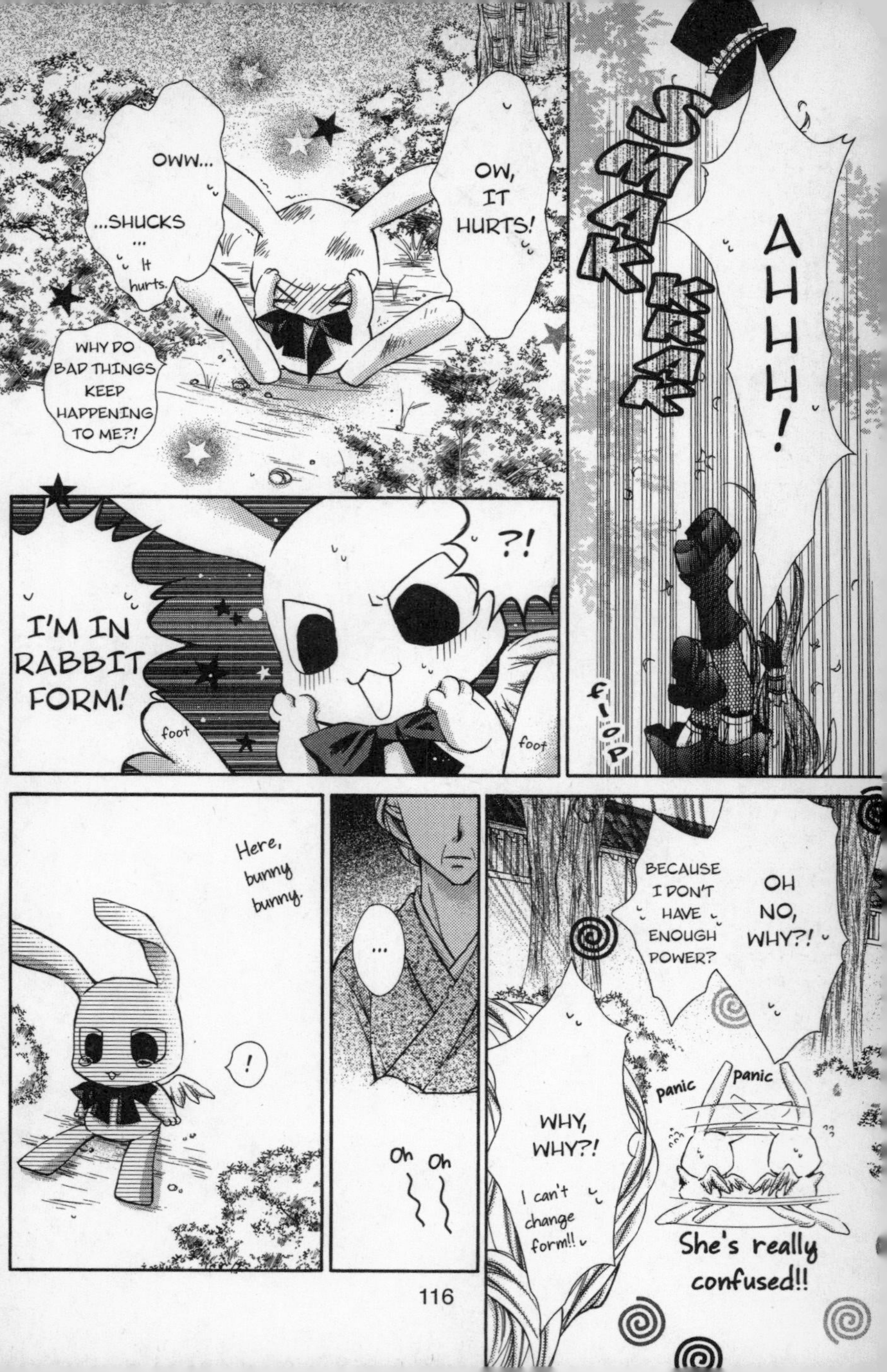
SMAK KAK
AHHH!
flop
OW, IT HURTS!
OWW...
...SHUCKS ...
It hurts.
WHY DO BAD THINGS KEEP HAPPENING TO ME?!
?!
I'M IN RABBIT FORM!
foot
foot
OH NO, WHY?!
BECAUSE I DON'T HAVE ENOUGH POWER?
WHY, WHY?!
I can't change form!!
panic
panic
She's really confused!!
...
Oh Oh
Here, bunny bunny.
!

O-oku (TV drama)
I love it. It's really interesting. In the beginning I started watching it because Miho Kanno is cute, but the Adachi Yumi-chan segment is very interesting too. I'm always on edge when I watch it as the story twists and turns!!

Hamtaro (TV anime)
I like this. I like the "couple," Sandy and Stan!! (Hamsters can get married even if they're siblings.) I like the couple Maxwell Sandy too. And of course Hamtaro!! He's just too cute!! Oxnard is good too! He says the strangest things!!
I bought most of the DVDs!!
I love the CD best too.

Gundam SEED (TV anime)
I was watching this because Houko Kuwahima is in it, playing two characters, but it's very interesting, and I've been watching it every week (uncommon for me). I am watching a lot of anime nowadays. It makes my heart beat fast. Gundam is so cool (although the only other one I've watched is the first one). I liked Char and Sayla.
I remember Haro fondly, too.

The Merry Moomin Family (TV anime)
This was on air when I was in seventh grade. The first series apparently wasn't too well done. This is the second series, but it was done by consulting closely with the author and it was shown in Finland, too.

I had two DVDs with my favorite stories, but I've been collecting the rest too. Little My and Snufkin LOVE!
Did you know these two are siblings with different mothers?! What a surprise!!

Boy, am I watching only anime.
Otaku otaku.

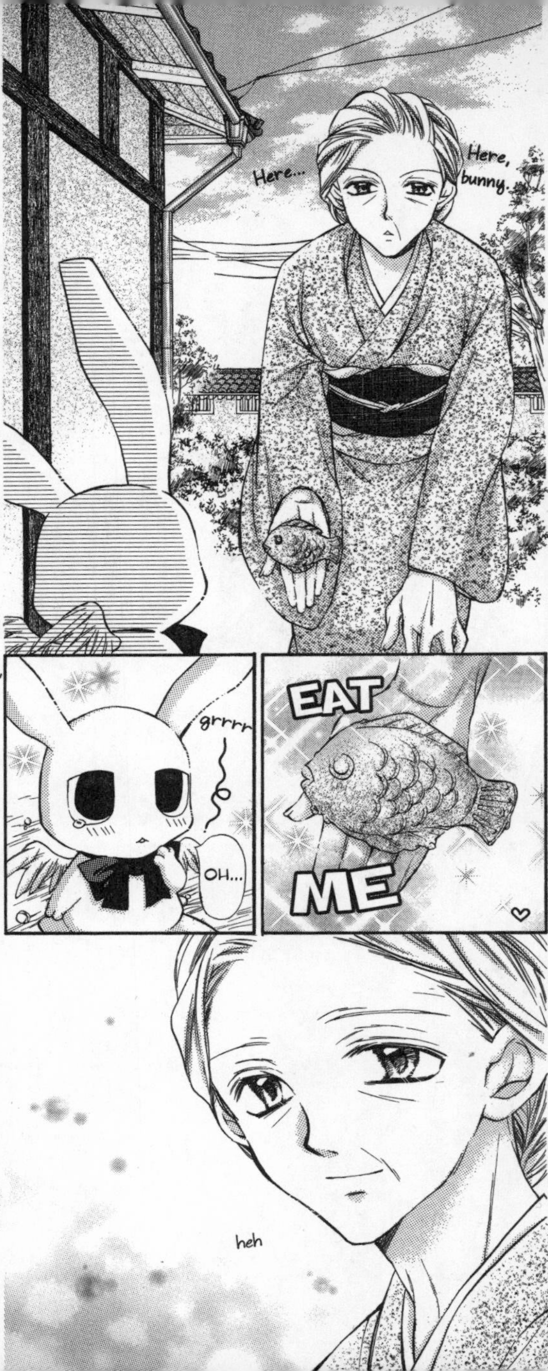
Here, bunny.
Here...
EAT ME
grrrr
OH...
heh

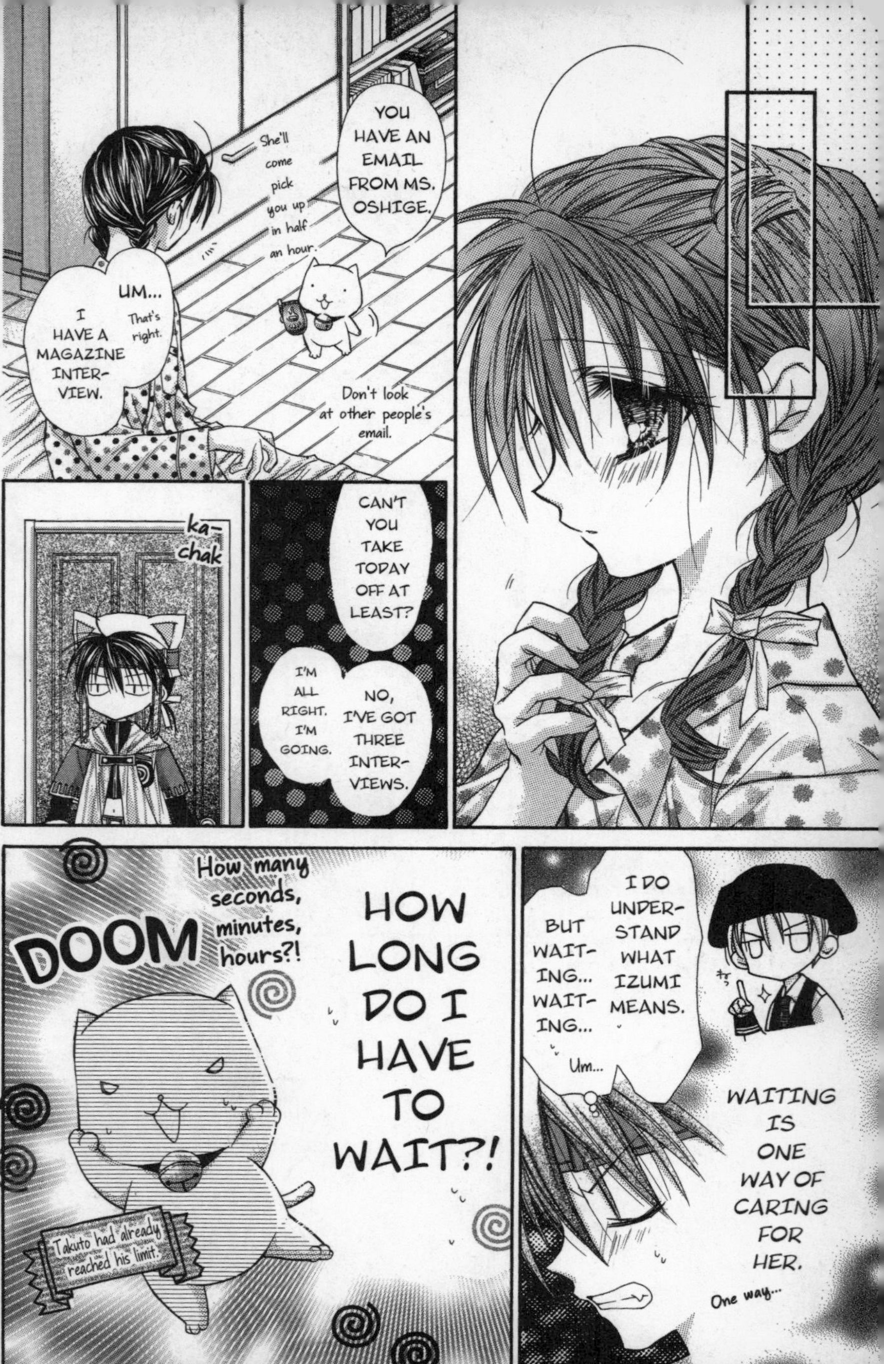
YOU HAVE AN EMAIL FROM MS. OSHIGE.
She'll come pick you up in half an hour.
UM...
That's right.
I HAVE A MAGAZINE INTER-VIEW.
Don't look at other people's email.
CAN'T YOU TAKE TODAY OFF AT LEAST?
NO, I'VE GOT THREE INTER-VIEWS.
I'M ALL RIGHT. I'M GOING.
ka-chak
I DO UNDER-STAND WHAT IZUMI MEANS.
BUT WAIT-ING... WAIT-ING...
Um...
WAITING IS ONE WAY OF CARING FOR HER.
One way...
HOW LONG DO I HAVE TO WAIT?!
How many seconds, minutes, hours?!
DOOM
Takuto had already reached his limit.

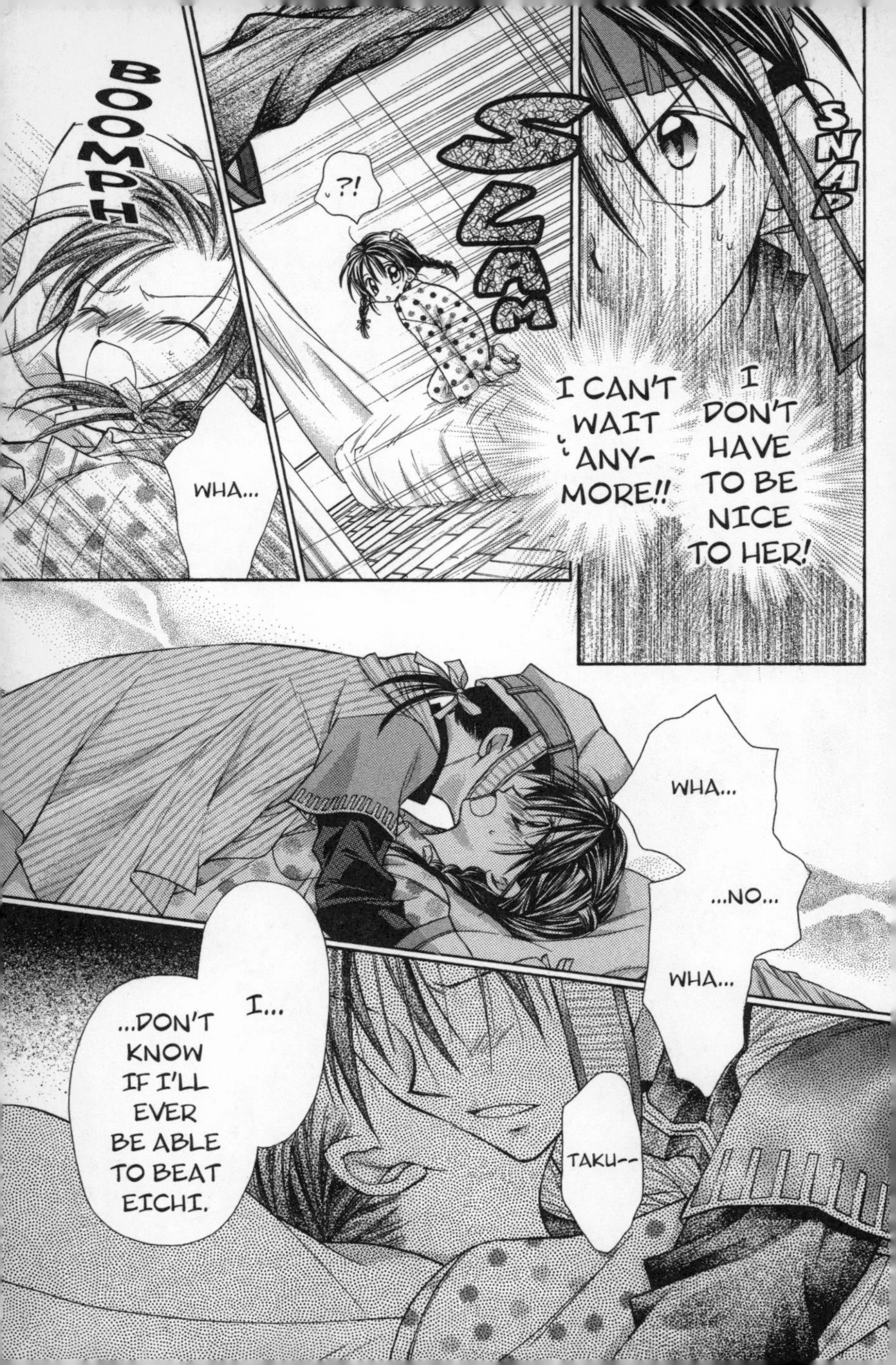
SNAP
I DON'T HAVE TO BE NICE TO HER!
I CAN'T WAIT ANYMORE!!
SLAM
?!
BOOMPH
WHA...
WHA...
...NO...
WHA...
TAKU--
I...
...DON'T KNOW IF I'LL EVER BE ABLE TO BEAT EICHI.

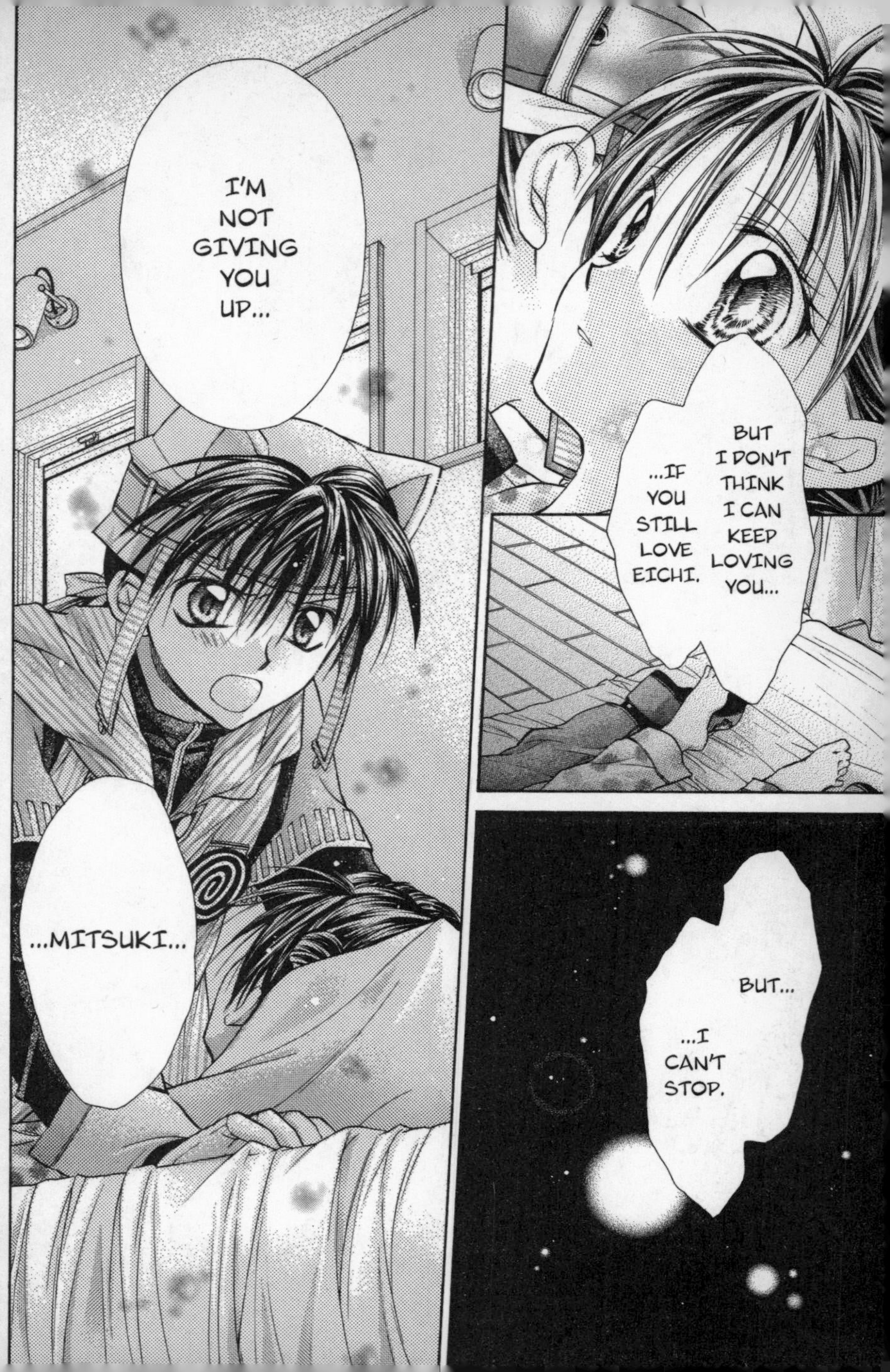
BUT I DON'T THINK I CAN KEEP LOVING YOU...
...IF YOU STILL LOVE EICHI.
BUT...
...I CAN'T STOP.
I'M NOT GIVING YOU UP...
...MITSUKI...

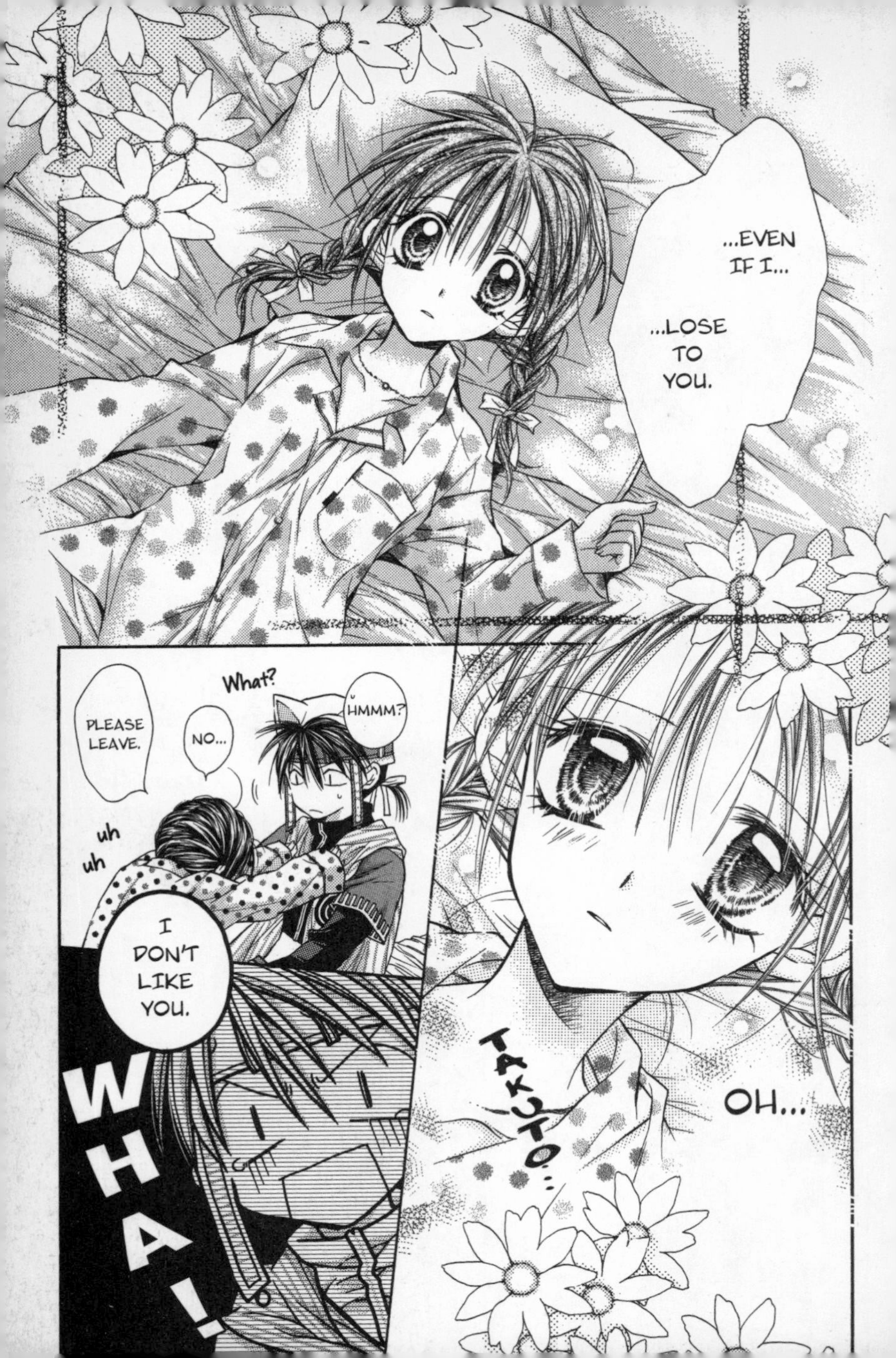
...EVEN IF I...
...LOSE TO YOU.
OH...
TAKUTO...
HMMM?
What?
NO...
PLEASE LEAVE.
uh uh
I DON'T LIKE YOU.
WHA!

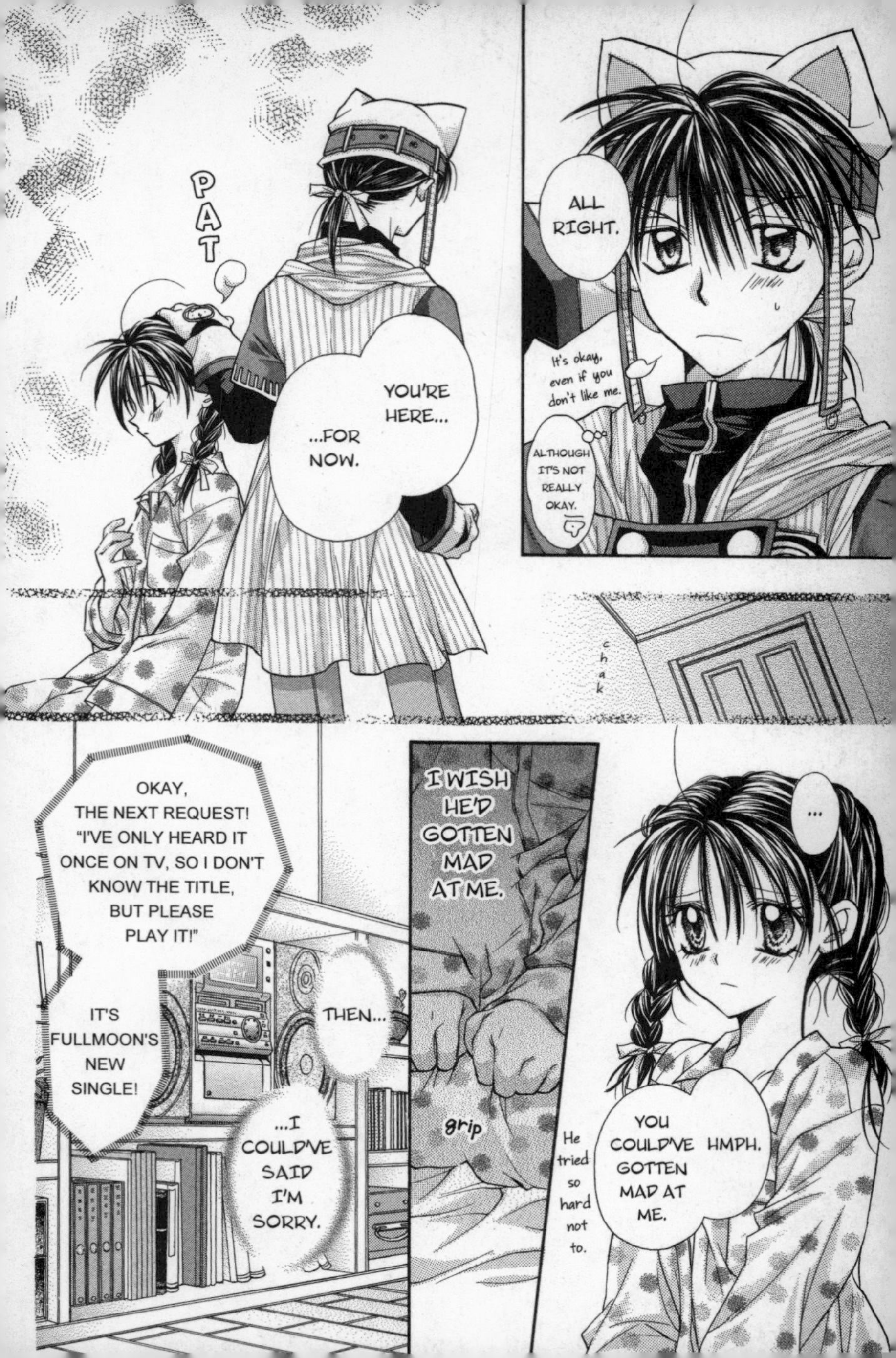
ALL RIGHT.
It's okay, even if you don't like me.
ALTHOUGH IT'S NOT REALLY OKAY.
chak
PAT
YOU'RE HERE...
...FOR NOW.
...
YOU COULD'VE GOTTEN MAD AT ME.
HMPH.
He tried so hard not to.
I WISH HE'D GOTTEN MAD AT ME.
grip
OKAY, THE NEXT REQUEST! "I'VE ONLY HEARD IT ONCE ON TV, SO I DON'T KNOW THE TITLE, BUT PLEASE PLAY IT!"
IT'S FULLMOON'S NEW SINGLE!
THEN...
...I COULD'VE SAID I'M SORRY.

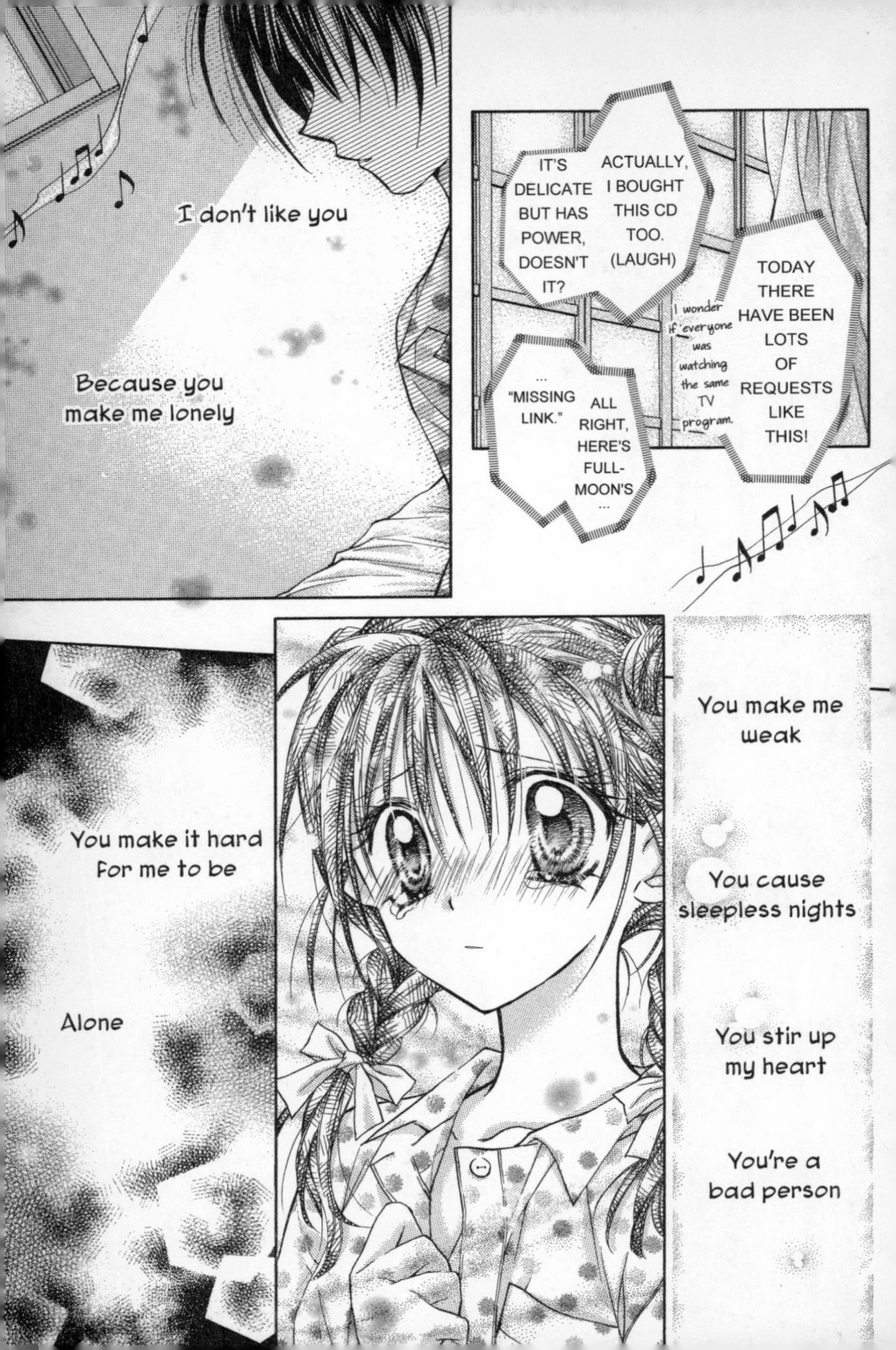
ACTUALLY, I BOUGHT THIS CD TOO. (LAUGH)
IT'S DELICATE BUT HAS POWER, DOESN'T IT?
TODAY THERE HAVE BEEN LOTS OF REQUESTS LIKE THIS!
I wonder if everyone was watching the same TV program.
ALL RIGHT, HERE'S FULL-MOON'S ...
... "MISSING LINK."
I don't like you
Because you make me lonely
You make me weak
You cause sleepless nights
You stir up my heart
You're a bad person
You make it hard for me to be
Alone

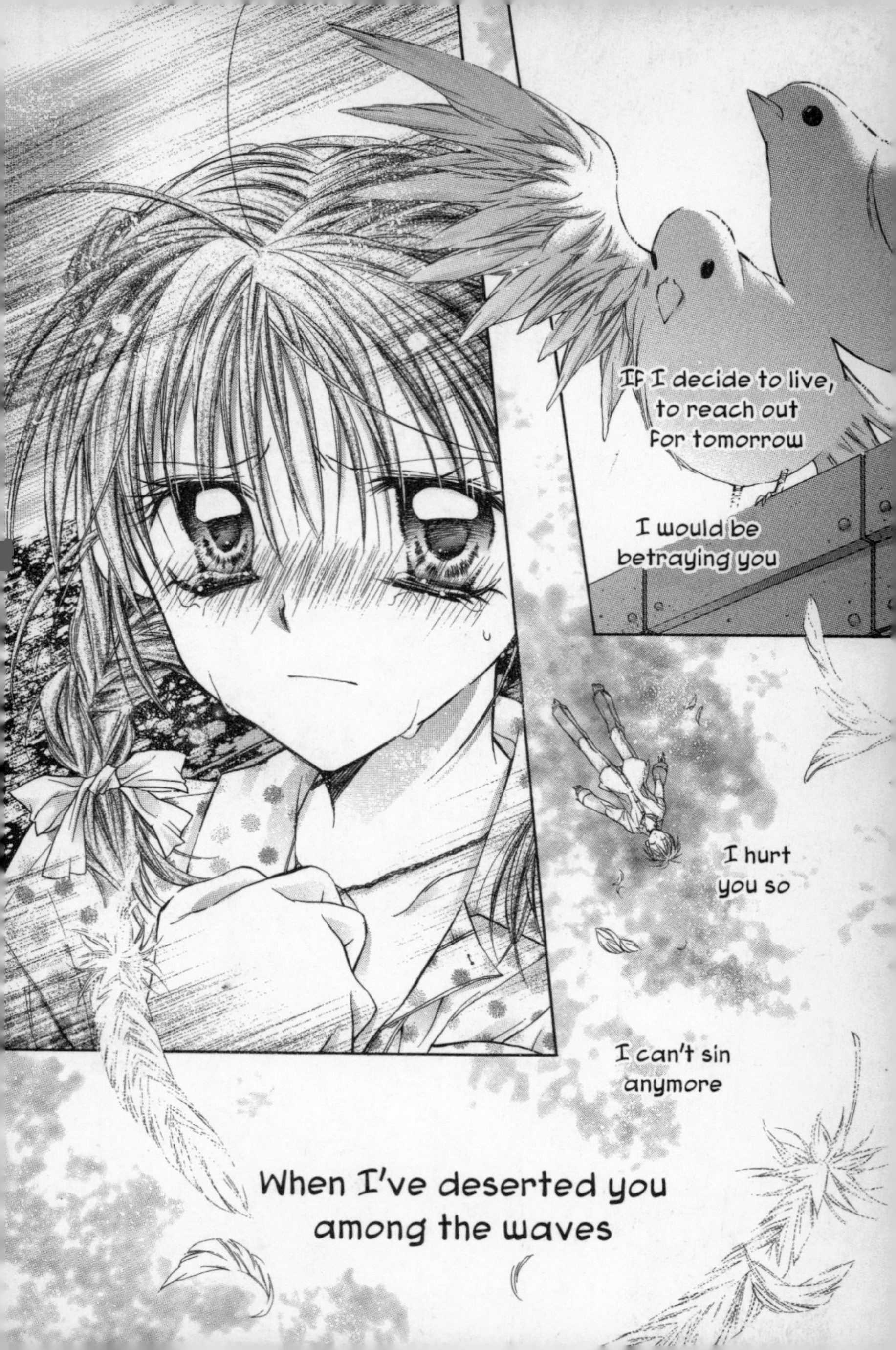
If I decide to live, to reach out for tomorrow
I would be betraying you
I hurt you so
I can't sin anymore
When I've deserted you among the waves

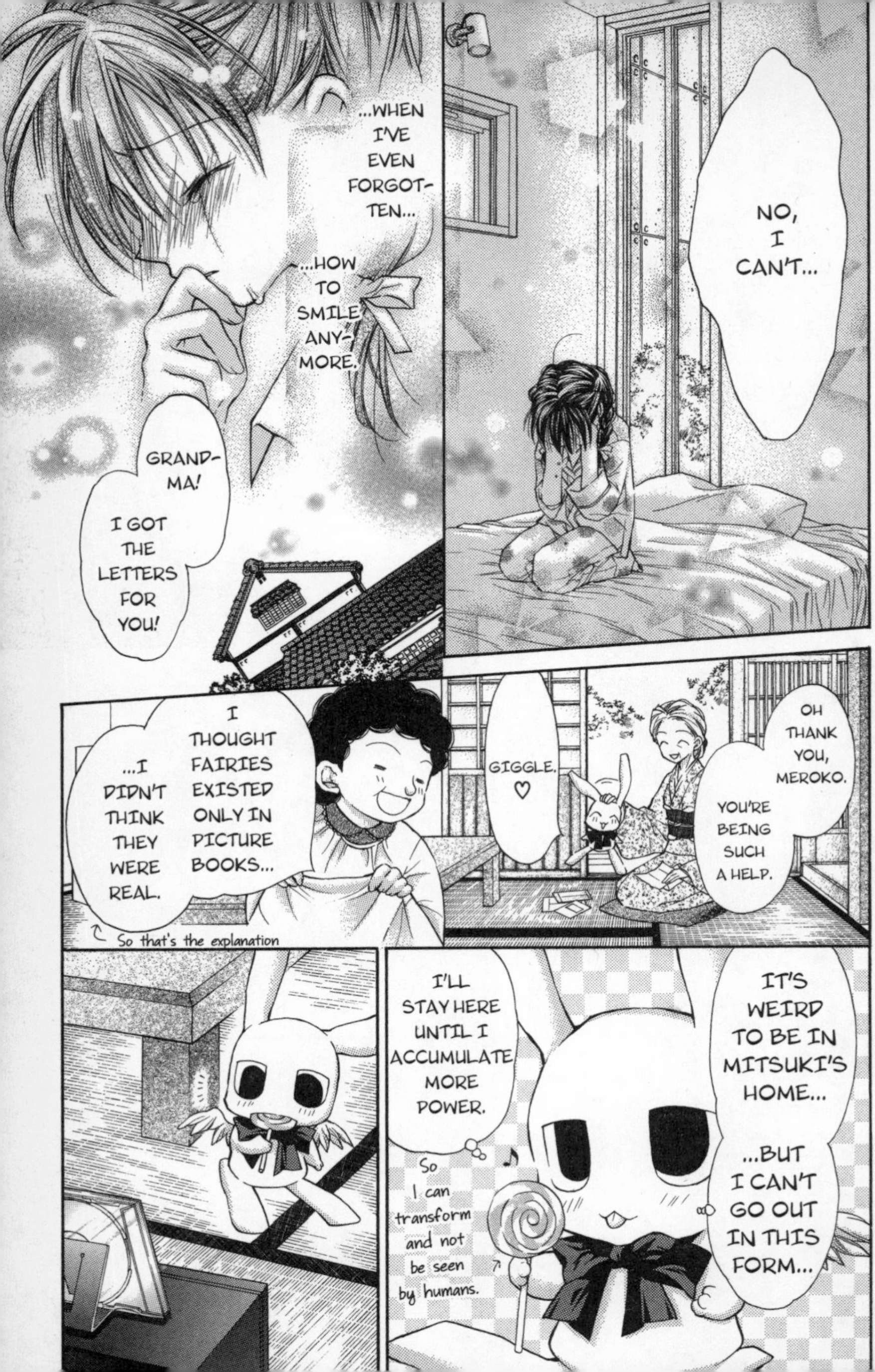
NO, I CAN'T...
...WHEN I'VE EVEN FORGOT-TEN...
...HOW TO SMILE ANY-MORE.
GRAND-MA!
I GOT THE LETTERS FOR YOU!
OH THANK YOU, MEROKO.
YOU'RE BEING SUCH A HELP.
GIGGLE. ♡
I THOUGHT FAIRIES EXISTED ONLY IN PICTURE BOOKS...
...I DIDN'T THINK THEY WERE REAL.
So that's the explanation
IT'S WEIRD TO BE IN MITSUKI'S HOME...
...BUT I CAN'T GO OUT IN THIS FORM...
I'LL STAY HERE UNTIL I ACCUMULATE MORE POWER.
So I can transform and not be seen by humans.

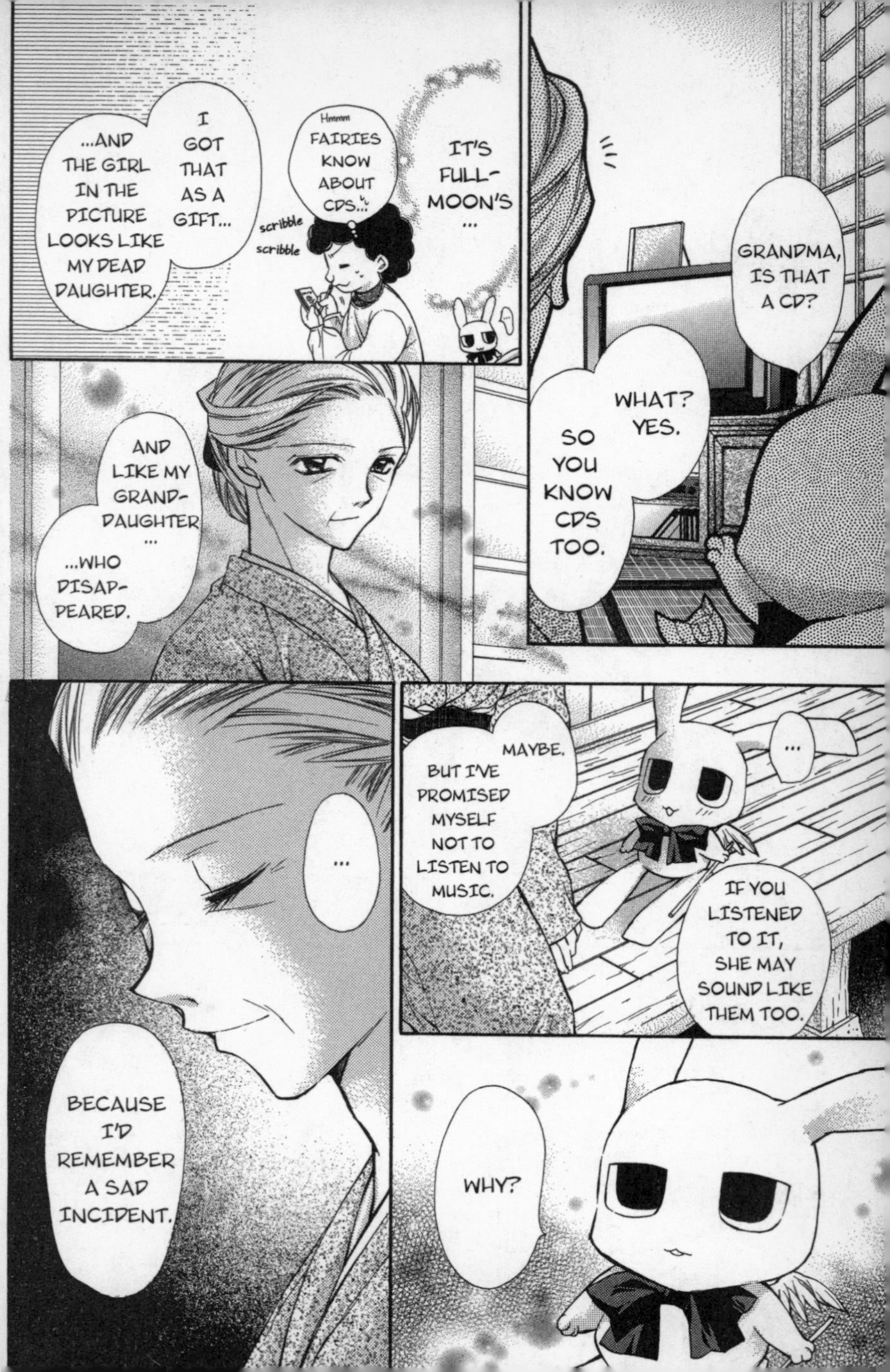
GRANDMA, IS THAT A CD?
WHAT? YES.
SO YOU KNOW CDS TOO.
IT'S FULL-MOON'S ...
Hmmm FAIRIES KNOW ABOUT CDS...
scribble scribble
I GOT THAT AS A GIFT...
...AND THE GIRL IN THE PICTURE LOOKS LIKE MY DEAD DAUGHTER.
AND LIKE MY GRAND-DAUGHTER ...
...WHO DISAP-PEARED.
...
IF YOU LISTENED TO IT, SHE MAY SOUND LIKE THEM TOO.
MAYBE. BUT I'VE PROMISED MYSELF NOT TO LISTEN TO MUSIC.
WHY?
...
BECAUSE I'D REMEMBER A SAD INCIDENT.

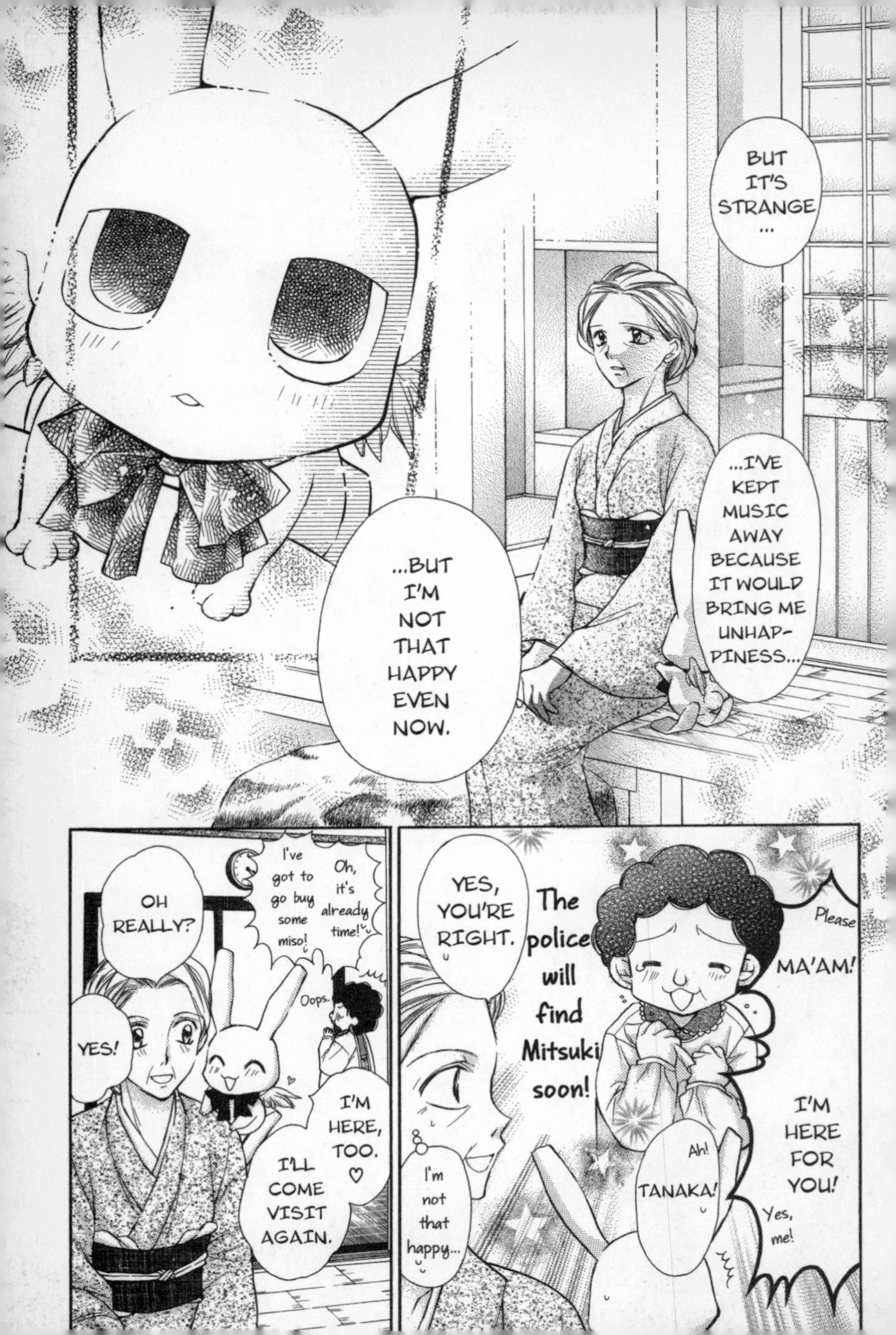
BUT IT'S STRANGE...
...I'VE KEPT MUSIC AWAY BECAUSE IT WOULD BRING ME UNHAP-PINESS...
...BUT I'M NOT THAT HAPPY EVEN NOW.
Please MA'AM!
I'M HERE FOR YOU!
Yes, me!
Ah! TANAKA!
The police will find Mitsuki soon!
YES, YOU'RE RIGHT.
I'm not that happy...
Oh, it's already time!
I've got to go buy some miso!
OH REALLY?
Oops.
YES!
I'M HERE, TOO. ♡
I'LL COME VISIT AGAIN.

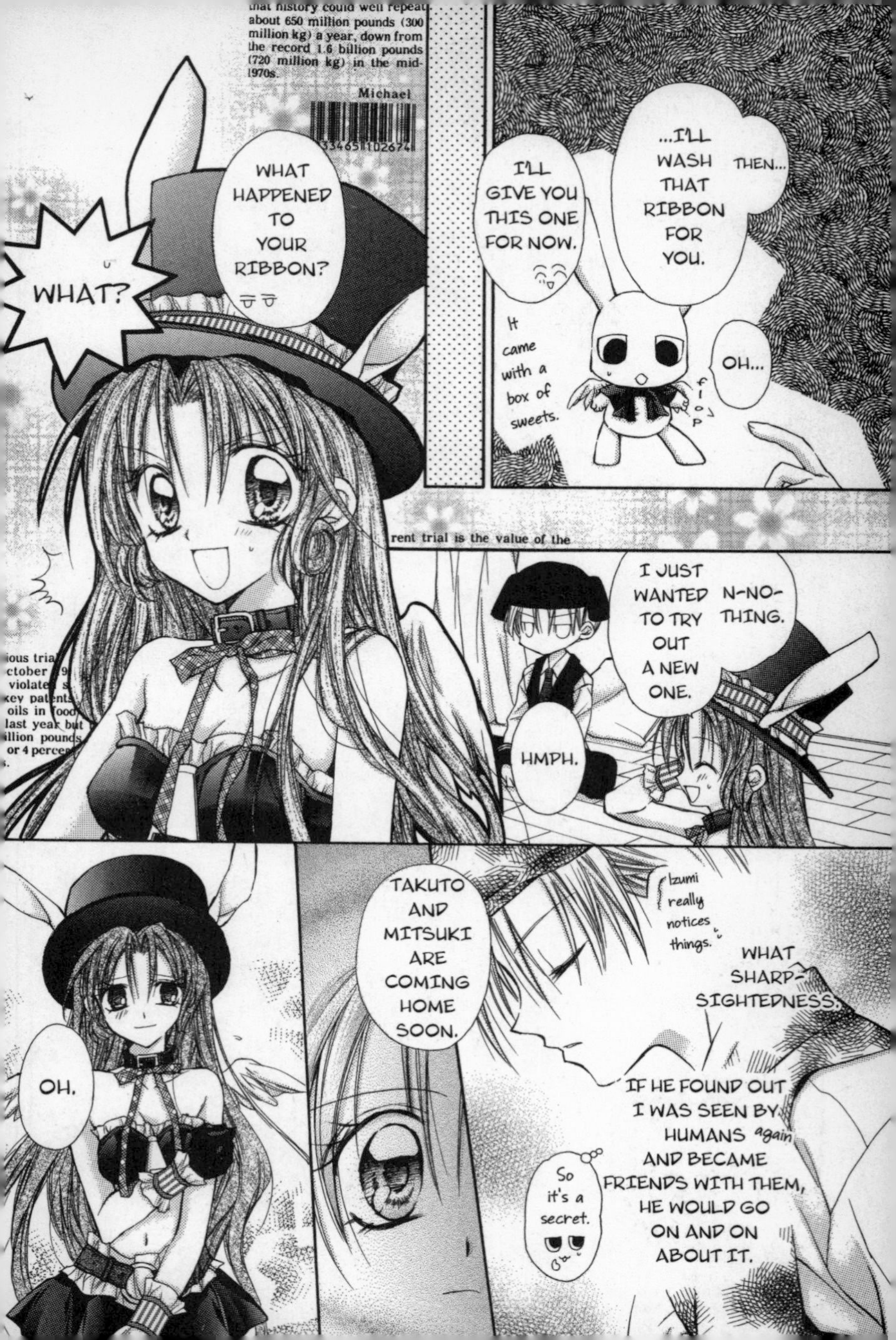

THEN...
...I'LL WASH THAT RIBBON FOR YOU.
I'LL GIVE YOU THIS ONE FOR NOW.
It came with a box of sweets.
OH...
flop
N-NOTHING.
I JUST WANTED TO TRY OUT A NEW ONE.
HMPH.
that history could well repeat about 650 million pounds (300 million kg) a year, down from the record 1.6 billion pounds (720 million kg) in the mid-1970s.
Michael
rent trial is the value of the
WHAT HAPPENED TO YOUR RIBBON?
WHAT?
TAKUTO AND MITSUKI ARE COMING HOME SOON.
Izumi really notices things.
WHAT SHARP-SIGHTEDNESS.
IF HE FOUND OUT I WAS SEEN BY HUMANS again AND BECAME FRIENDS WITH THEM, HE WOULD GO ON AND ON ABOUT IT.
So it's a secret.
OH.

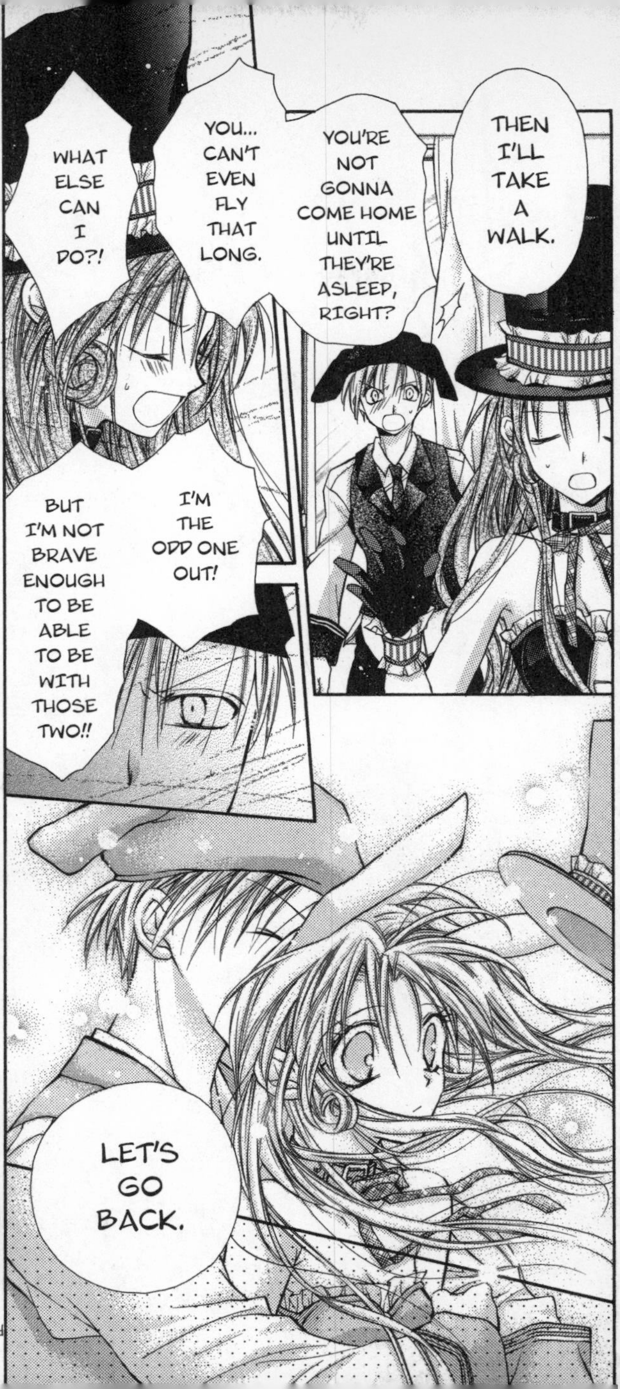
THEN I'LL TAKE A WALK.
YOU'RE NOT GONNA COME HOME UNTIL THEY'RE ASLEEP, RIGHT?
YOU... CAN'T EVEN FLY THAT LONG.
WHAT ELSE CAN I DO?!
I'M THE ODD ONE OUT!
BUT I'M NOT BRAVE ENOUGH TO BE ABLE TO BE WITH THOSE TWO!!
LET'S GO BACK.

Tanemura Arina's Penchi de Shakin

Episode 57

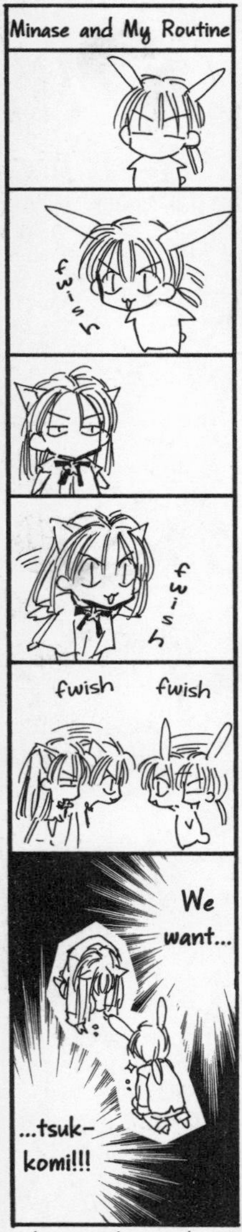
Minase and My Routine
fwish
fwish
fwish
fwish
We want...
...tsuk-komi!!!

Asano-san, please come!

"Tsukkomi" play the straight routine in Japanese two-person comedy. Minase and Tanemura are both playing the "boke" comic role. —Ed.

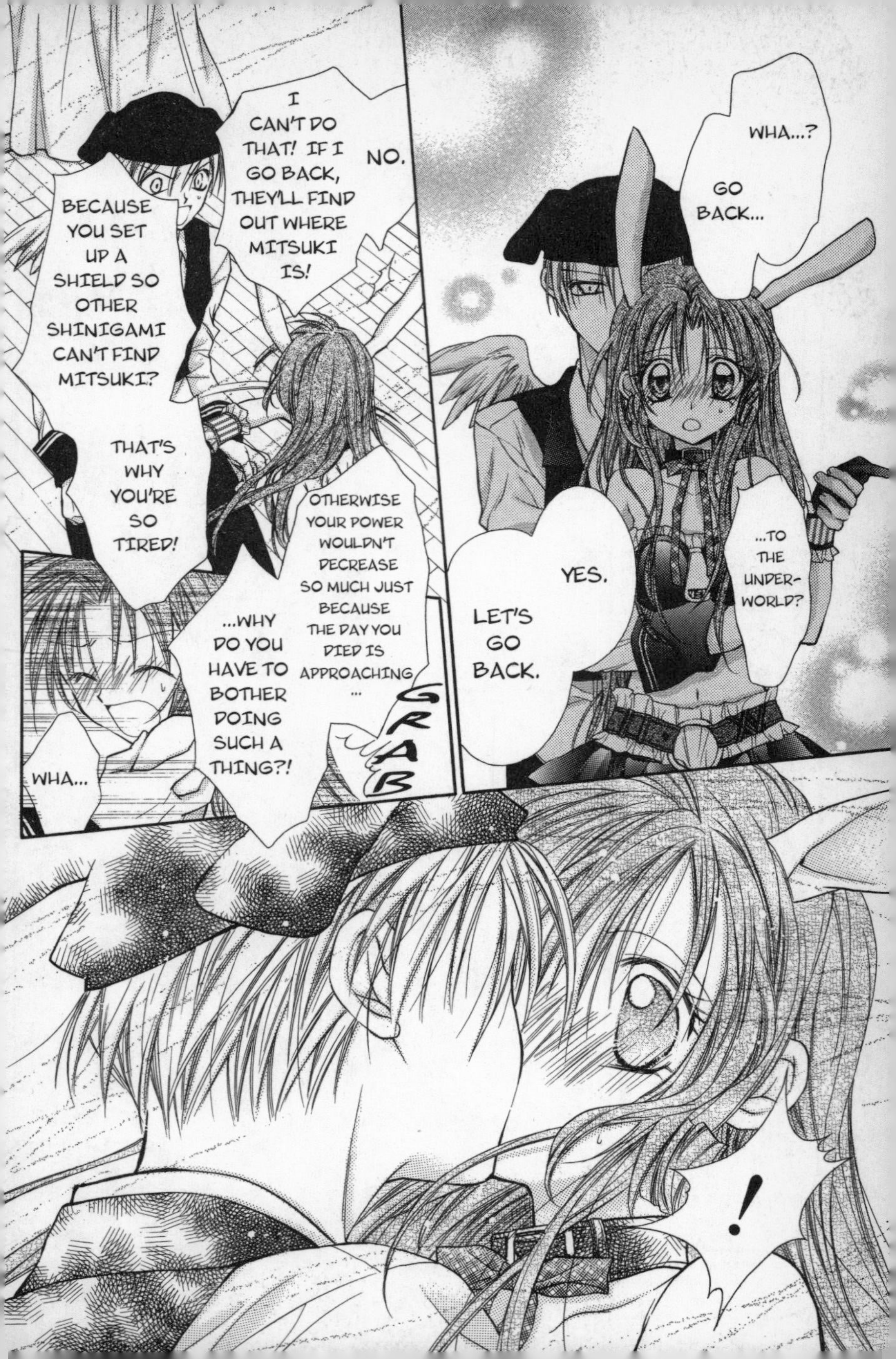
WHA...?
GO BACK...
...TO THE UNDER-WORLD?
YES.
LET'S GO BACK.
NO.
I CAN'T DO THAT! IF I GO BACK, THEY'LL FIND OUT WHERE MITSUKI IS!
BECAUSE YOU SET UP A SHIELD SO OTHER SHINIGAMI CAN'T FIND MITSUKI?
THAT'S WHY YOU'RE SO TIRED!
OTHERWISE YOUR POWER WOULDN'T DECREASE SO MUCH JUST BECAUSE THE DAY YOU DIED IS APPROACHING...
...WHY DO YOU HAVE TO BOTHER DOING SUCH A THING?!
GRAB
WHA...
!

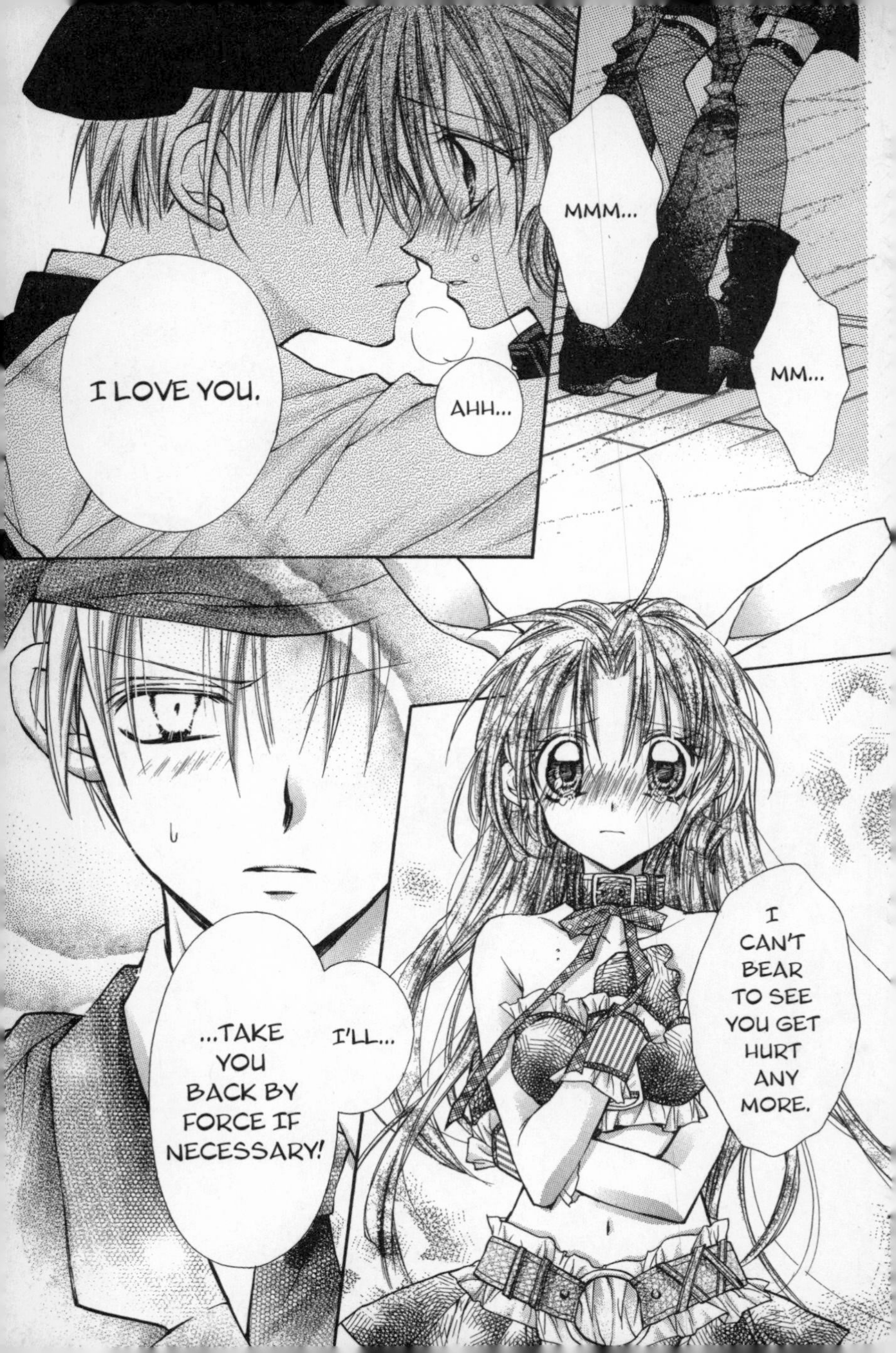
MMM...
MM...
AHH...
I LOVE YOU.
I CAN'T BEAR TO SEE YOU GET HURT ANY MORE.
I'LL...
...TAKE YOU BACK BY FORCE IF NECESSARY!

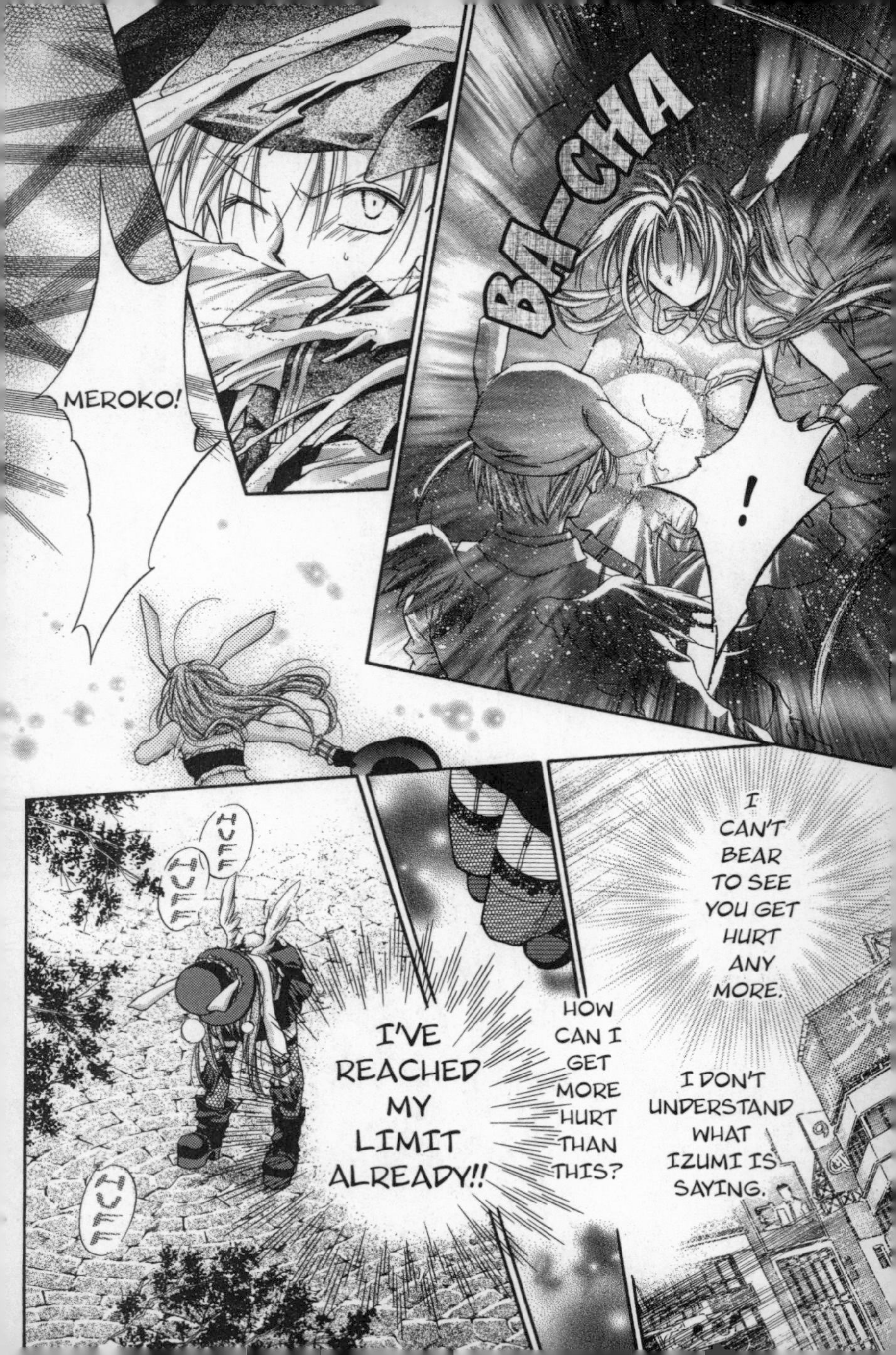
BA-CHA
!
MEROKO!
I CAN'T BEAR TO SEE YOU GET HURT ANY MORE.
I DON'T UNDERSTAND WHAT IZUMI IS SAYING.
HOW CAN I GET MORE HURT THAN THIS?
I'VE REACHED MY LIMIT ALREADY!!
HUFF
HUFF
HUFF

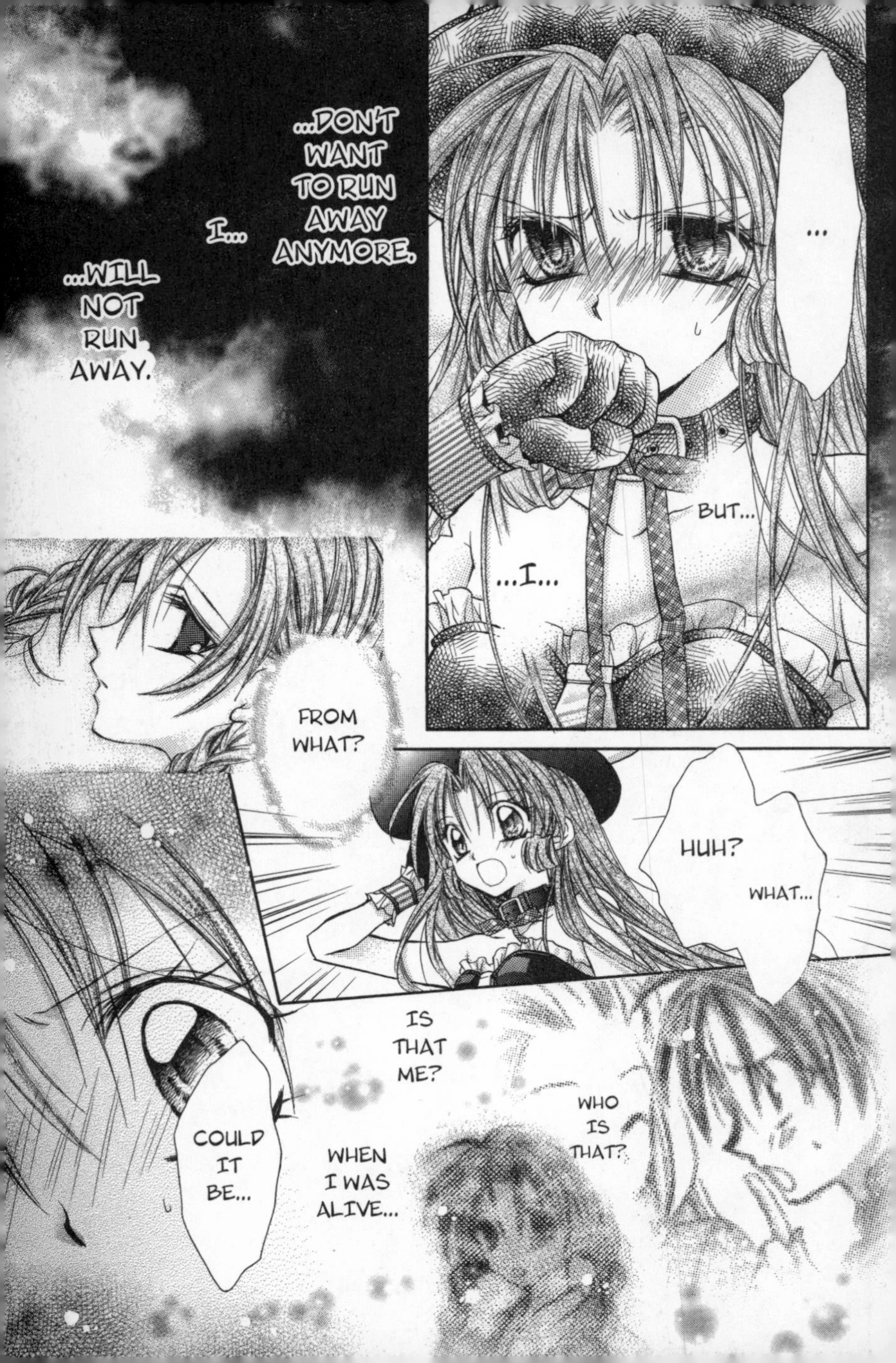
...
BUT...
...I...
...DON'T WANT TO RUN AWAY ANYMORE.
I...
...WILL NOT RUN AWAY.
FROM WHAT?
HUH?
WHAT...
IS THAT ME?
WHO IS THAT?
WHEN I WAS ALIVE...
COULD IT BE...

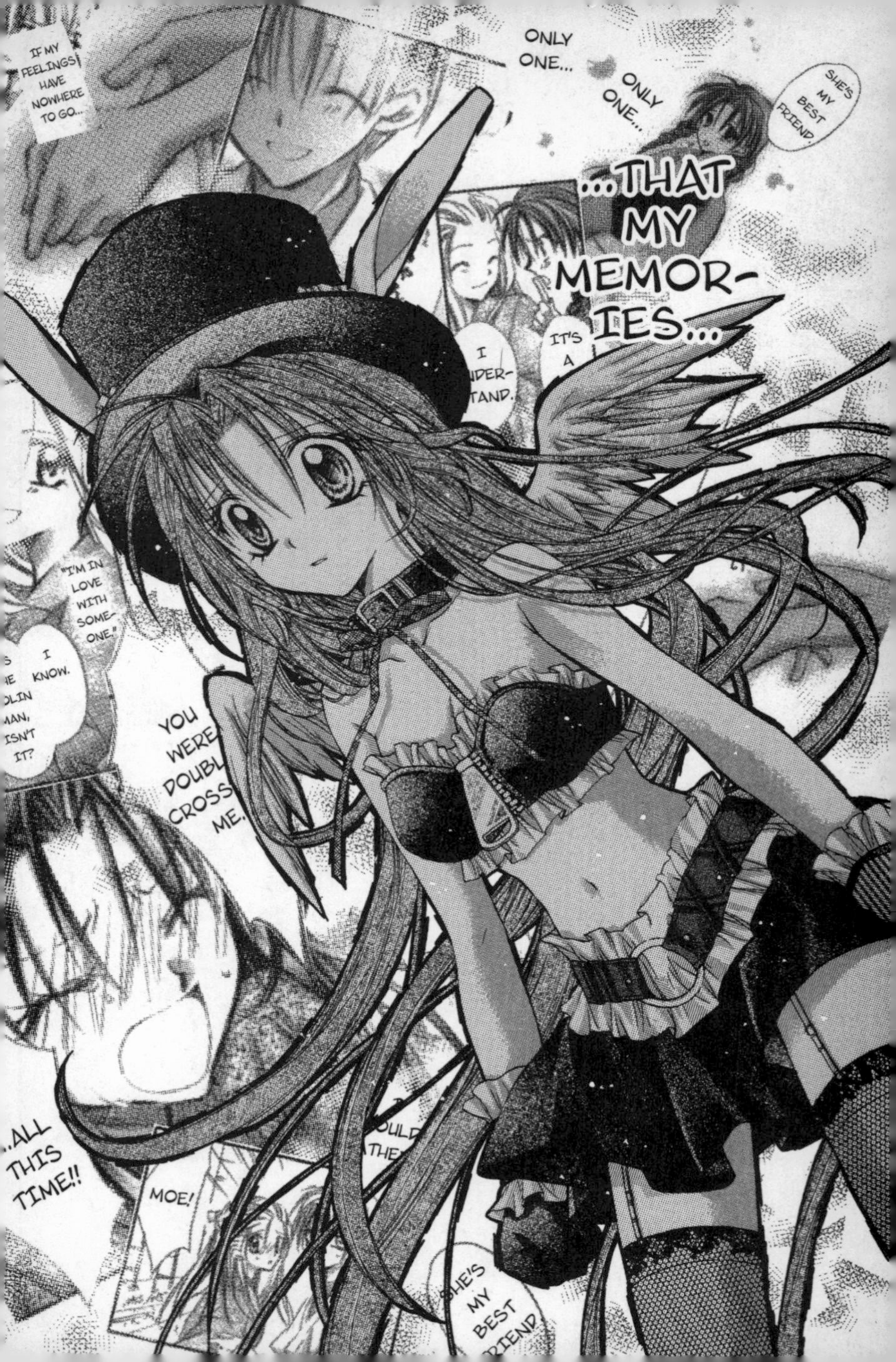
SHE'S MY BEST FRIEND.
ONLY ONE...
ONLY ONE...
...THAT MY MEMOR-IES...
IT'S A
I UNDER-STAND.
IF MY FEELINGS HAVE NOWHERE TO GO...
"I'M IN LOVE WITH SOME-ONE."
I KNOW.
YOU WERE
..ALL THIS TIME!!
MOE!
SHE'S MY BEST FRIEND.

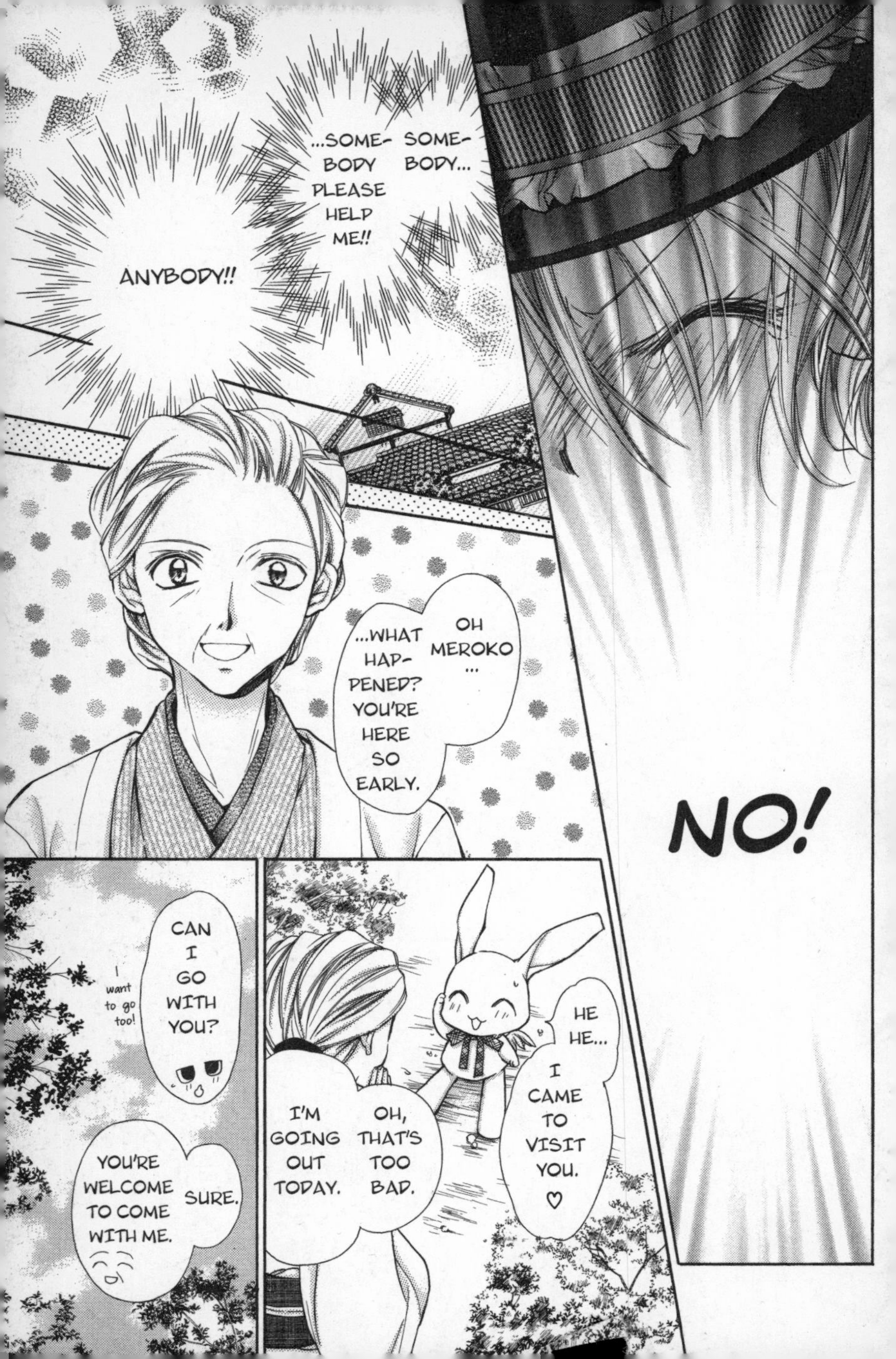
NO!
SOMEBODY...
...SOMEBODY PLEASE HELP ME!!
ANYBODY!!
OH MEROKO...
...WHAT HAPPENED? YOU'RE HERE SO EARLY.
HE HE... I CAME TO VISIT YOU. ♡
OH, THAT'S TOO BAD.
I'M GOING OUT TODAY.
CAN I GO WITH YOU?
I want to go too!
SURE.
YOU'RE WELCOME TO COME WITH ME.

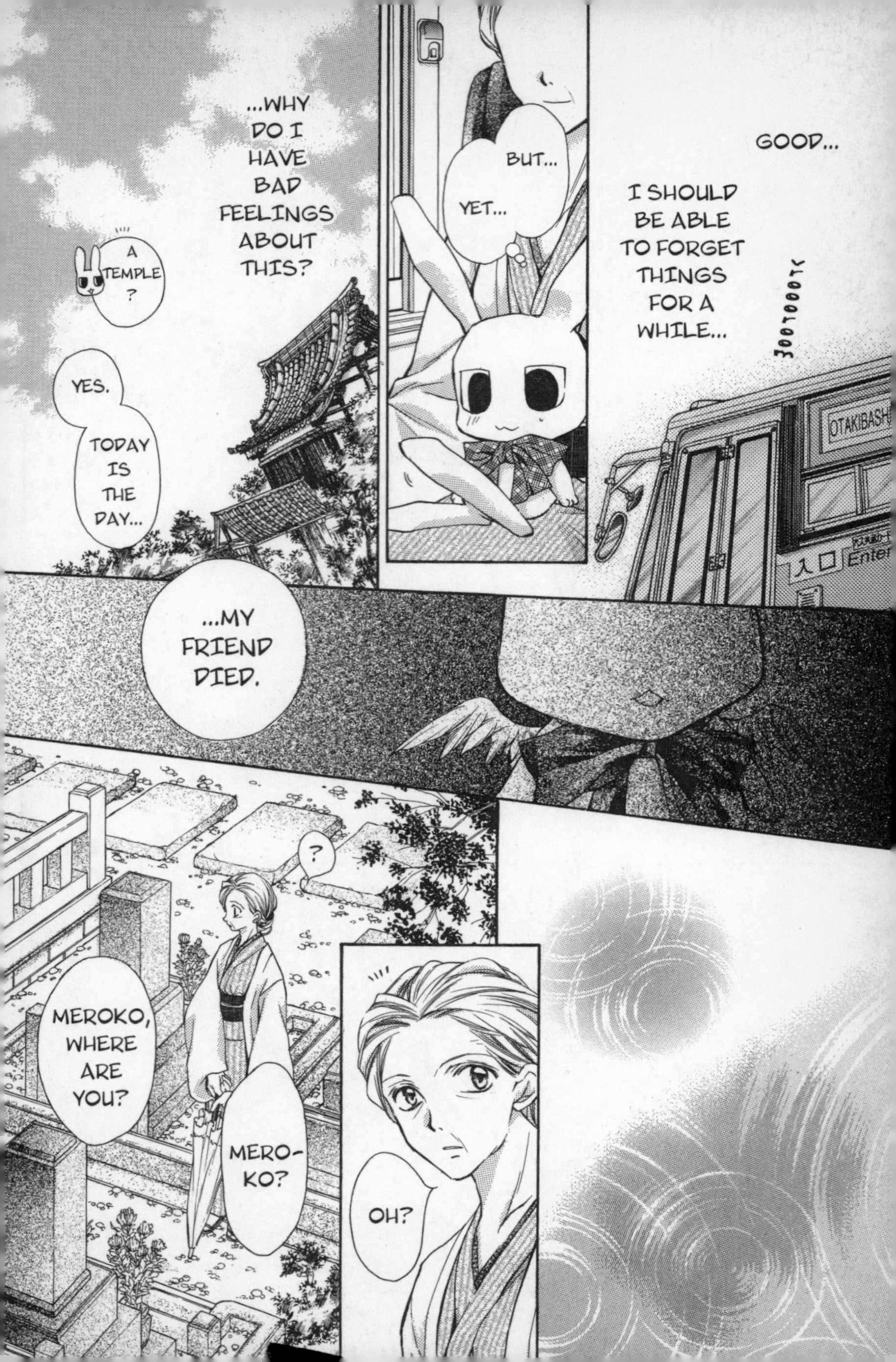
GOOD...
I SHOULD BE ABLE TO FORGET THINGS FOR A WHILE...
OTAKIBASH
入口 Enter
BUT...
YET...
...WHY DO I HAVE BAD FEELINGS ABOUT THIS?
A TEMPLE?
YES.
TODAY IS THE DAY...
...MY FRIEND DIED.
OH?
?
MEROKO, WHERE ARE YOU?
MERO-KO?

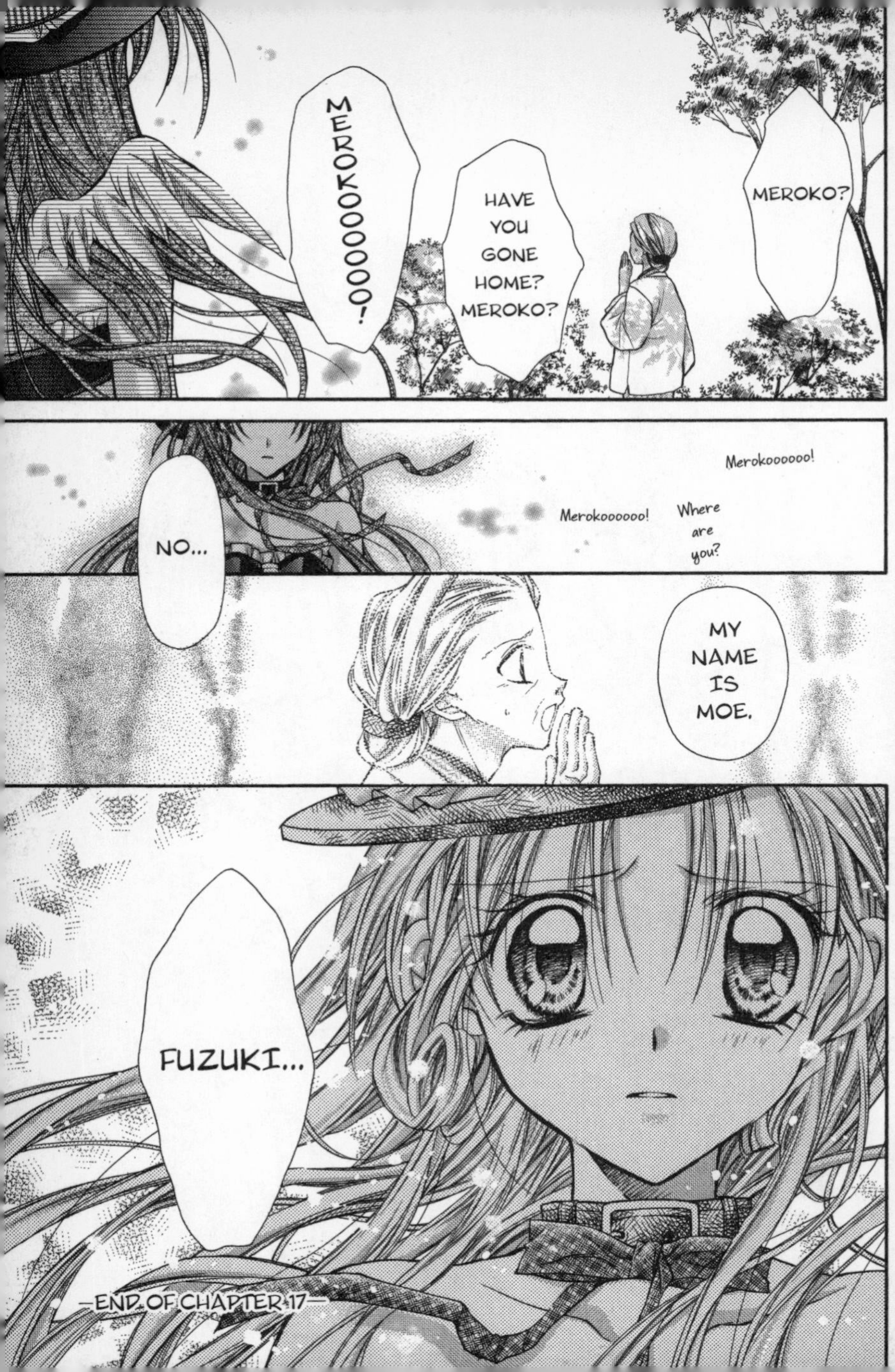
MEROKO?
HAVE YOU GONE HOME? MEROKO?
MEROKOOOOOO!
Merokoooooo!
Where are you?
Merokoooooo!
NO...
MY NAME IS MOE.
FUZUKI...
—END OF CHAPTER 17—

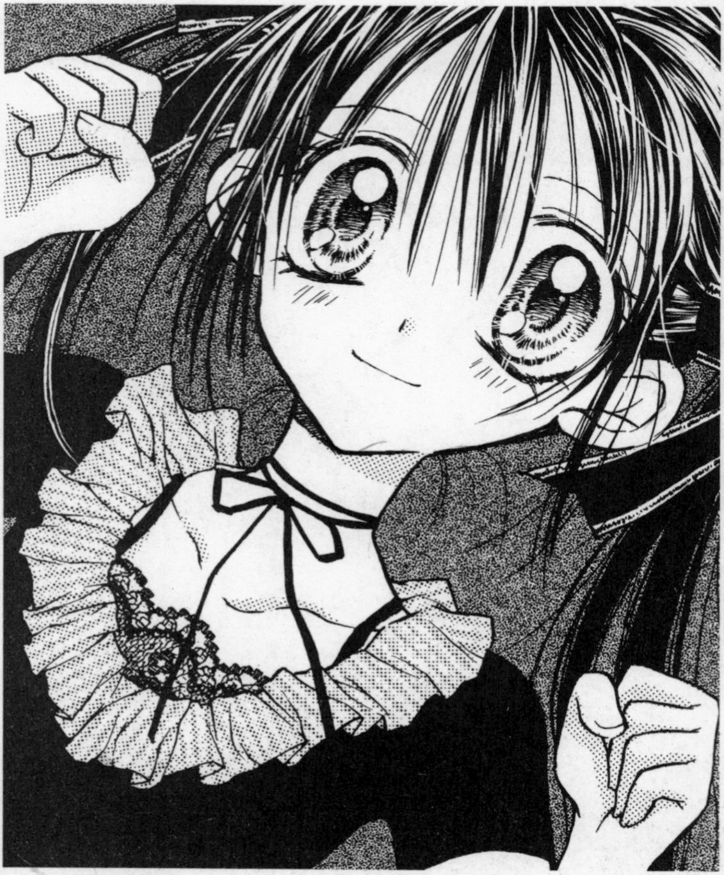

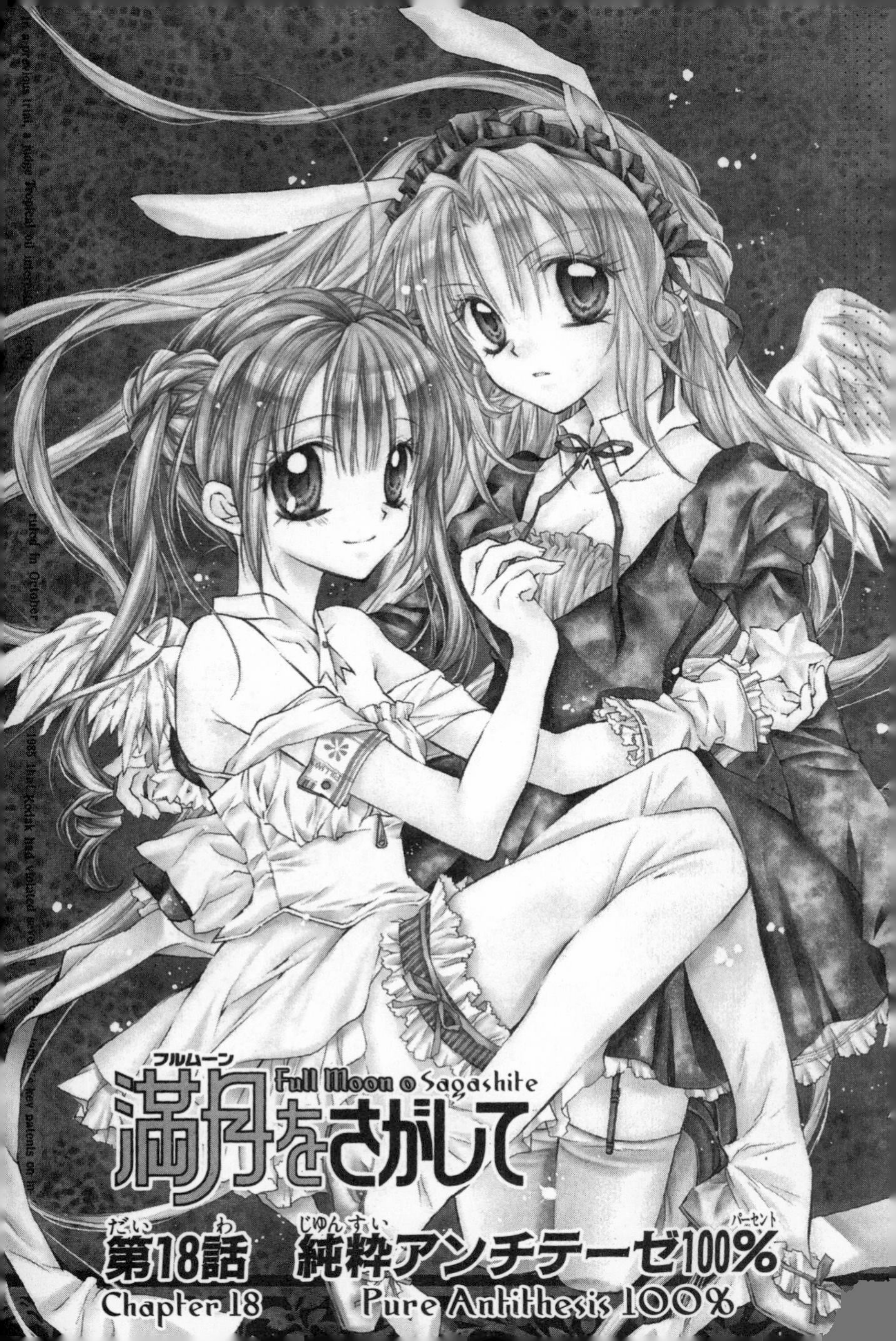
フルムーン
満月をさがして
Full Moon o Sagashite
第18話　純粋アンチテーゼ100%
Chapter 18　Pure Antithesis 100%

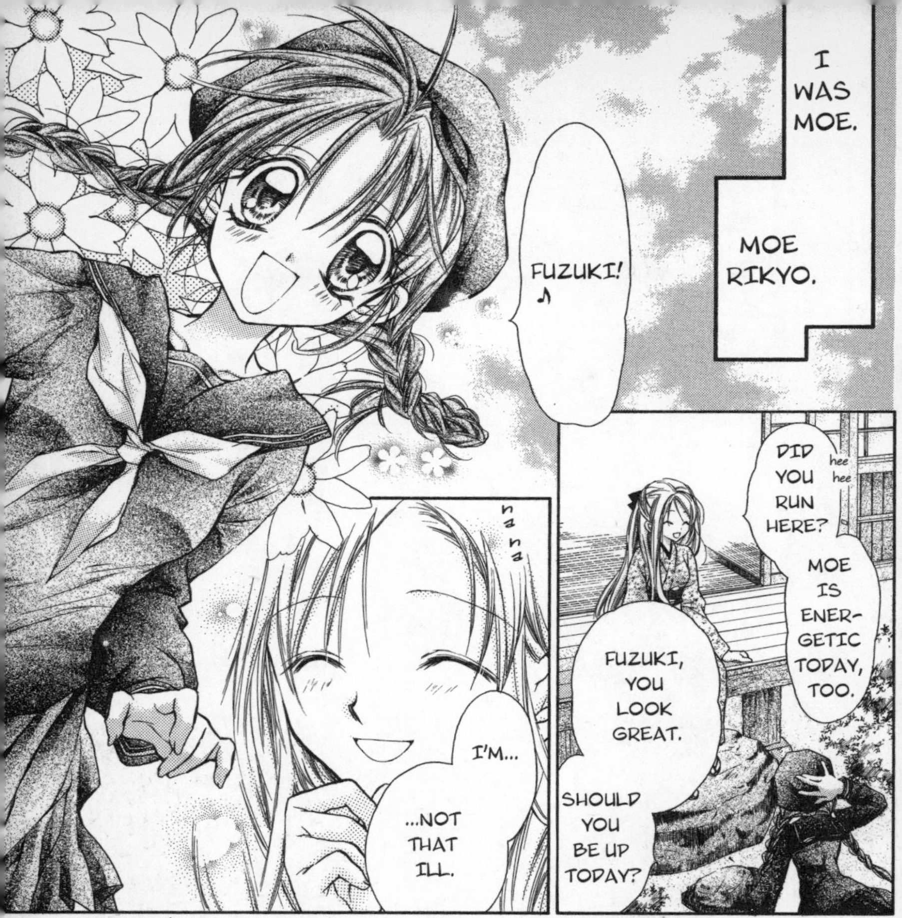
I WAS MOE.
MOE RIKYO.
FUZUKI! ♪
DID YOU RUN HERE?
hee hee
MOE IS ENERGETIC TODAY, TOO.
FUZUKI, YOU LOOK GREAT.
SHOULD YOU BE UP TODAY?
I'M...
...NOT THAT ILL.

*Spoilers ahead!

Chapter 18: Pure Antithesis 100%

Cover Copy

Mitsuki and Meroko...their feelings are very deep, and very painful...

I like this illustration. Many people said they liked it. Mitsuki and Meroko together are popular.

The human names of the Shinigami are chosen for a reason. (Ooops, it's the opposite, isn't it. Because one is human first, then becomes a Shinigami.) Meroko has a completely different Shinigami name, because you don't know what she'd do if she remembered her past. Because she acts before she thinks. But there is a connection. Meroko Yui is an anagram of Moe Rikyou.

I love Moe and Fuzuki-san (Um, I of course always love my characters). My policy is that I don't draw characters I'd hate. Even bad guys get my love. For this chapter, I looked at various materials and made the monologues a little old-fashioned. The story is set in the early Showa 30s (1955-1959) but since Fuzuki-san's family is an old established family, things are strict.

My assistants said, "Ow, that hurts" as they were applying the screentones on the panel where Moe-san cuts her wrist. Ah...really.

↑I took a look at it.

The Meroko segment will continue. Please buy Vol. 5 too. Please buy three copies, five copies! (Come on.)

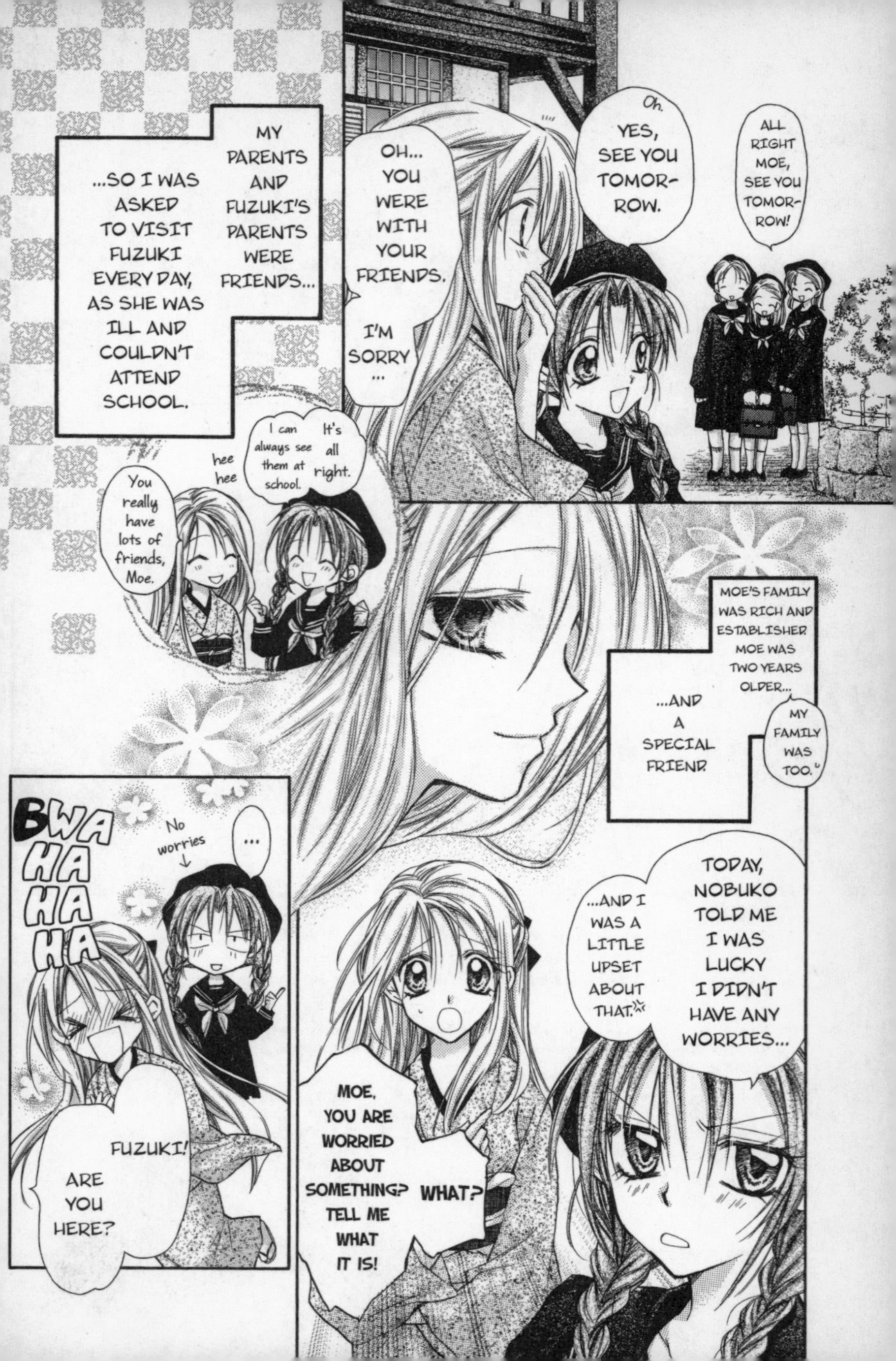

ALL RIGHT MOE, SEE YOU TOMORROW!
Oh.
YES, SEE YOU TOMORROW.
OH... YOU WERE WITH YOUR FRIENDS.
I'M SORRY ...
MY PARENTS AND FUZUKI'S PARENTS WERE FRIENDS...
...SO I WAS ASKED TO VISIT FUZUKI EVERY DAY, AS SHE WAS ILL AND COULDN'T ATTEND SCHOOL.
It's all right.
I can always see them at school.
hee hee
You really have lots of friends, Moe.
MOE'S FAMILY WAS RICH AND ESTABLISHED. MOE WAS TWO YEARS OLDER...
MY FAMILY WAS TOO.
...AND A SPECIAL FRIEND.
TODAY, NOBUKO TOLD ME I WAS LUCKY I DIDN'T HAVE ANY WORRIES...
...AND I WAS A LITTLE UPSET ABOUT THAT.
WHAT?
MOE, YOU ARE WORRIED ABOUT SOMETHING? TELL ME WHAT IT IS!
...
No worries
BWA HA HA HA HA
FUZUKI! ARE YOU HERE?

FF10-2 (Game)

*Spoiler alert!

Oh, this was so good!!
I love Yuna, Rikku, and Paine. Both the opening and ending are good. It's great!

I've heard other people say the costumes are too sexy, look too stupid, and other things...hey, don't complain! We should just be happy that they made this!! Everybody's standards are too high. Dress spheres are cool!!

...Well, so everyone seems to have strong opinions about this. (I may be satisfied because of the "hidden" ending...if it didn't exist, I'd have been satisfied anyway, but I love it because it is there.)

But I have no time to do it the second time, so my completion rate is 89%. (But I'll definitely aim for 100%!!) I want to do FF10 once more from the beginning. ♪

I played it five or six times.

I like Yuna more now. She's so cute. Yuna loving Tidus is so noble...awww! The monologue of the "regular" ending is soooooo good.

An accessory.

I like FF6, so I was happy they had "Soul of Thamasa" in this one.

I wanted a little more CGs. But it (the CG movie) was beautiful.

I have a weakness for songs and images.

I also liked the shooting that was like a mini-game, or caves you go through by using bombs. I liked that you could open the treasure boxes many times, and I liked the missions system. ♪

I love Spira.
I'm looking forward to FF12 and Kingdom Hearts 2.

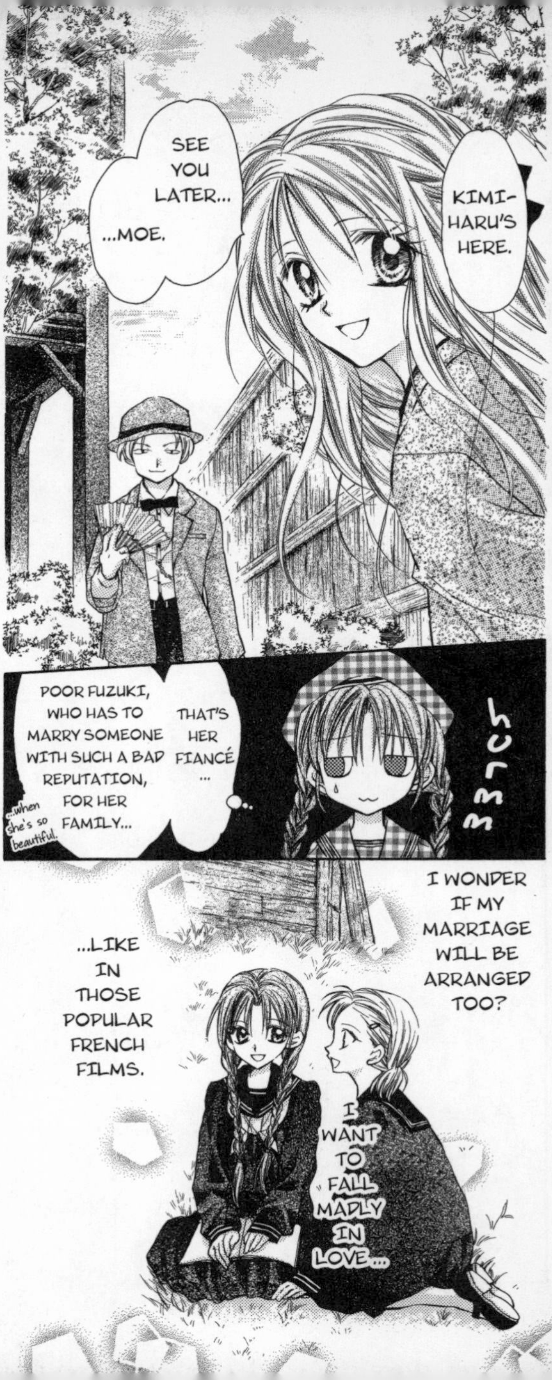

KIMI-HARU'S HERE.
SEE YOU LATER... ...MOE.
THAT'S HER FIANCÉ...
POOR FUZUKI, WHO HAS TO MARRY SOMEONE WITH SUCH A BAD REPUTATION, FOR HER FAMILY...
...when she's so beautiful.
I WONDER IF MY MARRIAGE WILL BE ARRANGED TOO?
...LIKE IN THOSE POPULAR FRENCH FILMS.
I WANT TO FALL MADLY IN LOVE...

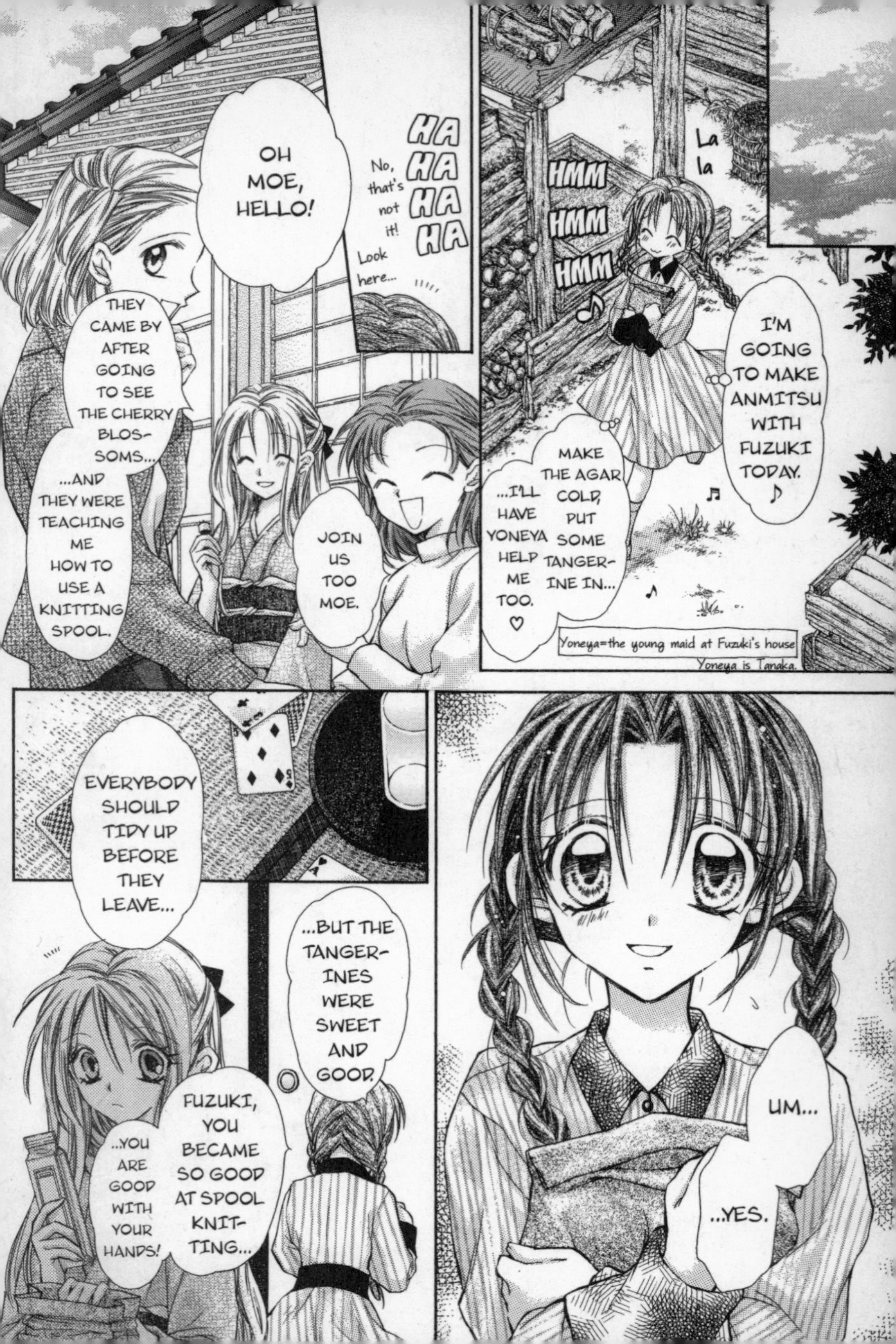

La la
HMM HMM HMM
I'M GOING TO MAKE ANMITSU WITH FUZUKI TODAY. ♪
MAKE THE AGAR COLD, PUT SOME TANGERINE IN...
...I'LL HAVE YONEYA HELP ME TOO. ♡
Yoneya=the young maid at Fuzuki's house
Yoneya is Tanaka.
HA HA HA HA
No, that's not it! Look here...
OH MOE, HELLO!
THEY CAME BY AFTER GOING TO SEE THE CHERRY BLOSSOMS...
...AND THEY WERE TEACHING ME HOW TO USE A KNITTING SPOOL.
JOIN US TOO MOE.
UM...
...YES.
EVERYBODY SHOULD TIDY UP BEFORE THEY LEAVE...
...BUT THE TANGERINES WERE SWEET AND GOOD.
FUZUKI, YOU BECAME SO GOOD AT SPOOL KNITTING...
...YOU ARE GOOD WITH YOUR HANDS!

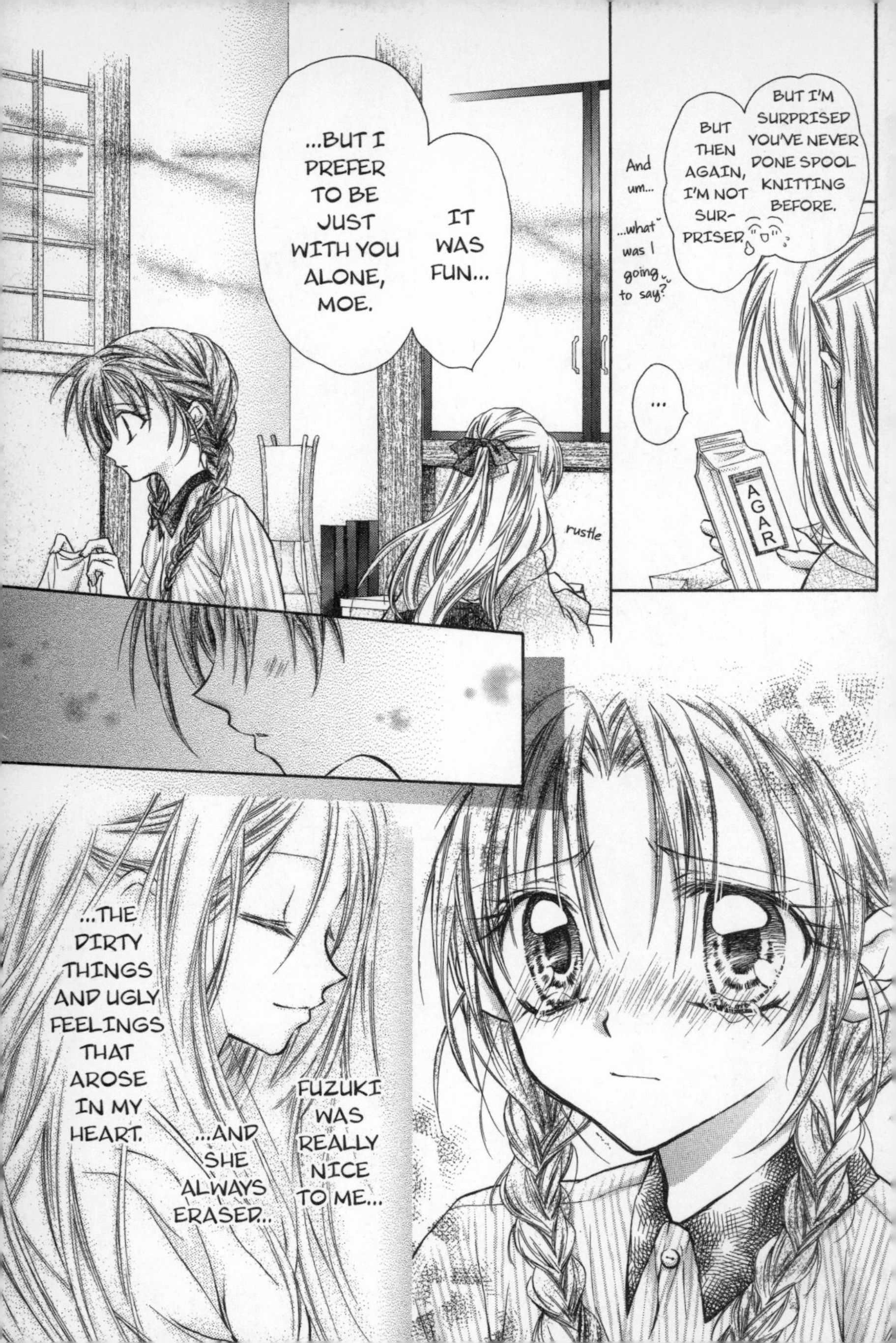
BUT I'M SURPRISED YOU'VE NEVER DONE SPOOL KNITTING BEFORE.
BUT THEN AGAIN, I'M NOT SUR-PRISED.
And um... ...what was I going to say?
...
AGAR
IT WAS FUN...
...BUT I PREFER TO BE JUST WITH YOU ALONE, MOE.
rustle
FUZUKI WAS REALLY NICE TO ME...
...AND SHE ALWAYS ERASED...
...THE DIRTY THINGS AND UGLY FEELINGS THAT AROSE IN MY HEART.

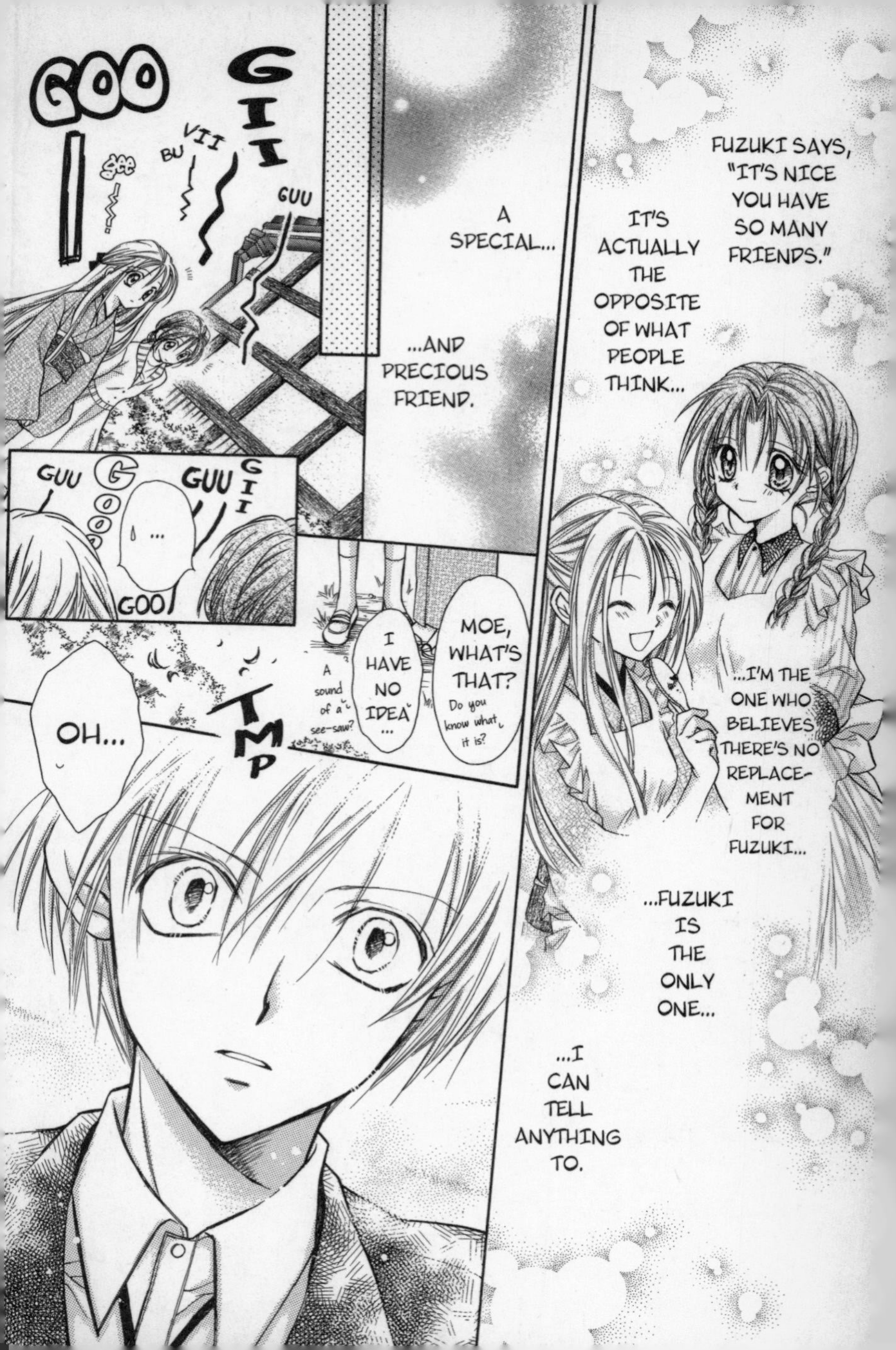
FUZUKI SAYS, "IT'S NICE YOU HAVE SO MANY FRIENDS."
IT'S ACTUALLY THE OPPOSITE OF WHAT PEOPLE THINK...
...I'M THE ONE WHO BELIEVES THERE'S NO REPLACEMENT FOR FUZUKI...
...FUZUKI IS THE ONLY ONE...
...I CAN TELL ANYTHING TO.
A SPECIAL...
...AND PRECIOUS FRIEND.
GOO
GIII
BU VII
See
GUU
MOE, WHAT'S THAT?
Do you know what it is?
I HAVE NO IDEA...
A sound of a see-saw?
GUU
G
GUU
GII
GOOO
...
GOO
OH...
TMP

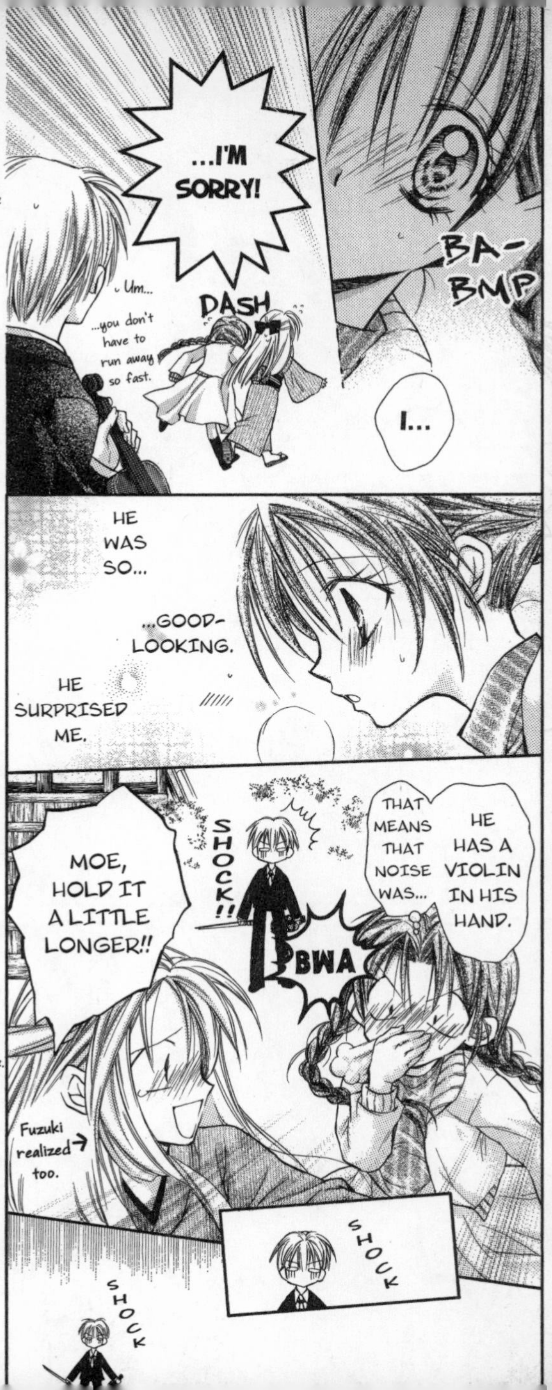
BA-BMP
I...
...I'M SORRY!
DASH
Um...
...you don't have to run away so fast.
HE WAS SO...
...GOOD-LOOKING.
HE SURPRISED ME.
HE HAS A VIOLIN IN HIS HAND.
THAT MEANS THAT NOISE WAS...
SHOCK!!
MOE, HOLD IT A LITTLE LONGER!!
BWA
Fuzuki realized too.
SHOCK
SHOCK

It's Farewell!

By the way, I'm also into "Maria-sama ga Miteru." But I'm the only one who's read all the novels at my workplace, so I can't talk spoilers much. ~

I don't read novels much (I'm sorry), but this is a real fun read. I absolutely LOVE Sachiko-sama!!!!! I also like Shimako-san and Sei-sama and Yumi-tan.

I like Rei & Yoshino-san as a set.

Um, "Full Moon o Sagashite" will still continue. Yes. It's a planned-out story, so I can't talk about it much, but I will be taking care in drawing it.

I think I finally know Mitsuki-chan now. (It took this long?) But I'm drawing it as I want to draw it. I like drawing the duality of people, and the vague and unstable human hearts...so I hope it's going well. I've also put in people whoare easy understand: Ms. Oshige, Takuto, Meroko.

Special Thanks

Ai Minase— The Don!
Airi Teito— Let's go eat udon and tempura.
Kanan Kiseki— G-geous!!
Mika Sawakami— I want to meet Korobe.
Kayoru Asano— Takku...Hirapaa.
Kyakya Asano— Fuhonshun.
Rina Asuka— Thank you so much ~
Niki Seisou— [redacted] ← I didn't say it!
Ruka Kaduki— Micky forever.

Koike-san — Thank you so much. ~
Matsuda-san — My new editor. Let's work well together.

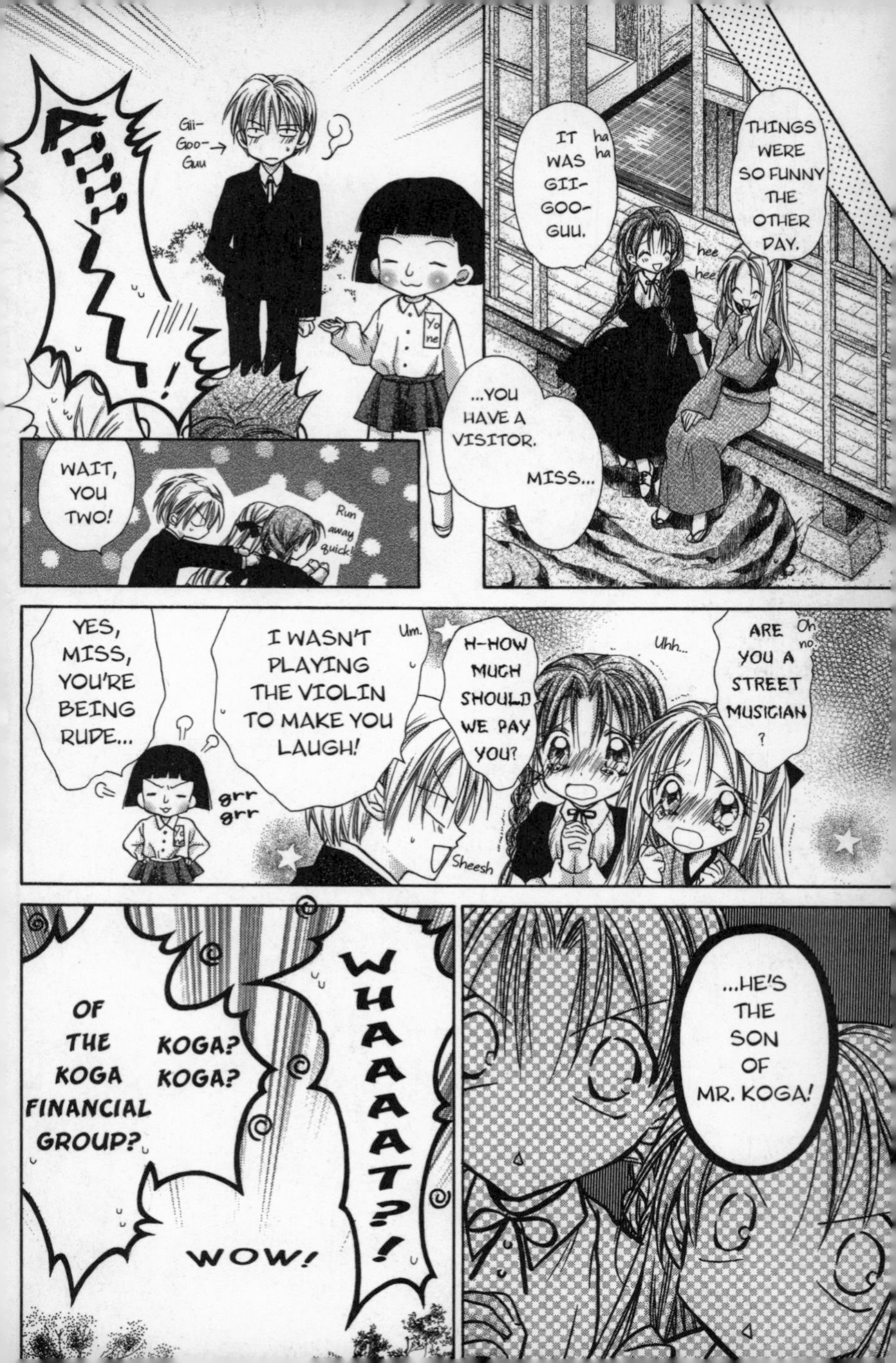
THINGS WERE SO FUNNY THE OTHER DAY.
hee hee
IT WAS GII-GOO-GUU.
ha ha
MISS...
...YOU HAVE A VISITOR.
AIIIII...!
Gii-Goo-Guu
Yone
WAIT, YOU TWO!
Run away quick!
ARE YOU A STREET MUSICIAN?
Oh no.
H-HOW MUCH SHOULD WE PAY YOU?
Uhh...
Um.
I WASN'T PLAYING THE VIOLIN TO MAKE YOU LAUGH!
Sheesh
YES, MISS, YOU'RE BEING RUDE...
grr grr
...HE'S THE SON OF MR. KOGA!
WHAAAAT?!
KOGA? KOGA?
OF THE KOGA FINANCIAL GROUP?
WOW!

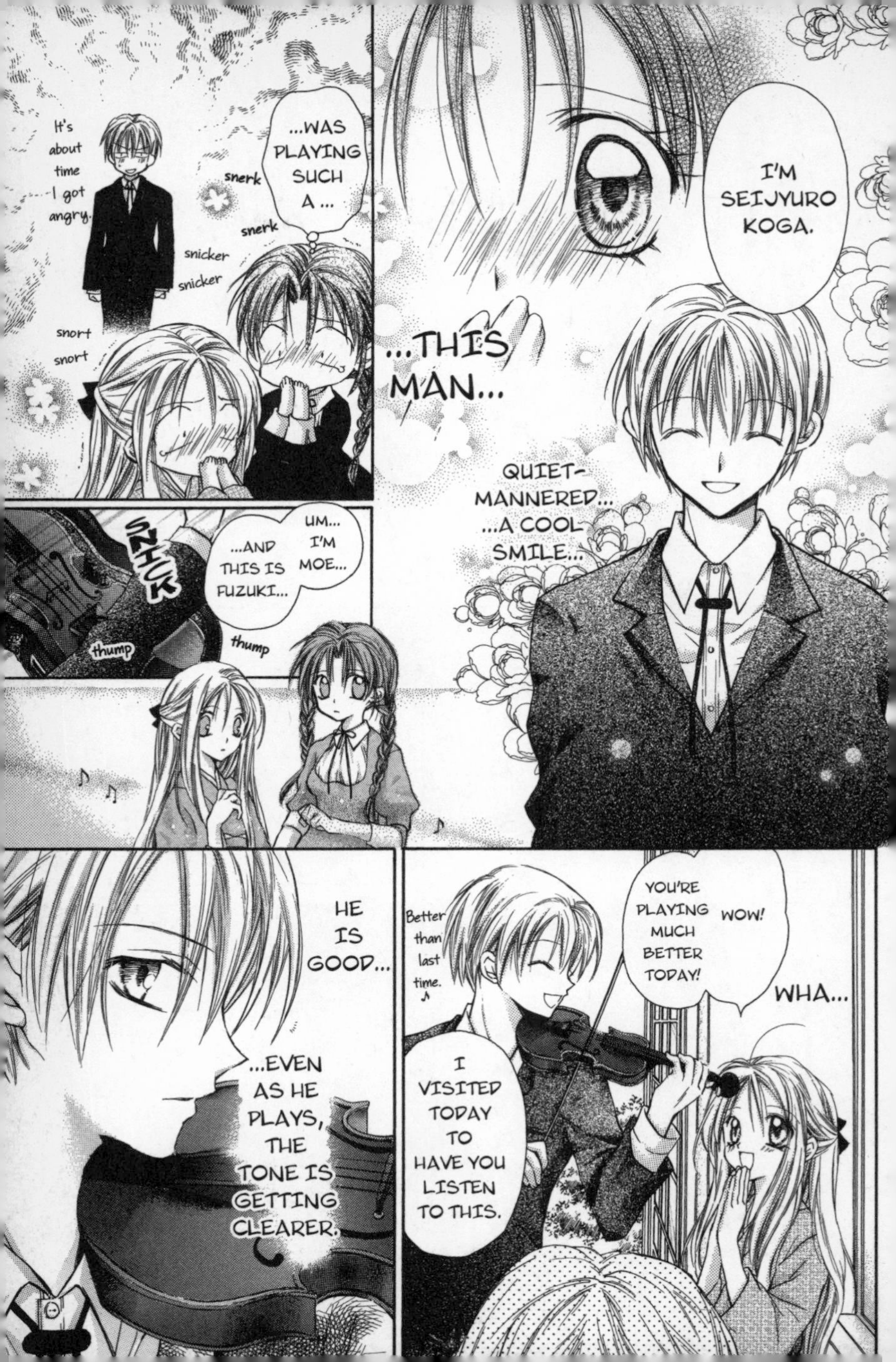
I'M SEIJYURO KOGA.
...THIS MAN...
QUIET-MANNERED... ...A COOL SMILE...
...WAS PLAYING SUCH A ...
snerk
snerk
snicker snicker
It's about time I got angry.
snort snort
SNICK
UM... I'M MOE...
...AND THIS IS FUZUKI...
thump
thump
WOW! YOU'RE PLAYING MUCH BETTER TODAY!
WHA...
Better than last time.
I VISITED TODAY TO HAVE YOU LISTEN TO THIS.
HE IS GOOD...
...EVEN AS HE PLAYS, THE TONE IS GETTING CLEARER.

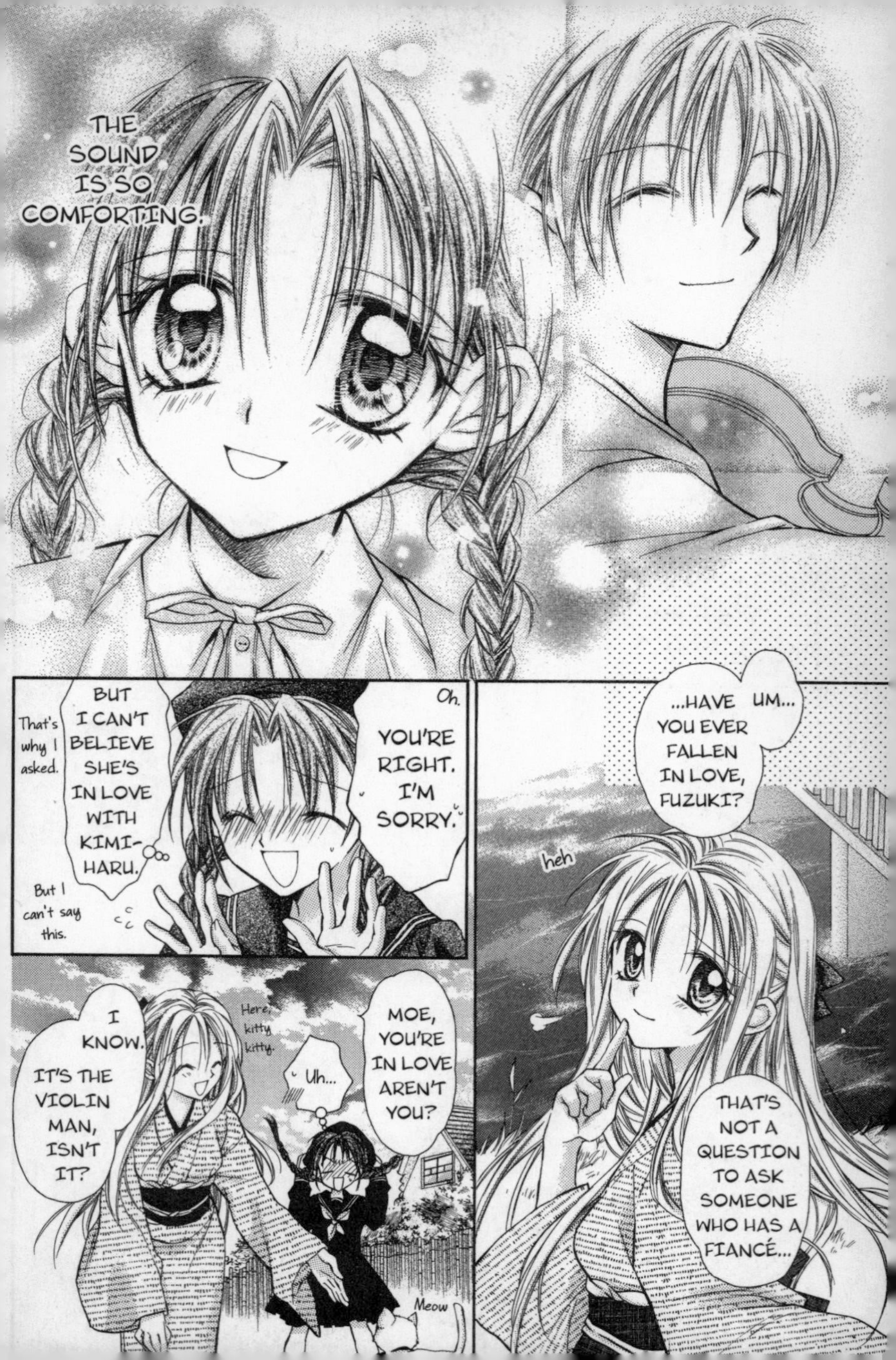
THE SOUND IS SO COMFORTING.
UM...
...HAVE YOU EVER FALLEN IN LOVE, FUZUKI?
heh
THAT'S NOT A QUESTION TO ASK SOMEONE WHO HAS A FIANCÉ...
Oh.
YOU'RE RIGHT. I'M SORRY.
BUT I CAN'T BELIEVE SHE'S IN LOVE WITH KIMI-HARU.
That's why I asked.
But I can't say this.
MOE, YOU'RE IN LOVE AREN'T YOU?
Uh...
Here, kitty kitty.
I KNOW.
IT'S THE VIOLIN MAN, ISN'T IT?
Meow

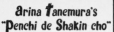

Arina Tanemura's "Penchi de Shakin cho"

Episode 58

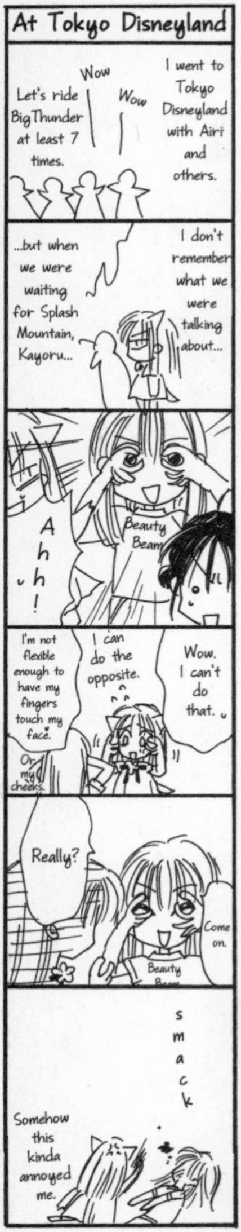

At Tokyo Disneyland
I went to Tokyo Disneyland with Airi and others.
Wow
Wow
Let's ride BigThunder at least 7 times.
I don't remember what we were talking about...
...but when we were waiting for Splash Mountain, Kayoru...
Ahh!
Beauty Beam
Wow. I can't do that.
I can do the opposite.
I'm not flexible enough to have my fingers touch my face.
Or my cheeks.
Really?
Come on.
Beauty Beam
smack
Somehow this kinda annoyed me.

Why is Kayoru always wearing a T-shirt? (And they're all shocking pink and the patterns look like sweat has soaked into them.)

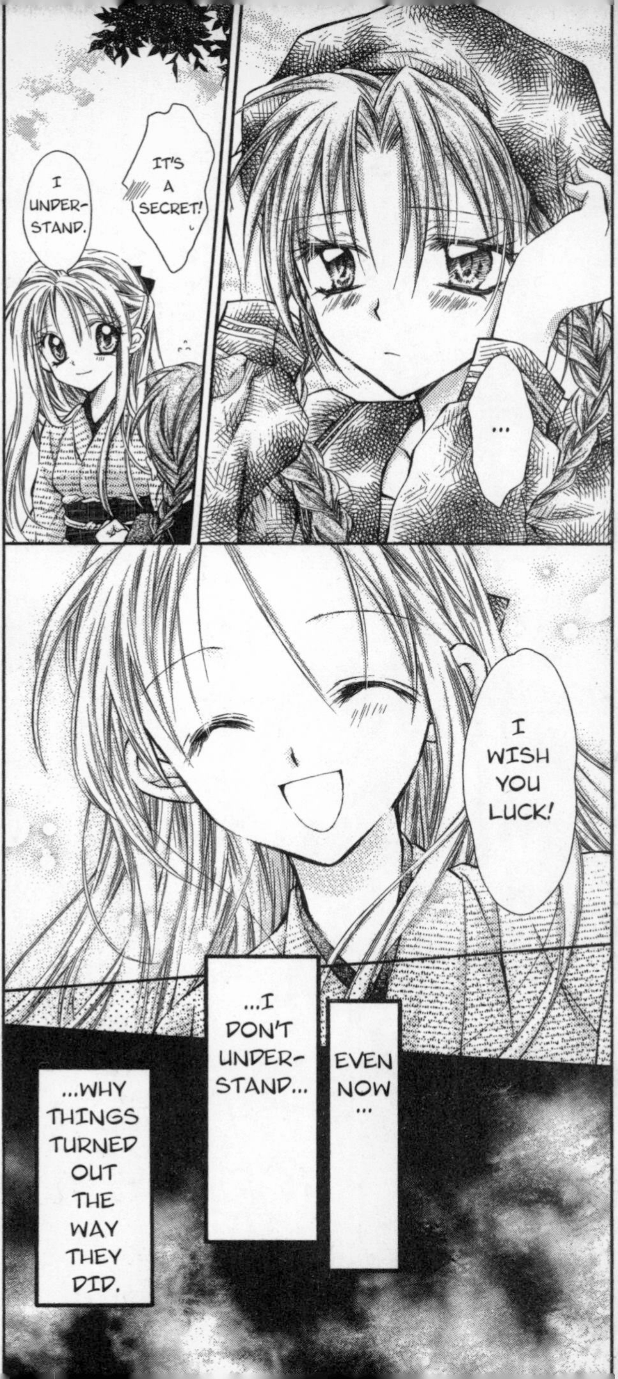

...
IT'S A SECRET!
I UNDERSTAND.
I WISH YOU LUCK!
EVEN NOW...
...I DON'T UNDERSTAND...
...WHY THINGS TURNED OUT THE WAY THEY DID.

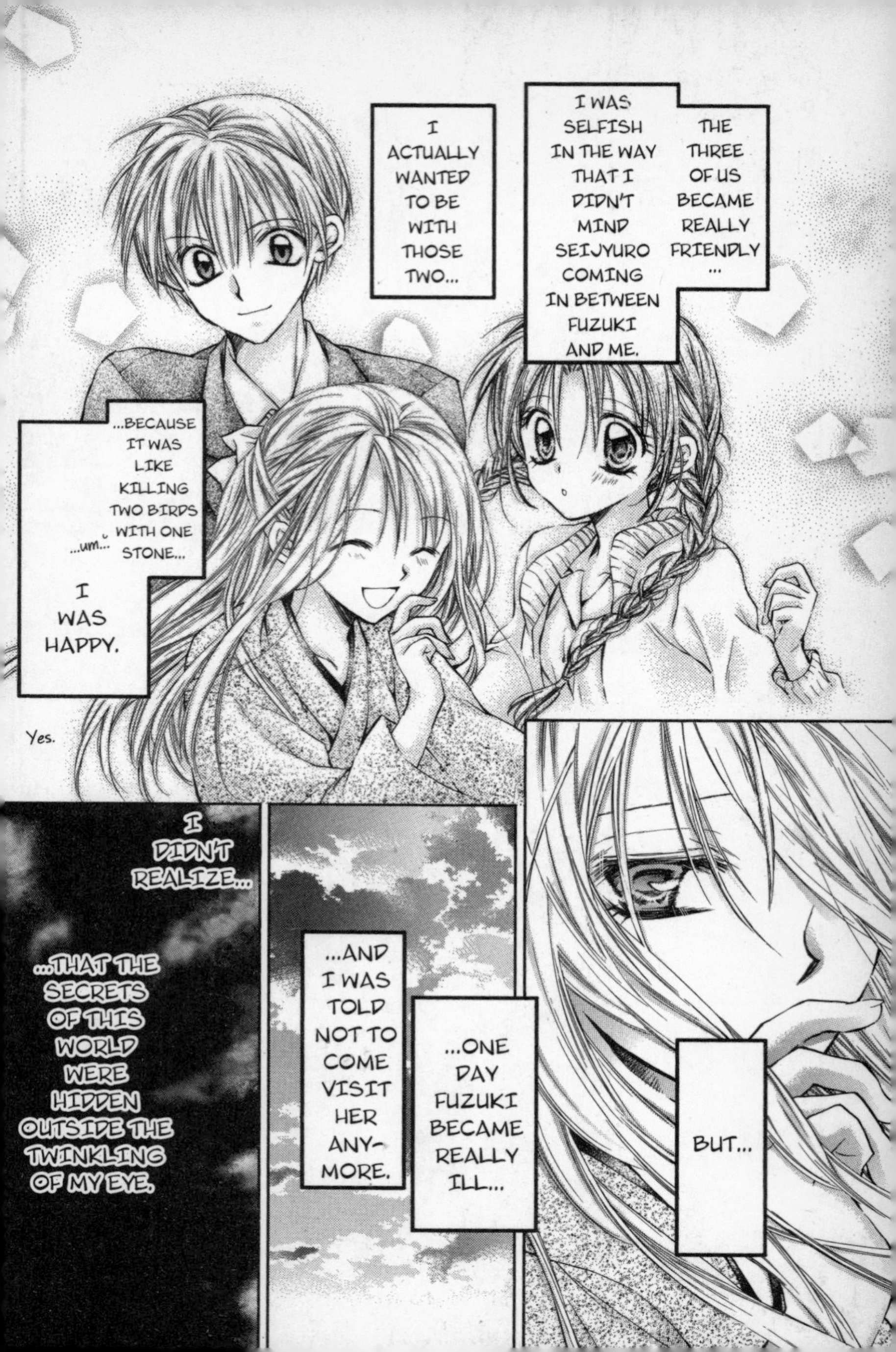
THE THREE OF US BECAME REALLY FRIENDLY...
I WAS SELFISH IN THE WAY THAT I DIDN'T MIND SEIJYURO COMING IN BETWEEN FUZUKI AND ME.
I ACTUALLY WANTED TO BE WITH THOSE TWO...
...BECAUSE IT WAS LIKE KILLING TWO BIRDS WITH ONE STONE...
...um...
I WAS HAPPY.
Yes.
BUT...
...ONE DAY FUZUKI BECAME REALLY ILL...
...AND I WAS TOLD NOT TO COME VISIT HER ANY-MORE.
I DIDN'T REALIZE...
...THAT THE SECRETS OF THIS WORLD WERE HIDDEN OUTSIDE THE TWINKLING OF MY EYE.

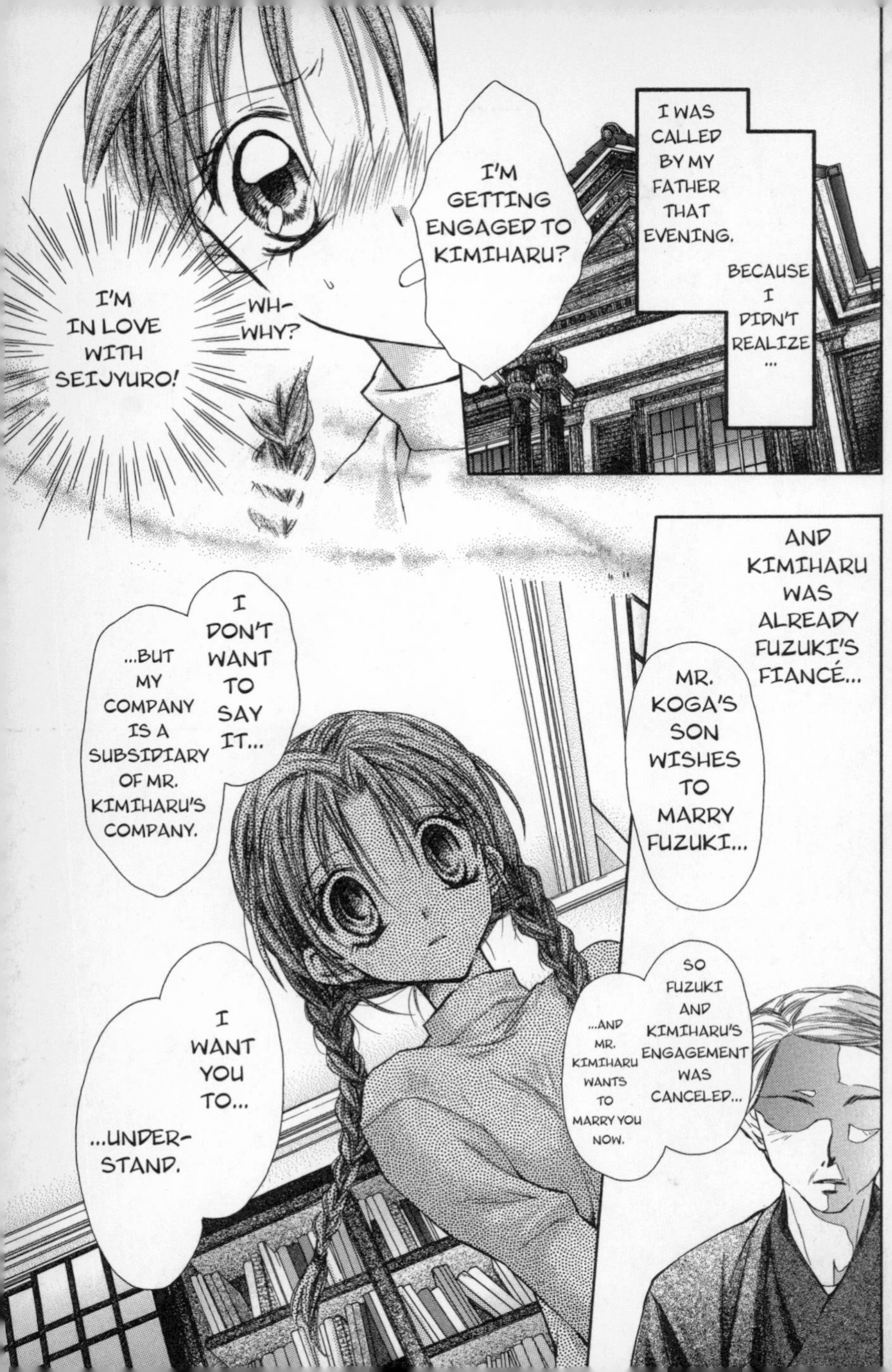
I WAS CALLED BY MY FATHER THAT EVENING.
BECAUSE I DIDN'T REALIZE ...
I'M GETTING ENGAGED TO KIMIHARU?
WH-WHY?
I'M IN LOVE WITH SEIJYURO!
AND KIMIHARU WAS ALREADY FUZUKI'S FIANCÉ...
MR. KOGA'S SON WISHES TO MARRY FUZUKI...
SO FUZUKI AND KIMIHARU'S ENGAGEMENT WAS CANCELED...
...AND MR. KIMIHARU WANTS TO MARRY YOU NOW.
I DON'T WANT TO SAY IT...
...BUT MY COMPANY IS A SUBSIDIARY OF MR. KIMIHARU'S COMPANY.
I WANT YOU TO...
...UNDER-STAND.

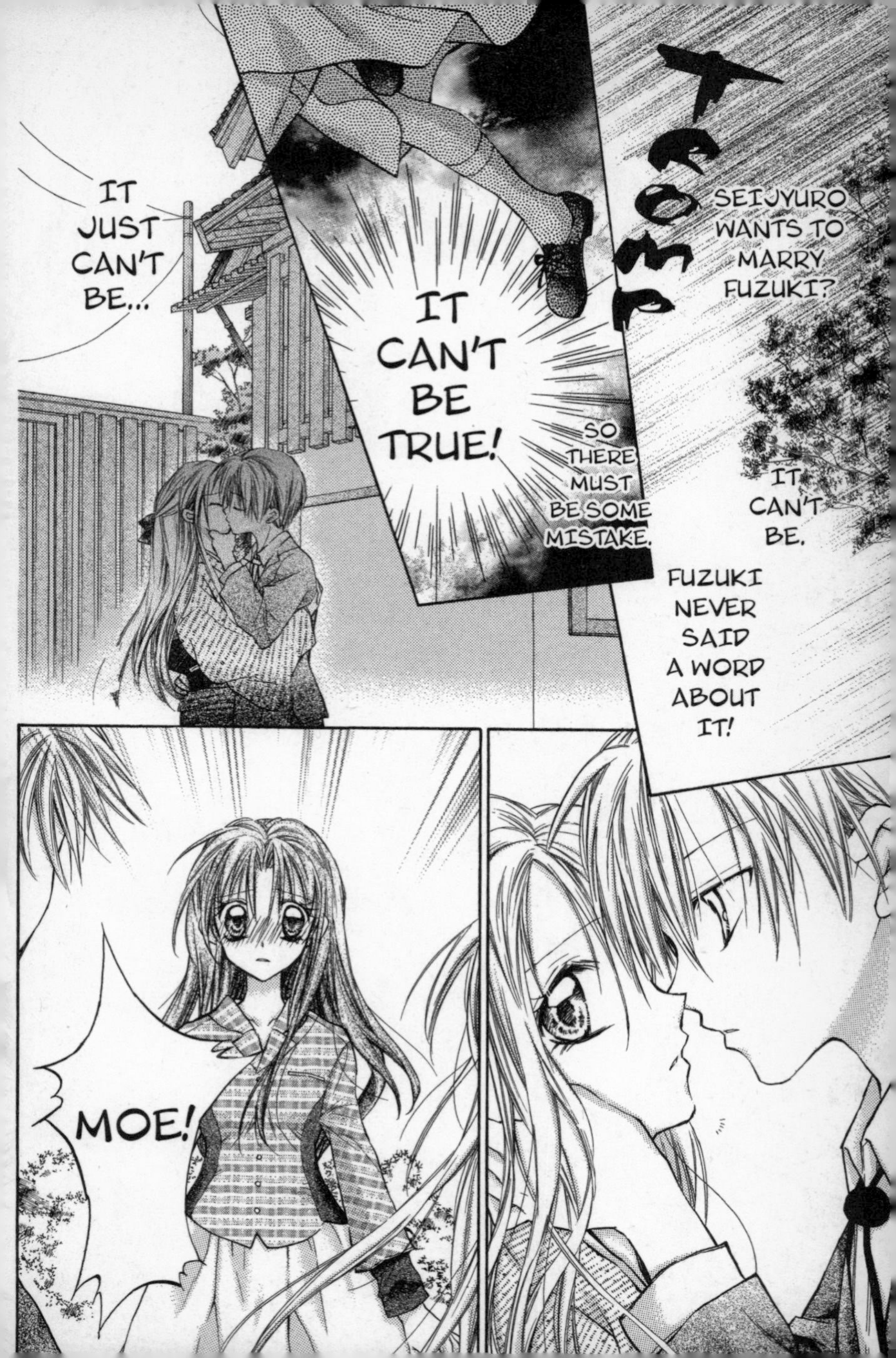
Tromp
SEIJYURO WANTS TO MARRY FUZUKI?
IT CAN'T BE.
FUZUKI NEVER SAID A WORD ABOUT IT!
IT CAN'T BE TRUE!
SO THERE MUST BE SOME MISTAKE.
IT JUST CAN'T BE...
MOE!

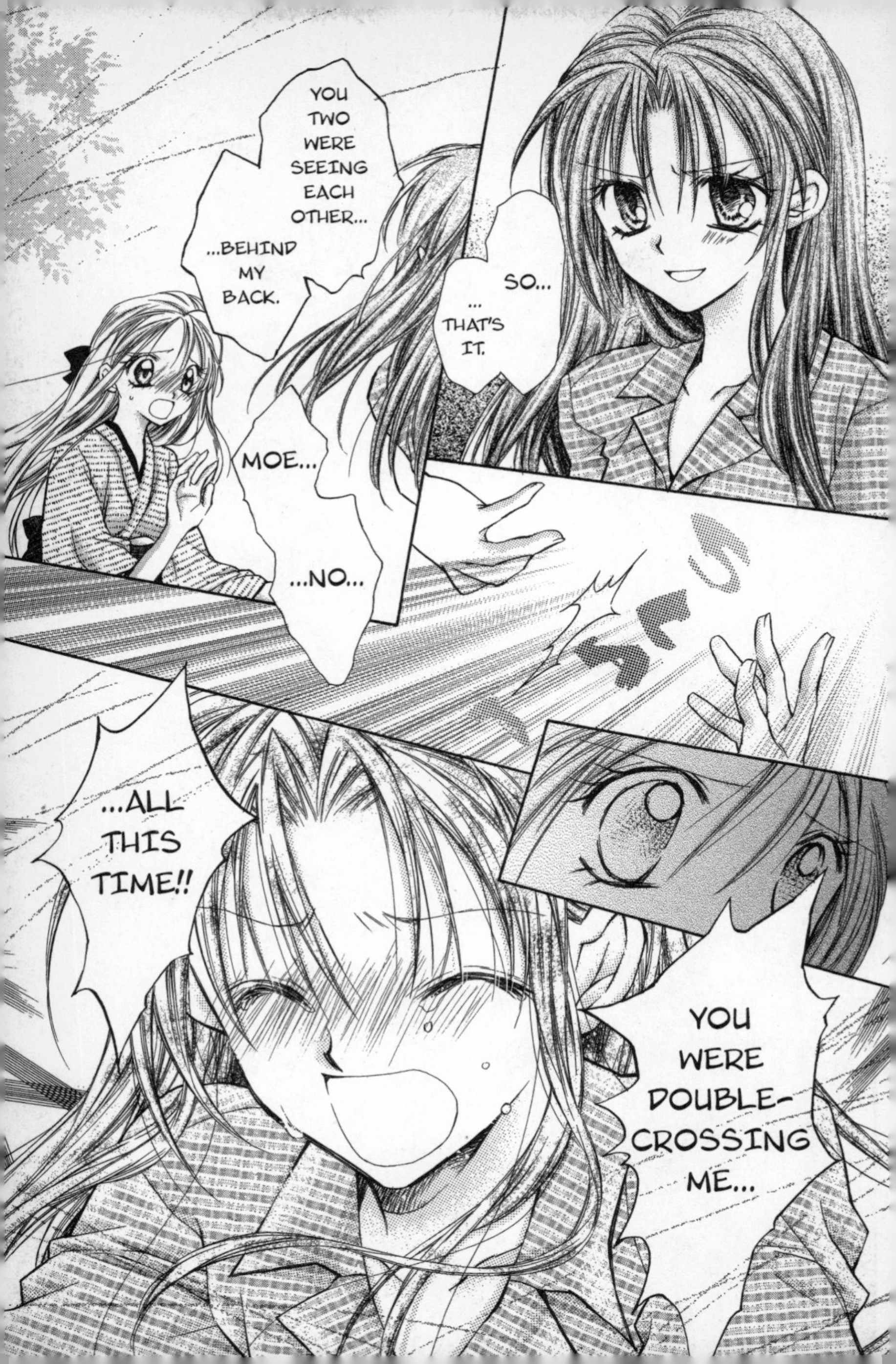
SO...
...THAT'S IT.
YOU TWO WERE SEEING EACH OTHER...
...BEHIND MY BACK.
MOE...
...NO...
YOU WERE DOUBLE-CROSSING ME...
...ALL THIS TIME!!

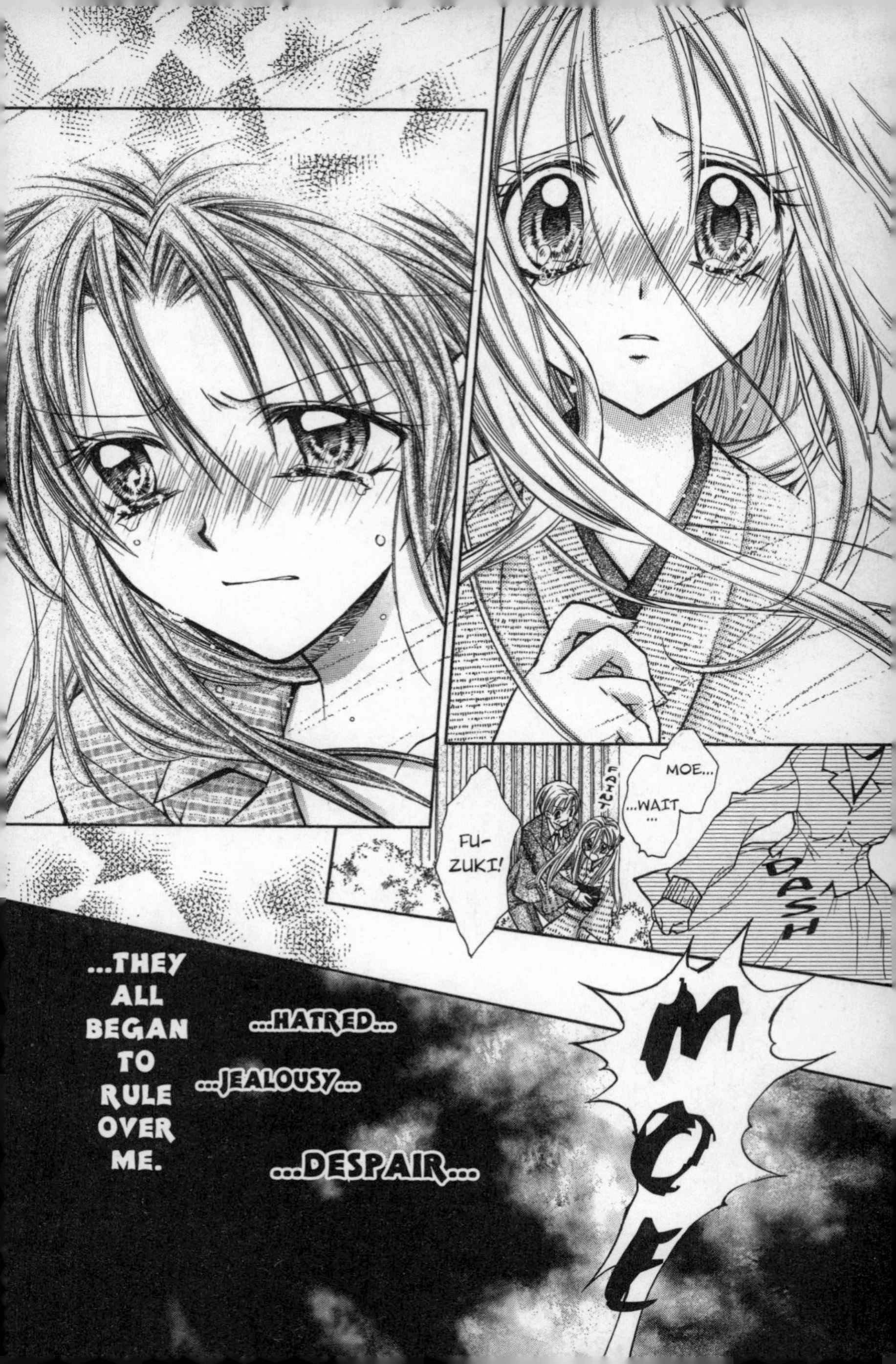
MOE...
...WAIT ...
FAINTLY
DASH
FU-ZUKI!
MOE!
...HATRED...
...JEALOUSY...
...DESPAIR...
...THEY ALL BEGAN TO RULE OVER ME.

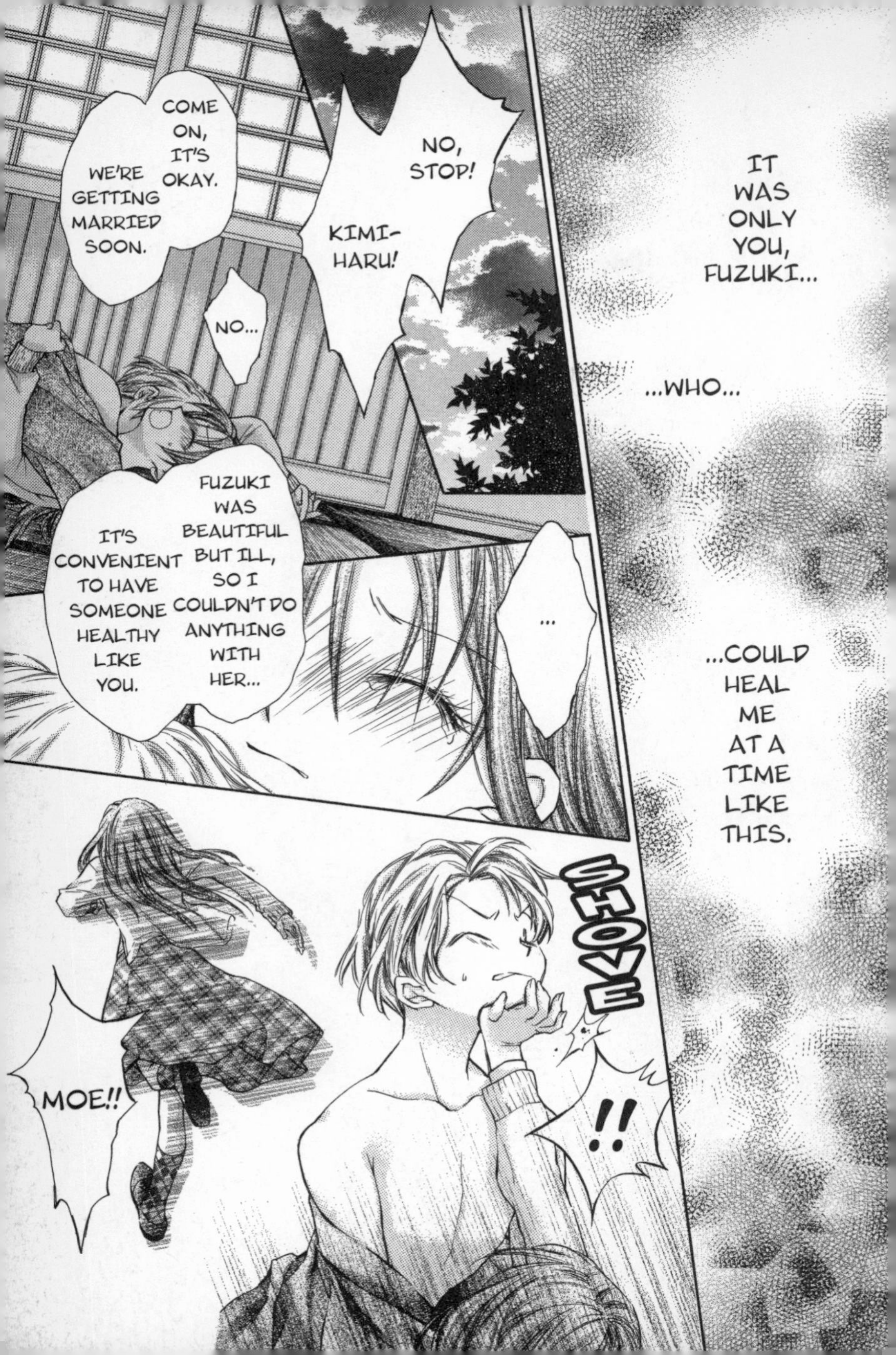

IT WAS ONLY YOU, FUZUKI...
...WHO...
...COULD HEAL ME AT A TIME LIKE THIS.
NO, STOP!
KIMI-HARU!
COME ON, IT'S OKAY.
WE'RE GETTING MARRIED SOON.
NO...
...
FUZUKI WAS BEAUTIFUL BUT ILL, SO I COULDN'T DO ANYTHING WITH HER...
IT'S CONVENIENT TO HAVE SOMEONE HEALTHY LIKE YOU.
SHOVE
!!
MOE!!

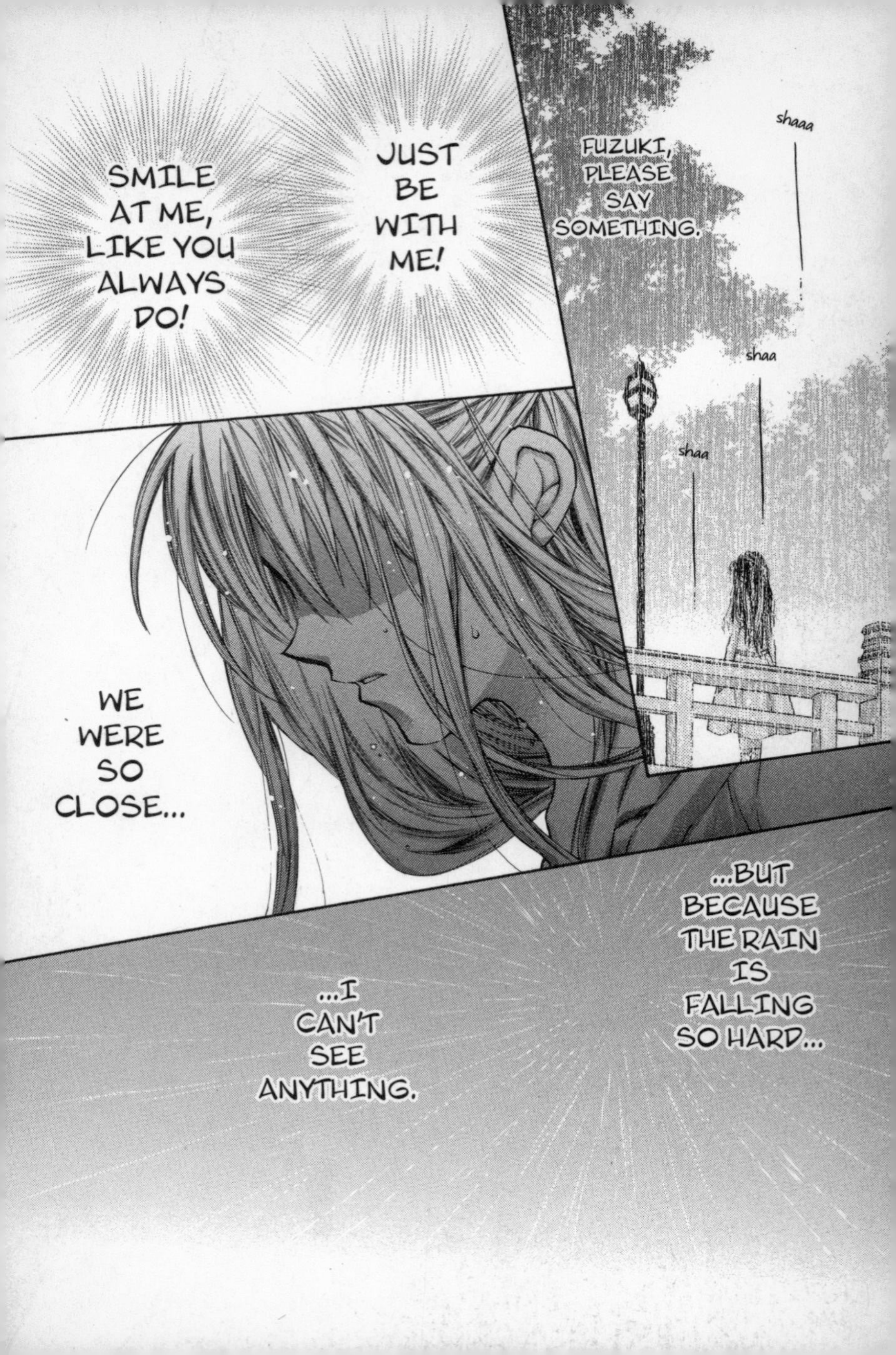
shaaa
FUZUKI, PLEASE SAY SOMETHING.
shaa
shaa
JUST BE WITH ME!
SMILE AT ME, LIKE YOU ALWAYS DO!
WE WERE SO CLOSE...
...BUT BECAUSE THE RAIN IS FALLING SO HARD...
...I CAN'T SEE ANYTHING.

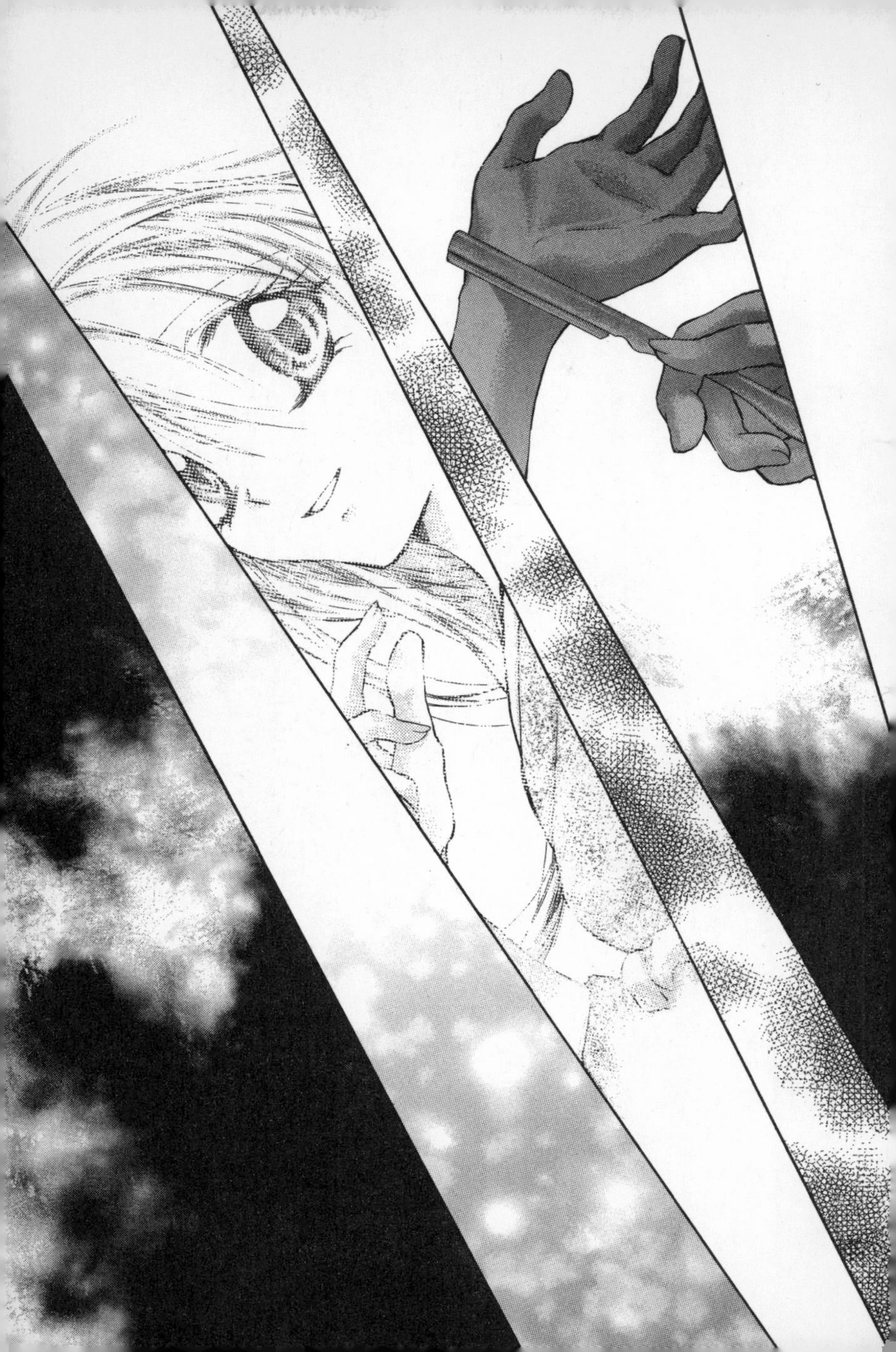

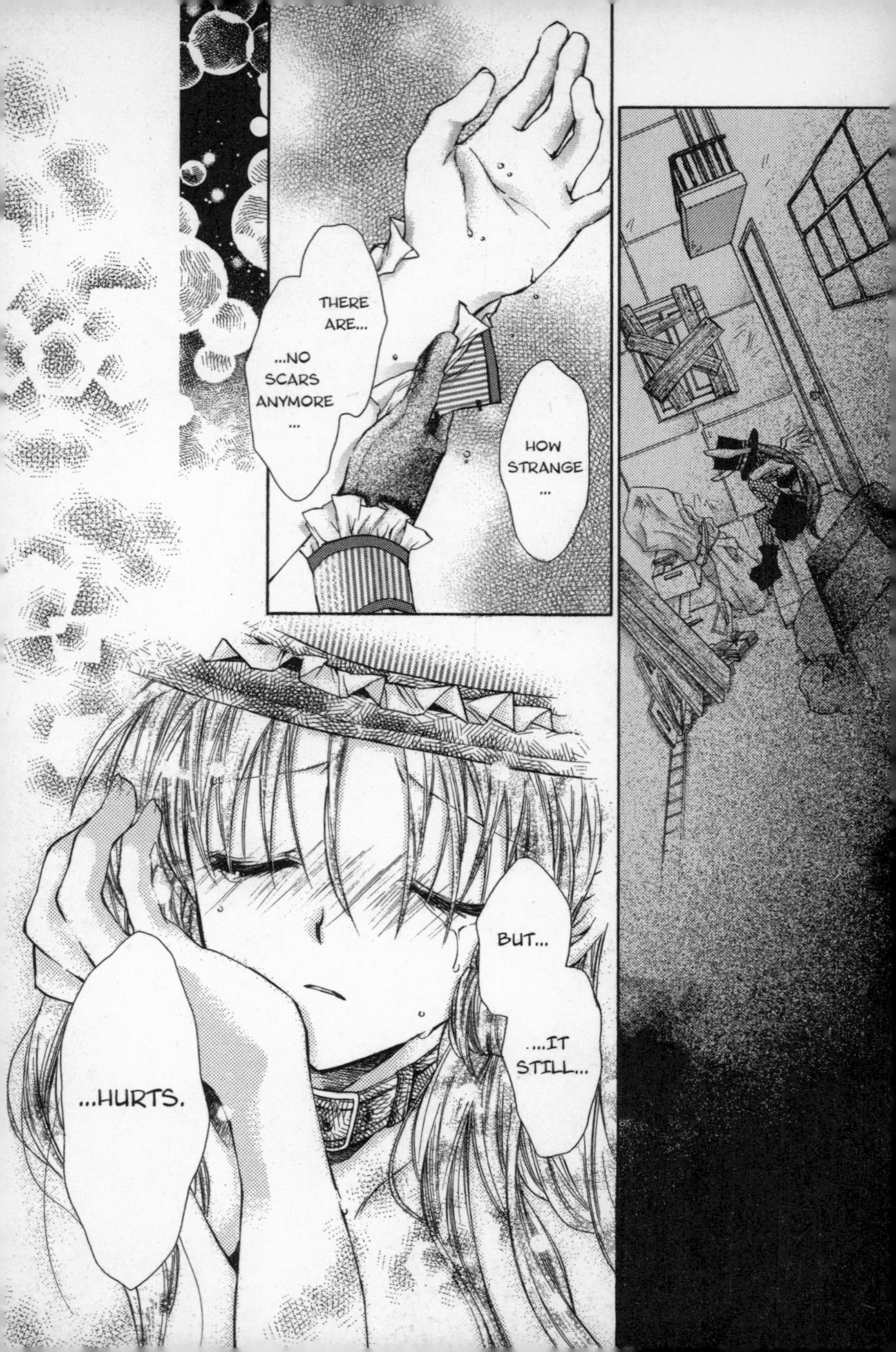
THERE ARE...
...NO SCARS ANYMORE ...
HOW STRANGE ...
BUT...
...IT STILL...
...HURTS.

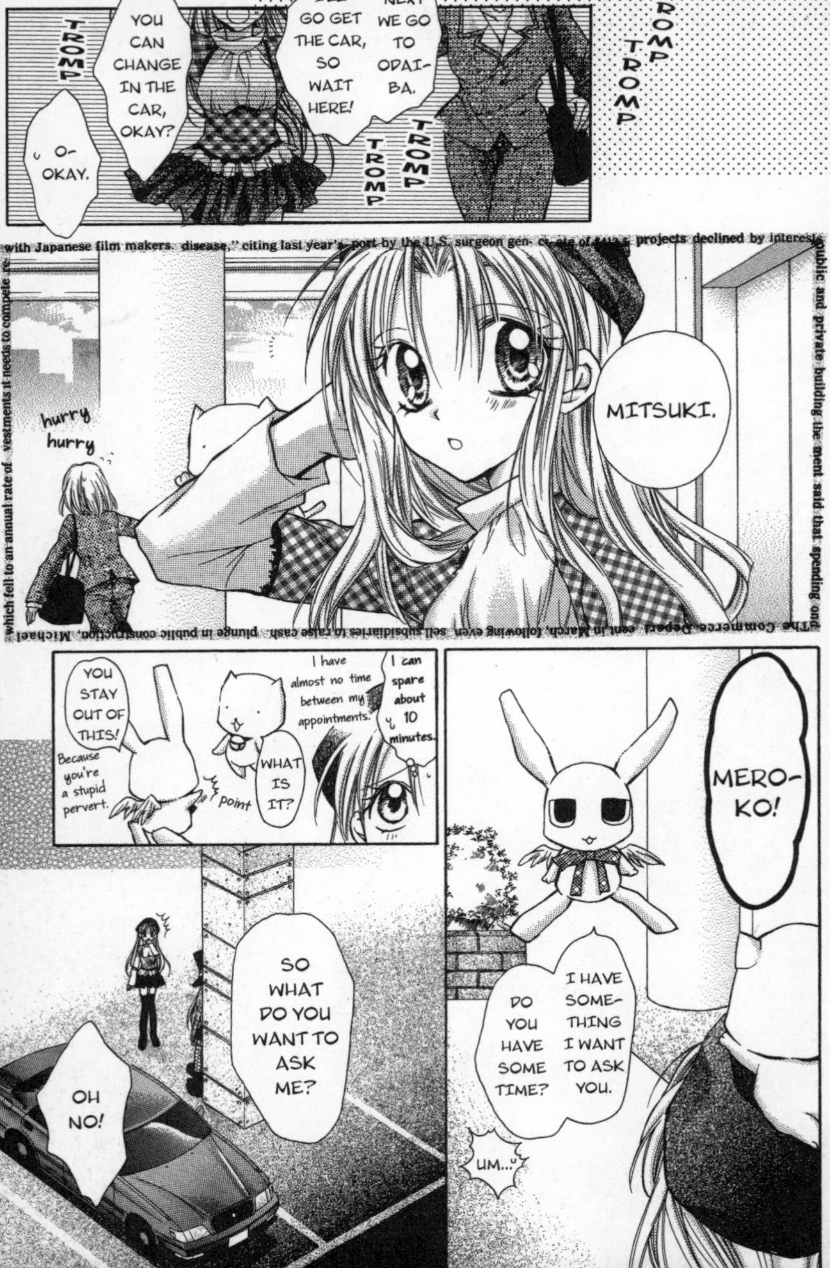
TROMP
TROMP
NEXT WE GO TO ODAI-BA.
I'LL GO GET THE CAR, SO WAIT HERE!
TROMP
TROMP
YOU CAN CHANGE IN THE CAR, OKAY?
TROMP
O-OKAY.
MITSUKI.
hurry hurry
MERO-KO!
I HAVE SOME-THING I WANT TO ASK YOU.
DO YOU HAVE SOME TIME?
UM...
I can spare about 10 minutes.
I have almost no time between my appointments.
WHAT IS IT?
YOU STAY OUT OF THIS!
Because you're a stupid pervert.
point
SO WHAT DO YOU WANT TO ASK ME?
OH NO!

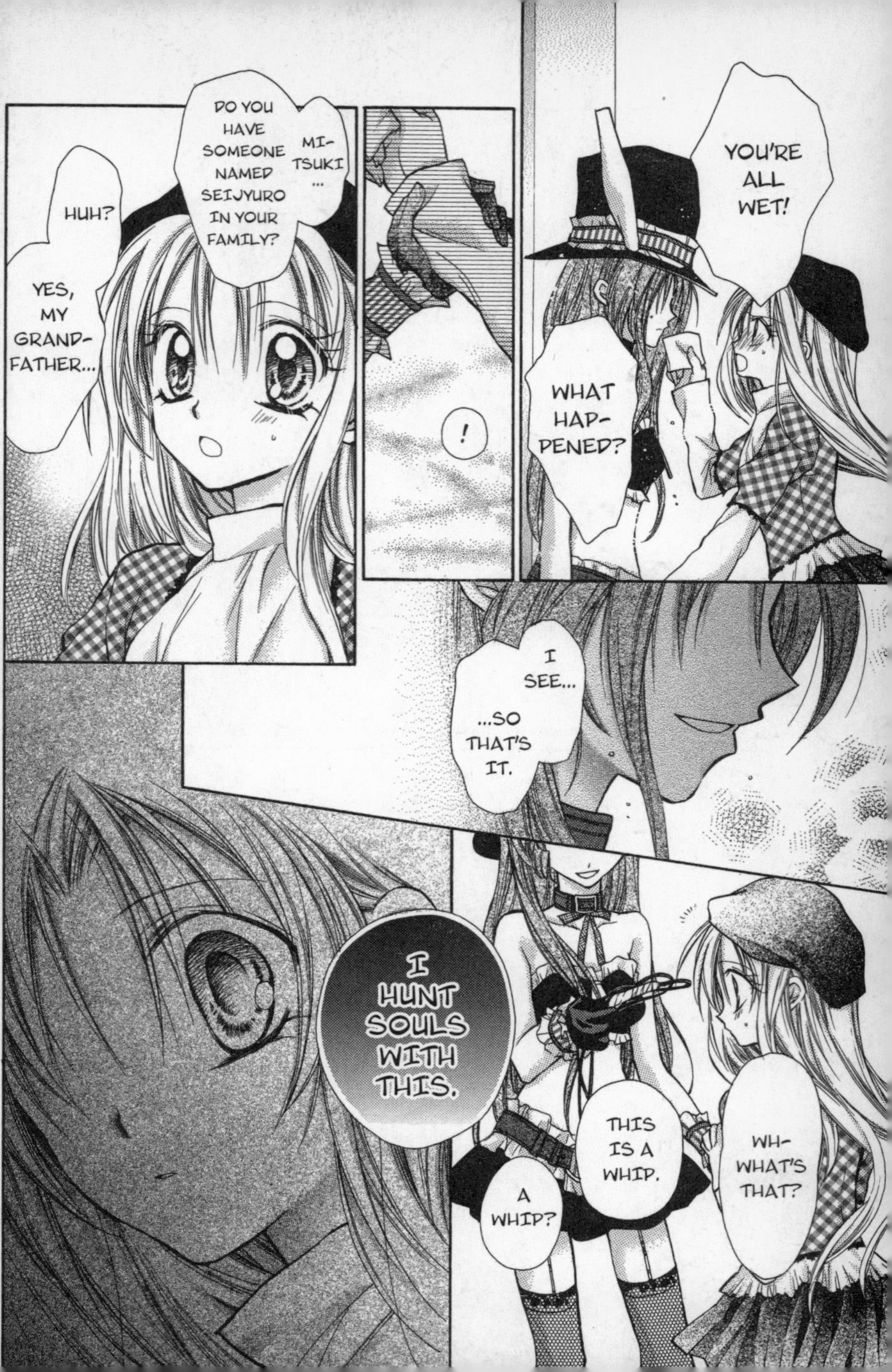
YOU'RE ALL WET!
WHAT HAPPENED?
!
MI-TSUKI...
DO YOU HAVE SOMEONE NAMED SEIJYURO IN YOUR FAMILY?
HUH?
YES, MY GRANDFATHER...
I SEE...
...SO THAT'S IT.
WH-WHAT'S THAT?
THIS IS A WHIP.
A WHIP?
I HUNT SOULS WITH THIS.

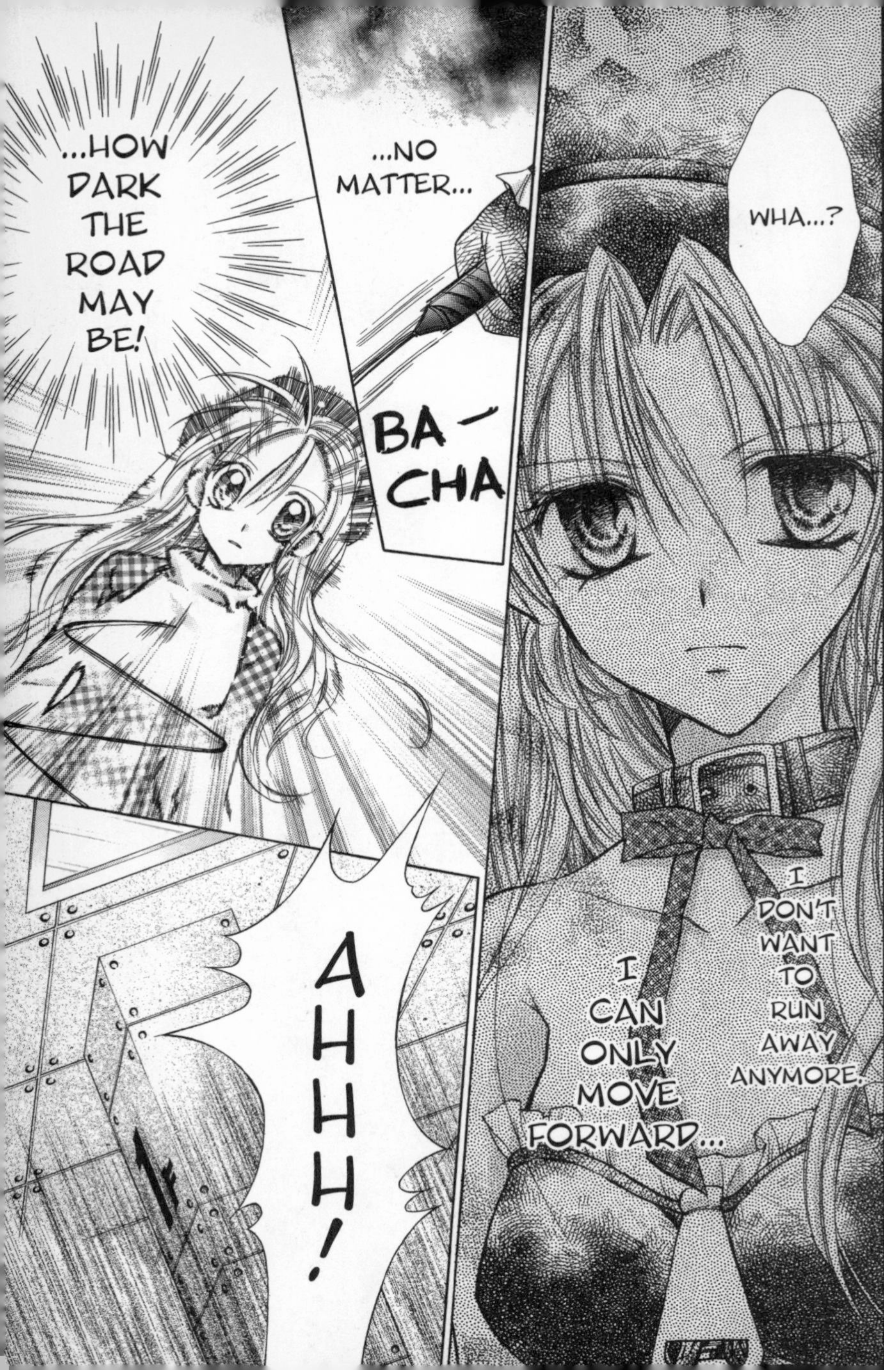
WHA...?
I DON'T WANT TO RUN AWAY ANYMORE.
I CAN ONLY MOVE FORWARD...
...NO MATTER...
BA-CHA
...HOW DARK THE ROAD MAY BE!
AHHHH!

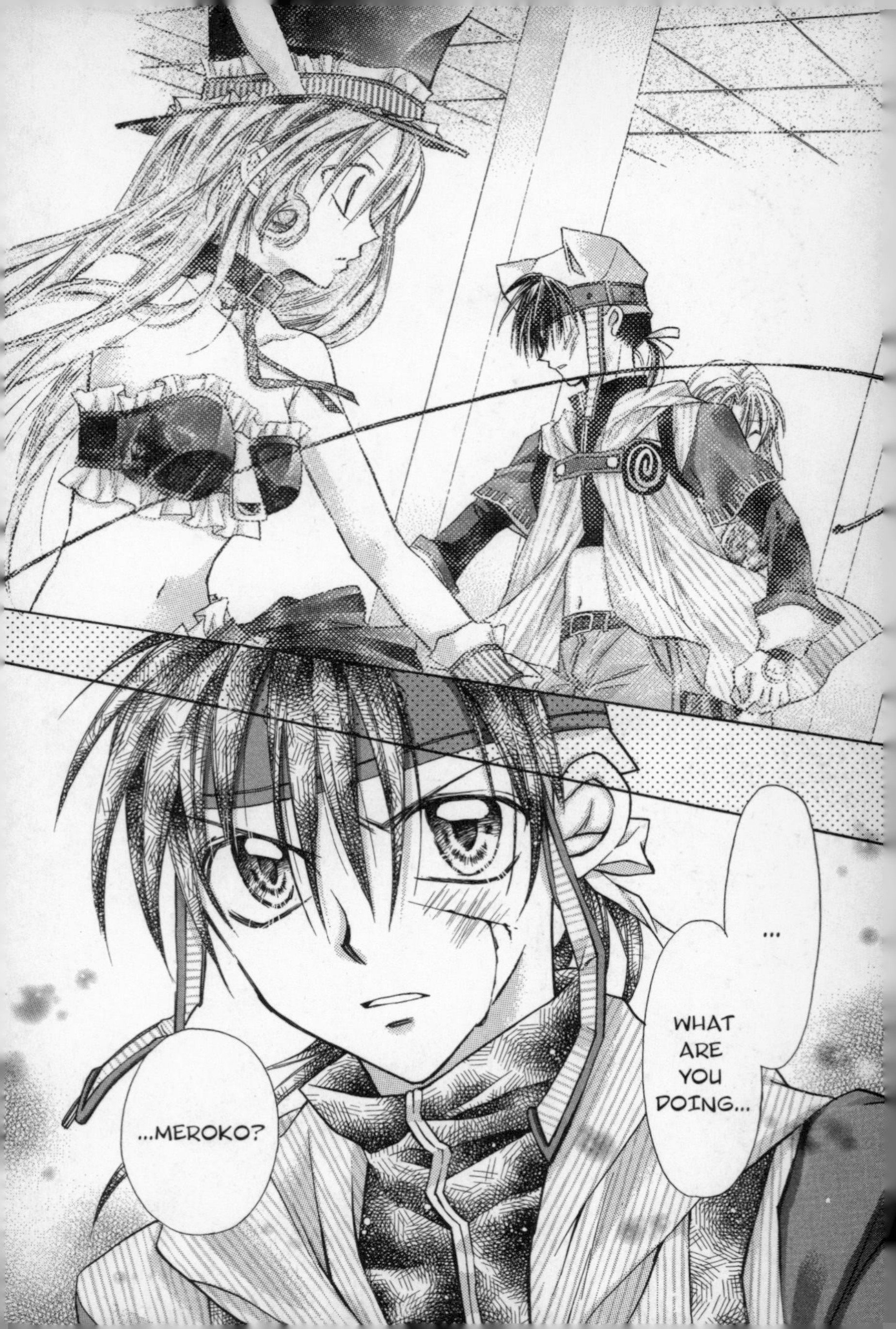
...
WHAT ARE YOU DOING...
...MEROKO?

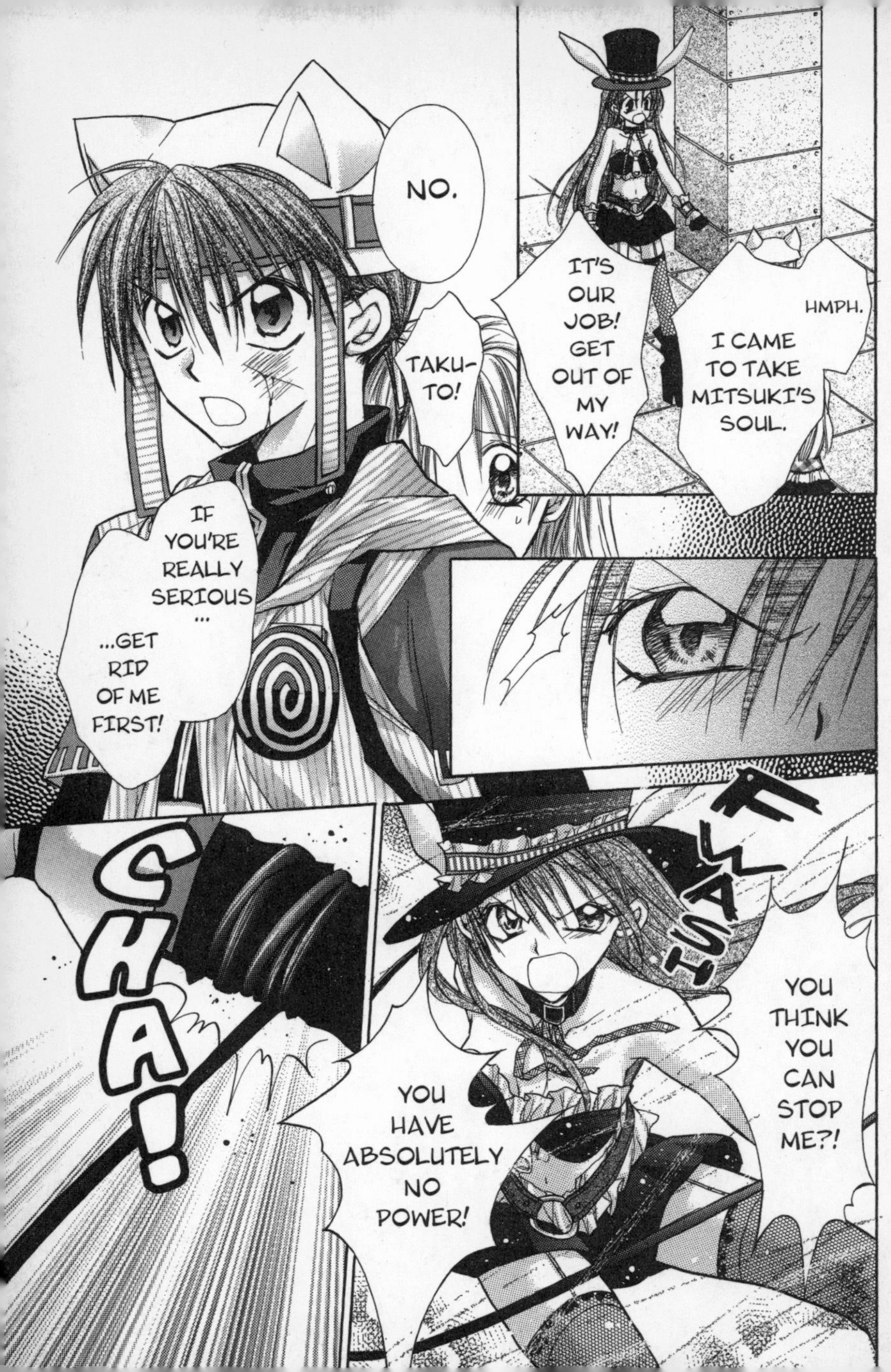
HMPH.
I CAME TO TAKE MITSUKI'S SOUL.
IT'S OUR JOB! GET OUT OF MY WAY!
NO.
TAKU-TO!
IF YOU'RE REALLY SERIOUS...
...GET RID OF ME FIRST!
FWASH
YOU THINK YOU CAN STOP ME?!
YOU HAVE ABSOLUTELY NO POWER!
CHA!

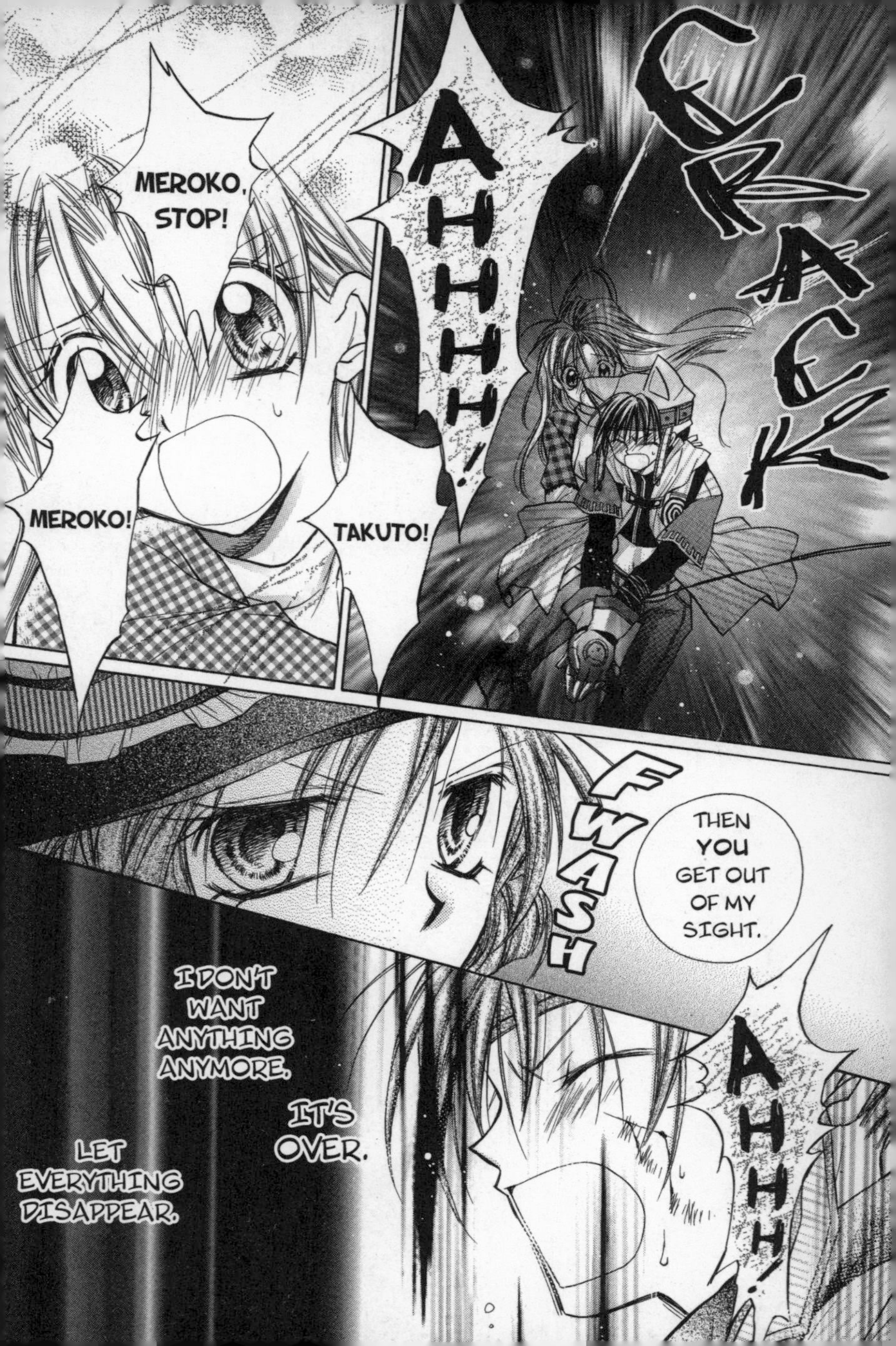
CRACK
AHHHH!
MEROKO, STOP!
TAKUTO!
MEROKO!
FWASH
THEN YOU GET OUT OF MY SIGHT.
AHHH!
I DON'T WANT ANYTHING ANYMORE.
IT'S OVER.
LET EVERYTHING DISAPPEAR.

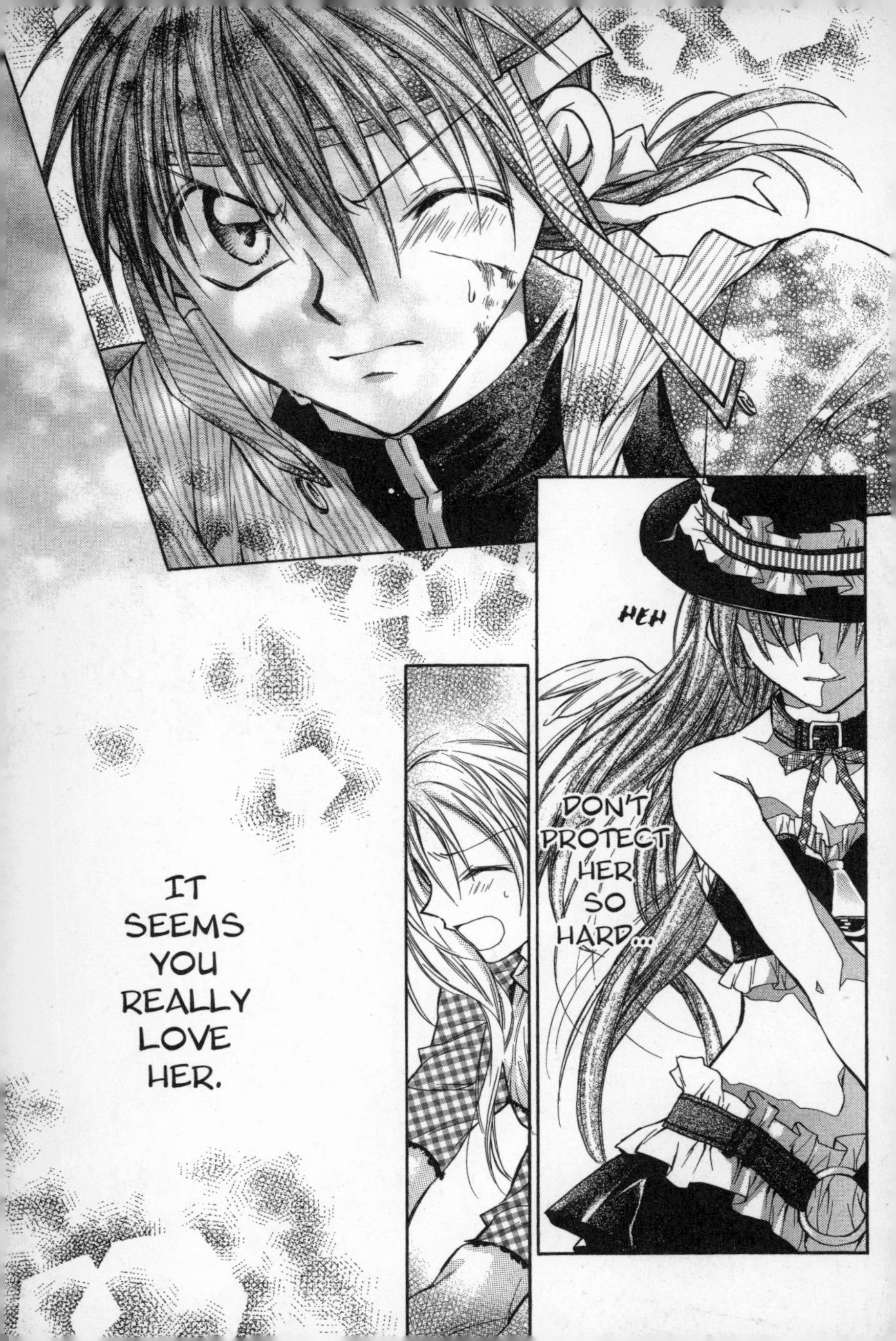
HEH
DON'T PROTECT HER SO HARD...
IT SEEMS YOU REALLY LOVE HER.

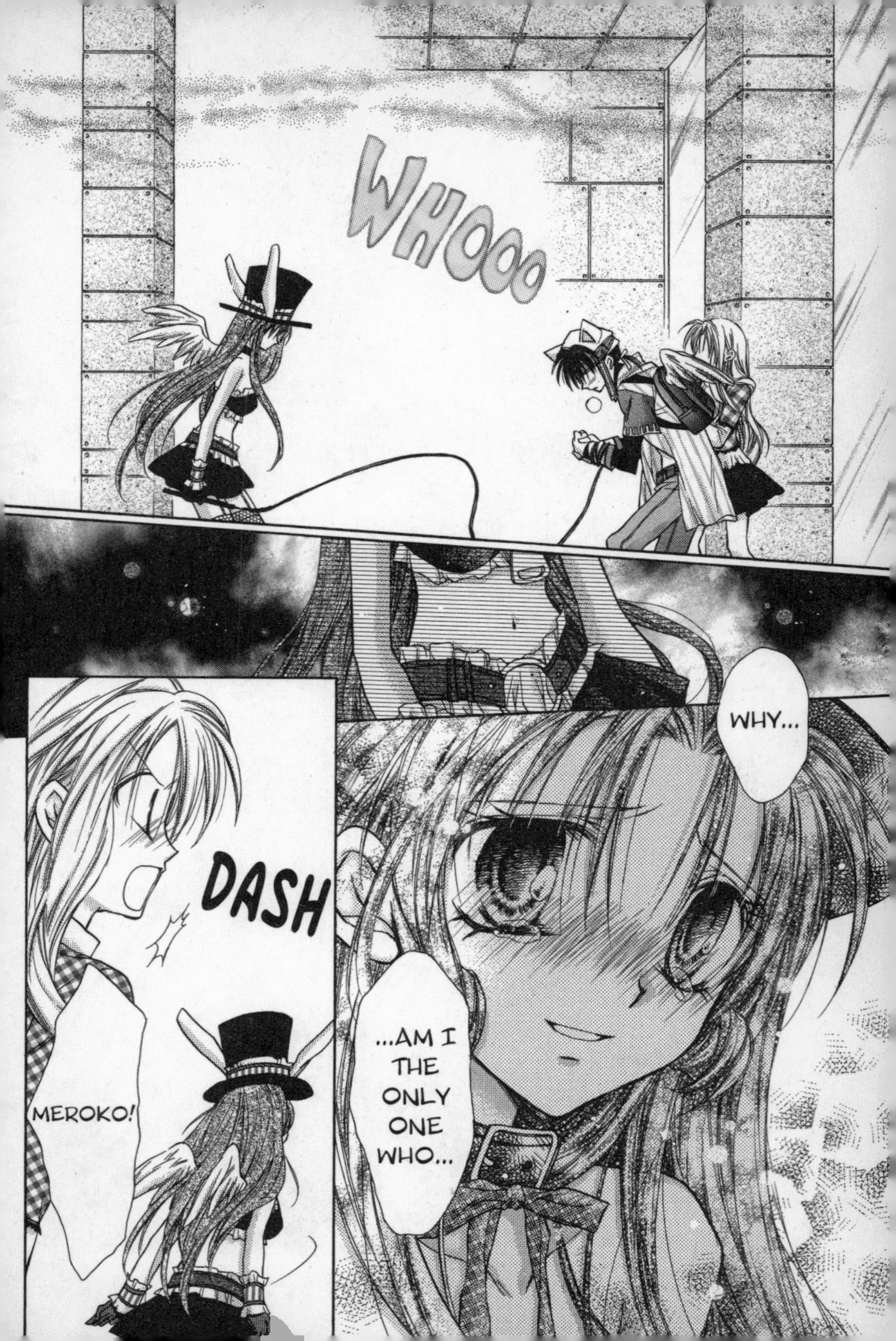
WHOOO
WHY...
...AM I THE ONLY ONE WHO...
DASH
MEROKO!

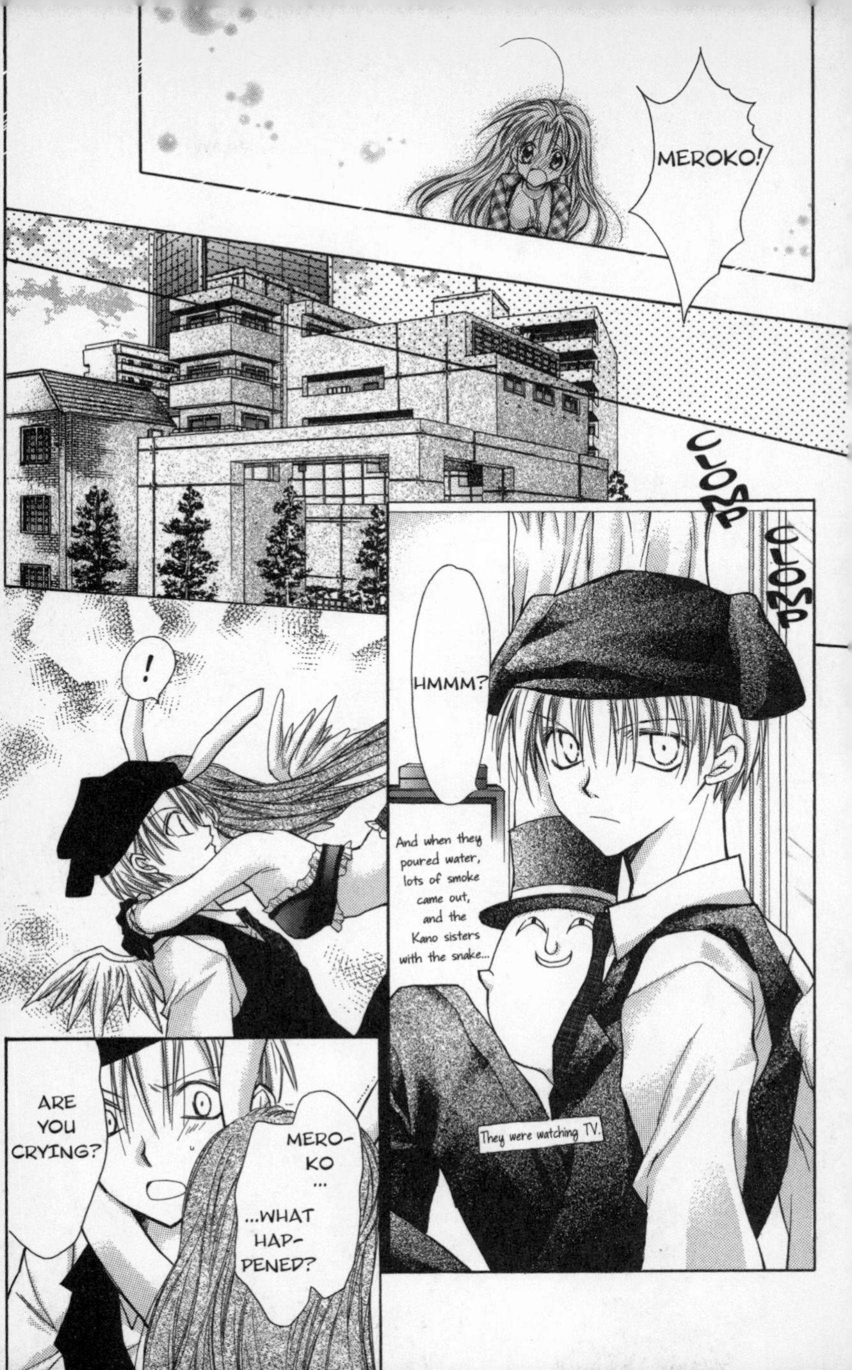

MEROKO!
CLOMP
CLOMP
HMMM?
And when they poured water, lots of smoke came out, and the Kano sisters with the snake...
They were watching TV.
!
MERO-KO ...
...WHAT HAP-PENED?
ARE YOU CRYING?

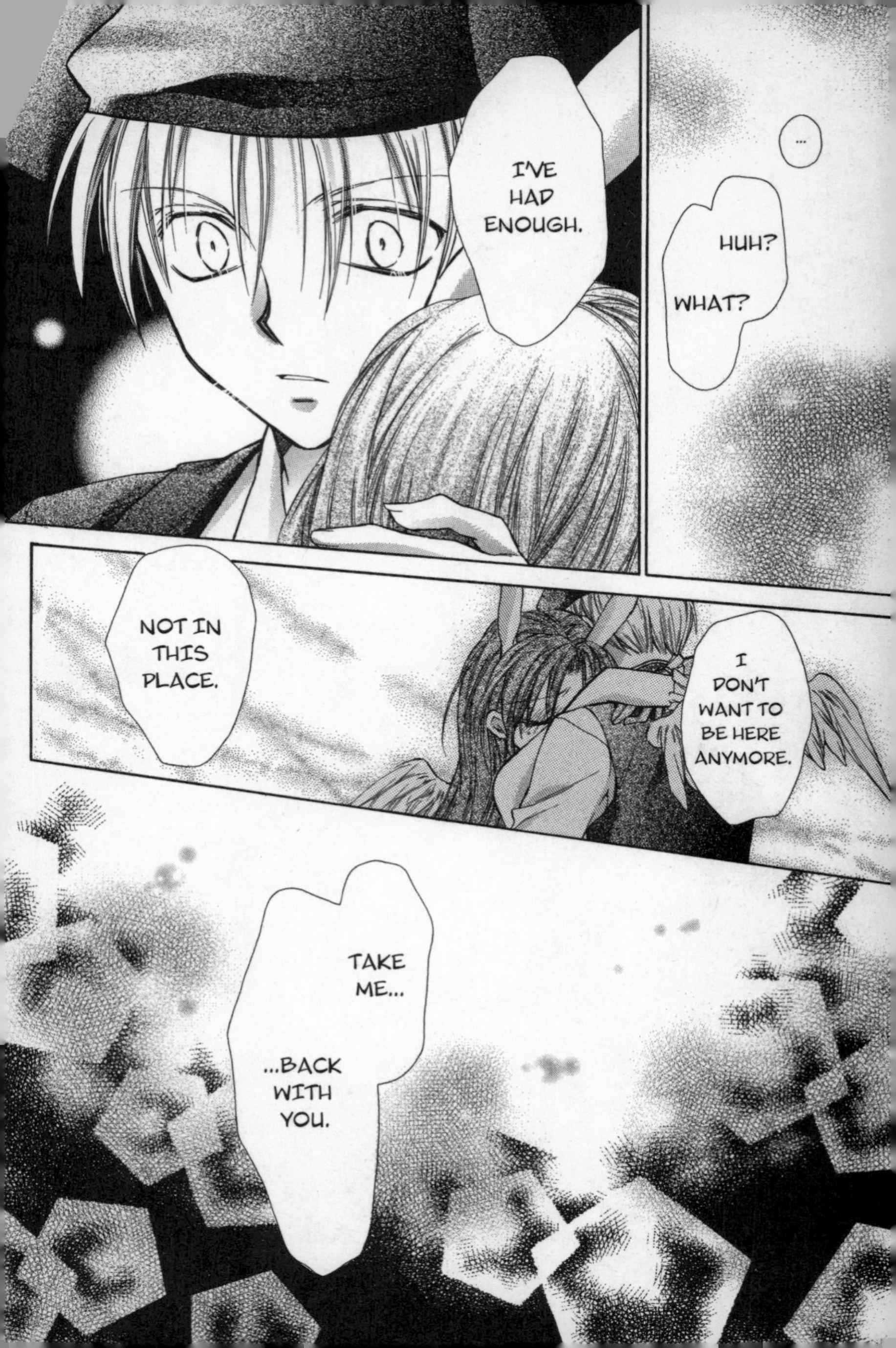
...
HUH? WHAT?
I'VE HAD ENOUGH.
I DON'T WANT TO BE HERE ANYMORE.
NOT IN THIS PLACE.
TAKE ME...
...BACK WITH YOU.

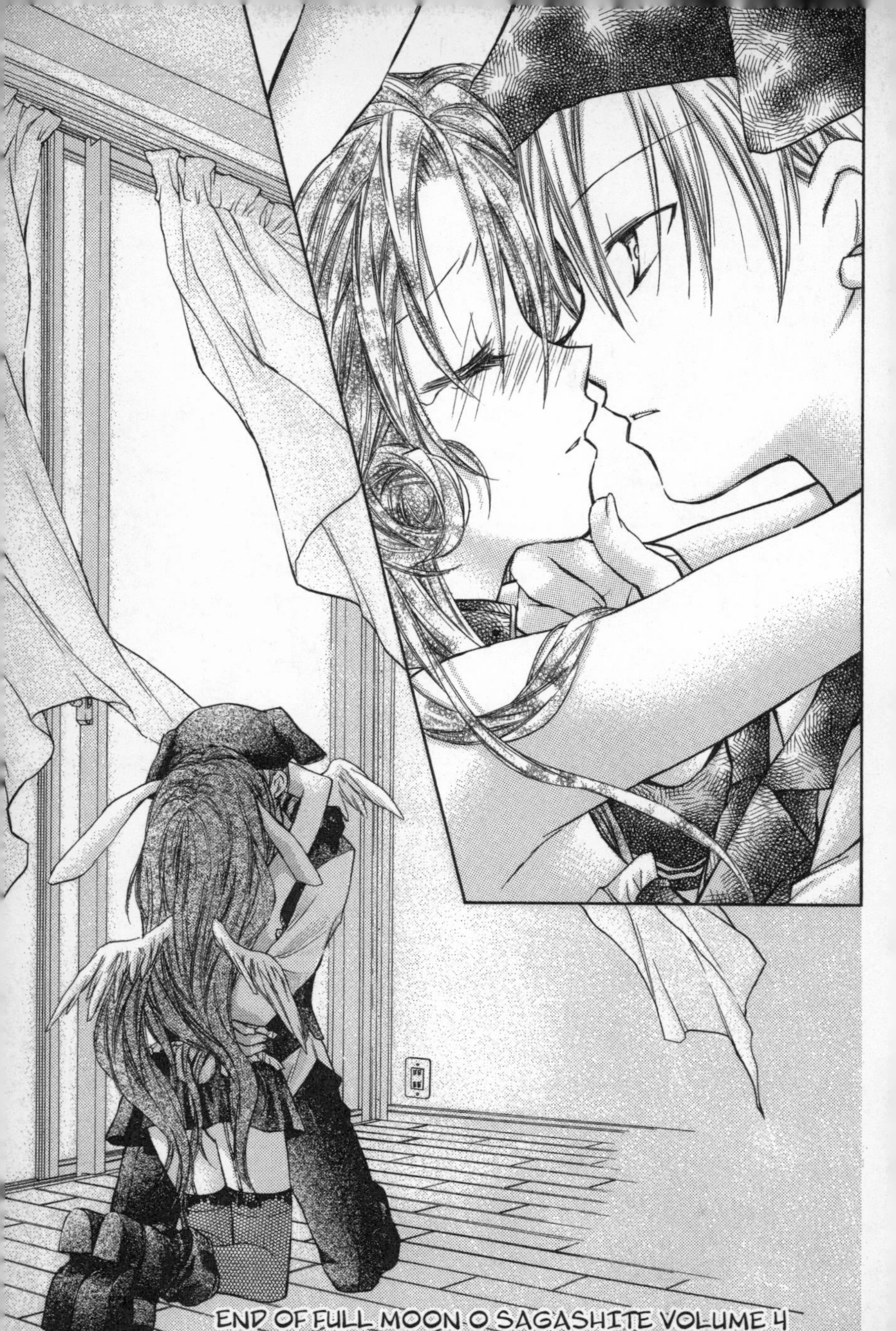

END OF FULL MOON O SAGASHITE VOLUME 4

Full Moon o Sagashite

TOTSUGEKI DOKODOKO☆ 4-PANEL MANGA

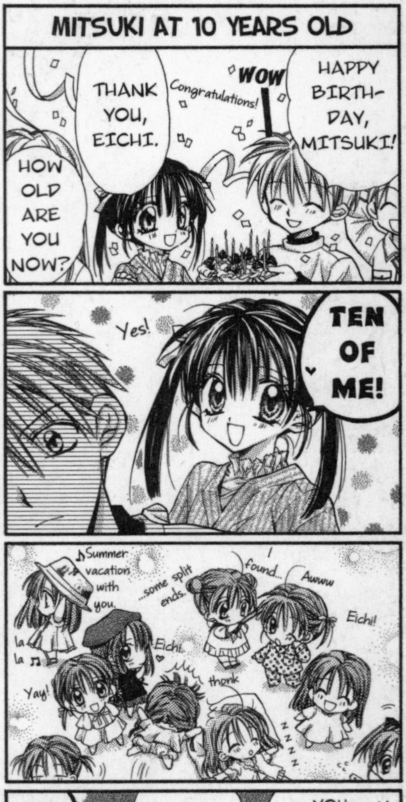
MITSUKI AT 10 YEARS OLD
HAPPY BIRTHDAY, MITSUKI!
WOW
Congratulations!
THANK YOU, EICHI.
HOW OLD ARE YOU NOW?
TEN OF ME!
Yes!
Eichi!
Awww
I found...
...some split ends.
Summer vacation with you.
Eichi.
la la
thonk
Yay!
No no.
YOU COUNT HOW OLD YOU ARE IN "YEARS."
IT'S ALL RIGHT, TEACHER.
TEN OF HER.
All mine.

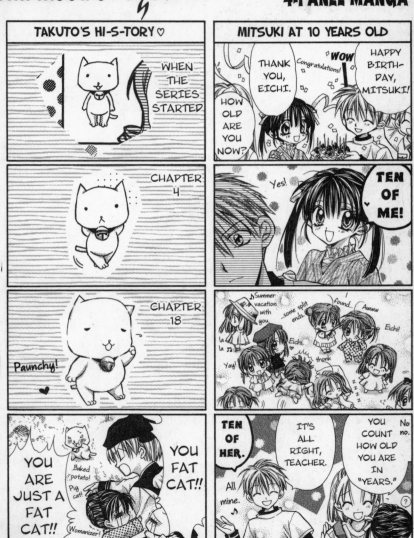

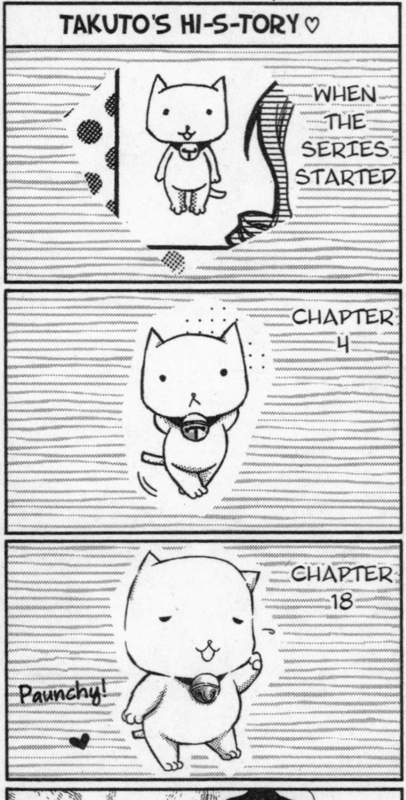
TAKUTO'S HI-S-TORY♡
WHEN THE SERIES STARTED
CHAPTER 4
CHAPTER 18
Paunchy!
YOU FAT CAT!!
Baked potato!
Pig cat!
Womanizer!
YOU ARE JUST A FAT CAT!!

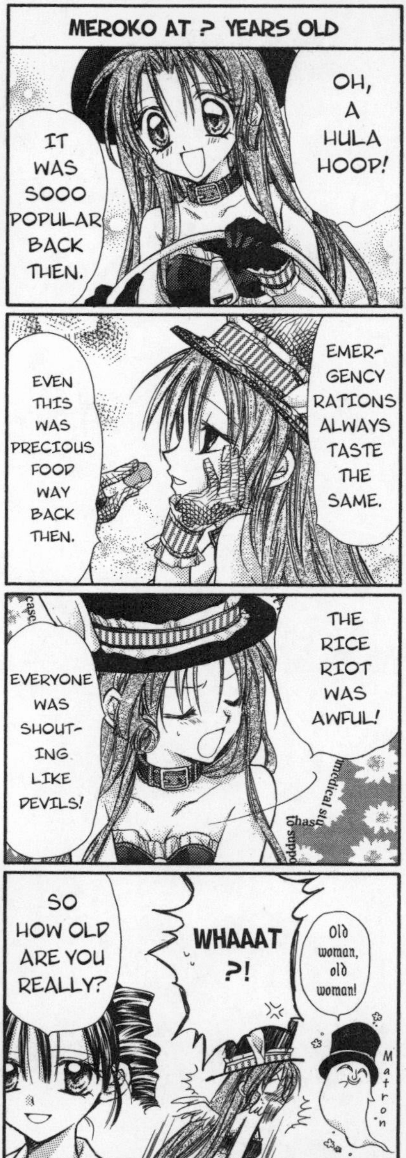
MEROKO AT ? YEARS OLD
OH, A HULA HOOP!
IT WAS SOOO POPULAR BACK THEN.
EMERGENCY RATIONS ALWAYS TASTE THE SAME.
EVEN THIS WAS PRECIOUS FOOD WAY BACK THEN.
THE RICE RIOT WAS AWFUL!
EVERYONE WAS SHOUTING LIKE DEVILS!
Old woman, old woman!
Matron
WHAAAT?!
SO HOW OLD ARE YOU REALLY?
She must be her grandmother's age.

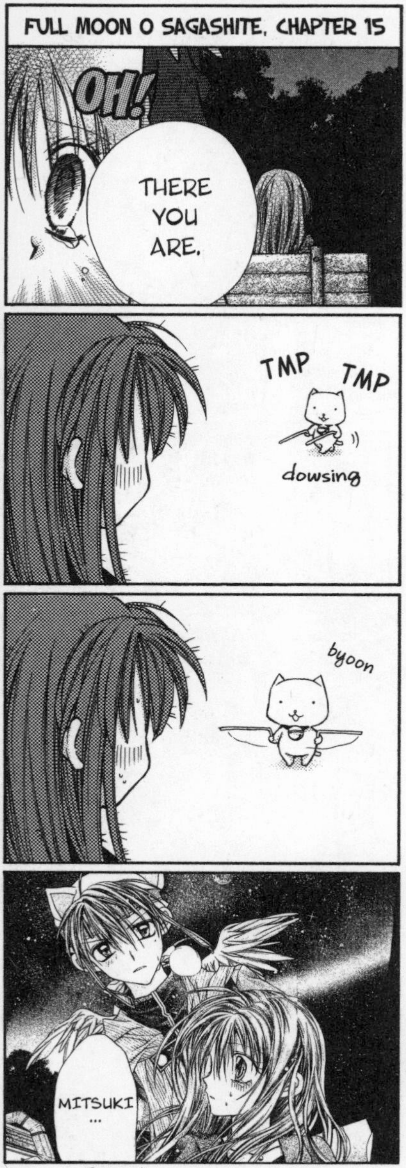
FULL MOON O SAGASHITE, CHAPTER 15
OH!
THERE YOU ARE.
TMP TMP
dowsing
byoon
MITSUKI...
This can't be.

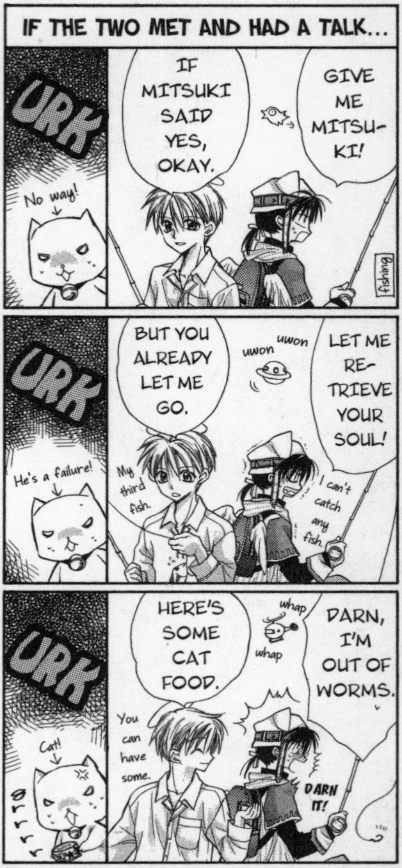
IF THE TWO MET AND HAD A TALK...
GIVE ME MITSUKI!
IF MITSUKI SAID YES, OKAY.
URK
No way!
fishing
LET ME RETRIEVE YOUR SOUL!
uwon uwon
BUT YOU ALREADY LET ME GO.
URK
I can't catch any fish.
My third fish.
He's a failure!
DARN, I'M OUT OF WORMS.
whap whap
HERE'S SOME CAT FOOD.
URK
DARN IT!
You can have some.
Cat!
grrrr
YOU ANNOY ME EVERY TIME YOU SPEAK!
I DON'T GET ANNOYED.
RAAAR!

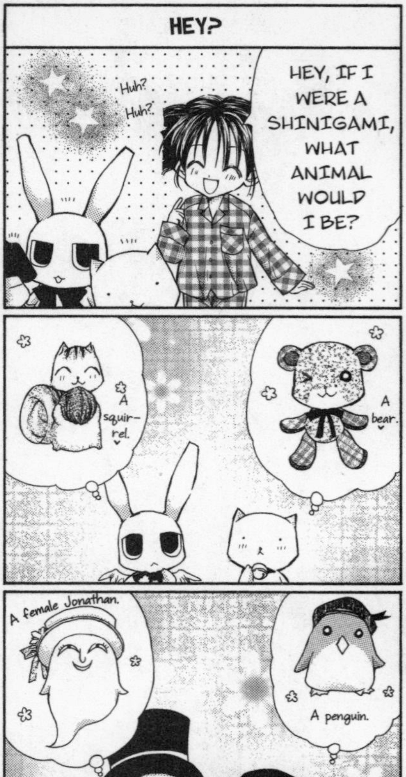
HEY?
HEY, IF I WERE A SHINIGAMI, WHAT ANIMAL WOULD I BE?
Huh? Huh?
A bear.
A squirrel.
A penguin.
A female Jonathan.
KONK

— END —

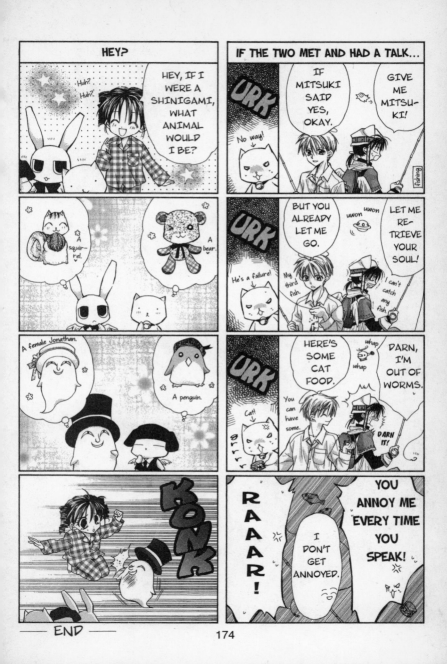

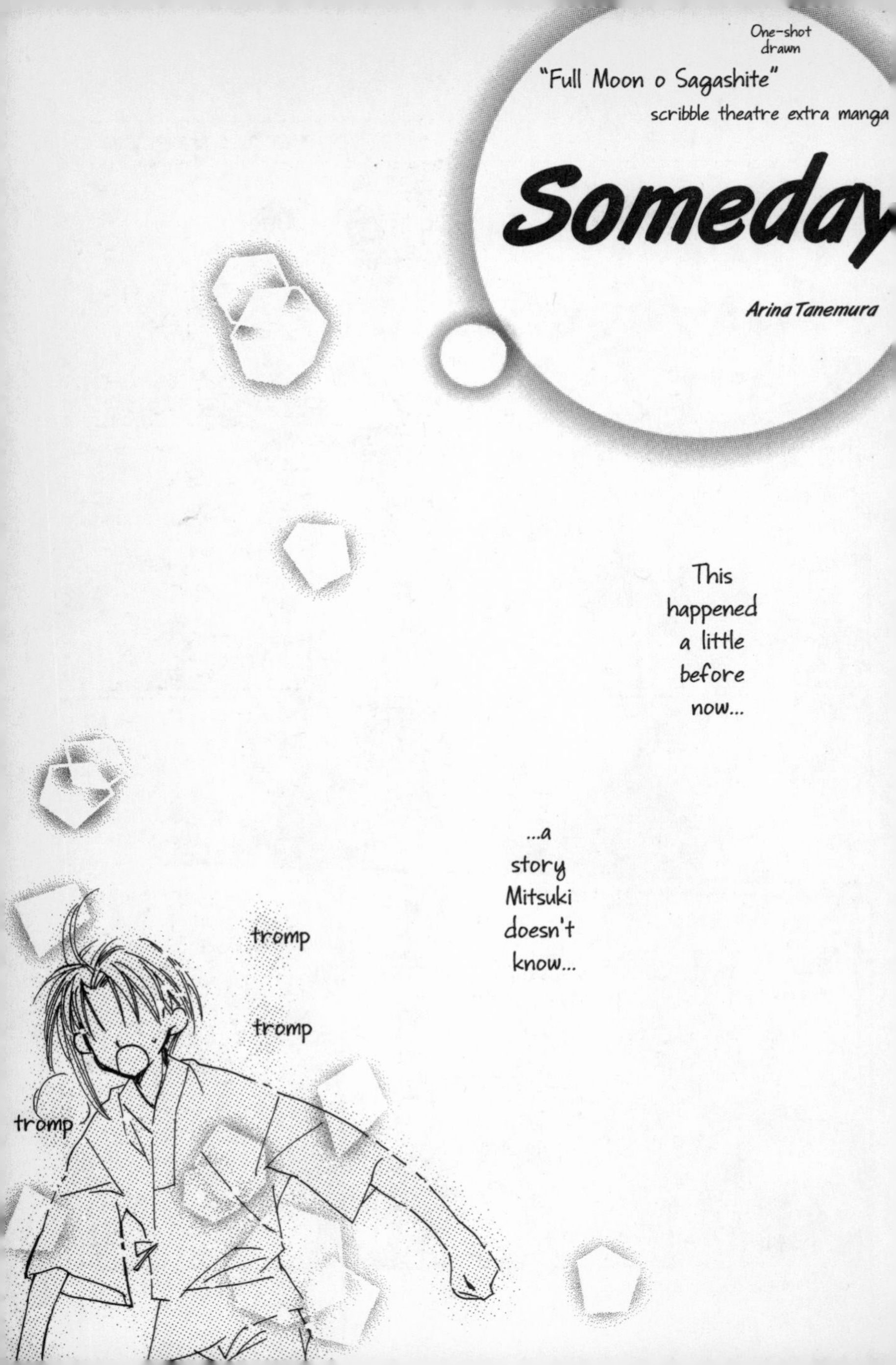
One-shot drawn
"Full Moon o Sagashite"
scribble theatre extra manga
Someday
Arina Tanemura
This happened a little before now...
...a story Mitsuki doesn't know...
tromp
tromp
tromp

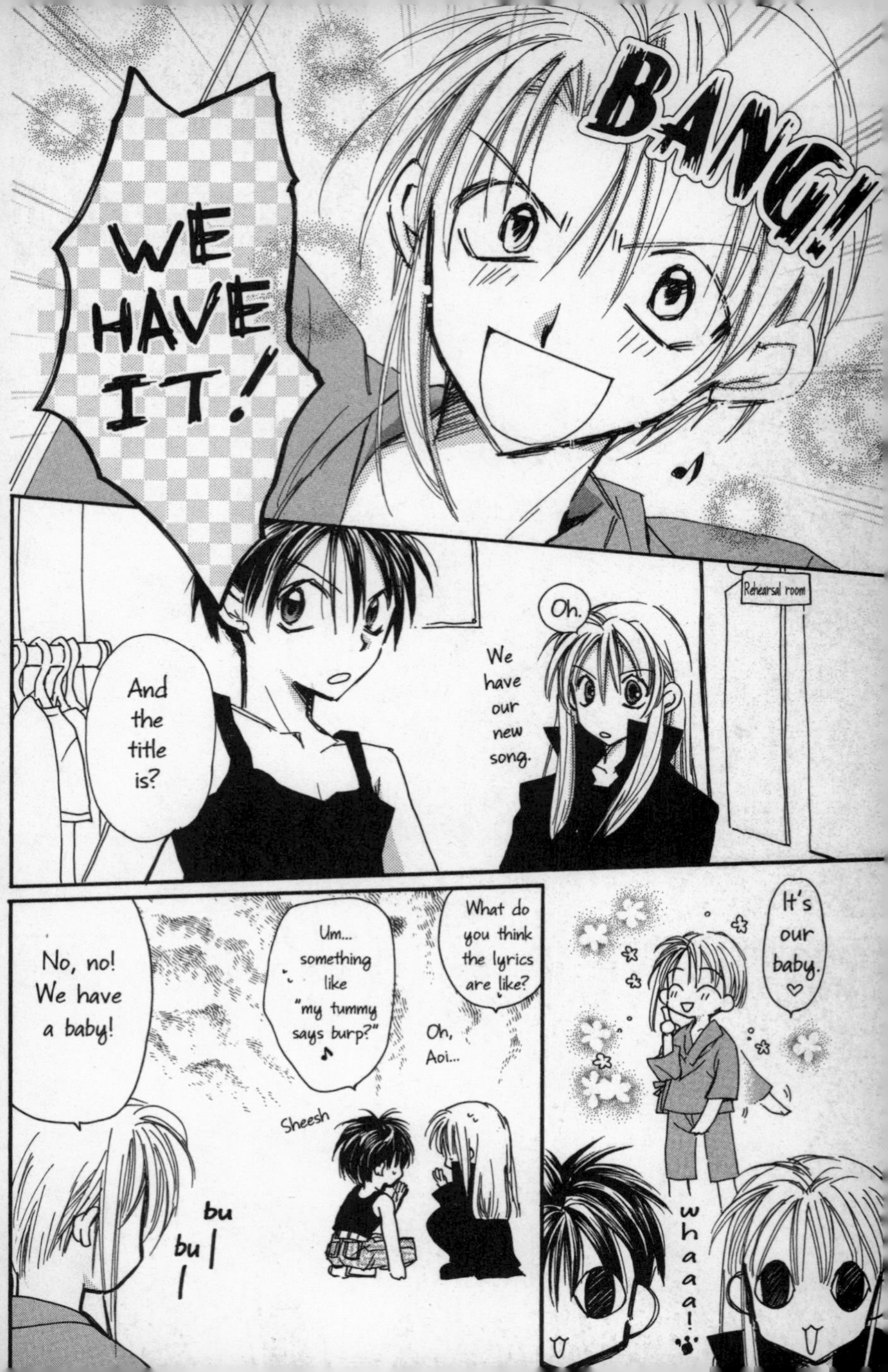
BANG!
WE HAVE IT!
Rehearsal room
Oh.
We have our new song.
And the title is?
It's our baby. ♡
whaaa!
What do you think the lyrics are like?
Um... something like "my tummy says burp?" ♪
Oh, Aoi...
Sheesh
No, no! We have a baby!
bu bu l l

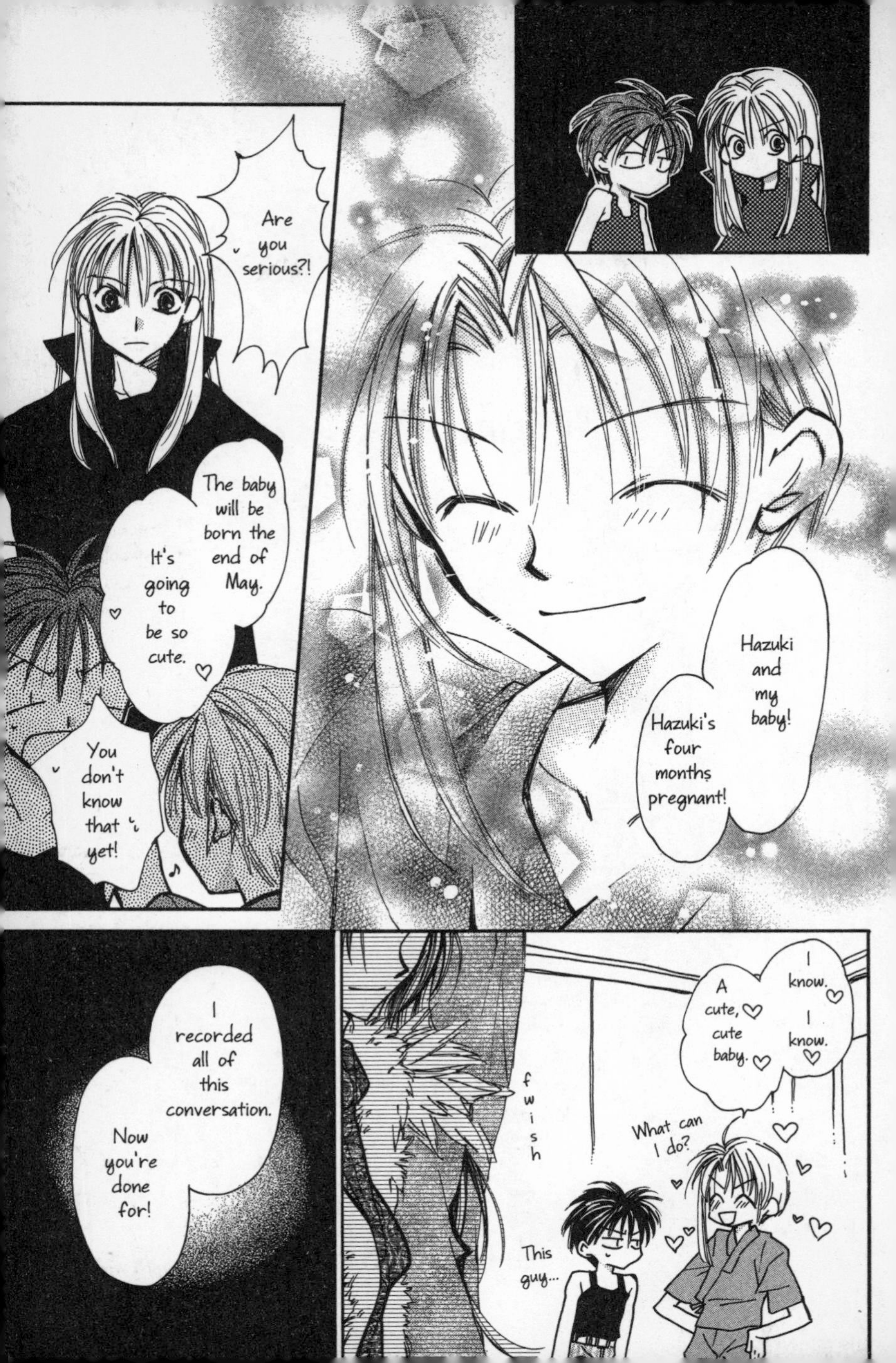

Hazuki and my baby!
Hazuki's four months pregnant!
Are you serious?!
The baby will be born the end of May.
It's going to be so cute.
You don't know that yet!
I know. I know.
A cute, cute baby.
What can I do?
fwish
This guy...
I recorded all of this conversation.
Now you're done for!

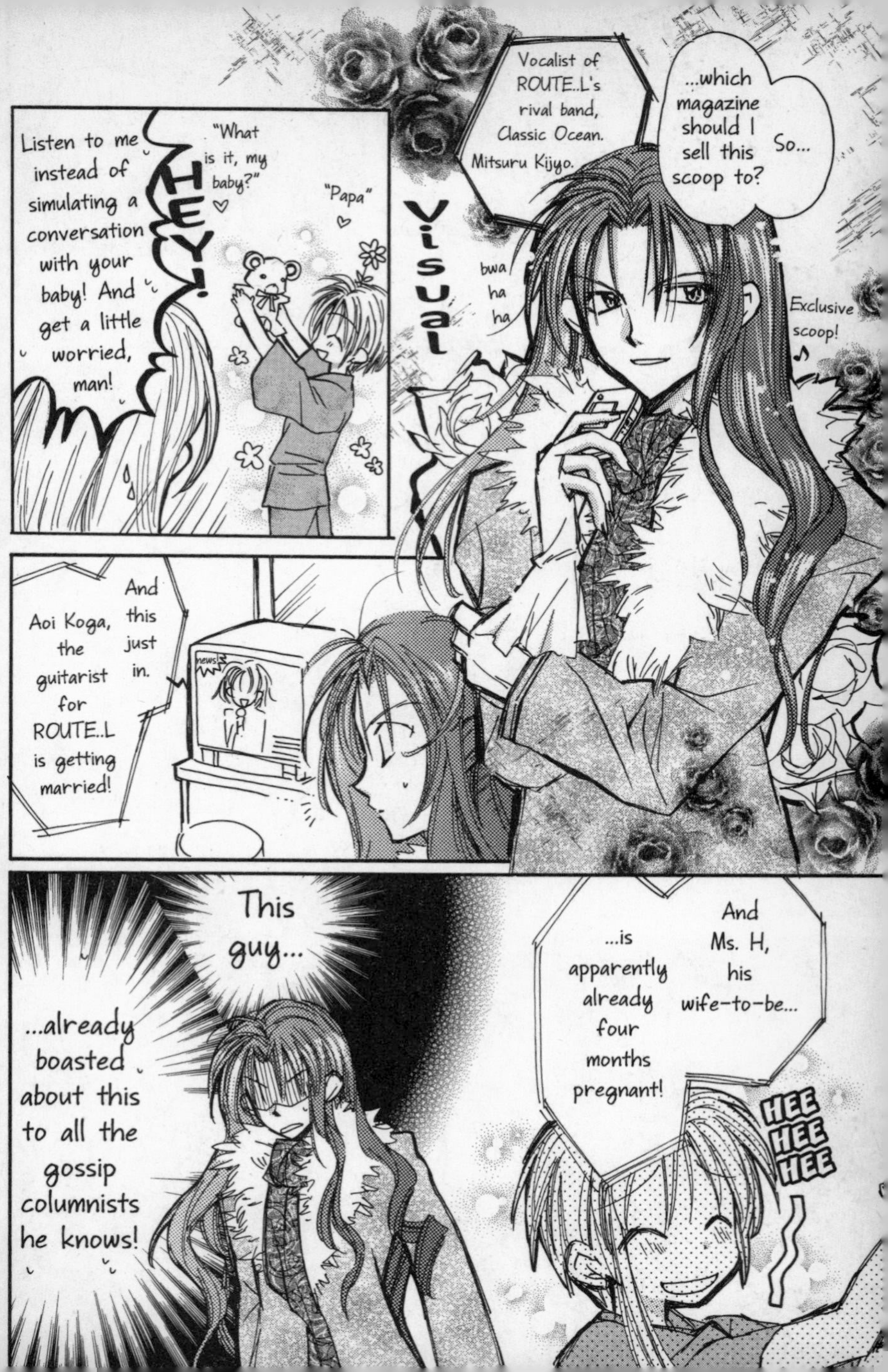
So...
...which magazine should I sell this scoop to?
Vocalist of ROUTE..L's rival band, Classic Ocean. Mitsuru Kijyo.
Exclusive scoop!
Visual
bwa ha ha
HEY!
Listen to me instead of simulating a conversation with your baby! And get a little worried, man!
"Papa"
"What is it, my baby?"
And this just in.
Aoi Koga, the guitarist for ROUTE..L is getting married!
news
And Ms. H, his wife-to-be...
...is apparently already four months pregnant!
HEE HEE HEE
This guy...
...already boasted about this to all the gossip columnists he knows!

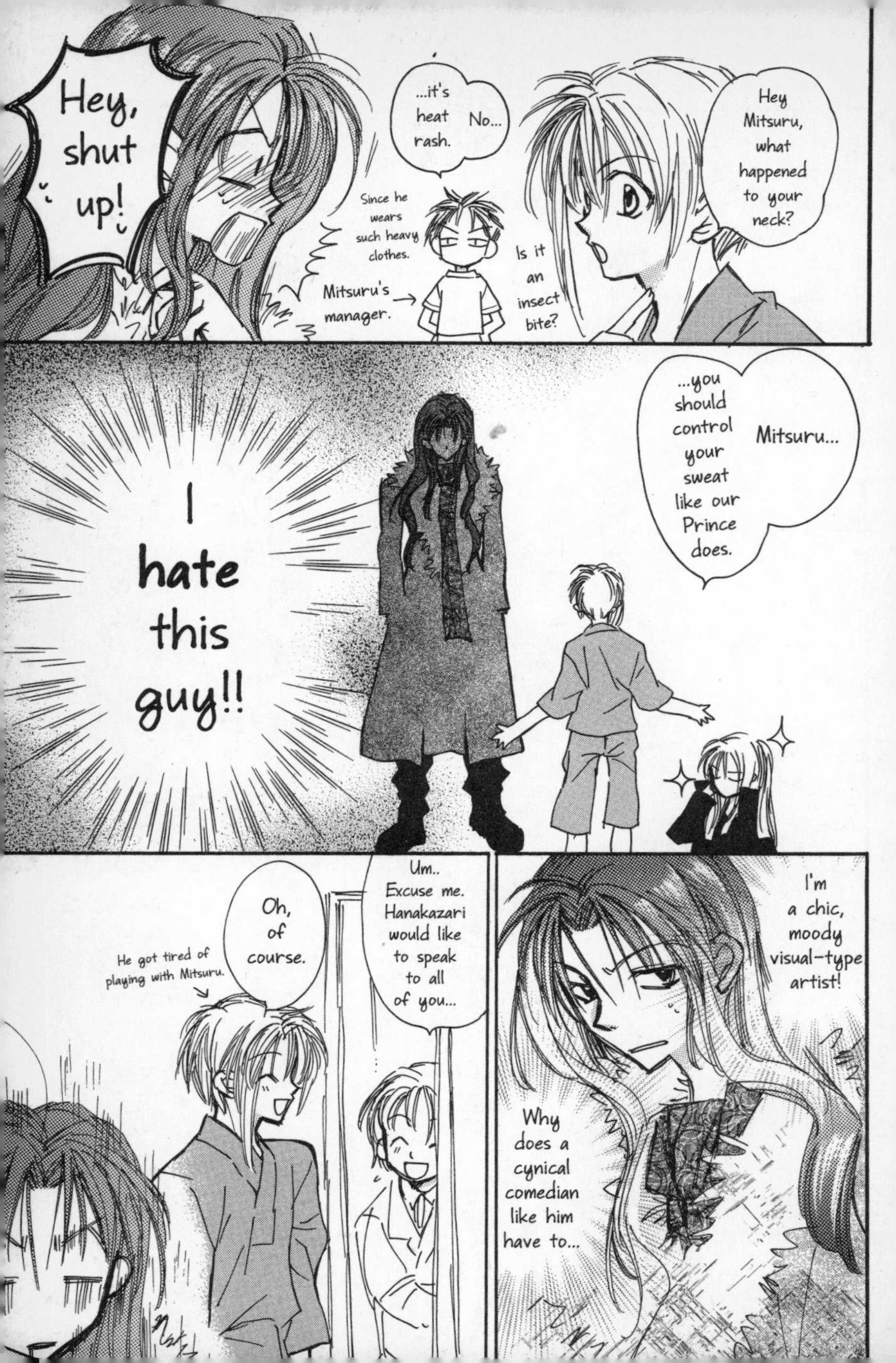
Hey Mitsuru, what happened to your neck?
Is it an insect bite?
No...
...it's heat rash.
Since he wears such heavy clothes.
Mitsuru's manager.
Hey, shut up!
Mitsuru...
...you should control your sweat like our Prince does.
I hate this guy!!
I'm a chic, moody visual-type artist!
Why does a cynical comedian like him have to...
Um.. Excuse me. Hanakazari would like to speak to all of you...
Oh, of course.
He got tired of playing with Mitsuru.

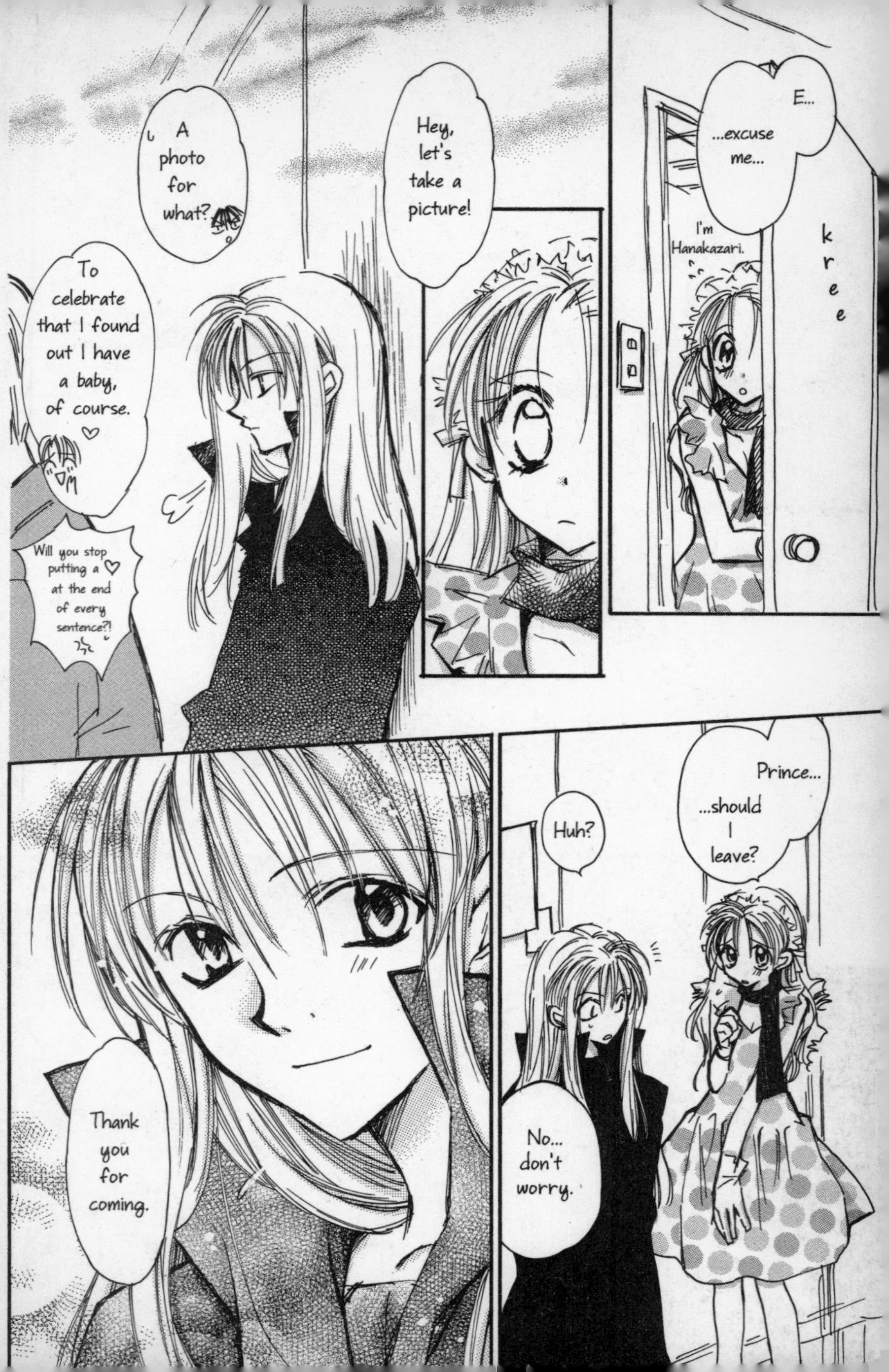
E...
...excuse me...
I'm Hanakazari.
kree
Hey, let's take a picture!
A photo for what?
To celebrate that I found out I have a baby, of course. ♡
Will you stop putting a ♡ at the end of every sentence?!
Prince... ...should I leave?
Huh?
No... don't worry.
Thank you for coming.

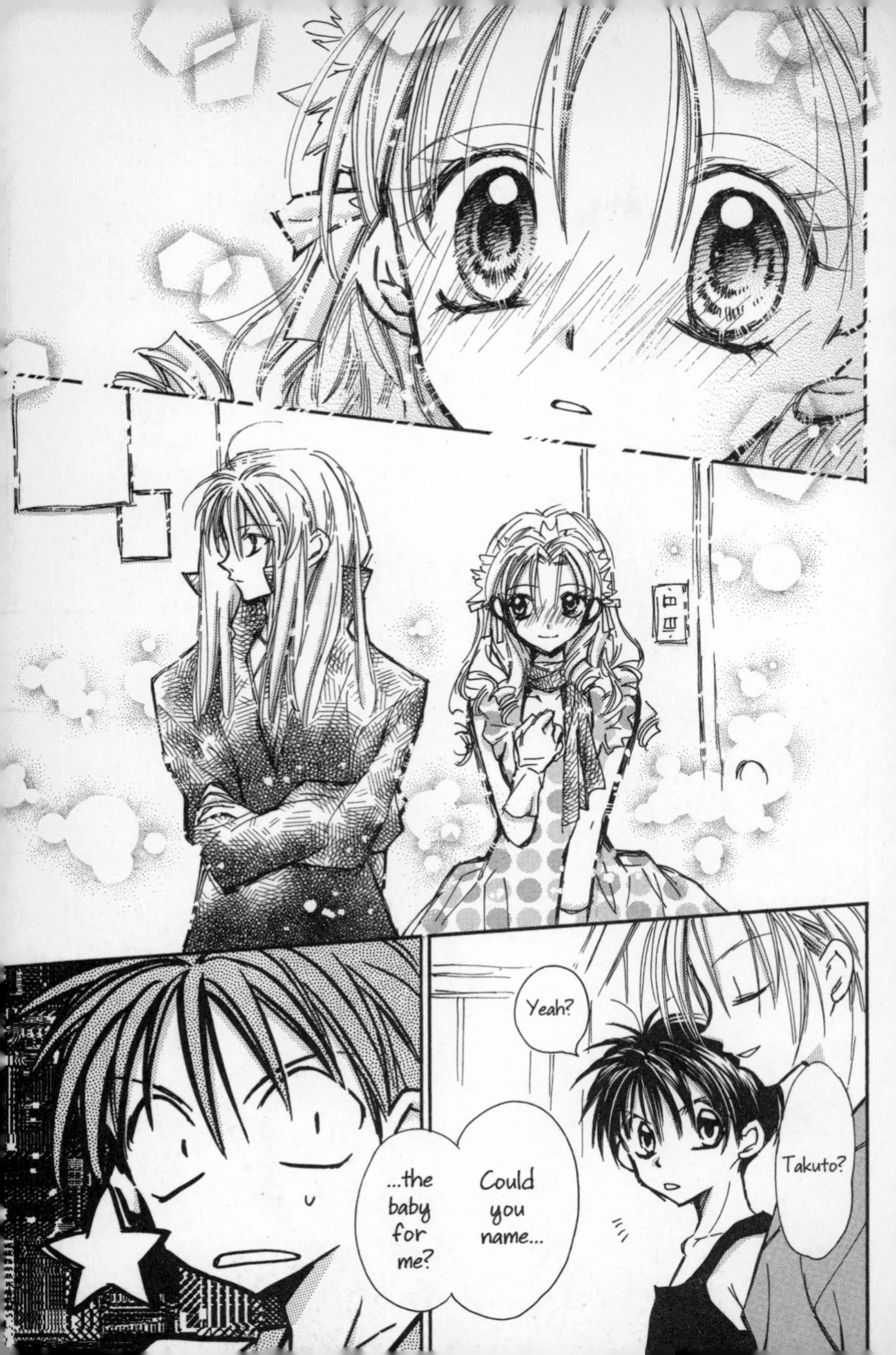
Takuto?
Yeah?
Could you name...
...the baby for me?

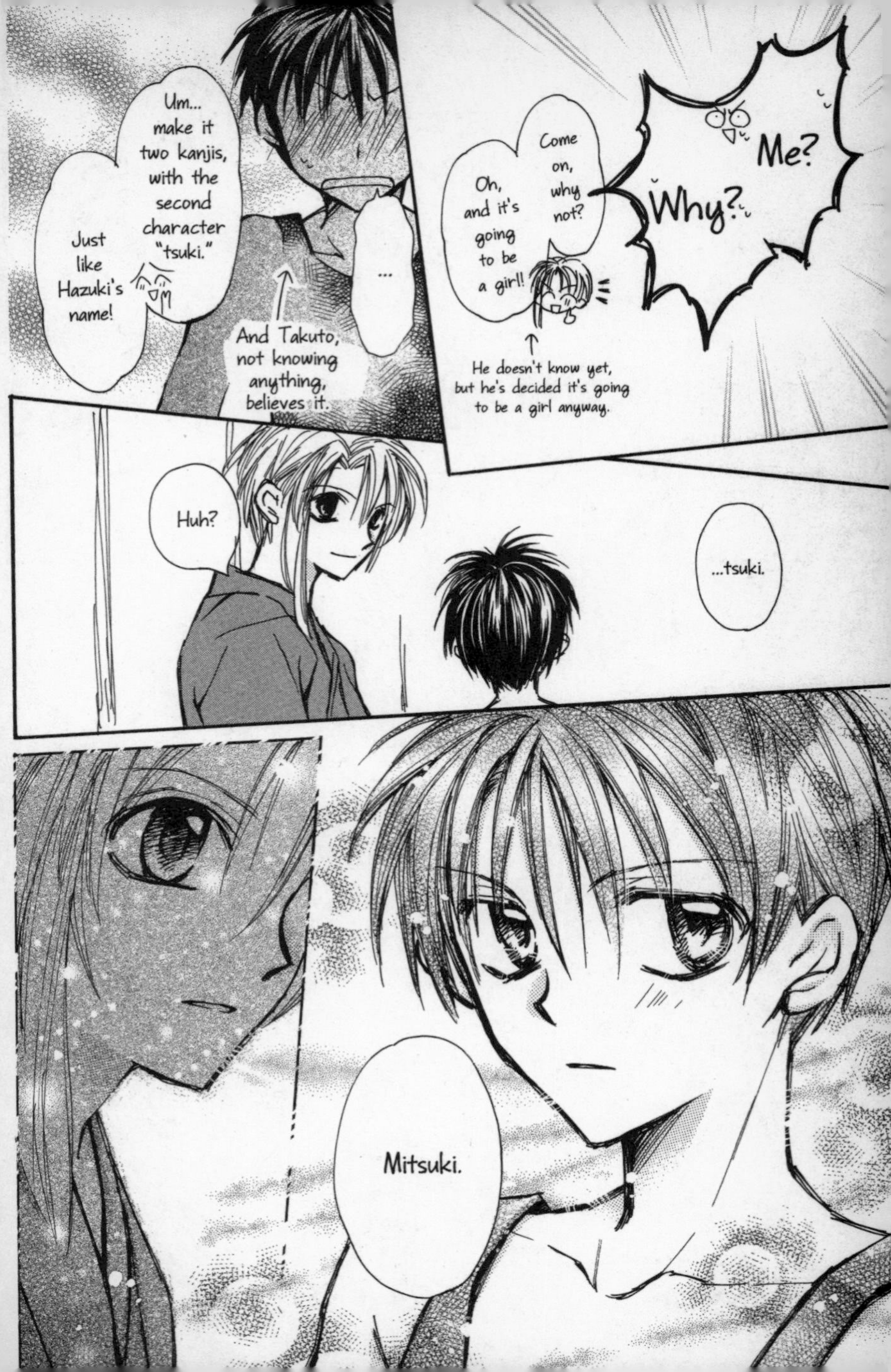
Me?
Why?
Come on, why not?
Oh, and it's going to be a girl!
He doesn't know yet, but he's decided it's going to be a girl anyway.
Um... make it two kanjis, with the second character "tsuki."
...
And Takuto, not knowing anything, believes it.
Just like Hazuki's name!
...tsuki.
Huh?
Mitsuki.

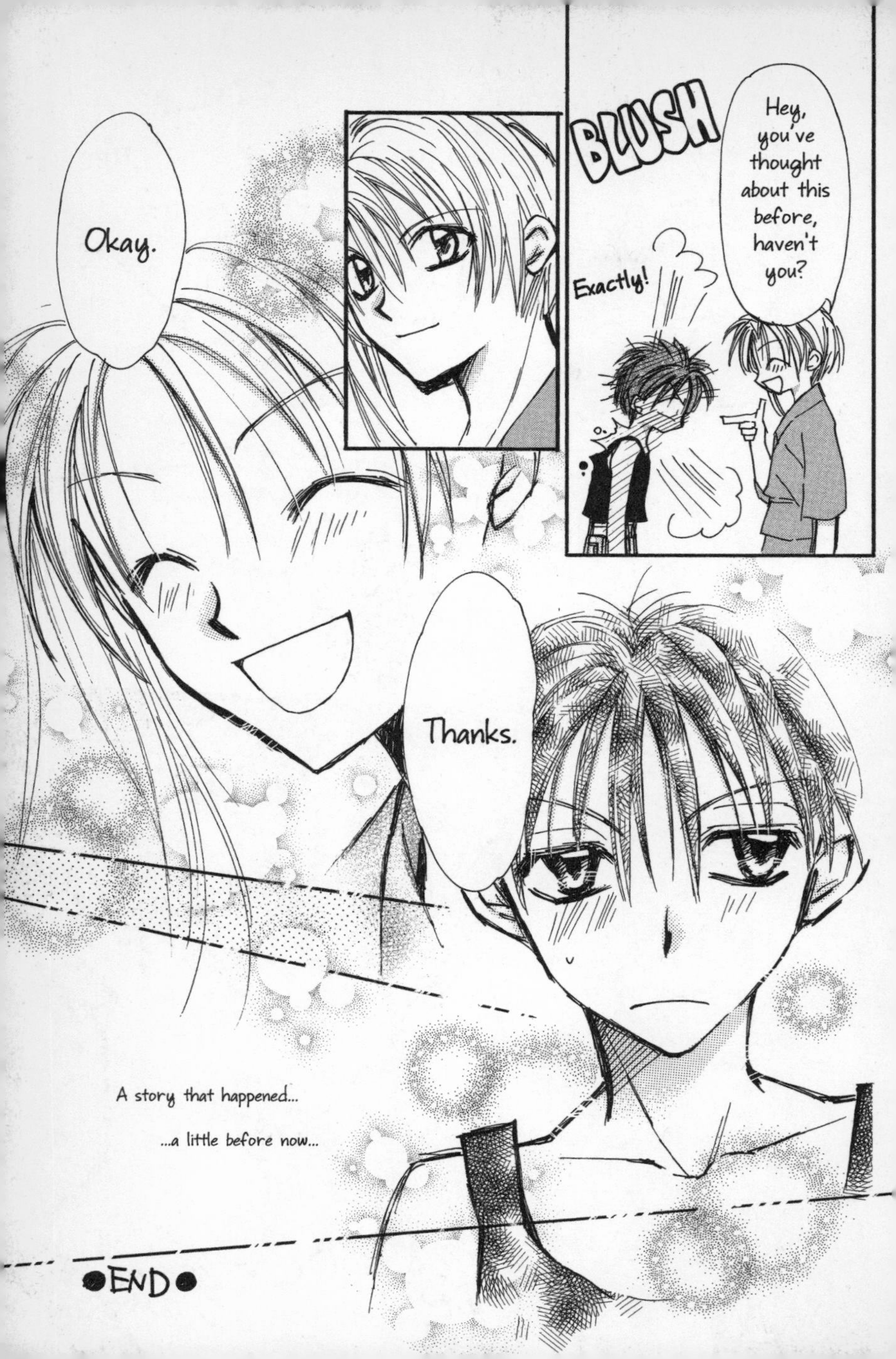
Hey, you've thought about this before, haven't you?
BLUSH
Exactly!
Okay.
Thanks.
A story that happened...
...a little before now...
END

Author Bio

Arina Tanemura was born in Aichi, Japan. She got her start in 1996, publishing *Nibanme no Koi no Katachi (*The Style of Second Love*)* in *Ribon Original* magazine. Her early work includes a collection of short stories called *Kanshaku Dama no Yuutsu* (Short-Tempered Melancholic). Two of her titles, *Kamikaze Kaito Jeanne* and *Full Moon,* were made into popular TV series. Tanemura enjoys Karaoke and is a huge *Lord of the Rings* fan.

Author's Note

The contents of this volume...are very serious, and it gave me satisfaction to draw it...(but the cover is "Love Love Angels" and I'm sorry). Nowadays, I just love Mitsuki + the Shinigami. These four (Jonathan is just an extra) are hot! I'm sorry my comments don't make much sense, as usual...

Full Moon o Sagashite

Vol. 4

The Shojo Beat Manga Edition

STORY & ART BY
ARINA TANEMURA

English Translation & Adaptation/Tomo Kimura
Touch-Up & Lettering/Elena Diaz
Graphics & Cover Design/Izumi Evers
Editor/Nancy Thistlethwaite

Editor in Chief, Books/Alvin Lu
Editor in Chief, Magazines/Marc Weidenbaum
VP of Publishing Licensing/Rika Inouye
VP of Sales/Gonzalo Ferreyra
Sr. VP of Marketing/Liza Coppola
Publisher/Hyoe Narita

Printed in Canada

Published by VIZ Media, LLC
P.O. Box 77064
San Francisco, CA 94107

Shojo Beat Manga Edition
10 9 8 7 6 5 4 3 2
First printing, November 2005
Second printing, May 2008

store.viz.com

RATED T FOR TEEN

PARENTAL ADVISORY
FULL MOON is rated T for Teen and is recommended for ages 13 and up. This volume contains themes of death.

ratings.viz.com

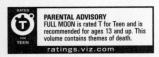

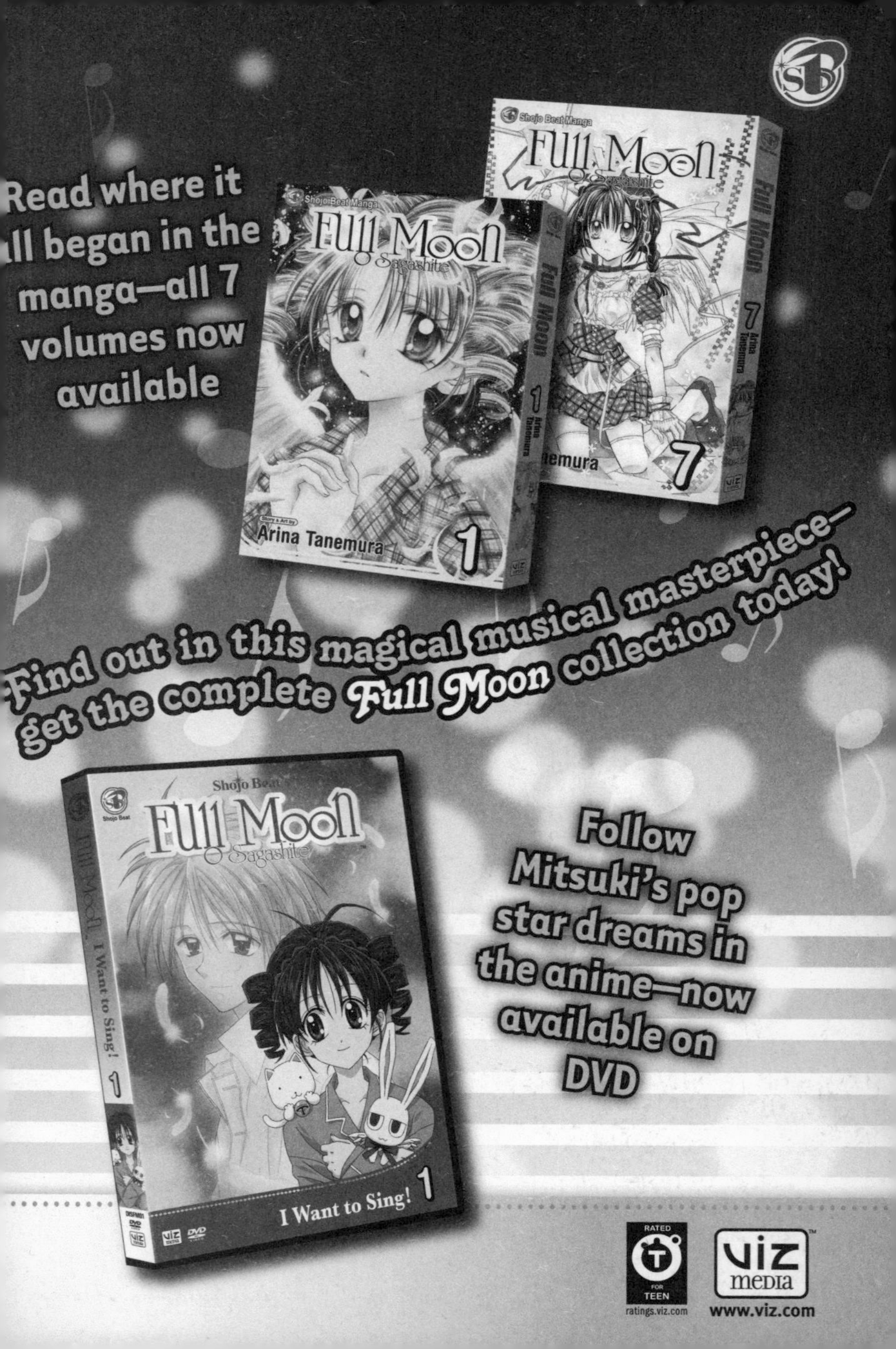
Read where it
ll began in the
manga—all 7
volumes now
available
Shojo Beat Manga
Full Moon
O Sagashite
Story & Art by
Arina Tanemura
1
7
Find out in this magical musical masterpiece—
get the complete Full Moon collection today!
Shojo Beat
Full Moon
O Sagashite
I Want to Sing! 1
Follow
Mitsuki's pop
star dreams in
the anime—now
available on
DVD
RATED
T
FOR
TEEN
ratings.viz.com
viz media
www.viz.com

Full Moon O Sagashite

By Arina Tanemura
creator of *The Gentlemen's Alliance* †

Mitsuki loves singing, but a malignant throat tumor prevents her from pursuing her passion.

Can two fun-loving Shinigami give her singing career a magical jump-start?

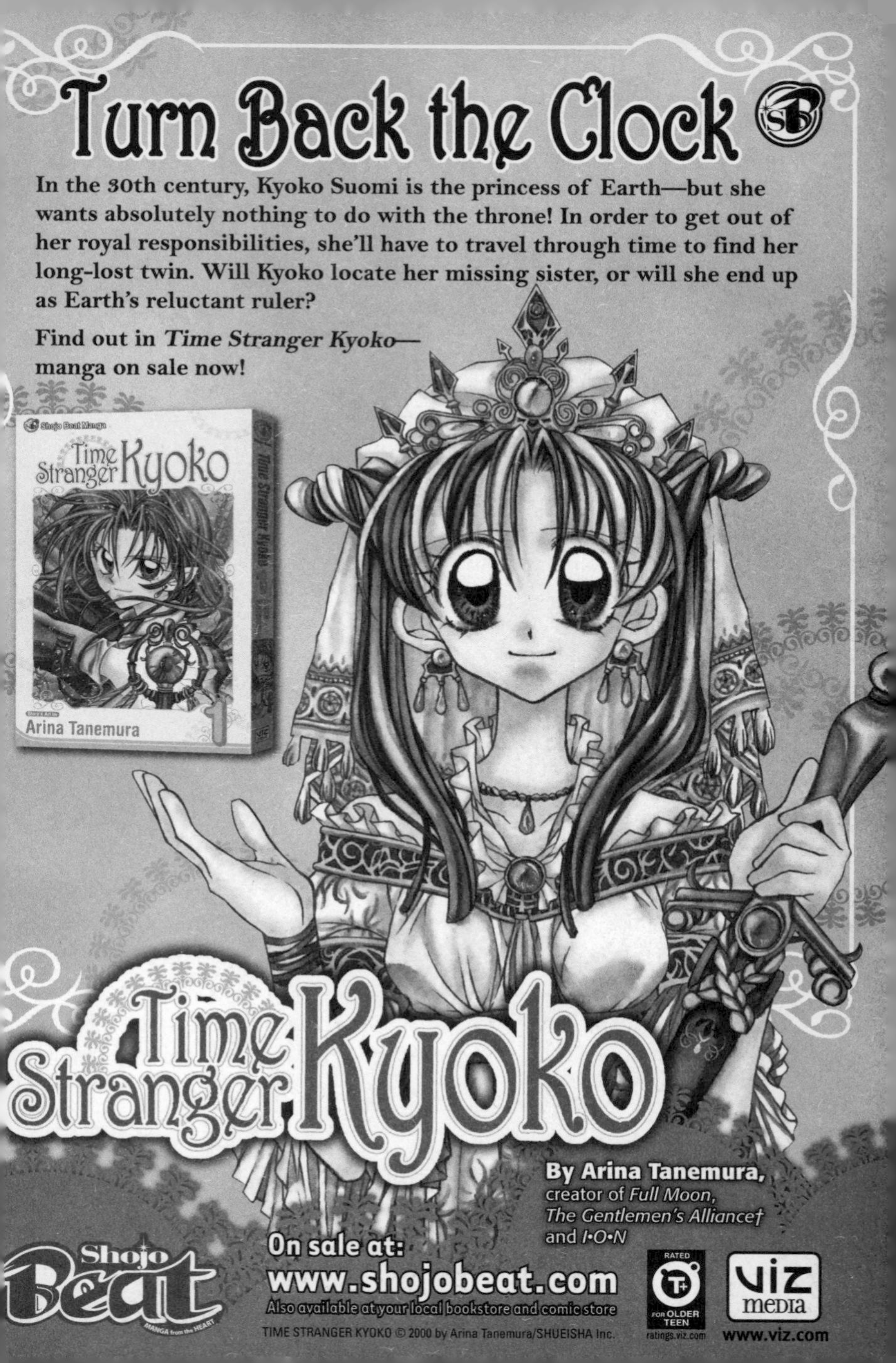
Turn Back the Clock
In the 30th century, Kyoko Suomi is the princess of Earth—but she wants absolutely nothing to do with the throne! In order to get out of her royal responsibilities, she'll have to travel through time to find her long-lost twin. Will Kyoko locate her missing sister, or will she end up as Earth's reluctant ruler?
Find out in Time Stranger Kyoko—manga on sale now!
Shojo Beat Manga
Time Stranger Kyoko
Arina Tanemura
1
Time Stranger Kyoko
By Arina Tanemura,
creator of Full Moon, The Gentlemen's Alliance† and I•O•N
On sale at:
www.shojobeat.com
Also available at your local bookstore and comic store
Shojo Beat
RATED T+ FOR OLDER TEEN
ratings.viz.com
VIZ MEDIA
www.viz.com
TIME STRANGER KYOKO © 2000 by Arina Tanemura/SHUEISHA Inc.

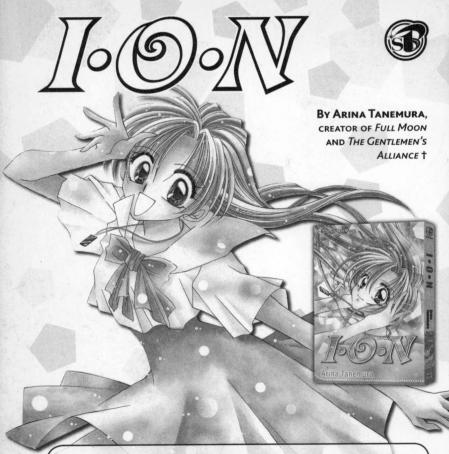

I·O·N

love ★ com

By Aya Nakahara

Sinjo Beat Manga
love ★ com
Lovely ★ Complex
Aya Nakahara
1

Class clowns
Risa and Ôtani
join forces
to find love!

Manga available now

On sale at **www.shojobeat.com**
Also available at your local bookstore and comic store

LOVE ★ COM © 2001 by Aya Nakahara/SHUEISHA Inc.

www.viz.com

Shojo Beat™

MANGA from the HEART

The Shojo Manga Authority

12 GIANT issues for ONLY $34.99*

That's 51% OFF the cover price!

The most **ADDICTIVE** shojo manga stories from Japan **PLUS** unique editorial coverage on the arts, music, culture, fashion, and much more!

Subscribe NOW and become a member of the ⓑ Sub Club!

- **SAVE** 51% OFF the cover price
- **ALWAYS** get every issue
- **ACCESS** exclusive areas of www.shojobeat.com
- **FREE** members-only gifts several times a year

Strictly VIP!

3 EASY WAYS TO SUBSCRIBE!

1) Send in the subscription order form from this book **OR**
2) Log on to: www.shojobeat.com **OR**
3) Call 1-800-541-7876